The Practice of WOODTURNING

The Practice of WOODTURNING

Mike Darlow

B T Batsford Ltd, London

First published in Great Britain in 1996 by

B T Batsford Ltd
4 Fitzhardinge Street
London W1H 0AH

ISBN 0 7134 7999 X

British Library Cataloguing-in-Publication Data

A catalogue record for this book is available from the British Library.

Printed in Australia

Contents

Preface   ix

Acknowledgments   xii

Terminology   xiv

1   WOOD   1

1.1   Tree and Wood Nomenclature   1
1.2   Tree Growth   3
1.3   Chemical Composition of Wood   5
1.4   Types of Extractives   5
1.5   Effects of Extractives on Wood Properties   6
1.6   Strength, Moisture Content, and Temperature   6
1.7   Internal Stresses   9
1.8   Fungal and Insect Attack   11
1.9   Intentional Staining   13
1.10   Turnability   13
1.11   Sources of Wood   13

2   DESIGN   14

2.1   The Production of a Design   15
2.2   Sources of Design   15
2.3   Treen   16
2.4   Design Nomenclature   16
2.5   The Physical Process of Designing   24
2.6   Design Guidelines   25
2.7   Aesthetic and Practical Considerations   28
2.8   Suitability for Use   29
2.9   Influences and Limitations on Design   29
2.10   Style, Fashion, and Taste   30
2.11   Marketing   31

3   **THE LATHE**   **33**

    3.1   History of the Lathe   34
    3.2   Types of Lathe   35
    3.3   Lathe Capacity   37
    3.4   The Lathe Bed   38
    3.5   The Stand   39
    3.6   The Headstock   41
    3.7   The Tailstock   43
    3.8   Tailstocks for Long-hole Boring   45
    3.9   The Banjo   47
    3.10   Toolrests   48
    3.11   Motor, Transmission, and Switchgear   49
    3.12   Driving Centres   51
    3.13   Tail Centres   53
    3.14   Outboard Turning Stands   54
    3.15   The Carriage   55

4   **LATHE ACCESSORIES AND ASSOCIATED EQUIPMENT**   **56**

    4.1   Measuring Equipment   56
    4.2   Faceplates   58
    4.3   Screwchucks   59
    4.4   Cupchucks   61
    4.5   Jacobs Chucks   61
    4.6   Sleeves   62
    4.7   Scroll Chucks   62
    4.8   Collet Chucks   68
    4.9   Homemade Chucks   69
    4.10   Vacuum Chucks   69
    4.11   Chuck Choice   70
    4.12   Mandrels   71
    4.13   Drill Bits   74

5   **TURNING THEORY AND TOOLS**   **76**

    5.1   Cutting Theory   77
    5.2   Tool Steels   92
    5.3   The Roughing Gouge   94
    5.4   The Skew Chisel   98

5.5   The Detail Gouge   101
5.6   The Parting Tool   105
5.7   Scrapers   106
5.8   Recommended Set of Tools   108
5.9   Tool Handles   108
5.10   Making Handles   110
5.11   Other Tools   111
5.12   Tool Grinding   113
5.13   Honing   119

6   WORKSHOP PROCEDURES   122

6.1   Workshop Safety   122
6.2   Lighting   123
6.3   The Stance   125
6.4   Turning Grips   125
6.5   Small-scale Turning   130
6.6   Turning Other Materials   130
6.7   Turning for Furniture Restoration   131
6.8   Sanding   132
6.9   Finishing   136

7   SPINDLE TURNING   139

7.1   Pencil and Pin Gauges   130
7.2   Preparation of Wood for Turning   144
7.3   Mounting the Wood Between Centres   147
7.4   Principles of Spindle Turning   149
7.5   Roughing   154
7.6   V-cuts   160
7.7   Leaving Squares   161
7.8   The Planing Cut   165
7.9   Bead Cutting   168
7.10   Cutting Fillets   179
7.11   Removing Waste with the Skew   181
7.12   Squaring Shoulders   181
7.13   Parting Tool Work   181
7.14   Use of the Detail Gouge   182
7.15   Parting-off   192
7.16   Copy Turning   194
7.17   Slender Turning   194

7.18 Split Turnings 201

7.19 Multiple-axis Turning 201

7.20 Laminating 209

7.21 Twists, Spirals, Fluting, and Reeding 209

7.22 Exercises 209

8 CUPCHUCK TURNING 215

8.1 Fixing the Work to the Headstock 215

8.2 Cupchucking a Knob 217

8.3 Turning an Egg Cup 221

8.4 Turning Lidded Boxes 225

8.5 Hollow Turning 232

9 FACEPLATE TURNING 234

9.1 Holding the Workpiece 234

9.2 Preparing the Workpiece 235

9.3 The Basic Faceplate Turning Cuts 235

9.4 Turning a Base 238

9.5 Hollowing in Faceplate Turning 241

9.6 Turning a Ring 243

10 BOWL TURNING 251

10.1 Bowl Design 253

10.2 Wood for Bowls 257

10.3 Wood Preparation for Rough-turning of Bowls 258

10.4 Outline Turning Procedures 270

10.5 Seasoning 273

10.6 Stabilisation 274

10.7 Bowl Chucking 275

10.8 Tool Choice and Presentation 289

10.9 The Turning of Bowls 294

10.10 Turning the Waste from the Bottom 315

10.11 Bowl Sanding 319

References 321

Gallery 322

Index 331

Preface

One of the standard books on management is *The Practice of Management* by Peter F. Drucker. In that book a practice is shown to combine art, science, and technology, plus the essential ingredients of human effort and ingenuity. Woodturning also demands these qualities and I have therefore shamelessly stolen three-quarters of Mr. Drucker's title.

When I started to learn woodturning, I had no thought of it being other than a hobby. However, I was fortunate in gaining entrance to the three-year woodturning course at Sydney Technical College which was staffed by professional woodturners. Being somewhat of a bookworm, I also read as much as possible on the subject. It quickly became apparent that there were major discrepancies, disagreements, and omissions in and between my tuition and my reading. In particular, the books were almost universally pitched at too low a level. This book was therefore started within a year of my commencing to learn woodturning with the objectives of, firstly, filling the gaping hole in the literature and, secondly, providing a framework within which to conduct researches of my own to determine the best turning equipment and techniques. I hope that the early start on the book has enabled me to cover those points which beginners find difficult while providing plenty of meat for the ambitious and professional turners.

Since spending some time teaching woodturning, I have become conscious that most people taking up the practice neither have access to professional tuition nor are able to watch expert turners in action. In short, they attempt woodturning in isolation with books and magazines as their only source of instruction. I have therefore attempted to properly explain and illustrate the fundamentals by describing not only the how but also the why of woodturning. My own turning techniques still develop and change in line with new thoughts and experiences, so that I can only state that this book attempts to describe what I believe are the optimum practices at the time of writing. It would, however, be irresponsible of me merely to describe these practices. More importantly, I have laboured to fully explain and support my recommendations in order that you, the reader, may make up your own mind.

This book concentrates on those areas of turning to which I believe I have something fresh to add, something to explain, or something to correct. Hence, some aspects of turning are covered in less detail than in other publications. This may be because I personally have little interest in these aspects, or because there is more research to be done. The book also seeks to show the reader the true potential of woodturning, although this can require extra expenditure on equipment. Finally, the designs and subjects for turning illustrated in much of the literature are often poor, and I hope that this book goes some way to correcting this.

It is of course difficult to understand one particular aspect of turning in isolation. Those of you new to turning should read through the book fairly quickly a couple of times before becoming involved with the detail. As stated at the beginning of this introduction, turning is a practice and its techniques need to be practiced so that they become almost automatic. When this stage is reached, you can concentrate on achieving the exact shape and finish that you want instead of being distracted by details of technique. You should also try to see as many other turners in operation as possible. Hopefully this book will enable you to select the beneficial and reject the harmful from others' practices.

Professional hand woodturners are now relatively rare. Other materials have superseded wood for many applications and the still large amount of woodturning required is mainly done by fully or partially automatic lathes. Not only is wood being superseded for technical reasons, it is also becoming relatively more expensive and also more difficult to obtain the clear straight-grained stock preferred for spindle turning. Is there then any future for woodturning? I believe that there is for the following reasons:

1. Leisure time and discretionary income are rising. Woodturning is a useful and rewarding hobby.
2. As wood becomes more expensive, it is becoming more appreciated. Hence, there is a growing market for products which are of wood and display the features of wood.
3. There remains a considerable demand for short-run production work, uneconomical for automatic lathes because of the small numbers required.
4. The demand for the turning for repairs and replacements as well as for new work is not now decreasing.
5. Besides actually producing, there are viable areas such as teaching, supplying equipment and requisites, and even writing.

However, the majority of this book's readers will practice woodturning for enjoyment, and indeed woodturning should be an emotional experience. Woodturning books tend to dwell on the technical aspects, and with reason, for only when skills are assured and equipment is right can you really revel in the practice. The sweet feeling of a truly sharp tool cutting, the dancing movements of a skew chisel, the controlled power of heavy cuts: these are what woodturning is really about. It should mean much more to you than a high-speed process for carving circular cross-sections. It should be like playing a musical instrument; there must be life, involvement, light, and shade. Plus, there is the satisfaction of having created a turning which is beautiful and in most cases functional.

In short, woodturning offers enjoyment, satisfaction, and even remuneration, in addition to frustration, anger, and exasperation. I hope that this book assists you in realizing and perhaps expanding your woodturning ambitions.

In conclusion, I would like to think that this book will not become outdated. However, I am sure that it will as others and I learn, discover, and experiment further. Any comments or corrections that you have may be sent to me through the publishers. They will be considered and answered.

PREFACE TO 1995 EDITION

This book's first edition was published in 1985. During the following eight years woodturning knowledge increased enormously and my seven-hour video released in 1993, also titled *The Practice of Woodturning*, reflects this. The resulting discrepancies between the book and the video resulting from the eight year gap showed a need for the book to be revised, and this edition is the result.

Most instructional woodturning books describe their author's personal techniques. Confusingly, each author promotes techniques which differ to some extent from those promoted by other authors. How can the woodturning student select those techniques which will best suit him or her? Unfortunately this question is based upon the common, but false, assumption that different techniques suit different turners.

I believe that for each woodturning situation:

1. There is one best method, or for some situations two or more equal-best methods.
2. The best methods are properly determined by how and with what result an edge creates a fresh surface on the wood.
3. The best methods are the same for all turners irrespective of their physical characteristics, nationalities, personalities, etc.
4. Those who teach woodturning have a duty to their students to teach the best methods known at that time.

The personal methods used by instructors are not without interest, but would students knowingly seek to learn demonstrably inferior methods. This completely revised edition of The Practice of Woodturning therefore attempts to describe what I believe are in late 1995 the best methods.

I cannot guarantee that the methods in this book are the best which are known in late 1995, but I have attempted to substantiate their worth, particularly in Chapter 5. I invite those who believe that this book's methods are not the best to substantiate why. If those substantiations are convincing, woodturning knowledge will be progressed, a benefit for all turners.

A review of 1986 criticised this book for focussing on traditional turning. It did not, and it does not now. It attempts to give you the knowledge to be able to turn what you design irrespective of whether that design is traditional or otherwise.

The amateur turns occasionally and therefore needs sounder technique than the professional who is always 'in practice'. Many who learn to turn have to teach themselves. This book therefore is long and detailed: firstly, to enable me to pass on a large body of knowledge; and secondly, to avoid the all-too-common superficiality which leaves you lost.

The use of technical terms such as rake, side rake, and subsurface damage is intentional. They are fully explained and then used because they contribute clarity, surely an essential in a book which seeks to explain both the 'why' and the 'how' of the best woodturning methods.

MIKE DARLOW

Acknowledgments

What turning expertise I have is in great part due to the excellent teaching that I received at Sydney Technical College from George Sutton, John Ewert, and George Hatfield and my thanks are due to them. George Sutton in particular has a knowledge of both the how and the why of turning which exceeds that of any other turner that I have met, and much of the advice and analysis in Chapters 7 and 8 will be familiar to him.

Other turners that I have visited have always freely discussed their individual approaches and I should like to thank Cecil Jordan, Ray Key, and Richard Raffan, all in England. Australian woodturners who have made contributions include Alan Hayes, Chris Lorrimer, Alan Schoultz, and Bruce Leadbeatter.

Thanks are also due to J.A. Simpson of the Forestry Commission of New South Wales for his advice on the chemical treatment of wood. Jane Burns of the Crafts Council of Australia gave valuable nontechnical advice.

Peter Johnson has remained a great friend despite near electrocution during the photography sessions and the results are a tribute to his patience and ability. We have taken the hard way, and have tried to show the turner's view in the instructional shots, thereby (we hope) aiding comprehension.

Special thanks are due to Kim Mawhinnew who retyped the manuscript innumerable times and with unfailing enthusiasm.

The writing of this book was spread over two and a half years. During that time I have received encouragement and support from many friends. In particular Marilla Burgess, Judith Brotherton, O.R. Linka, Aureole MacArogher, David and Francis Walsh, and Claude and Pippa Bilinsky. My parents have given tremendous support throughout, while during the final months my wife Aliki's help was critical in finally finishing the thing off.

ACKNOWLEDGMENTS FOR 1995 EDITION

I have gleaned widely since this book was first published in 1985. Frank Bollins, Dale Hageman, George Hatfield, Leonard Lee, Bob Shepherd, George Sutton, Stephen Waite and Vic Wood have each contributed technical advice.

In 1993 Albert LeCoff organised the first World Woodturning Conference. He was brave enough to invite me. This enabled me to establish and renew international contacts. Jerry Glaser was perhaps the most valuable, and our meeting was aided by a common friendship with Neil Jones.

Many of the excellent photographs taken by Peter Johnson for the 1985 edition have been retained. The new photographs have been taken by me, often with Dale Hageman supplying the hands. These photographs would have been far worse but for the advice and help of David Cumming, Mark Connors, and Rowan Fotheringham.

The original edition was scanned and the many rewritings and revisions tirelessly word-processed by Barrie Randerson and Andrew Ball.

The writings of other woodturners are always of interest. Keith Rowley's depiction of roughing cuts has influenced Figure 7.15 and I am not alone in adopting Richard Raffan's depiction of groups of cuts.

Readers familiar with earlier editions will, I hope, be impressed by how much more information is in this one. Greg Burrows has assembled the text and illustrations, and his expertise has resulted in a larger whole of greater clarity in the same space.

It is not enough to produce a book. You also have to get it into the market place. Ray Key, Rick Mastelli, and particularly Ken Raffe have helped with this.

Most professional woodworkers will confirm the need for a working wife and for children who will stand the pressures and sacrifices which the trade demands. I have indeed been fortunate, and thank Alice, Joshua and Samuel.

Terminology

Descriptions of three-dimensional motions and forces can be confusing, and in wood-turning there may often be the additional complication of there being two different axes: the lathe axis and the axis of the tool itself. Thus, when the tool axis is perpendicular to the lathe axis, a lateral movement of the tool with respect to its own axis (that is, to the turner's left or right) is equally a longitudinal movement with respect to the lathe axis. To ensure clarity special care is taken with sentence construction and the wording conforms to the definitions which follow:

Axially, *adv.* Along an axis.

Axis, *n.* Imaginary line about which a body rotates or revolves. Unless otherwise stated or inferred, the axis of rotation of the lathe headstock spindle. The term may also be applied to the axis of symmetry of an object.

Backward, adv. In spindle turning when referring to the tool, moving horizontally and perpendicularly to the lathe axis toward the turner.

Centrifugal, *adj.* Tending to move away from the axis.

Centripetal, *adj.* Tending to move toward the axis. Hence, when an object is whirled round on a string, the string exerts a centripetal force on the object which is equal and opposite to the outward centrifugal force induced by the object's circular motion.

Circumference, n. Line enclosing a circle, that is, the perimeter of a circle.

Forward, adv. In spindle turning when referring to the tool, moving horizontally and perpendicularly toward the lathe axis away from the turner.

Fulcrum, n. Pivot about which a lever turns.

Lateral, *adj.* In a sideways direction, that is, horizontally and at right angles to the axis.

Longitudinal, *adj.* Parallel to the axis.

Moment, *n.* Rotational force, that is, similar to that exerted when using a wrench (spanner).

Normal, *n.* Line at right angles to a tangent which passes through the point of intersection between the curve and the tangent.

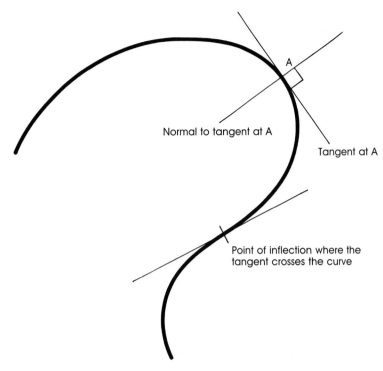

Tangent, normal, and point of inflection

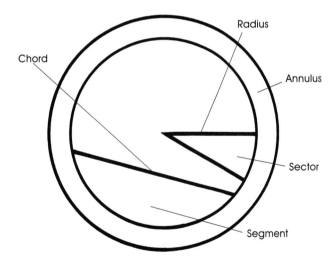

Parts of a circle

Periphery, *n.* External surface of a body.

Perpendicular, *adj.* At right angles to any line or plane.

Perpendicular, *n.* Line at right angles to a line or plane.

Point of inflexion, *n.* Point at which the curvature of a curve changes from convex to concave.

Radial, *adj.* Toward or away from a center along a radius.

Reaction, *n.* Equal and opposite force resisting an applied force.

Revolve, *v.* To perform a circular motion about an axis which is not coincidental with the axis of symmetry of the body in question.

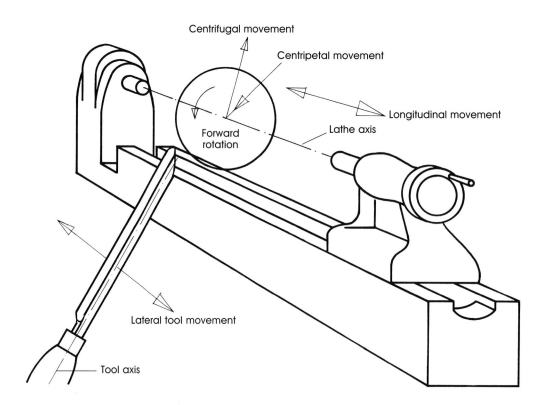

Axes and movements

Rotation, *n.* Motion of a body revolving around its own axis of symmetry.

Tangent, *n,* Straight line touching a curve at one point. Therefore the minute length of curve in contact with the line is parallel to the line.

Transverse, *adj.* At right angles to an axis.

Velocity, *n.* Speed in the direction of motion.

Pointing arrows	
Dimensioning arrows	
Movement arrows	
Force arrows	
Center lines and axes	
Hidden detail	

Wood — side grain	
Wood — end grain	
A length left square in cross-section	

1
Wood

In this age of mass production, synthetic materials, and the rapid depletion of the world's forests, wood is at last becoming accepted as a luxury material by the public. In some cases, even, the appeal of the wood itself may exceed that due to the design and workmanship. Therefore, it is important that the woodworker is both knowledgeable and enthusiastic about his raw material so that he can, firstly, use it sensibly and sensitively, and secondly, inform and enthuse the public, both directly and through the medium of his own work.

1.1 TREE AND WOOD NOMENCLATURE

The naming of woods is fraught with confusion and inconsistency. However, as public awareness of wood increases, so it behooves us to tighten up on both nomenclature and identification. The problems stem from the potentially large number of names by which a particular wood species may be known. Each tree species has a unique botanic name, and many woods have standard trade names. However, some trees and timbers also have local names, and these or similar names may be applied to different species in other localities. Then, of course, many trees are felled without being correctly identified and someone along the supply chain ventures a name which is then accepted absolutely.

Woodturners use a greater range of species than other woodworkers and it is therefore important that we develop expertise in tree and wood identification and are consistent and correct in our naming. Many guides and manuals exist for tree identification, and your local forestry office will also be prepared to assist. Similarly with the identification of wood, although it is more difficult because you have much less to go on. With both wood and tree data and vegetative samples, a positive identification is usually possible without having to resort to one of the wood identification laboratories or herbariums.

The identification and naming of trees has a long history. Theophrastus, a pupil of Aristotle, described 480 plant species in about 300 BC. Another Greek, Dioscorides, wrote a herbal in the first century AD. which held sway until the first modern classification was published in 1583. This volume, *De Plantis*, was published by Professor

Caesalpinus at the University of Pisa. Research, for botany was a respected field for both professional and amateur, proceeded apace, and by 1703 John Ray's book *Methodus Plantarum* was able to refer to 18,000 plant species.

However, it was Carolus Linnaeus (1707-78) who introduced the modern classification for plant identification in his book *Species Plantarum* (1753). He classified plants according to their sexual organs (that is, stamens and pistils), a method since considered too narrow, and proposed a naming system known as binomial nomenclature. A sound system of nomenclature is obviously necessary, for there are about 250,000 species in the plant kingdom. Note that a species is a plant which will reproduce itself identically.

In the binomial nomenclature, the two words which form the plant's name are written in italics, with the first word denoting the genus and having its first letter in the upper case. The second word denotes the species and is composed of all lower-case letters. Consider, for example, the tree whose botanic name is *Caesalpinia sappan*. The genus name honours Professor Caesalpinus. The species name refers to the medieval name of the wood. This Asian wood yields a bright red dye known as bresil, and it was the discovery of another wood in South America giving a similar dye which led to the naming of Brazil. This other wood, *Caesalpinia echinata*, has the standard trade name pernambuco (after the territory where the best specimens grow) and is prized for violin bows.

The science of classification, taxonomy, is based upon a tiered system in which the units comprising a tier are then each subdivided to form the next tier below. The tiers are:

Plant Kingdom
Subkingdom
Division
Class
Subclass
Order
Family
Genus
Species

Being specifically interested in wood, we need be concerned with only two divisions and these are described in Figure 1.1.

There is a natural aversion to using latinised botanic names, and rarely do they in any way physically describe the wood. Hence, standard trade names have been agreed upon for most commercial timbers. However, even these can be confusing and they are necessarily restricted to a small proportion of the approximately 30,000 tree species in the world.

Perhaps the difficulties in naming can be illustrated by looking at the oaks. In the genus Quercus (from the Latin name for an oak tree) there are about 500 species. All true oaks bear acorns, and species are identified by the forms of their leaves, flowers, and acorns. These trees, which are native in Europe, Asia, and North America, fall into three groups based on their wood structure: white oaks; red oaks whose timber is coarser, less durable, and permeable to liquids; and evergreen oaks whose wood is closer-grained and without conspicuous annual rings.

All true oaks have pale-coloured timbers with prominent *medullary rays*, radial groups of cells which facilitate radial transmission of nutrients and wastes. However, the picture is complicated by the tendency for many timbers with large medullary rays to be incorrectly called oaks. Thus in Australia, for example, there are many unrelated species known as oaks, such as the brown tulip oak, *Heritiera trifoliata*; the silky oaks, *Grevillea robusta*, *Orites excelsa*, and *Cardwellia sublimis*; and the sheoaks, genus *Casuarina*. Similar confusion occurs with walnuts, ashes, maples, cedars, mahoganies, etc.

Figure 1.1 Tree Classification

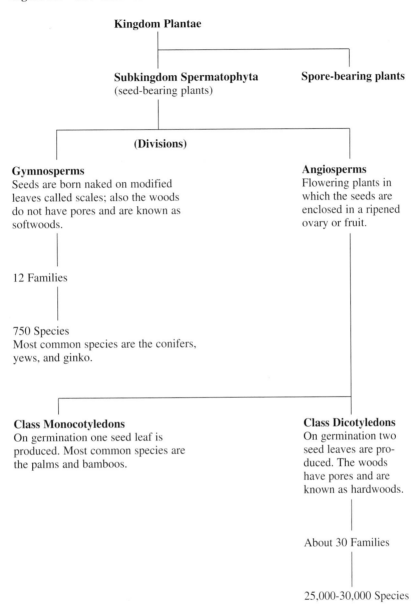

The problems associated with correct naming are therefore considerable, but it is far better to admit the ignorance or uncertainty, which is surely to be expected with 30,000 possibilities, than to continue with the sloppiness which has characterised much timber identification and naming to date.

1.2 TREE GROWTH

Trees grow in height by cell production at the growing tips. Increase in diameter results from the cell-forming activity at the cambium, a zone at the junction of the wood and the bark (Figure 1.2). The material used in the creation of new tissue is manufactured by the process of photosynthesis. In this process, water and minerals (sap) are conveyed from the roots via the outer wood (sapwood) to the leaves. In the leaves, the green compound chlorophyll converts the sun's radiant energy into chemical energy. This permits water from the sap to combine with the 0.03 percent of carbon dioxide in the air to form sugars, starches, and amino acids. Oxygen is also produced and released into the air. The minerals in the sap act mainly as catalysts.

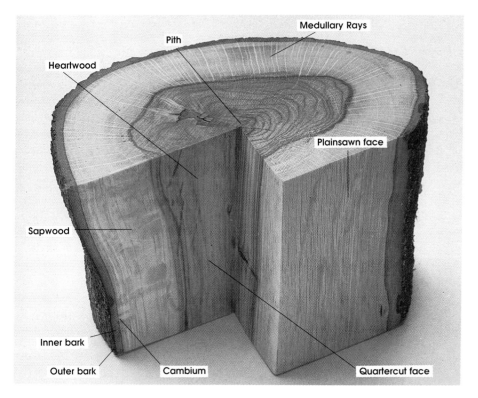

Figure 1.2   A small log of English oak (*Quercus robur*). Although this species is ring porous, the annual rings of this log are not prominent because of the mild winters in Australia.

The compounds produced in the leaves are then conducted down the inner bark to feed the cell production which takes place in the cambium. Cells which are produced on the inner surface of the cambium become sapwood; those produced on the outer surface become bark. Obviously, sapwood cannot be added without the bark increasing in girth, and this is enabled by the bark splitting or being shed.

Particularly in cool climates, the rate of growth varies during the year, being perhaps nil in the winter, rapid in the spring, and slower in the summer and autumn. This variation in growth rate often gives rise to the phenomenon known as annual rings (see Figure 1.3). Hardwoods exhibiting annual rings are known as ring porous. Tropical hardwoods grow all year and are therefore known as diffuse porous (Figure 1.4).

In the section on nomenclature, trees were divided into softwoods and hardwoods —the difference being the respective absence or presence of vessels or pores which are large linear cells. On hardwoods, end-grain vessels show as small circles or dots depending on size (see Figure 1.4). They are absent from softwoods (see Figure 1.3). Although both hardwoods and softwoods have medullary rays, they can be especially large only in hardwoods.

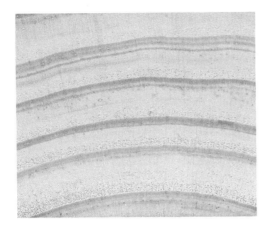

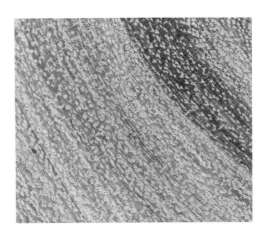

Figure 1.3 A cross-section of radiata pine (*Pinus radiata*) showing annual rings. The paler wood is softer and results from the rapid spring growth.

Figure 1.4 End-grain blackbean (*Castanospermum australe*), a tropical hardwood. The prominent pale dots are sections through the pores.

1.3 CHEMICAL COMPOSITION OF WOOD

Wood is composed of carbon, oxygen, and hydrogen. Besides water these elements form four groups of compounds:

1. *Cellulose*, which forms almost half the weight of dry wood. It is the source of wood's tensile strength, and forms wood fibres in combination with hemicelluloses and lignin.
2. *Hemicelluloses*, which are closely allied with cellulose.
3. *Lignin*, which bonds the wood fibres together to give the characteristic woodiness, that is, high structural strength which distinguishes trees from the soft tissue plants. It comprises about 30 percent by weight of softwoods and 20 percent of hardwoods. Lignin is plastic when hot and therefore enables the process of steambending in which the lignin is softened by heating to 212°F (100°C).
4. *Extractives*, which are compounds that give many timbers their special characteristics. They are so called because they can be extracted with solvents, and in some cases distilled out. Extractives give colour, durability, and smell. They are concentrated in the heartwood, particularly in its outer region. Hence, the sapwood and inner heartwood are more subject to fungal and insect attack.

1.4 TYPES OF EXTRACTIVES

There are five types of extractives:

1. *Carbohydrates*, in the sap or stored in the cells.
2. *Terpenes*, in the forms of volatile oils and nonvolatile resins. They are frequently the cause of characteristic wood odours.
3. *Phenolic compounds*, which are present mainly in the heartwood and account for heartwood's darker colour and, due to their toxicity, greater durability. Tannin is the best-known phenolic compound.

4. *Nitrogen compounds*, present in the sapwood. The presence of these renders the wood susceptible to attack.
5. *Inorganic compounds*, which are the constituents of wood ash. The amount is usually below 1 percent but may be up to 5 percent. Silica can also occur as free grains, and when more than 0.5 percent is present, rapid blunting of tools is experienced. Softwoods are generally silica-free, but some hardwoods have large proportions, for example, teak up to 1.4 percent and Queensland walnut up to 1.1 percent.

1.5 EFFECTS OF EXTRACTIVES ON WOOD PROPERTIES

Extractives can affect wood properties in several ways:

1. *Colour*. The three basic compounds comprising wood are pale or colourless. Extractives provide colour and their uneven distribution gives rise to colour variations in wood. They are sensitive to ultraviolet light which tends to yellow them. Ultraviolet absorbers are therefore often incorporated into clear finishes.
2. *Staining*. Iron and ammonia both react with tannin to give dark colourations. Some colouring compounds are water soluble and wetting of timbers containing them can lead to water marks.
3. *Durability*. The toxic nature of phenols and the avoidance of them by insects and funguses are important reasons for the greater durability of heartwood. High resin concentrations in softwoods also discourage attack.
4. *Allergies*. The highly irritant nature of the dust and sap of some species is due to extractives.
5. *Effect on finishing*. Oleoresins occur in some softwoods and can exude as sticky globules through some finishes. Some hardwoods also exude extractives which harm finishes, and even if extractives are not actually exuded, some slowing of the drying rate or poor adhesion of glue may be noticeable.

1.6 STRENGTH, MOISTURE CONTENT, AND TEMPERATURE

The living tree is saturated with water and the proportion may vary from 30 to over 200 percent of the dry weight of the wood substances. Dense timbers have low moisture contents; vigorously growing softwoods generally have much higher figures. Sapwood has a higher moisture content than heartwood, but being more permeable because it is actively conducting sap, it dries more quickly and will therefore distort and crack more than heartwood during seasoning.

With the exception of green-turned bowls (see Section 10.4), finished turnings should be produced in seasoned timber because:

1. They will be dimensionally far more stable.
2. There is a much reduced likelihood of fungal decay, staining, and insect attack.
3. Weight is reduced.
4. It will take finishes and gluing better.
5. If the products are containers, the contents will not mildew.
6. Strength and hardness are greater.

The moisture content of a piece of wood is expressed as a percentage of the oven-dry weight; that is:

$$
\begin{aligned}
\text{Percentage moisture content} &= \frac{\text{Weight of moisture}}{\text{Oven-dry weight}} \times 100 \\
&= \frac{\text{Wet weight} - \text{Oven-dry weight}}{\text{Oven-dry weight}} \times 100 \\
&= \left(\frac{\text{Wet weight}}{\text{Oven-dry weight}} - 1 \right) \times 100
\end{aligned}
$$

Truly accurate determinations of moisture content are done by taking a wood sample back from the ends of the piece, weighing, oven-drying, and weighing again. This is obviously not usually feasible and therefore two alternatives exist. You can weigh the wood regularly, and when its weight remains constant conclude that it is seasoned to the corresponding average ambient relative humidity. Note that the accuracy of this conclusion declines with increasing wood thickness and density. Alternatively, you can use a battery-operated moisture meter. There are probed and probeless. With probed, steel electrodes are driven in, and the electrical resistance of the wood between them, which is higher with drier wood, is measured and enables the moisture content to be determined. The newer probeless meters measure moisture content by creating electromagnetic fields.

Air contains water, and the maximum weight of water which air at a given temperature can contain is a measure of its absolute humidity. However, if the air holds less than its maximum weight of water vapour, it will tend to absorb water, and it is therefore its relative humidity which determines its drying effectiveness. For example, air at 85°F (29°C) can hold up to 12 grains of water per pound (1.7 grams per kilogram) of dry air. Therefore, if the air contains only 3 grains, it is 25 percent saturated and hence has a relative humidity of 25 percent. The relative humidity of air will vary considerably, being high on damp days and low on clear, windy days. It will be, on average, much higher in wet coastal regions than in deserts. In addition, the average annual relative humidity of the outside air in a region will be appreciably higher than that in heated or air-conditioned premises.

Timber is hygroscopic and therefore its moisture content will vary with changes in the ambient air's relative humidity. Table 1.1 shows the equilibrium moisture content of wood for various constant humidities.

**TABLE 1.1   RELATIONSHIP BETWEEN RELATIVE HUMIDITY AND
EQUILIBRIUM MOISTURE CONTENT AT 70°F (21°C)**

Relative Humidity of the Air, %	Corresponding Equilibrium Moisture Content of Wood, % at 25°C
10	3.0
20	4.5
30	6.5
40	8.0
50	10.5
60	11.5
70	13.5
75	15.0
80	17.5
90	22.0

The tendency of a piece of wood to season without warping and cracking (that is, without *degrade*) varies according to species and to the grain characteristics of the particular piece. Woods with large medullary rays are prone to radial splits because ray tissue shrinks at a different rate from the rest of the wood structure. Dense woods allow moisture to escape only slowly, so that although having initially low moisture contents, steep moisture-content gradients develop which cause high internal stresses and attendant cracking. Contorted grain structures will also encourage excessive degrade.

Moisture in wood is present as *free water*; that is, it is held in cell cavities and other spaces within the wood. In addition, water is held firmly within the cell walls and this is known as *combined water*.

During seasoning, the free water is first to evaporate and this takes place relatively quickly. When all the free water has gone, the fibre saturation point is reached; at this stage the moisture content is 25 to 35 percent. The combined water will then start to evaporate, albeit much more slowly, and shrinkage will commence.

Unfortunately, wood does not dry evenly. The free water in the outer layer will evaporate quickly, allowing evaporation of the combined water in the outer layer to commence. The outer wood layer will start to shrink. Meanwhile, evaporation from the inner wood is proceeding at a slower pace, and so free water will still be present and there will have been no tendency for shrinkage of these inner layers to occur. Tension stresses will therefore result in the outer layers, and cracking may occur.

Two other factors contribute markedly to degrade: variations in shrinkage coefficients, and variations in permeability to moisture.

In the majority of timbers, shrinkage of cells in the radial direction of a log is about half that of shrinkage in the tangential direction (that is, at right angles to the rays). Longitudinal (axial) shrinkage in the log is negligible, being about one-fiftieth of the radial shrinkage. Obviously, degrade will be more prone in species whose shrinkage coefficients are high and in species whose radial and tangential coefficients are very different from one another. Table 1.2 shows a representative range of coefficients which are expressed as the percentage reduction in dimension experienced when the wood is seasoned from wet to 12 percent moisture content.

TABLE 1.2   EXAMPLES OF WOOD SHRINKAGE COEFFICIENTS

Species	Radial Shrinkage, %	Tangential Shrinkage, %
Indonesian kauri (*Agathis alba*)	1.1	1.7
Radiata pine (*Pinus radiata*)	2.5	3.9
Turpentine (*Syncarpia glomulifera*)	7.0	14.5
Peppermint (*Eucalyptus piperita*)	9.5	20.5

Uneven drying is also promoted by the variation in velocity of moisture movement. The ratios of longitudinal:radial:tangential moisture movements are approximately 10 to 25:2 to 4:1. Hence the importance of sealing exposed end grain during seasoning.

The methods of seasoning and stabilisation particularly relevant to woodturning are described in Sections 10.5 and 10.6.

Wet wood is always easier to turn than dry wood. Long ribbon shavings flow silkily in contrast to the small chip-like shavings from seasoned timber. In addition, the tool's cutting edge is kept cool by the moisture in the wood so that sharpness is retained for much longer. However, the problems associated with distortion and cracking as wet wood seasons have been described. As well, wet wood is weaker and less cohesive, so that the off-the-tool finish from wet wood is inferior.

In turning, the relative velocity of the wood at the cutting edge is high, and hence high temperatures are generated in both the wood and the tool. This is well illustrated by the very hot shavings produced when heavily scraping end grain in cupchuck work. This rise in temperature is helpful as the wood is weakened and therefore cuts more easily.

Some turnings are highly stressed during their working life; Windsor chair legs are a notable example. In such work it is most important that the grain be straight and truly axial. For instance, if the grain is at 15° to the axis of the member, the strengths in compression, bending, and tension will drop to 80, 70, and 50 percent, respectively, of their axial grain values.

1.7   INTERNAL STRESSES

In Figure 1.5 the part of the tree above trunk cross-section A-A exerts a vertically downward force. If the tree is straight, vertical, and symmetrical, the stress (force per unit area) across A-A is of constant magnitude. However the wood in branches, in leaning or in unsymmetrically-loaded trunks, or in trees subjected prevailing winds, grows in an unevenly stressed condition. This unevenness of stress results in a tendency for such wood to distort during woodworking operations, and to a lesser extent thereafter.

Consider the branch in Figure 1.5. To support its own weight the branch grows with the fibres in the upper section of the branch in tension, and those in the lower section in compression (Figure 1.6). The stresses are highest at the extreme top and bottom of the branch.

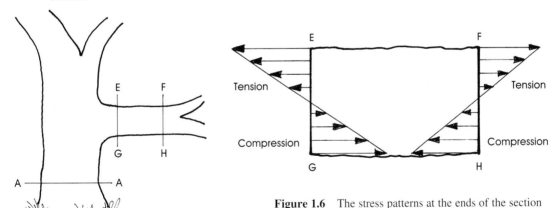

Figure 1.5   A living tree.

Figure 1.6   The stress patterns at the ends of the section of living branch E,F,G,H. The stresses across E,G are higher than those across F,H because of the self-weight of E,F,G,H.

Trees have a tendency to develop extra wood to cope with uneven stress situations. Softwoods produce compression wood which is denser and may be darker in colour (Figure 1.7). Hardwoods produce tension wood which is woollier than normal (Figure 1.8).

When a tree is felled the wood remains in a stressed condition. By cutting along the

Figure 1.7
A cross-section through the branch in Figure 1.5 showing the compression wood which would be produced below the pith if the tree was a softwood.

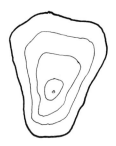

Figure 1.8
A cross-section through the branch in Figure 1.5 showing the tension wood which would be produced above the pith if the tree was a hardwood.

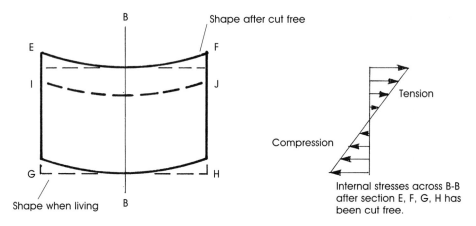

Figure 1.9 How branch section E,F,G,H would deform once freed from the tree and therefore from the external stresses imposed by the living branch to the right of section E,G in Figure 1.5. The new internal stressing is indicated at the section ends.

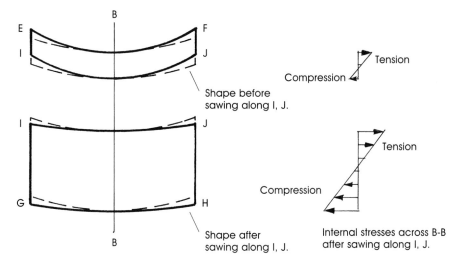

Figure 1.10 The deformations and residual stress patterns after sawing along I,J.

grain, planks, etc. of smaller cross-sectional area are produced. These are more flexible and are able to distort to a greater extent, thus relieving some of the internal stressing. This process in which wood distorts during and after cutting as its internal stresses adopt a new equilibrium is called *relaxation*.

If the length of branch E,F,G,H in Figure 1.5 were cut away, its fibres at E,G and F,H would no longer be subjected to tensile and compressive stresses due to the branch's own self-weight. The fibre stresses in E,F,G,H would therefore change, they would lessen as shown in Figure 1.9 and allow the branch section to bow. The bowing due to this relaxation would however be barely perceptible because it would be resisted by the section's stiffness.

Consider cutting a sector shaped plank from the top of E,F,G,H. As you cut along I,J, the two resulting pieces will bow as shown in Figure 1.10 as the internal stresses relax into a new equilibrium. This relaxation is a two-stage process. As the cut is being made there is instantaneous distortion. Then follows a long-term relaxation at a gradually reducing rate until a new equilibrium is reached. This second-stage relaxation usually produces significantly less distortion than that due to the first stage.

Prior to cutting along I,J the adjacent wood is in tension. When sector E,F,I,J is freed, its face I,J is no longer subject to the 'external' force exerted by the wood along the top face of I,J,G,H. Therefore the bottom surface I,J of the sector is able to lengthen, and the internal stresses can relax into a new equilibrium. Similarly the top surface of I,J,G,H is no longer restrained, and it too can lengthen. The resultant bowing of I,J,G,H will be much less obvious than that in E,F,I,J because of the former's greater stiffness.

Variations in internal stress are a continuing problem for those who work in solid wood. The most common instance is when ripsawing a plank. As the wood is cut, the two resulting pieces either converge and bind on the riving knife, or diverge. The result: two banana-shaped pieces from one straight piece. Woodturners too are bedevilled. Turning a spindle removes wood and so may cause considerable bowing due to stress relaxation. Even turning a bowl from a disk causes some distortion, both due to further seasoning and stress relaxation during and after hollowing. Peter Child in *The Craftsman Woodturner* gives a graphic analogy for such relaxation, "An abdominal operation... causes some doubling up in most humans!"

1.8   FUNGAL AND INSECT ATTACK

In addition to degrade due to drying, wood is also subject to attack from both funguses and insects.

Funguses are forms of plant life that do not possess the chlorophyll which enables green plants to manufacture their own nutrients. Funguses therefore feed on other plants, either alive or dead. Infection is spread by airborne spores with some funguses producing millions of spores per hour. Attack is possible only in warm, damp conditions, and sapwood, with its high level of nutrients, is particularly susceptible.

The staining funguses are our main source of concern. Colours produced include brown, orange, red, yellow, and blue-black called *bluestain*. These stains do not alter the structural properties of the wood. Speedy conversion into sawn sizes followed by rapid seasoning will prevent attack. Alternatively, a number of chemical treatments can be used to prevent both fungal and insect attack, but they are, to varying extents, toxic to man. The effects of exposure during proper treatment and storage of the wood and from the dust during turning may well be negligible for some chemicals, but I hope that readers will excuse my reluctance to make positive recommendations.

More serious fungal attack leads to decay, also known as rot. Structural deterioration becomes serious and may be accompanied by very attractive colour changes. Spalting (see Figure 1.11) is a particular form of white rot which is accompanied by softening and embrittlement of the wood.

Wood is also attacked by insects. Different insects attack at different moisture contents. Even when turning dry wood, we may experience an occasional flash of spray as another larva meets an early end!

Attack may be by the adult insects or, more commonly, by the larvae. The five common classes of attacking insects are:

1. Those that attack live trees—mainly *longhorn beetles.*
2. Those that attack freshly felled logs—*pinhole borers.*
3. Those that attack seasoned and seasoning wood—mainly *powder-post beetles.*
4. Those that attack timber in buildings and furniture—*furniture beetles.*
5. Those that attack wood in any condition—*termites.*

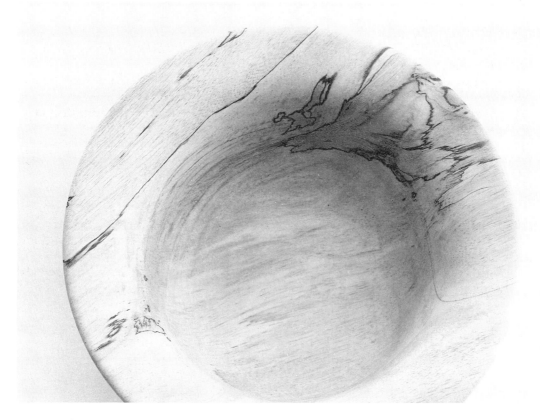

Figure 1.11   Spalting in lemon wood (*Citrus limonia*).

The pinhole borers tend to die out once the timber starts to dry, so it is the powder-post beetles (Lyctids and Bostrychids) which are most troublesome to the turner. Bostrychids are mainly tropical; Lyctids are dwellers of both tropical and temperate zones. Lyctids do not attack softwoods or small-pored hardwoods. Visible signs are exit holes about $1/16$ inch (1.5 mm) in diameter and small piles of dust. The larvae are about $1/4$ inch (6 mm) long, must have starch, and do not therefore attack heartwood, although the beetles may exit through it. Prevention may be achieved by physical removal of the sapwood, or by immersion in a suitable chemical solution. Heat is also effective in killing Lyctids.

1.9   INTENTIONAL STAINING

In certain circumstances the appearance of some woods, particularly pale woods, can be enhanced by allowing mould attack, particularly bluestaining. To facilitate bluestain, you should dimension the wood, seal the ends, then stack in the original log shape without stickers in order to impede seasoning. Occasionally, say every two weeks, open up the log and inspect progress. When staining is sufficient, or when not progressing any further, restack with stickers and season normally. Intentional staining is also brought about by fully waxing the wood or by wrapping it in plastic, these methods being especially suitable for rough-turned bowls.

1.10   TURNABILITY

The mechanical and physical properties of most woods are listed in reference texts, but there is no mention of that property of wood which most concerns us and which I have called turnability. It is not a property which has been quantified. Nor does it seem to be related to the commonly listed properties of wood.

Almost all woods can be spindle turned, though with varying ease. When you are hollowing during cupchuck turning, a number of woods crush on their end grain. However, it is during bowl turning that variations in turnability are most noticeable. Some woods turn like cheese and require virtually no sanding, others pick out on end and uphill grain, others squash under the tool, yet others pull out along the grain. Therefore, as bowls are to a large extent priced on size, it is rarely worthwhile for professional turners to bother with species of poor turnability.

As with all wood properties, an average turnability could be ascribed to a particular wood species. The turnability of a particular sample of a species may, however, be very different. It will be affected by the genetic make-up of that particular tree; by the soil, climate, and surroundings in which the tree grew; by the treatment of the wood after the tree was felled; and by the particular part of the tree from which the sample was taken.

The turnability of a particular workpiece will influence the turning methods employed, and these are described where appropriate.

1.11   SOURCES OF WOOD

Woodturners can use a far greater range of sizes, species, and sections of tree than other woodworkers. Hence, the range of potential wood sources is correspondingly greater, and includes:
1. Lumberyards and specialist wood suppliers.
2. Sawmills.
3. Auctions.
4. Old furniture and other redundant wooden items.
5. Demolition sites.
6. Road widening and building sites.
7. Offcuts from sawmills and furniture factories.
8. The local dump.
9. Swaps with other woodworkers.
10. Domestic and urban tree felling, pruning, and surgery.
11. Butts and branches left as waste in woodland after the trunk logs have been removed to sawmills.
12. Trees which the woodturner receives permission to fell.

2
Design

We live in an environment which is increasingly designed. Man-made, and therefore designed, structures and artefacts cover a greater area and occupy more space than ever before. The trend will continue, especially now that design has become an established profession with the whole panoply of formal courses, qualifications, and professional institutions. Various well-defined specialties within design have been created, and we even accept the designing of nature, that is, landscape design.

As our surroundings become more designed and therefore more artificial, we may attempt to compensate by designing more 'naturally'. We may use more natural materials such as stone and wood, and emphasise them by contrasting them against plastic, chromium plating, and lacquer.

The true importance of design is realised, except among those who become distracted by technique or equipment. Therefore it is still common to see well-turned and well-finished articles which are both ugly and ill-suited for their intended use. In the related sphere of furniture, it is surely significant that we remember the designers and designer-makers rather than those who were solely cabinetmakers.

What is design? It is the process which results in the creation of a design. A wood-turning design is usually simple—black lines which may be straight, convex, or concave, on a white background. We recognise the result, what is the process?

In woodturning, the design spectrum is bounded at one end by reproduction or copying, and at the other by original design. Most designs combine copying and originality in various proportions.

What is an original design and how is it produced? As intelligence is useless without knowledge, so is an inborn design aptitude useless without knowledge related to design. The supposedly original part of a design is the spark or the inspiration. This might spring from an error or an association with something just experienced or recalled, or it might come apparently out of the blue. It can even be conceived as a result of concentrating on a design problem. The technique of brainstorming can also lead to apparently original ideas. It is obvious that in design, as in other fields, Pasteur's statement "Chance favours only the prepared mind" applies.

Often those engaged in design cannot afford the luxury of waiting for inspiration.

They have to force designs out. However, forced design often gives the feeling of being forced in the same way that a greenhouse-reared plant is usually a bit too lush.

2.1 THE PRODUCTION OF A DESIGN

Presumably the ability to produce original concepts varies between individuals. However, the concentration and knowledge necessary to produce a viable finished design from an initial inspiration are just as necessary. The transformation of an idea into a design is a series of steps, sometimes confused, sometimes orderly. The steps may include:

1. Assumptions followed by trial and error.
2. Further ideas.
3. The use of knowledge, either consciously or subconsciously, of other styles and designs.
4. The need to satisfy functional requirements, if any.
5. The requirement to conform to relevant requirements or limitations.
6. Interacting with other people to obtain their ideas and opinions.
7. Making compromises, for example, beauty versus cost, size versus material availability.

Being a natural and nonplastic material, wood and the processes by which it is worked exert particular influences and limitations on the production of a design. However, many memorable designs are the results of intentionally violating the accepted technical limitations, and indeed of violating the accepted design conventions.

As you have seen, the production of a design requires knowledge and concentration. The remainder of this chapter looks at these requirements in greater detail under the following headings:

Sources of design
Treen
Design nomenclature
The physical process of designing
Design guidelines
Aesthetic and practical considerations
Suitability for use
Influences and limitations on design
Style, fashion, and taste
Marketing

2.2 SOURCES OF DESIGN

Design knowledge is important, even essential, for those who wish to design. Both the possession of design knowledge and the process of acquiring it can stimulate the generation of ideas. It is important not only that you study both antique and recent designs, but that you keep up-to-date. Sources of design knowledge which can be relevant to woodturners include:

1. Museums, galleries, collections, and exhibitions.
2. Natural forms. Shapes derived from animals, plants, and even geological formations can stimulate new ideas, particularly where you are prepared to do some carving and use other techniques or incorporate other media.

3. Machinery and technology. For example, the shapes of some components are adaptable for woodturning and can even be incorporated into the finished product.
4. The world around us generally. Wherever you are, there are objects and shapes which offer possibilities to the woodturner.
5. Books and magazines on the following subjects:
   Woodworking
   Woodturning
   Furniture
   Interior design and architecture
   Arts and crafts using media other than wood
   Design
   Antiques
   Arts and artefacts of other cultures
   Publicity and advertising
   Treen.

2.3 TREEN

If turning is to continue to flourish, turners must become more adventurous. Too many turning exhibitions are just bowl after bowl after bowl.

One almost inexhaustible source of ideas is treen. *Treen* is the collective noun for wooden items which are not furniture and are not architectural. It is therefore already the main field of endeavour for most turners. Undoubtedly the best reference is *Treen and Other Wooden Bygones* by Edward H. Pinto (G. Bell & Sons Ltd, London, 1969). His collection is now excellently displayed at the Birmingham Museum and Art Gallery in England.

There is, of course, no need to just copy antique forms. Turners should be introducing new designs and searching for new opportunities. There must be an effort not to restrict output to functional items only.

The restriction that turned items are circular about an axis is not as onerous as the public believes, but it is nevertheless liberating to use other materials and techniques in addition.

2.4 DESIGN NOMENCLATURE

Design is essentially visual, although the other senses, especially touch, may play a part. When, however, you need to describe designs verbally or in writing, a good knowledge of design nomenclature is essential. Also, a good knowledge of historical and standard turning details is required if you are to be able to design quickly and efficiently under the eyes of potential clients. This section attempts to clarify the confusion of nomenclature which has grown up.

Obviously, designs can only be composed of lines or surfaces which are convex, concave, or straight. The general term for a convex turned surface on a spindle is a *bead*; the term for a concave turned surface is a *hollow*. Figure 2.1 shows an example of spindle turning incorporating the various simple classes of these basic curves.

In the past, various combinations of curves have been found particularly useful or attractive in both furniture and architecture. They are known as *mouldings* and are equally applicable to woodturning (see Figure 2.2). In mouldings, the ratios of height to width are flexible and the curves do not necessarily conform to any specific mathematically definable shape. The governing factors are the directions of the tangents to the curve at its ends and whether the curve is concave, convex, or a mixture as in cyma and ogee profiles.

Some combinations of curves and mouldings have become favoured for particular turned items, especially furniture components. These are described below.

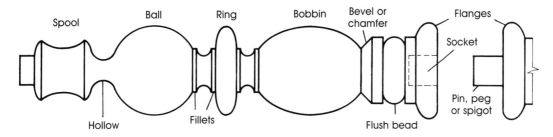

Figure 2.1 Basic curve nomenclature.

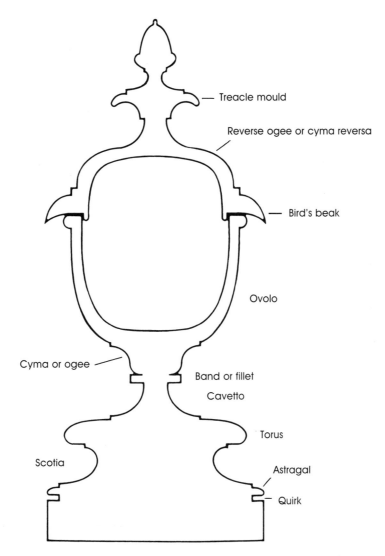

Figure 2.2 A cross-section through an urn showing common moulding profiles.

Feet

Turned feet of the ball type (Figure 2.3) have been popular for several centuries, with their heyday in England being from the mid-seventeenth to the early eighteenth century. *Trumpet foot* is an American term for a ball-type foot on a high flared pad.

Club feet were commonly used on furniture legs, both in England and America, during the first half of the eighteenth century. They may also be found with a ball instead of the more usual pad.

Stump foot is a contemporary eighteenth-century term for a short turned foot, without a castor, supporting a piece of case furniture. The French term for their form of the stump foot is *toupie*. The characteristic stump foot shapes were also stretched and used on chairs, tables, and other furniture with longer legs.

Turning was also used sometimes to produce legs and feet square in cross-section. *Marlboro' foot* (a late eighteenth-century term) is applied to the spade-shaped foot used commonly on English Sheraton or American Federal furniture. In the therming process, a number of legs were strapped onto a large drum which was then rotated and the required profile turned. Four operations were obviously required. The apparently flat sides of the turnings are therefore slightly convex.

Spindles

Spindles is the generic term for turned members, often bounded at their ends by cross members, whose length is considerably greater than their maximum diameter. Spindles commonly occur as stretchers, in chair backs, and to form screens when arranged in rows. Perhaps the most frequent use of a screen of spindles is the balusters supporting a stair handrail. A range of typical spindle forms is shown in Figure 2.4. Many curve combinations are common to spindles and to legs and columns, and some are considered in the following section.

Legs and Columns

Figure 2.5 shows a representative range of types. Several profiles which are common in antique turnings have specific names and these are illustrated, as are frequently used decorative carvings. The difference between a twist and a spiral should perhaps be highlighted. In a *twist*, the integral cross-sectional shape is twisted around its own axis of symmetry. In a *spiral* (or coil), each stem (or bine) is revolved around the central axis of a column. In extreme cases, a rod may be passed down this central axis.

A column with straight sides will appear slightly waisted and hence weak. To correct this illusion, such columns are turned with a slight *entasis*, or swelling. On small work this is eyed in, but for large work you may find it necessary to calliper diameters. The graphical method for developing the entasis is shown in Figure 2.6.

Robert Chitham's *The Classical Orders of Architecture* (Architectural Press, London, 1985) is one of many sources giving proportions for column capitals and bases. He also proposes the method described below for calculating shaft entasis or diminution:

> Divide the column shaft into *n* parts of equal height. Referring to Figure 2.6, the cosine of the diminution angle AOC is shaft diameter AB divided by shaft diameter CD (typically about 0.85). The diminution angle is determined from this cosine (I use log tables). For a diminution of 0.85 the diminution angle is 31°47'. For such a column, the diameter at the top of, say, the third of seven column parts would be:

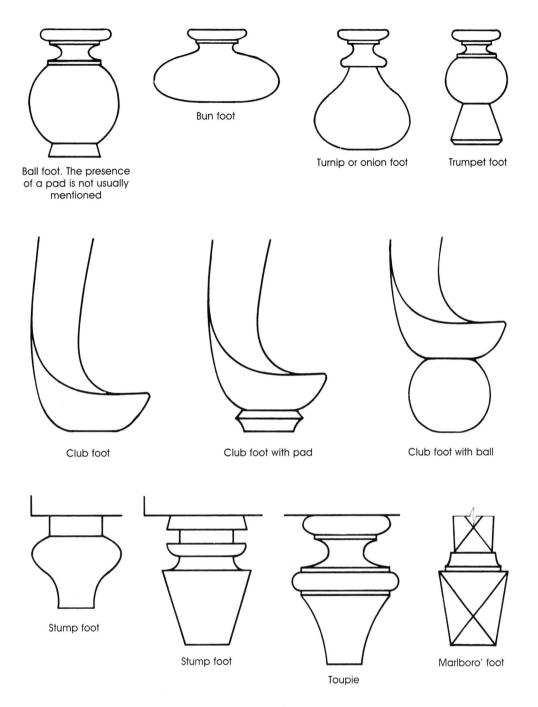

Ball foot. The presence
of a pad is not usually
mentioned

Bun foot

Turnip or onion foot

Trumpet foot

Club foot

Club foot with pad

Club foot with ball

Stump foot

Stump foot

Toupie

Marlboro' foot

Figure 2.3 Turned feet.

Column diameter at base x cosine $\dfrac{(3 \times 31°47')}{7}$

= CD x cosine 13°37'

= CD x 0.9719

For relatively slender architectural columns Chitham keeps the bottom third of the shaft of constant diameter, and calculates entasis only on the top two thirds.

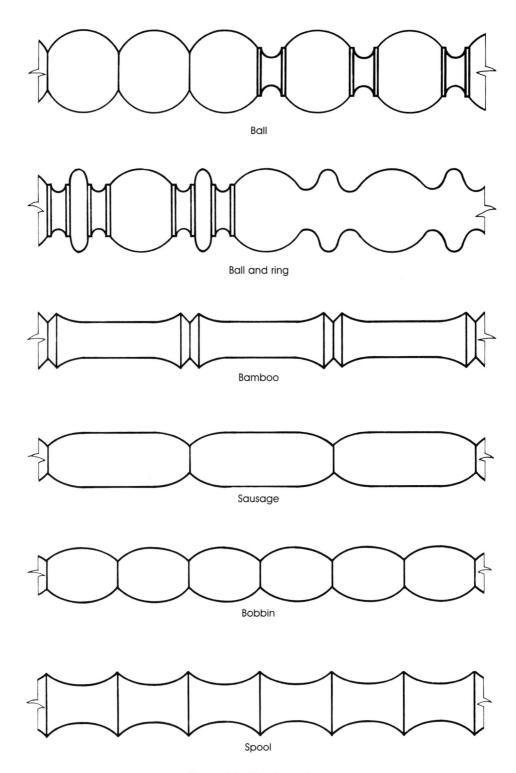

Ball

Ball and ring

Bamboo

Sausage

Bobbin

Spool

Figure 2.4 Spindle turnings.

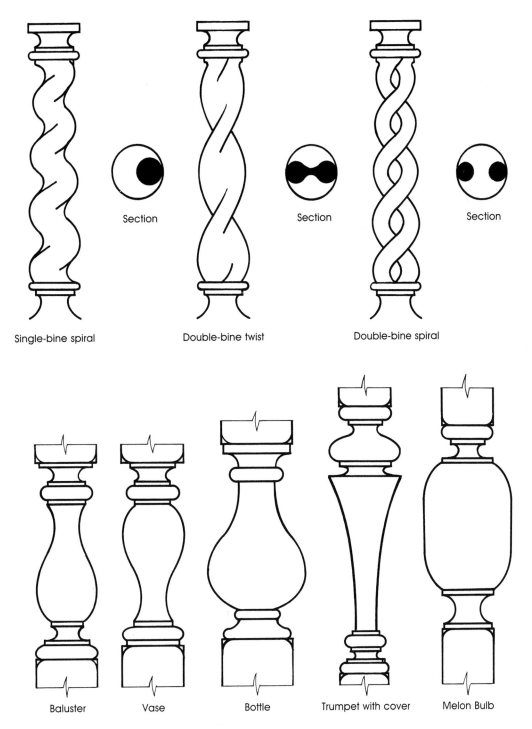

Figure 2.5 Legs and columns.

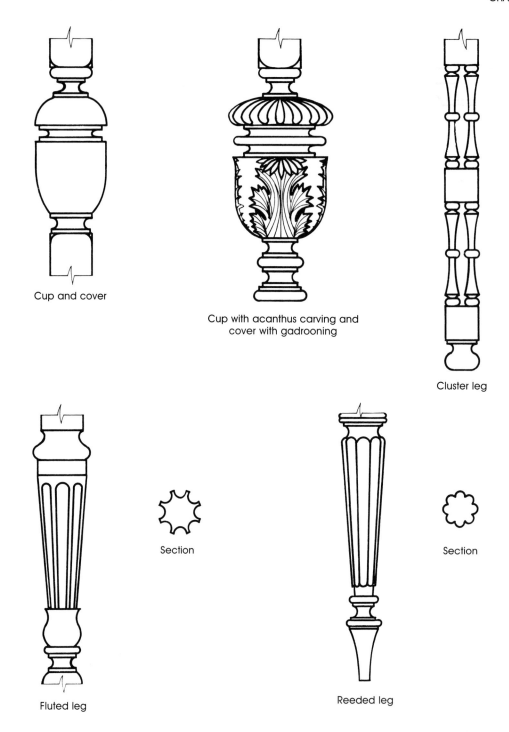

Cup and cover

Cup with acanthus carving and
cover with gadrooning

Cluster leg

Fluted leg

Section

Reeded leg

Section

Figure 2.5 Legs and columns.

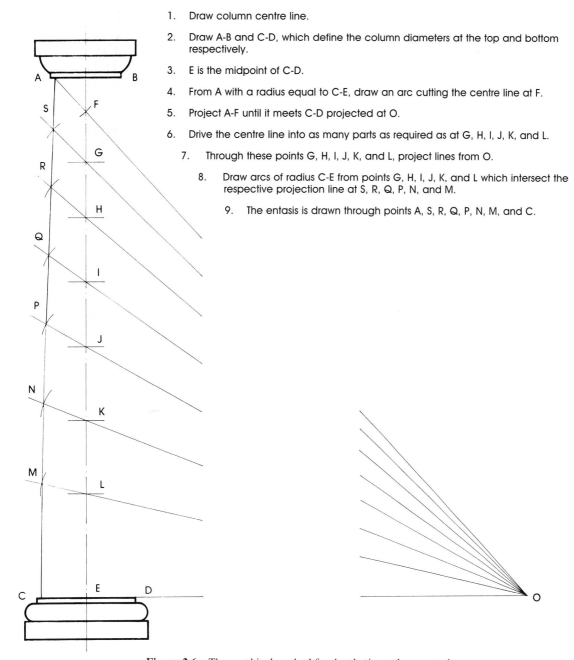

1. Draw column centre line.

2. Draw A-B and C-D, which define the column diameters at the top and bottom respectively.

3. E is the midpoint of C-D.

4. From A with a radius equal to C-E, draw an arc cutting the centre line at F.

5. Project A-F until it meets C-D projected at O.

6. Drive the centre line into as many parts as required as at G, H, I, J, K, and L.

7. Through these points G, H, I, J, K, and L, project lines from O.

8. Draw arcs of radius C-E from points G, H, I, J, K, and L which intersect the respective projection line at S, R, Q, P, N, and M.

9. The entasis is drawn through points A, S, R, Q, P, N, M, and C.

Figure 2.6   The graphical method for developing column entasis.

Finials and Knobs

The design of *finials* and *knobs* (Figure 2.7) is a good indication of age and origin. Finials were turned integrally with spindles, or turned separately and then dowelled on. Inverted finials are known as drops.

Fortunately for restoration turners, wooden knobs were very much in fashion during the nineteenth century. Sometimes they were turned with a pin, but more often they were tapped and affixed with a wooden screw. This enabled them to be removed so that the door or drawer could be more easily polished.

Urn finial   Urn and flame finial   Acorn finial   Thistle finial

Mushroom top to a
seventeenth-century American
chair front post

Mushroom-shaped knob

Back post finial to a
seventeenth-century American Brewster chair

Figure 2.7 Finials and a knob

2.5   THE PHYSICAL PROCESS OF DESIGNING

Drafting ability is desirable for woodturners. It is far more efficient to solve design and production problems on paper than in the lathe. Designs should be drawn to scale, preferably full size, with elevations, plans, and sections as required. Any modifications can easily be made to these drawings, which should include dimensions, a cutting list, and details of methods and special chucks, etc.

Obviously, certain equipment is required: paper, drawing board and T square or drafting machine, drawing instruments, triangles, etc. Squared paper will be found particularly useful for sketches.

The translation of the drawings into the finished turning is dealt with in later chapters, but for the expert turner that is not usually too difficult—the essential foundation of woodturning is design and it is all too often neglected.

2.6   DESIGN GUIDELINES

In 1933 William H. Varnum's book *Industrial Art Design* was published (Manual Arts Press, Peoria, Illinois). This attempted to lay down quantitative design rules, particularly on proportion. Franklin H. Gottshall used these rules in several of his books, notably *Design for the Craftsman* (Bruce Publishing, Milwaukee, 1940). I and others have found these guidelines valuable in the production of designs and in analysing designs which do not look quite right. However, the guidelines are not rigid rules which must be followed blindly, and indeed many successful pieces do not conform.

Varnum divides design into three phases:

1. *Structural design*, establishment of major proportions and space relationships and placing of major elements.
2. *Contour enrichment*, using curves to make the design more pleasing.
3. *Surface enrichment*, such as carving, painting, or inlay.

In Varnum's structural design, the silhouette of the basic outline of the object is known as the *primary mass*. In the primary mass, enclosed spaces are considered as filled in and small projections are ignored. The nine guidelines listed below are not quoted exactly from Varnum, but are adaptations which are more focussed at woodturners.

GUIDELINE 1:   The primary mass, unless required to be square, should be definitely horizontal or vertical (Figure 2.8). Furthermore it is preferable if the height-to-width ratios are not easily recognised—for example 1:1, 2:1, or 1:3—or the eye will tend to find the piece boring. The proportion 1.62:1 was discovered by the Greeks and was thought to be the ideal. It is known as the Golden Proportion (see Figure 2.9).

GUIDELINE 2:   When a primary mass is divided by horizontals into two parts, the parts should be of unequal height (see Figure 2.8).

GUIDELINE 3:   When a primary mass is divided by horizontals into three parts, all areas may be unequal, with the largest placed between the other two. Alternatively, the areas may be placed in order of height with either the tallest or the shortest at the base (see Figure 2.9).

GUIDELINE 4:   If a primary mass is to be divided by horizontals into more than three parts, it should first be divided into two or three major sections by guideline 2 or 3, and these major parts should then subdivided again using guidelines 2 and 3 (see Figure 2.10).

GUIDELINE 5:   If a primary mass is to be divided by verticals into two parts, it is preferable if the areas are alike in size and form (see Figure 2.11).

GUIDELINE 6:   When a primary mass is divided by verticals into three parts, it is preferable if the central part is the largest and the two outside parts are of equal width (see Figure 2.12).

GUIDELINE 7: When a primary mass is to be divided by verticals into more than three parts, it should first be divided into two or three major sections by guideline 5 or 6, and these major parts then subdivided again using guidelines 5 and 6.

GUIDELINE 8: To avoid a top-heavy or unstable look, the primary mass will usually decrease in width and depth toward the top.

GUIDELINE 9: An appendage is an addition to the primary mass. Whether an appendage is actually part of the primary mass is often a moot point. However, the appendage should:

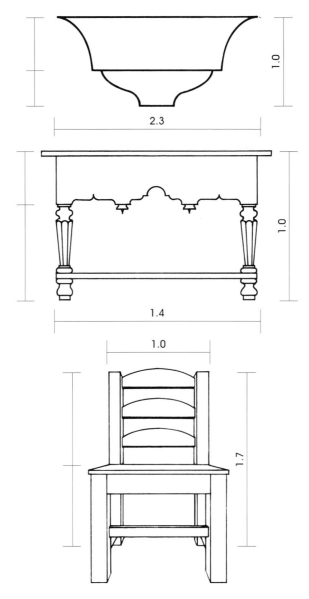

Figure 2.8   Illustration of design guidelines 1 and 2

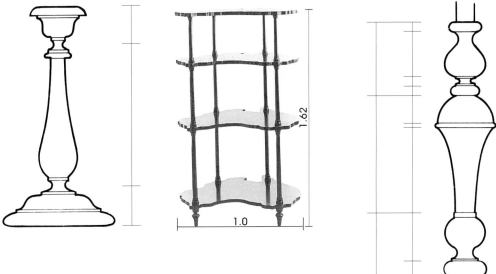

Figure 2.9   Illustration of design guideline 3.

Figure 2.10   Illustration of design guideline 4. A lowboy leg.

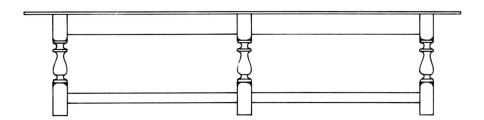

Figure 2.11   Illustration of design guideline 5. A dining table.

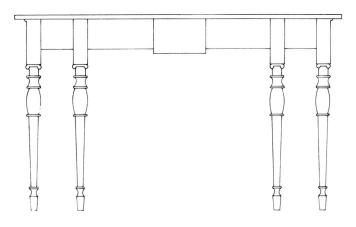

Figure 2.12   Illustration of design guideline 6. A side table.

1. Be designed in unity with the primary mass.
2. Have the appearance of flowing smoothly and, if possible, tangentially from the primary mass.
3. If possible, echo or repeat the features of the primary mass.

Varnum's guidelines, like eighteenth and nineteenth century pattern books, enable sound design, even classical design, and are distilled from a long line of writings on proportion and beauty stretching back to ancient Greece. But beauty is not necessarily or even desirably the sole objective of the designer. The romantic approach saw design as emotional, even spiritual. Wonder, distaste, or laughter are therefore valid reactions to a design which seeks to communicate. There are two further design objectives: the fulfilment of utilitarian function, and the need to satisfy restraints. A rolling pin is primarily a functional object, but your design freedom could be restricted by the non-availability of your preferred wood or by a particular client requirement. Therefore when you design you will be usually seeking to satisfy not one but several criteria. Although these criteria will rarely be equally important, in turning aesthetic beauty is usually desired and Varnum's guidelines will help you to achieve it. Even their intentional rejection will be relevant if your design intent is aesthetic discordance.

2.7 AESTHETIC AND PRACTICAL CONSIDERATIONS

In the detailing of designs and during the turning process, there are many points which form the basis of 'good practice'. Good practice not only simplifies the turning process, but gives the finished product a finer appearance. Fifteen examples are given below:

1. Fillets should be parallel or at right angles to the lathe axis, and usually all of the same width. They should be wide enough to indicate the points of inflection, but not wide enough to destroy the fluidity of the curves on which they lie.
2. Curves should meet fillets at right angles.
3. Fillets may be canted:
    (a) When a change to a smaller skew chisel would be required solely to cut the fillet.
    (b) In order to accentuate relatively shallow curves necessitated usually by strength considerations.
4. Simple curves should be definitely shaped, for example: circular, elliptical, or well skewed.
5. Curves should be smooth and not include small, unintentional straight sections, bumps, or hollows. Compound and reverse curves need to be defined, or else in repetition turning they will vary considerably from one piece to another.
6. Try to minimise wastage of wood. If a piece is to be turned to a finished maximum diameter of 2 inches (50 mm), then the sawn size 3 inches × 3 inches (75 mm × 75 mm) may have to be used and 55 percent of the wood wasted. Reducing the leg to a maximum finished diameter of $1^3/_4$ inches (44 mm) greatly reduces waste and may not significantly affect the leg's appearance or serviceability.
7. Do not monotonously repeat details. However, repetition of a design theme is desirable.
8. Do not be overelaborate. Messy, cluttered detail may impress the ignorant, but it is usually a sign that the basic design lacks structure and elegance. Flush beads and V-cuts are particularly prone to overuse.

9. Remember that wood moves. It will vary in both thickness and width with mois-ture-content variations, and platelike turnings will cup unless perfectly quarter-sawn. Movements will also occur as internal stresses relax into a new equilibri-um. Hence, wide bases of the sort used for traditional candlesticks will eventual-ly rock, and bowls with lids where bowl or lid (or both) has its grain direction nonaxial will tend to lose their original fit.

10. When a square section is left on a spindle, it is more serviceable to curve back the corner projections or perhaps use an ogee. It is common practice to leave a cylin-drical section adjacent to the square so that the risk of damaging the square when turning details next to it is avoided.

11. Keep slenderness in mind. When designing how one section dowels into another, try to avoid weak projections which could be damaged before the components are joined. Ensure that the assembled section will have sufficient strength.

12. Design so as to minimise callipering. Ask yourself if the appearance of the turn-ing would be significantly affected if all details which varied slightly in diameter were turned with the same diameter.

13. Design so that the minimum number of turning tools are used the minimum num-ber of times. Deep, narrow hollows, for instance, will require a small gouge and usually a small skew chisel which probably will not be needed for any other part of the turning.

14. Try to avoid awkward cuts, for example, in spindle turning a downhill cut from a ring, a small bead next to a section left square, or a half hollow whose bottom is bounded by a ring.

15. During the design stage, consider how modifications might simplify turning or chucking. It may be more efficient to do some of the work out of the lathe; for example end boring might be better done using a drilling machine or horizontal borer.

2.8   SUITABILITY FOR USE

Although many turned pieces are decorative or designed to amuse or even disturb (sure-ly all legitimate functions), woodturning has traditionally been concerned with the pro-duction of useful items. That each design should efficiently satisfy its intended uses is obvious. However, in the same way that an original design is rarely purely original, so is a functional design rarely purely functional. A sewing needle is probably one of the few purely functional items. In producing a functional design, we unconsciously or con-sciously make stylistic decisions and balance and compromise between function, aes-thetics, and cost.

The advantages and disadvantages of wood as a material are considered in the next section, and it is obvious that wood continues to be widely used on aesthetic grounds long after it has been made obsolete by metal and plastic. Therefore, functionality is less important relative to beauty than it once was, and you should not be afraid to design pieces which are more than purely functional.

2.9   INFLUENCES AND LIMITATIONS ON DESIGN

Design and production do not exist in a vacuum. They should be related to the materials available, the equipment and skills at hand, and even the preferences and requirements of the end user. This section discusses these points in detail.

Properties of Wood

Wood has particular properties which vary considerably between species and even within a single tree. It is, however, reasonable to generalise:

1. Wood is resilient, but its surface is easily damaged.
2. It is a good insulator and therefore warm to touch.
3. Its strength properties vary considerably according to species and the direction in which they are measured relative to the grain direction.
4. With varying moisture content it shrinks, expands, and warps; again these properties are not isotropic.
5. Applied finishes can enhance, preserve, or change its appearance.
6. Woods come in a wide variety of colours, many of which change with exposure. Note that the appearance of the wood clear-finished can be approximated by wetting the raw wood. The grain structure of the wood and the way in which colour is characteristically distributed may dictate whether it is preferable to plainsaw or quartersaw the log.
7. The availability of wood varies considerably, with seasoned, straight-grained, large cross-sections always being difficult to obtain, whatever the species.
8. Some woods, especially those with prominent medullary rays, split easily and would therefore be unsuitable for, say, tool handles.
9. Because of smell or oil exudation some woods are unsuitable to be in contact with food. Similar wood properties may be desirable, say, to repel moths.
10. Turnability varies greatly. Some woods are hard; some have interlocked grain; some contain abrasive silica; some cannot be faceplate turned without requiring excessive sanding; some are so weak or open that they crush rather than stand up and allow themselves to be cut.

The Influences of Equipment and Skills

Obviously, someone with a small lathe and without a bandsaw is really not equipped to produce any large pieces which he may design. Nevertheless, it is possible to disregard safety, overload equipment, and accomplish the apparently impossible. In considering new designs, the professional turner needs to compare the cost of new specialised equipment against the expected returns. Alternatively it may be better to sublet the work or to hire the equipment.

Not only do designs sometimes require new equipment, they will also sometimes require new skills. Obviously, skills and equipment are intimately related, and for the one-off piece hand skills are a feasible alternative to new equipment. Indeed, it is, in general true that the advances in woodturning have been developed in response to the dictates and requirements of new designs for finished products. Perhaps the main criticism of present-day woodturning writing is that much of it presumes that readers are unwilling both to acquire the skills and to purchase or develop the equipment necessary to lift their woodturning from its present mundane level.

2.10 STYLE, FASHION, AND TASTE

We say that a style is in fashion when it is considered to be popular and therefore in demand. We speak of styles being classical when we believe that they have characteristics which ensure that they are always popular. Somehow classical also implies that the designs are verging on the purely functional, and that therefore fashionableness is a property of the decoration of the piece rather than its basic structure.

Today, fashion is commercially manipulated. Technological advances mean that there is an advantage to be gained by promoting new materials or new styles which utilise new forming processes. Variations in the prices and availabilities of materials dictate which are to be promoted as desirable. New styles are even manufactured regularly to ensure that the public continues to spend more than it needs to. Woodturning too, despite the limitations that its products must be of wood and have round cross-sections, has a history of stylistic change even though its technology has remained relatively stagnant.

Simpler woodturning styles are in vogue today, presumably following the overall trend toward plain surfaces and streamlining which has occurred during the past hundred years. The introduction of automatic woodturning lathes has also necessitated a reduction in the amount of detail, and this lead has been followed by hand turners whose level of skill, particularly with the skew chisel, is now lower. The improvements in headstock and chuck designs, introduction of new glues and accurate table saws, and advances in wood seasoning and stabilisation have permitted larger sizes of workpiece to be used, facilitated an increase in cupchuck and faceplate turning relative to spindle turning, and enabled laminations to be turned easily and safely.

Despite today's simpler styles, it is possible to distinguish many individual styles in turning. Obviously, unless a particular style is specified by the client, it is an advantage to have your own individual style. Pieces in a style will have recognisable attributes in common. It may be the use of certain woods, particular combinations of curves, or uncommon proportions or thicknesses. It could be the turning of particular types of items or the use of specialised techniques or equipment. Individual styles can be purposely invented, but in the main they evolve naturally from the nature of the craftsman and his particular circumstances. However as individuality becomes seen as more desirable there is a tendency to confuse it with merit; to take the short cut of plagiarism, and hope for an ill-informed clientele.

But what of those who unintentionally but unavoidably promote plagiarism? If those who have achieved recognisable styles derive income from supplying the special equipment and teaching the special techniques associated with their styles, they should not be too surprised if they spawn imitators.

This design chapter extensively shows antique forms. I believe that a knowledge of them is desirable. But this and the absence of illustrations of work by contemporary stylists does not dictate that you should design in traditional styles. Indeed, most of the design advice is generally applicable, even to work of communicative rather than functional or aesthetic intents.

A fascinating sidelight of the importance of style and fashion is the public's reaction to woodturning. Although people's reactions vary enormously, it is possible to generalise. Because we are vitally interested in wood and woodturning, we assume that others are. In the main they are not. They are unable to discern good woodturning from bad, from both technical and design standpoints. Even among the informed public there is an astonishing divergence in taste. Some are conservative, and even though they may appreciate a new or unusual piece, they are unlikely to buy it. People, in general, are ignorant about wood, and any holes or cracks conjure up an image of the piece instantly disintegrating as soon as they get it home. However, the public is, on the whole, receptive, and surely the creation of interest and thereby demand is one of the main functions of marketing.

2.11 MARKETING

In the Western world, labour is far more expensive than in the less developed countries. Woodware is imported freely from the latter and retailed at prices sometimes below the value of the wood itself. There is also, of course, Western mass-produced woodware read-ily available. These factors would suggest that hand turning cannot be viable.

With high labour rates, heavy overheads, high labour content, and highly priced raw material, hand turning must be expensive, indeed a luxury, no matter what its quality. Obviously, if it is for sale at a luxury price, it must be seen to be a luxury product. First-class design, attractive woods, and high quality of turning and finish are prerequisites for successful sales. Once your products are suitable, it is then the job of marketing to achieve sales by placing your work before those already likely to buy and by attempting to convert the disinterested into woodturning aficionados.

It is not my intention to provide instant and exhaustive expertise in marketing tech-niques. However, I list a few points to note:

1. The value of the wood is normally a relatively low proportion of the total cost of an item. Marketability is greatly increased while production cost is only margin-ally so by the use of especially attractive woods.
2. Some woods have a mystique or high reputation, and are therefore preferred.
3. What hourly rate should you use in costing? Woodturning is not protected by leg-islation which perpetuates professional monopolies and therefore allows exorbi-tant rates to be charged. Many amateurs wish to show and sell their work, and are content to charge low prices. Woodworking is assumed to give great pleasure and satisfaction which are somehow thought to lessen a person's needs for food, clothing, and shelter. Finally, there is the public belief that woodturning is craft not fine art, and is the domain of bohemians and the elderly. In short, there are strong downward pressures on woodturning hourly rates which most turners seem only too ready to accept masochistically.
4. It is assumed that markets provide a suitable outlet for woodturnings. However, people go to markets with little money and the expectation of being able to buy things cheaply. They are quite prepared to pay considerably more for the same items from shops or galleries.
5. Because of the higher labour contents, woodturnings should be considerably more expensive than similar objects in glass or clay. Wood should therefore be dis-played separately, or the impression is created that it is overpriced.
6. Although resilient and therefore resistant to total destruction, wood has an easily damaged surface. It is thus unsuitable to be left for sale on consignment.
7. Other media tend to be nonspecific; that is, they could come from anywhere, like clay or glass. The use of wood from local or even famous trees can add sales appeal. Indeed, a tree's previous owner is almost certain to want something made from it.
8. Marketability will be enhanced if the wood species and the turner's name or sig-nature are written on the piece. A pyrograph is excellent for this.

Of course, the foregoing assumes that your production will be retailed, whereas many turners do a high proportion of bespoke work such as replacement parts for antique furniture restorers. However, here again there is a general expectation that low rates will be charged.

3

The Lathe

Traditionally, a woodturning lathe was a machine for turning wood which was held in a horizontal position between adjustable centres and rotated against cutting tools. This description remains true today with the addition that wood can now be held only at one end (cupchucked), and that wooden disks may be held by one face for faceplate or bowl turning.

This chapter deals specifically with the lathe plus those other items which remain attached to the lathe under normal circumstances, and starts with a diagram of a lathe (Figure 3.1) and a brief history.

Figure 3.1 A patternmaker's lathe showing the major components.

3.1 HISTORY OF THE LATHE

It is possible to date with reasonable accuracy many of the discoveries or inventions which have constituted advances in turning technology. There was often, however, a considerable delay before these advances became widely used in woodturning, and even today I suspect that the medieval woodturner would be quite at home in some workshops.

Rudimentary lathes are thought to have originated in Europe or in the Middle East in about 1000 BC, although the first pictorial record is Egyptian and dated about 300 BC. The drive was by a cord wrapped around the work itself or around a driving mandrel, with the turner or an assistant applying a reciprocating motion to the driving cord by hand or by bowing. By the thirteenth century the bowstring principle was developed into the pole lathe which enabled one-man operation. The pole lathe's bowstring was connected to a foot treadle below the lathe bed. After passing around the mandrel or workpiece, the bowstring's upper end was attached to the end of a length of sapling (the pole) which acted as a return spring. The turner was therefore able to power the lathe while having both hands free to control the tool. Rotation of the workpiece was, as in the earlier lathes, continually reversing and no cutting could be done on the return stroke. The lathe had a wooden bed with two tailstocks each equipped with a fixed metal centre. One tailstock was fixed in position, the other was moveable along the bed.

By the latter half of the sixteenth century several major improvements had been invented, but that they were all soon adopted by Mr Average Woodturner is doubtful. The inventions were the:

1. 'Great Wheel' drive.
2. Two-bearing headstock.
3. Stepped pulley.
4. Treadle, crankshaft, and flywheel drive.
5. Adjustable tail centre.
6. Slide rest.
7. Harnessing of water power.

The Great Wheel was a wooden flywheel about 6 feet (1800 mm) in diameter. It was mounted between trunions and separate from the lathe itself. The Great Wheel was cranked by an assistant, and by an endless cord it applied a unidirectional drive to a stepped pulley mounted on the headstock spindle. Later, introduction of the treadle, crankshaft, and flywheel drive enabled the unidirectional drive to be retained and the luckless assistant to be sacked.

The slide rest, first illustrated in Germany in 1480, was eventually utilised for wood machining in the patternmaker's lathe.

Although woodturning remained an important trade, from the seventeenth century innovative effort was largely channelled into ornamental turning lathes and lathes for making clocks and scientific instruments. Henceforth, therefore, improvements in woodturning lathes were almost entirely a result of the search for advances in metal turning. These were, in turn, a result of the demands for greater accuracy and economy in the manufacture of, among other things, steam engines, sewing machines, bicycles, and automobiles.

Below is a list of the major innovations which have led to the modern woodturning lathe and its associated equipment.

1701   Cast, split, soft-metal bearings are illustrated in *L'art du tourneau* by Charles Plumier. These are not superseded until the introduction of rolling friction bearings at the end of the nineteenth century.

1751	In Sheffield, Benjamin Huntsman commences commercial production of crucible carbon steel. Carbon tool steel was used for the manufacture of most woodturning tools until about 1980.
1800	The Industrial Revolution gathers momentum with the large-scale manufacture of James Watt's steam engine.
1808	William Newbury patents the bandsaw, although its widespread adoption could not commence until the introduction of cushioned wheel rims and spring-steel blades in France in about 1853.
1819	Thomas Blanchard of Philadelphia invents the copy-lathe (originally for producing rifle stocks).
1820	William Fairburn in Britain introduces efficient line-shafting, thereby allowing many machines to be driven using leather belts from a central steam engine.
1842	James Dundas introduces the self-centring scroll chuck.
1868	In Gloucestershire R.F. Mushet produces a tungsten tool steel. Further research in America by F.W. Taylor leads to the modern high-speed tool steels.
1873	Theophile Gramme demonstrates a machine driven by its own electric motor, although it takes a further 50 years before the forest of line-shafts and belting is really on the retreat.
1877	F.B. Norton in America takes out a patent for vitrified emery wheels. Emery, a naturally occurring aluminium oxide, is displaced in 1880 by corundum (almost pure aluminium oxide). In 1897 C.B. Jacobs discovers artificial corundum, and by 1906 the Norton Company has switched over completely to the manufacture of artificial corundum wheels.
1891	E.G. Acheson rediscovers silicon carbide (carborundum), an abrasive harder but more brittle than aluminium oxide.
1899	L. Schuler fits ball bearings to a lathe spindle, although their general introduction was probably not until the 1920s.
1930	V-belts start to replace leather belting.
1980 onwards	High-speed steel starts to replace carbon tool steel for turning tools. The expansion of hobby and studio turning gathers pace and catalyses the introduction of new equipment and techniques and the rediscovery of forgotten ones.
1990 onwards	Continuous speed variation, both mechanical and electronic, augments the sensible trend to more lathe speeds. Miniature turning and lathes become popular. The relatively greater rise in the popularity of bowl turning causes more lathes to have an outboard turning facility or a swivelling headstock.

Needless to say, woodturning technology is continuing to develop, particularly with the renewed interest in it by thinking professional turners and by amateurs expert in other but relevant fields such as pneumatics, machine design, and electronics.

3.2   TYPES OF LATHE

With the universal availability of electric power, operator-powered lathes are properly relegated to curiosities in museums or at fairs. Below are described the main attributes of the various types of electrically powered lathes available (see Figure 3.2):

1. Some manufacturers produce attachments which enable portable electric drills to be converted into very small and rudimentary lathes.

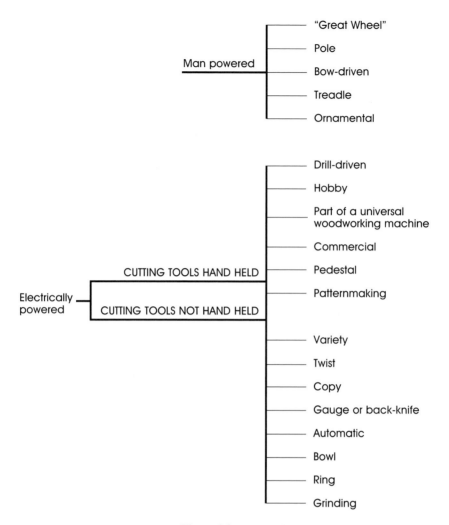

Figure 3.2 Types of lathe.

2. Hobby lathes normally swing between 6 and 16 inches (150 and 400 mm) in diameter and up to 36 inches (915 mm) between centres. Construction is usually light with pressed steel or tubular beds; detailing is sometimes primitive to save cost. Cast-iron miniature lathes of high quality started to become available from about 1990.

3. Lathes forming the basis for universal woodworking machines are usually similar to hobby lathes. The demands of the other functions prevent these being more than hobby machines.

4. Modern commercial lathes are relatively rare. Many manufacturers have gone out of business and the others now aim at the large-volume school and hobby markets. Furthermore, as the market for commercial lathes shrinks, the unit cost becomes relatively higher.

   Commercial and serious hobby lathes usually have cast and fully machined beds and heavy headstocks and tailstocks. They swing at least 16 inches (400 mm) diameter over the bed. The headstock and tailstock spindles are drilled for No. 2 Morse taper or larger. Anyone wishing to take woodturning really seriously will need the greater rigidity and potential of these machines.

   Although most beds take 36 inches (915 mm) between centres, longer beds are often an option. A wide range of accessories is usually available and some have optional carriages. Not all commercial lathes permit outboard turning.

When wooden beds were common, headstocks, tailstocks, and banjos were available to install on a bed and stand of one's own making. These are still to be found and provide a cheaper alternative for those whose main work will be spindle turning.

5. Pedestal lathes are basically commercial headstocks on stands, and are used for faceplate and bowl turning. With some, a short cantilever bed is available.

6. Patternmaking requires precision and hence patternmaking lathes are specifically made to enable the wood to be both hand turned and machined in the same way that metal is turned on an engineer's centre lathe. Wooden patterns for castings are often large so that these lathes frequently have swings of over 3 feet (1 metre) and almost all permit outboard turning. Carriages are often powered, but there is usually no direct gearbox connection between the headstock spindle and the carriage drive shaft which would permit thread cutting.

Lathes Where the Tools Are Not Hand Held

Although contact with these lathes is minimal for most turners, you should know something about them. They divide into two categories: those in which the wood rotates at speeds similar to those in hand turning; and those in which the wood rotates slowly and the cutters rotate or revolve at high speed. Their introduction has taken away the drudgery and boredom of hand turning long runs of identical items. For the professional, knowledge of the capacities and availabilities of these lathes in your area should lead to a two-way flow of business.

3.3   LATHE CAPACITY

A lathe's nominal capacity (Figure 3.3) is designated by the maximum diameter (swing) which can be turned over the bed and by the maximum length which can be accepted between centres. Some lathes have a recess in the bed immediately to the right of the headstock, this 'gap' permitting the turning of disks of larger than nominal capacity. However, whether a lathe can safely be used to turn work sized near to its nominal capacity depends on many factors which will be clarified later in this chapter.

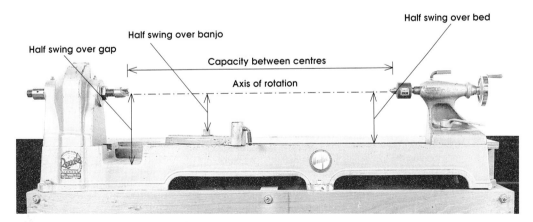

Figure 3.3   Lathe capacities.

3.4 THE LATHE BED

The bed is the basis of the lathe. The best material is cast iron because of its weight and rigidity. Unlike steel, it has the advantage that it is a poor transmitter of vibration because its cementite crystals are surrounded by insulating free graphite. However steel sections if strong and heavy provide a valid and cheaper alternative.

Cast-iron beds should be heavy with ample cross bracing. The bedways should be accurately machined on their tops, insides, and undersides. Machining the tops and insides of the bedways is essential if the tailstock is to align precisely with the headstock axis of rotation. Machining the undersides allows the banjo and tailstock clamping blocks to slide easily and minimises the amount of tightening and loosening required.

Heavy wooden beds, often with steel wearing strips along the ways, were once common, and are adequate for most work. However, there are occasions when it is critical that headstock and tailstock align, and this is most unlikely except on fully rigid and fully machined beds.

Metal-turning lathes usually have inverted V-section bedways to guide the tailstock and carriage. They are rare in woodturning lathes because the extra precision thereby achieved does not warrant the considerable extra cost, and because of the problems of fixing the banjo. Those who wish to adapt such a metal-turning bed for woodturning will need a special mounting block for the banjo.

A gap is a useful feature as long as it does not weaken the bed or be so long as to

Figure 3.4   A concrete lathe stand, the ultimate in weight ($2^{1}/_{2}$ tons, $2^{1}/_{2}$ tonnes) and rigidity. Bolts were cast into the concrete to hold the fabricated steel bed. The cast-iron headstock, tailstock, and banjo were purchased separately. An outboard stand is shown on the left (Figure 3.16). Note also the sandpaper rack. This lathe is not totally satisfactory because longitudinal vibrations tend to be transmitted along the steel bed making heavy cupchucking impossible.

Figure 3.5 A bench lathe with a cast-iron bed; a good size and quality for hobby and small commercial use. The heavy hardwood stand has a diagonal brace to prevent racking.

prevent a banjo being located close to the headstock. The gap permits large faceplate work to be turned inboard, but is rarely wide enough to permit gouges to be held in a near-vertical presentation when bowl turning.

The bed design should permit the easy escape of shavings and allow for the passage of the transmission belting from a motor preferably positioned beneath the bed and below the headstock.

Finally, the normal bed length giving a capacity between centres of about 36 inches (915 mm) is usually sufficient unless you intend doing architectural turning such as veranda and newel posts, or turned bed components. For this long spindle turning, long one- or multiple-section beds are available, although heavy timbers, or steel rectangular hollow-sections or tubes sometimes filled with concrete, or steel bars or beams are often used.

3.5 THE STAND

The stand not only supports the bed, it usually houses the motor and sometimes the controlling switchgear, provides bench space behind the bed, and can be used to mount an

Figure 3.6   A close-up of the tool rack shown in Figure 3.5. The handles pass through holes 2 inches (50 mm) in diameter at 3-inch (75-mm) centres and are supported by a l-inch (25-mm) dowel. This arrangement does not become clogged with chips.

outboard turning toolrest and tool racks.

Stands can be cast iron, steel, concrete (Figure 3.4), or wood (Figure 3.5). The essentials are the same: vibration-damping weight and rigidity. Diagonal bracing is recommended to increase the rigidity of fabricated stands. To further increase effective mass and rigidity, the stand should be strongly fixed to the floor and can be weighted with bricks, sand, etc.

Some lathes are available as bench models with sheet steel stands as an optional extra. These stands are rarely sufficiently rigid or heavy and may not even be worth trying to beef up, so it is usually better to buy the bench model and make your own stand. Stands fabricated from heavy steel-sections are usually sufficiently rigid and easy to improve.

Although using a seat on a swing arm similar to that used on many modern panel saws should be possible, a turner stands to turn. For work between centres, the lathe axis should be an inch or two (25 to 50 mm) above elbow height when you are standing straight up. An axis that is too low results in a sore back and neck. For a pedestal lathe used for bowl turning, the axis may be higher, say midway between the elbow and the shoulder. The stand should not foul your feet when standing. It should house the motor in a situation relatively free of dust and shavings, and it should allow for easy egress of shavings falling through the bed. A bench top is built behind and just below the top of the lathe bed. When the bed is of steel sections, the lathe is generally mounted on the bench top. Above and behind it, a rack for turning tools and small equipment is often located (Figure 3.6).

3.6 THE HEADSTOCK

Obviously, the iron casting (preferred because of its vibration-damping properties) or steel fabrication requires to be fully rigid and machined such that the spindle axis is parallel to the bedways and aligns with the tailstock spindle. It should also be compact and free of projections which may get in the turner's way when working adjacent to or reaching over the headstock.

The headstock design should ideally enclose the driving pulleys while allowing suf-

Figure 3.7 A Woodfast MC908 headstock. The inboard end of the spindle has a No. 2 Morse taper swallow and is threaded 30mm x 3.5mm pitch. A hexagonal flange allows the spindle to be held for the tightening and removal of accessories. Outboard turning is possible. The large end-flange of the Poly-V pulley is drilled with 24 holes and an indexing pin is provided. The pulley's five steps give lathe speeds of 2700, 2000, 1200, 650, and 370 rpm with a 1440 rpm electric motor.

TABLE 3.1 MORSE TAPERS

Number of Morse Taper	Diametrical Taper, inches per foot*	Diameter at Gauge Line A, inches*	Exposed Length C, inches*	Contact Length M, inches*	Diameter at Small End H, inches*	Length of Arbor from Gauge Line K, inches*
1	0.59858	0.4750	$^1/_8$	$2^1/_{16}$	$^{11}/_{32}$	$2^3/_{16}$
2	0.59941	0.70	$^3/_{16}$	$2^1/_2$	$^{17}/_{32}$	$2^{21}/_{32}$
3	0.60235	0.9380	$^3/_{16}$	$3^1/_{16}$	$^{23}/_{32}$	$3^5/_{16}$
4	0.62326	1.2310	$^1/_4$	$3^7/_8$	$^{31}/_{32}$	$4^3/_{16}$
$4^1/_2$	0.6240	1.50	$^1/_4$	$4^5/_{16}$	$1^{13}/_{64}$	$4^5/_8$
5	0.63151	1.7480	$^1/_4$	$4^{15}/_{16}$	$1^{13}/_{32}$	$5^5/_{16}$

NOTE: The Morse taper of about 1 in 20, or $^5/_8$ inch per foot, is a self-gripping taper.
*To convert inches to millimetres, multiply by 25.4.

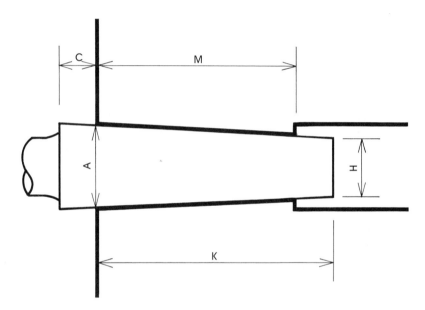

ficient access to change speeds (Figure 3.7). If the pulleys are between the two headstock bearings, the headstock spindle will have to be removed in order to replace the belt. It is good practice to also replace the bearings when this is done. As bearings are easily damaged when being fitted or removed, ensure that the correct procedures are used.

It is not uncommon to wish to use a flat-bed engineer's lathe headstock for woodturning. Rather than do expensive modifications to the original headstock, it is generally better to replace it with a ready-made woodturning lathe headstock.

The headstock spindle should be amply large in diameter, with a central through hole, and a Morse taper swallow at the right-hand end (see Figure 3.8 and Table 3.1). Spindles usually have a right-hand threaded nose at their right-hand end. Where it is required to do bowl turning, a nose with a left-hand thread should be provided at the left-hand end unless there is a facility to swivel the headstock. However, where you want to do very heavy turning, threaded noses are unsuitable — it is both difficult and dangerous to screw on or remove heavy chucks or heavily laden faceplates. Also, if any form of spindle braking is employed, the faceplate can unscrew with spectacular results. A spindle nose such as the American long taper nose (Figure 3.9) overcomes such problems. It is, however, a much more expensive nose and so are the matching faceplates, but these faceplates can be used on either end of the spindle.

Figure 3.8 An older style of headstock using a flat belt for power transmission. Notice that the faceplate has a hexagonal boss so that it can be removed easily. A No. 2 Morse taper driving centre in a No. 2 to 3 Morse taper sleeve is about to be pushed into the lathe spindle swallow.

A headstock spindle has two bearings. These are usually single deep-groove ball or tapered roller bearings. For those spindles with noses at both ends, bearing systems should permit force to be taken from either the right or the left. Also, it should be possible to preload the bearings to eliminate undue play.

Particularly where screwed noses are employed, it is important to be able to lock the spindle. Faceplates and chucks are screwed up tight against the true machined flanges, and turning from the nearside of the lathe serves to tighten them on further. Hence, a facility to lock the spindle, preferably in any position, is desirable so that accessories can be removed easily. An indexing facility (Figure 3.7), although more common, is less important and not necessarily strong enough to be used for spindle locking.

3.7 THE TAILSTOCK

The tailstock serves to locate the right-hand end of work being turned between centres or, less often, to hold drill bits. For the latter, it is critical that the tailstock spindle axis aligns

0

Figure 3.9 A large headstock with an American long taper spindle nose. Relative rotation between the chuck backing plate and the spindle is prevented by the key which mates with the keyway in the boss. The loose locking ring which butts against a flange on the spindle engages on the external thread of the boss and thereby enables the backing plate to be firmly pulled up the taper.

truly with that of the headstock. The spindle at its left-hand end is bored with a Morse taper. Longitudinal spindle adjustment is by a handwheel.

There are two basic types of tailstock. In the conventional one the tail centre is automatically ejected when the spindle is fully retracted. In the 'drilling' tailstock, the tail centre has to be removed with a drift or knock-out bar. This second type allows long-hole boring bits to be fed through the hollow spindle.

The tailstock spindle should slide easily, but there should not be any slop. A heavy handwheel about 5 inches (125 mm) in diameter is preferred as it can be spun and the spindle thus moved quickly without having to wind laboriously. Large handwheels also enable sufficient leverage to be exerted to push the wood properly onto the driving centre prongs.

The usual methods for locking the tailstock in position on the bed use a bolt, a nut, or a lever-operated cam device (Figure 3.12).

Patternmaker's lathes with a carriage often have a set-over adjustment whereby the top part of the tailstock can be moved horizontally and at right angles to the bed (Figure 3.10), thus enabling tapers to be turned without having to continuously adjust the cross-slide of the carriage (Figure 3.19).

Quick-acting and drilling tailstocks which incorporate lever operation to move the spindle longitudinally are not commonly available now.

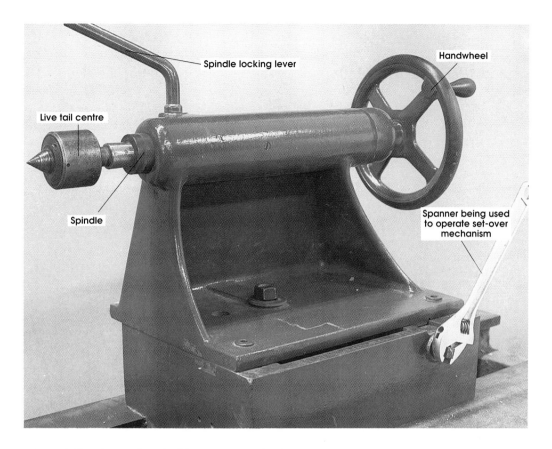

Figure 3.10 A large tailstock with a set-over mechanism.

3.8   TAILSTOCKS FOR LONG-HOLE BORING

When axially drilling long work, it is preferable to rotate the work and to use shell-type bits (lamp standard augers, Figure 4.20) or gun drills. With gun drills, the chips are blown out with compressed air which passes through the bit. The bit therefore does not have to be withdrawn to clear the chips.

For long-hole boring, it is necessary to locate the tailstock end of the work and allow access to the centre of that end for the feeding of the bit and the removal of chips. Some lathes have tailstocks with hollow spindles which are used with special hollow cup centres to hold the workpiece's right-hand end and centre and align the drill bit. Alternatively, a special-purpose drilling tailstock can be made by bolting a ball-bearing into or onto a wooden or steel tailstock structure such that the ball bearing is centred about the lathe axis (see Figure 3.11). If you have a conventional tailstock you can use a long-hole boring attachment similar to a hollow cup centre which fits into the banjo. During drilling, the headstock end of the work is gripped by a pronged driving centre or better by a chuck.

The procedure for drilling is as follows:

1. If using a supplementary ball-bearing tailstock similar to that in Figure 3.11, pre-turn a suitable taper or shallow shoulder and a short spigot on the tailstock end of the workpiece. The taper or shoulder and spigot should fit neatly against and inside the ball-bearing inner race to provide proper location of the right-hand end of the workpiece during drilling.

Figure 3.11   A plywood long-hole boring tailstock with a lamp standard auger protruding. The bearing is of the self-aligning type. It is preferable to have a fixed bearing housing.

If your lathe tailstock allows you to drill through it, use a hollow cup centre with the through hole having the same diameter as that of the drill bit. The centre will then act as a drill brush and perfectly align and centre the bit.

If using a banjo-mounted long-hole bearing attachment, use an appropriately sized twist drill or rod mounted in the tailstock to align the attachment.

2. Mount the work in the lathe and set the speed to about 1000 rpm.

3. If the 'tail centre' does not act as an accurately-sized and axial bush, it is best to bore a pilot hole into the workpiece's right-hand end using a twist drill mounted in the tailstock.

4. To avoid hitting the driving centre or chuck, use a piece of adhesive tape to mark the drilling depth on the auger. Note that for very long holes it may be necessary to drill from both ends of the workpiece.

5. Push the auger axially into the workpiece, and after drilling no more than 1 inch (25 mm), withdraw it with the flute facing upwards to remove the waste. Repeat until the required depth is reached. If you push the auger in too far, the waste chips are compressed and enlarge the hole, thus enabling the bit to wander off-line.

Figure 3.12 A banjo with cam locking. The underside of the tailstock to the right demonstrates the cam-lock mechanism.

3.9 THE BANJO

The toolrest holder is sometimes called a banjo because of its vague similarity to that instrument when viewed in plan (see Figure 3.12). There are several systems for locking the banjo to the bed

1. A bolt or threaded stem passing through the banjo to a clamping block beneath the bedways (this means that for safety the lathe should be stopped when the banjo has to be moved).
2. A lever-operated cam locking mechanism which, however, prevents the stem of the banjo being located over the centre of the bed.
3. A wedge or locking nut under the bed.

The toolrest stem is usually locked in position in the hollow stem of the banjo by a radial screw. The screw should be able to be located in preferably four alternative positions in plan. This is so that when the banjo is used in different positions, the locking screw can be relocated so that it does not foul the workpiece or your hand. The banjo stem should not extend higher than 2 inches (50 mm) below the lathe axis.

Where the banjo is locked to the bed by a nut or bolt, operation is facilitated by having the top and insides of the banjo along the slot machined. (The underside of the banjo must always be machined).

3.10 TOOLRESTS

The steel stem of the rest should not be less than 1 inch (25 mm) in diameter for normal lathes; 1¼ inches (32 mm) is recommended for large lathes. The stem should be neatly welded to the top because a projecting boss interferes with the tied-underhand turning grip and may interfere with tools being used at steep presentations.

The best shape of cross-section for the top piece of the toolrest seems to have been the cause of some debate in recent times. As I recommend tied-underhand turning and like the rest to be at about ³⁄₄ inch (19 mm) from the wood to provide sufficient working room, I want a section which is small enough to get my finger under and strong enough not to deflect during turning. It should also be constant along its length, and provide a fulcrum for the tool blade as near as possible to the work. The preferred cross-section for spindle and cupchuck turning is shown in Figure 3.13; it should be constant along the whole length of the top of the toolrest.

Wooden rests are not recommended – they are too bulky. Mild steel rests are adequately hard. Any nicks or dents which occur are easily filed out, and are minimised by arrising the corners of your skew chisels and parting tools.

Most turning can be accomplished with a straight toolrest 16 inches (400 mm) long. A variety of other lengths will be found useful (see Figure 3.14). Long toolrests may have two or three stems. To enable them to be positioned easily, the extra stem(s) should be slightly reduced in diameter. A right-angled rest will be found useful for both cupchuck and faceplate turning.

It will be shown in Chapter 10 that curved toolrests are of great benefit in bowl turning. Their cross-section should be such as to minimise tool overhang, allow the curve to be forged, and have sufficient stiffness not to deflect in use (Figure 3.13).

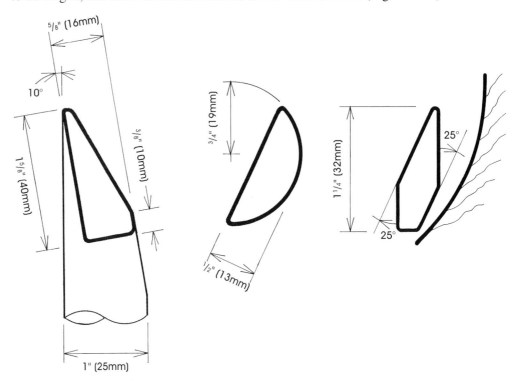

Figure 3.13 *Left:* the recommended toolrest cross-section for spindle and cupchuck turning.
Centre and right: toolrest cross-sections for turning inside bowls. The toolrest in the centre is cheaper to manufacture being round bar which has been slit.

Figure 3.14 Toolrests for spindle and cupchuck turning. The right-angled toolrest (middle left) and the cantilever toolrest (bottom left) are both useful in cupchuck turning. The cantilever toolrest has a U-shaped plate welded to its end. A tool can be located between and levered off the arms of the U.

3.11 MOTOR, TRANSMISSION, AND SWITCHGEAR

Lathe motors are generally between one-half and 3 horsepower, with 1 horsepower being ample for most lathes. Three-phase motors, although not feasible for most turners, are cheaper and easier to reverse. Reversing switches are available for single-phase motors, the reversing facility being used to speed sanding during faceplate turning.

The maximum optimum lathe speed for turning a short, 3 inch (75 mm) diameter workpiece is 2000 rpm. This equates to a velocity of the wood relative to the tool of 26 feet per second (8 metres per second). You can in practice turn at far lower speeds and sometimes should. Further, if you have set the lathe speed according to the workpiece's maximum diameter, the bulk of the turning will often be accomplished without problem at far lower relative velocities of wood to tool. Therefore although you need to be able to vary lathe speed, the increments of variation need not be too small.

There are three further reasons for requiring a lathe's speed to be variable: to reduce vibration when turning heavy, slender, or eccentric work; to set the speed when drilling to that optimum for the particular drill bit; and to prolong cutting edge life by reducing the speed for abrasive or very hard woods.

The most common method of lathe speed variation uses stepped pulleys, between three and eight in number, the more the better. The speeds will generally be within the range 200 to 3200 rpm. The pulleys on the motor and lathe spindle are connected by belts. Flat belts (Figure 3.8) lack the wedging action which enables V-belts to transmit high torques. V-belts come in various cross-sections, with Z or A being used for hobby lathes. To enable a greater speed range without unduly increasing pulley diameters, Poly-V belts (a hybrid of flat and multiple V-belts) are being increasingly used. Toothed V-belts are useful when you want to drive smaller than usual V-belt pulleys.

Where only the right-hand end of the headstock spindle is used to mount work, the stepped pulley is often mounted immediately to the left of the left-hand bearing. Where both ends of the spindle are nosed, the stepped pulley will be located between the two bearings.

The electric motor needs to be mounted so that the two stepped pulleys align perfectly, the motor is protected from dust and shavings, the belt and pulleys are guarded, and the motor is easily accessible and adjustable in distance from the headstock spindle so that the belt can be changed from one pair of pulleys to another to vary the speed. In lathes used in schools there is often an electrical cutout which switches off the motor when its access door is opened. A common and efficient motor mounting employs a hinged motor platform. The motor position should be adjusted so that the belts can only be twisted about a quarter of a rotation by hand.

Stepped pulleys are not the only means of mechanically varying the lathe speed. One method uses a friction disk driven directly by the motor. The disk in turn drives a power take-off wheel whose radial distance from the friction disk axis is variable. Pairs of pulleys with adjustable diameters can be used, although some designs are noisy. To increase the speed range with stepped or adjustable pullets a lay-shaft may be added, but again there is an undesirable increase in noise.

Finally the motor speed itself can be varied. Motors are available with multiple windings to give two or even more speeds. It is also possible, to vary motor speed continuously.

Motors are made to operate on either direct or alternating current. DC motors require a rectifier if they are to operate off AC supply. However, the speed of DC motors can be easily and continuously varied. The common method is by varying the voltage, which gives a constant torque. AC motors, both single-phase and three-phase, are readily available, although single-phase motors are usually limited to a maximum of about 2 horsepower. Using electronics, you can vary speed, direction, and even acceleration and braking, although at considerable expense. The convenience and flexibility of such systems make them apparently feasible for woodturning lathes; however, their constant torque characteristic (that is, horsepower output is proportional to motor speed) means that the motor should be oversized and stepped pulleys used in conjunction.

Normal AC motors have a very high starting torque, and the work is therefore brought to full speed almost instantaneously. The situation can be improved by using a capacitor start or a clutch or by intentionally slipping the V-belt, but these facilities are rarely provided as standard. A clutch arrangement promoted by American Del Stubbs uses a foot pedal to move the motor up and closer to the headstock, thereby allowing the belt to slip. A facility to brake the headstock spindle is very worthwhile as considerable time can be lost while the lathe slows to a stop in work requiring frequent stop-start. This braking can be manually operated, and may utilise a mechanical brake. An electric brake which reverses the field direction can be employed, although this stops rotation almost instantaneously. Alternatively, a mechanical brake can be electrically operated so that no extra manual operation is required and a more gradual braking is obtained. Brake motors are available which are normal three-phase motors incorporating a solenoid-operated disk brake. The disadvantage of always having the brake on when the motor is off can be overcome by an override switch.

Lathe operation can be greatly facilitated by having convenient control switching. On-off is essential, and forward-reverse is useful if much faceplate turning is contemplated. Protection from overload and overheating is recommended in case the work jams or the motor is stopped and started too frequently. Speed, acceleration, and braking controls are much less common.

The usual place for lathe controls is on the nearside of the bed below the headstock. This is fine for general spindle turning on small lathes, although a stop button on the front of the right-hand end of the bed allows the turner to switch off from a safe position and wind the tail centre in if he feels that the work is about to fly out. A superior arrangement (retain the extra stop button), especially when outboard turning is envisaged, is to have the switches on a console which is on a lead. This allows the console to be moved to the position most convenient for that turning operation. Yet another alternative is double switching with one set of switches on the left-hand side of the left-hand end of the lathe and the other set in the usual position below the headstock on the lathe's nearside.

3.12 DRIVING CENTRES

A driving centre (Figure 3.15) has two roles: to centre the wood's left-hand end, and to grip the wood so that the headstock spindle's rotation can be transferred without slippage to the workpiece.

A driving centre should have a Morse taper matching that of the headstock spindle swallow, a number of prongs, and a pointed centre pin. Driving centres have been manufactured with two, three, and four prongs. Four is preferable, giving more grip and allow-

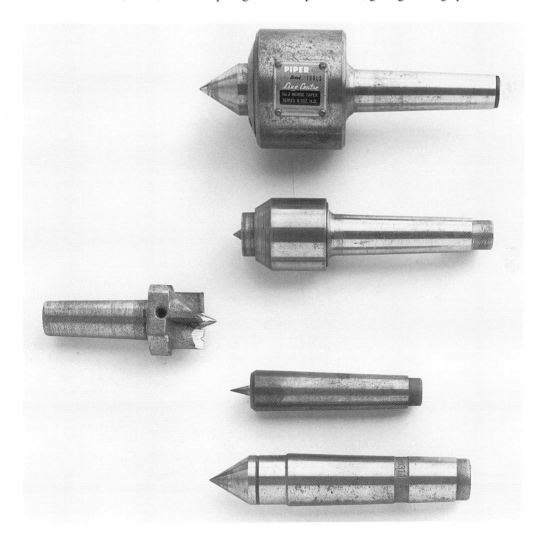

Figure 3.15 Driving and tail centres. *Left:* a four-prong driving centre. Its centre pin projection should be about ¼ inch (6 mm). Two flats are milled on it so that it can be removed using a spanner. Note the notch filed in the lower prong which assists exact recentring. *Right:* tail centres, from top to bottom, a live cone centre, a live cup centre, a plain cup centre, a plain cone centre.

ing two prongs to hold each half of the wood when turning split turnings (see Section 7.18). On most lathes, the diameter across the prongs is about 1 inch (25 mm), which is adequate. For large work, the diameter across the prongs should be correspondingly greater. Alternatively, a faceplate may be modified, or a self-centring chuck or engineer's face driver may be utilised.

The ends of the prongs should be kept sharp with a file and they should be long enough to allow for many resharpenings. Somehow, when you are recentring work on the driving centre, it rarely centres exactly as it did before. Therefore, file a notch in the centre of one prong so that the work can always be recentred with the same orientation with respect to the driving prongs.

The centre pin generally has an apex angle of about 30. The pin's optimum projection from the face of the prongs is $^1/_4$ inch (6 mm). If longer, the wood is hard to push past

Figure 3.16 A fabricated outboard turning stand. The centre stanchion is a hollow steel section, 4 inches x 4 inches (100 mm x 100 mm), but even so it has a slight tendency to flex; further diagonal bracing would eliminate this.

the point onto the prongs. Too long a point may be shortened by filing with the driving centre rotating at high speed in the lathe. If much shorter, there is insufficient projection to rest the end of the wood on while locating the wood at its tailstock end.

The driving centre may be removed by hammering a rod (known as a knock-out bar) through the hollow spindle. Alternatively, the centre should have two flats so that a sharp jerk with a spanner can be used.

3.13 TAIL CENTRES

The traditional solid cone-shaped tail centre has now been superseded by rotating (called live) centres. Although a 90° apex angle is sometimes recommended, 60° is the angle used for metal-turning centres and therefore the one readily available. This more acute angle does not seem to have a significantly greater tendency to split the wood, but it does make adjusting the centring of the workpiece's right-hand end more difficult.

The ring (or cup) centre is also available now as a revolving one. It gives excellent location and tends to hold the wood together. Hence, it is good for wood liable to split and for split turnings. The centre pin of the cup centre should be similar in size and shape to that of a driving centre, that is, projecting $^{1}/_{8}$ to $^{1}/_{4}$ inch (3 to 6 mm) and having an apex angle of about 30°. Hollow cup centres (both live and dead) which you can long hole bore through are also available. The diameter of the through-hole should match that of your

Figure 3.17   A cantilever plate outboard stand. The steel plate is $1^{1}/_{2}$ inches (37 mm) thick. This type of stand can be easily provided for any type of bench lathe.

drill bit so that the centre acts as a bush.

In addition to the rotating (or live) tail centres with fixed noses, centres are available with interchangeable and threaded noses. These allow a greater range of centring possibilities.

3.14 OUTBOARD TURNING STANDS

With swivelling headstock lathes or on lathes on which you can turn outboard, special adjustable, cantilever, sideboard or outboard toolrest holders are usually available. If you are contemplating large-diameter outboard turning, free-standing stands (see Figure 3.16) are preferred because they can be moved into any position. However, unless a concrete floor is present, the outboard stand is unsuitable because it will bounce under the variable forces exerted on the tool by the wood. In addition, unless the stand itself is exceedingly rigid and heavy, it will spring under the variable loadings which will often be most extreme when the tool is being used far from the centre of the stand.

An alternative type of outboard stand is the cantilever plate. This rigid steel plate is bolted under the headstock end of the bed (Figure 3.17). It should project a minimum of 8 inches (200 mm) to the left of the left-hand face of the left-hand faceplate. A much taller banjo is obviously required. Additional stability is provided if the left-hand end of the

Figure 3.18 A cantilever plate screwed onto the wooden bearers which support the lathe. The bearers are specially extended to the left of the headstock.

plate is propped off the floor. A packing plate of the same thickness as the cantilever plate will also be required under the right-hand end of the bed to level the lathe.

A similar facility can be achieved by screwing a steel plate to the bearers which support the lathe and are extended past the left-hand end of the headstock (Figure 3.18).

3.15 THE CARRIAGE

Patternmaker's lathes have a carriage so that the wood can be machined when necessary in a way similar to that used for metal (Figure 3.19). A feed shaft sometimes powers the longitudinal motion of the carriage. In patternmaker's lathes that do not have a feed shaft, the carriage is wound along by hand.

Most carriages just have a simple tool post mounted on the cross-slide (the cross-slide enables the tool post to be moved horizontally at right angles to the lathe axis). More sophisticated carriages have a compound cross-slide.

For general woodturning, the carriage has little application except for the turning of large diameter dowels. It can be useful in cupchucking if you require hollowing with exactly parallel sides or the fronts of workpieces to be scraped to a particular profile. A router can also be mounted on the cross-slide and be used for fluting and reeding.

Figure 3.19   A lathe carriage which is moved along the bed with the large handwheel or the rotating feed shaft..

4

Lathe Accessories and Associated Equipment

This chapter describes those items of equipment used in woodturning which are easily mounted on and removed from the lathe. In addition, it discusses other equipment used away from the lathe.

4.1 MEASURING EQUIPMENT

Figures 4.1 and 4.2 give a range of the additional measuring equipment which turners will find useful. Points to note are:

1. Firm-joint callipers are not really satisfactory for setting diameters with the wood rotating as they tend to open. The spring type is preferred, but the jaws of all callipers need to be smoothly rounded so that they will slip sweetly over the rotating wood. Note that the adjusting knob on some spring callipers may unscrew when callipering rotating wood due to the vibration, so that it will be necessary to add a lock nut, or tape or hold the callipers in such a way that the adjusting knob is prevented from rotating.

2. The large firm-joint callipers have turned wooden ends and are used in bowl turning to check wall thicknesses. The wooden ends eliminate the danger of damaging

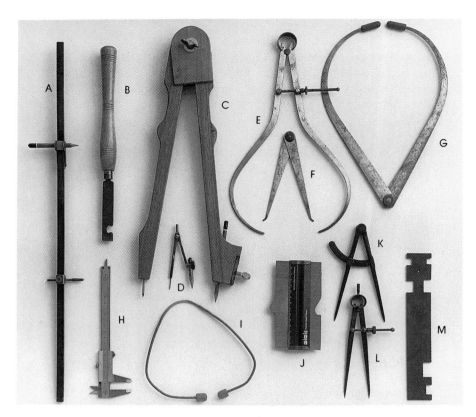

Figure 4.1 Measuring equipment. A, trammel heads; B, diameter gauge; C, large pencil compasses; D, pencil compasses; E, spring outside callipers; F, firm-joint inside callipers; G, firm-joint outside callipers with protective wooden ends; H, vernier callipers; I, flexible steel rod with protective wooden ends for measuring in inaccessible situations; J, Mimic; K, wing dividers; L, spring dividers; M, multiple diameter gauge.

Figure 4.2 Using a homemade centre finder.

the bowl surfaces.

3. Vernier callipers are ideal for measuring diameters and the lengths of work which have to be duplicated and for setting diameters with the wood rotating. The jaws, however, will need to have their ends rounded. Poor-quality callipers will not stand up to the rigours of turning. Check also that there is a strong and positive locking screw.

4. Two pairs of pencil compasses will be useful. The normal size can be bought; the large ones (about 19 inches high, 475 mm) may have to be made. They are particularly used in bowl work. Trammel heads are less suitable than compasses unless the diameters being scribed are extremely large.

5. A length of mild steel rod, about $^3/_{16}$ inch (5 mm) in diameter, may be useful for callipering in restricted situations. Again, as in point 2 above, wooden ends are recommended.

6. Wing dividers will be found best for making circles on the ends of the wood when cupchucking or on the flat faces of disks because the setting can be locked, whereas for spring-type dividers the setting is only prevented from enlarging, not decreasing.

7. Although possession of vernier callipers will eliminate the necessity of other callipering equipment, at least in the small-diameter range, additional gauges for frequently required diameters will prove useful. Two types are commonly used. The first (Figure 4.1B) is made from steel about $^1/_4$ inch (6 mm) thick. The second (Figure 4.1M) is similar in principle, but has multiple diameters; it is made from $^1/_8$ inch (3 mm) steel. You can also use the ends of open-ended spanners as gauges. To set a diameter, a gauge is used with a parting tool or gouge.

8. A centre finder (Figure 4.2) is especially useful for determining the centres of disks or marking diameters.

9. The Mimic's chief use is when copy-turning faceplate mouldings such as circular picture frames or bolection mouldings. With these jobs, it is difficult to judge radial distances and thicknesses. In spindle turning, it is quicker to use pencil and pin gauges, callipering, and most importantly your eyes to compare and judge shapes (see Section 7.1).

4.2 FACEPLATES

A right-hand faceplate is usually supplied with a lathe, as should a left-hand one when there is a facility for outboard turning (Figure 4.3). It is useful to have extra faceplates because homemade chucks and partially completed jobs can be left mounted on them.

Six inches (150 mm) in diameter is the most common size, but depending on your lathe, larger and especially smaller diameters will also prove useful. There is a tendency for some manufacturers to make their faceplates too thin so that they can deflect in use. For instance, a faceplate 6 inches (150 mm) in diameter needs to be at least $^1/_4$ inch (6 mm) thick.

The usefulness of being able to lock the spindle was mentioned in discussing the headstock (Section 3.6). This facility, in turn, needs to be mated with some way of applying a strong rotational force in order to unscrew faceplates and other equipment. The boss of the faceplate should therefore be faceted so that a normal spanner (wrench in North America) can be used, or be notched or drilled for use with a C-spanner.

It is often important to be able to mount a disk-shaped workpiece with its centre truly coincident with the lathe axis. Most faceplates have a central hole (the thread inside the faceplate boss is usually taken right through) which allows the centre of the disk to be centred visually. An alternative solution is a sprung centre spike.

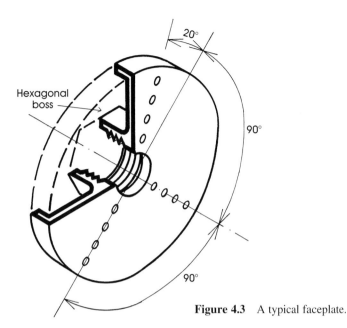

Figure 4.3 A typical faceplate.

Disks are mounted on the faceplate by screwing through from the back; four 10-gauge screws with penetrations of $^3/_8$ inch (10 mm) are usually ample. Four radial rows of screw holes are usually provided lying on two diameters at right angles. A fifth row at about 20° to, and used in lieu of, one of the original rows is useful because it ensures that work or equipment can be remounted only in its original orientation. Alternatively, mark a permanent reference point on the rim of the faceplate, and pencil a mark on the work, which is then lined up with the reference point when the work is remounted. The holes for screwing through the faceplate should, of course, be sized for the gauge of screw likely to be used.

When work whose base diameter is smaller than the faceplate diameter is to be mounted, a small plywood spacing disk is used to allow tool access. When thin disks whose diameters are much larger than the faceplate diameter are to be turned, a thick plywood, wood, or medium density fibreboard (MDF) supporting disk will prevent the workpiece flexing.

4.3   SCREWCHUCKS

Screwchucks (Figure 4.4) work by the screw pulling the workpiece back against the face of the chuck, and it is the latent friction between the front face of the screwchuck and the rear face of the workpiece which holds the workpiece secure.

This latent frictional force is proportional to both the pull of the screw and the roughness of the surfaces. Obviously, the pull can also be improved by increasing the depth of penetration of the screw, although $^1/_2$ inch (13 mm) will be sufficient for most items. Penetration can be varied by using plywood packing disks. The roughness of the face of the chuck can be increased by gluing on fine-abrasive paper.

Many lathes have screwchucks available as an additional accessory. Most of them copy the excellent Glaser screwchuck which uses a rectangular thread form and requires a $^1/_4$ inch (6 mm) pilot hole. You can adapt a faceplate to make a screwchuck as shown in Figure 4.5.

Screwchucks are generally between $1^1/_2$ and 6 inches (37 and 150 mm) in diameter. Wood up to twice the chuck diameter can be turned satisfactorily. Predrill a pilot hole.

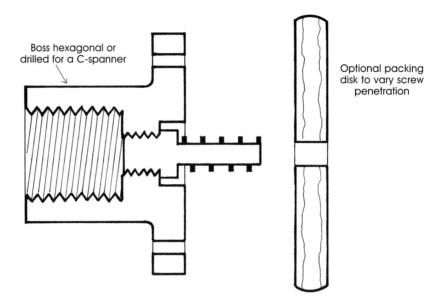

Figure 4.4   A section through a typical screwchuck.

When screwing work on, be careful not to overtighten to the point that the wood thread is stripped. Again, as with faceplates, use a reference point on the rim to minimise misalignment if remounting.

The work mounted on screwchucks is usually faceplate work and you are therefore screwing into side grain. Axially grained work can be held, but it should be small and have a long screw penetration to overcome the poor holding power of long grain.

For turning, outboard left-hand-threaded screw chucks are available.

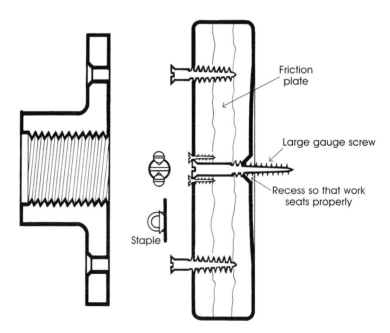

Figure 4.5   Converting a faceplate to a screwchuck. A staple may also be used to prevent the holding screw rotating. The slight hollowing on the front face of the friction plate is optional.

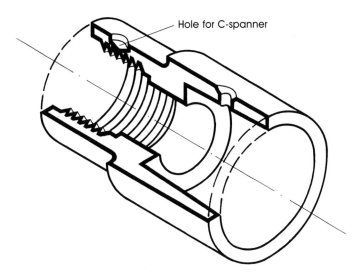

Figure 4.6 A cupchuck. The diametrical taper of the inside of the bell is typically 1 in 20. The bell is about $1^{1}/_{2}$ inches (37 mm) to 2 inches (50 mm) deep depending on diameter.

4.4 CUPCHUCKS

In cupchuck turning, described in detail in Chapter 8, the wood is held by its left-hand end and has its grain direction parallel to the lathe axis. This method of holding allows full access to the work's right-hand end. Like the screwchuck, the cupchuck (Figure 4.6) utilises friction to hold the wood, but this time the friction is between the inside of the wall of the chuck and the periphery of the matching taper turned on the wood. The arrangement is similar to the self-gripping Morse tapers in the headstock and tailstock spindles. Holding power is very high. Cupchucks require accurate preturning of the waste which will be held in the chuck, and are slower to use than the scroll and collet chucks described in Sections 4.7 and 4.8. The cupchuck is very safe, having no projections, and is compact in diameter, therefore allowing you to work close up to the end of the chuck. A C-spanner is commonly used to screw on and remove the chuck. Cupchucks can be made in a wide range of sizes, but $1^{3}/_{4}$ and $2^{3}/_{4}$ inches (44 and 70 mm) are the most useful.

There is a related chuck like an engineer's die called a Screw Cupchuck manufactured by Woodfast. The chuck socket is threaded and cuts a thread on the workpiece's preturned spigot as the spigot is screwed in. The spigot should project from a true radial shoulder. The spigot should be screwed in such that the shoulder bears against the face of the chuck. This increases the strength of the hold, and enables the accurate rechucking of a workpiece, something not possible with a cupchuck.

4.5 JACOBS CHUCKS

Jacobs chucks (Figure 4.7) are available in maximum capacities up to ¾ inch (19 mm). They should be fixed onto Morse tapered arbors so that they can be held in either the headstock or the tailstock swallow. When held in the headstock spindle, they provide a safe and convenient way of cupchucking small work or of providing the end fixity desirable when turning small-diameter slender work (see Section 7.17). Jacobs chucks are most commonly used to hold drill bits.

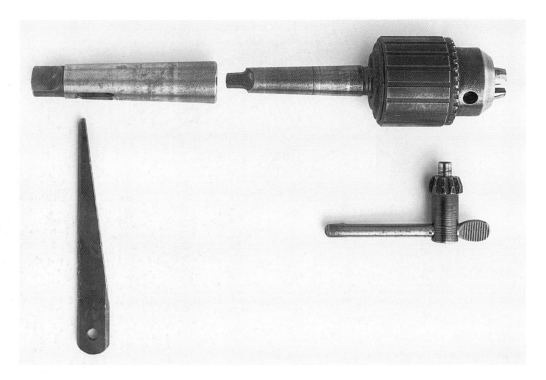

Figure 4.7 A Jacobs chuck mounted on an arbor. *Top left:* a 2 to 3 Morse taper sleeve.
Bottom left: a drift for ejecting the arbor. *Top right:* a Jacobs chuck mounted on a No. 2 Morse taper arbor.
Bottom right: the key for the Jacobs chuck.

4.6   SLEEVES

Sleeves (Figure 4.7) are precision-ground tapered tubes which enable accessories with a
certain Morse taper to be used in swallows which have a larger Morse taper. The narrow
end of a sleeve has a slotted hole so that a tapered tool known as a drift can be knocked
through to eject the accessory. The device which allows a larger taper to be held in a
smaller taper is called an extension socket.

4.7   SCROLL CHUCKS

Engineer's chucks are used very extensively in metal turning, but less often in woodturning. They are available with independently moveable jaws, or with self-centring (called
scroll) actions in which the jaws move radially in and out in unison. Certainly independent chucks have applications, but these are very limited compared with the almost universal usefulness of the self-centring, or scroll, variety.

 Engineer's chucks are available with two, three, four, or six jaws. For our purposes,
three or preferably four jaws are used, the latter giving greater gripping area and allowing square sections to be gripped without preliminary turning. A variety of jaws are available: inside-gripping (Figure 4.8), outside-gripping, bar, two-piece hard, and soft blank.
When you are using the chuck in the role of a cupchuck, four bar jaws will give the maximum contact area between the jaws and the wood. Soft blank jaws are plain and supplied
in the annealed state. After being machined for the particular application, they are then
hardened prior to use. Table 4.1 gives details of typical chucks.

 The advantages and disadvantages of engineer's chucks are as follows:

TABLE 4.1 STANDARD ENGINEER'S THREE- AND FOUR-JAW SCROLL CHUCKS

Diameter of Body		Diameter of Centre Hole		Weight	
inches	mm	inches	mm	pounds	kg
4	100	1.00	25.4	6.6	3.0
5	125	1.38	35.0	10.3	4.7
6	160	1.81	45.9	17.8	8.1
7.87	200	2.16	54.8	31.3	14.2
10	250	2.99	75.9	58.6	26.6

Figure 4.8 A four-jaw scroll chuck with inside-gripping jaws. The headstock stepped pulleys are flat-belt driven.

Figure 4.9   A plywood and plastic chuck guard. The shallow hybrid gouge (see Section 5.3) is ground so that it can be used to rough close to the guard and yet give a skewed cutting action on the whole of the workpiece.

1. They are expensive and will need a backing plate in order to be able to be mounted onto your spindle nose.
2. They are heavy so that hobby lathe bearings will usually not accept diameters larger than 5 inches (125 mm).
3. They are dangerous with sharp projections from the front face and often from the periphery. They should therefore be well guarded (see Figure 4.9). A partial guard can be readily made by stretching a short length of inner tube around a chuck's cylindrical periphery.
4. They are precision-made, are very quick in operation, have a wide range of adjustment, and are very versatile.
5. If they are used for cupchucking, the diameter of the chuck is usually considerably greater than the diameter of the workpiece. Therefore, tool access to the wood immediately to the right of the jaws is difficult.
6. Whether they are inside- or outside-gripping, the contact area is small and, therefore, if the wood projection is other than minimal, the wood must be compressed under the jaws in order to be held securely.
7. Self-centring chucks are very convenient for gripping other chucks, faceplate bosses, etc.
8. They will occasionally become clogged with wood dust and then need to be disassembled and cleaned.

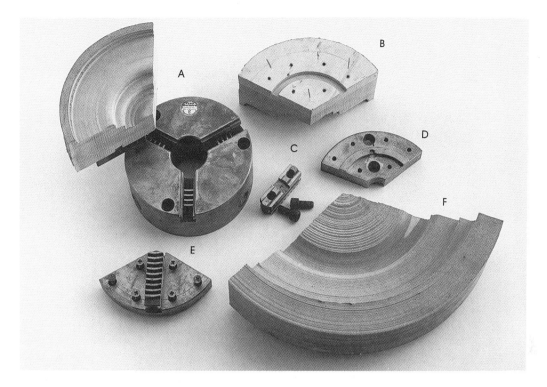

Figure 4.10 The components of the chuck plate system. A, front view of a three-jaw scroll chuck with a fully assembled chuck plate sector; B, the underside of a supplementary plate sector, the annular recess is located by the annular ridge in the top of the chuckplate D; C, top view of the bottom half of a two-piece jaw; D, the top of a chuck plate; E, the underside of a chuck plate with a half jaw screwed on; F, a larger supplementary plate which can still be used with the chuck plates shown.

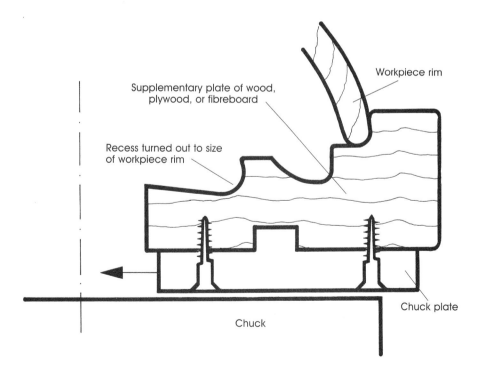

Figure 4.11 Outside gripping with chuck plates.

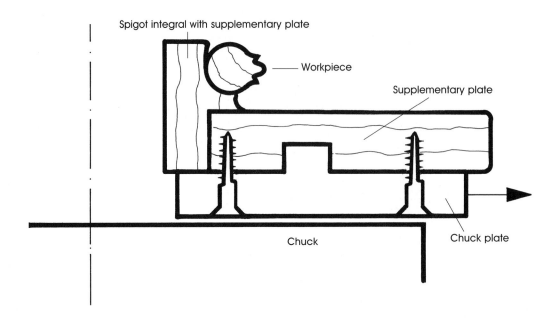

Figure 4.12   Inside gripping with chuck plates.

9. They can be adapted to securely grip finished surfaces without damage by the use of my invention, chuck accessory plates.

In plan the steel chuck plates are sectors of a circle (Figure 4.10). They are bolted onto the bottom halves of standard two-piece jaws and therefore can be moved radially in or out in unison. Similarly, sector-shaped plates of an easily turnable material such as wood, plywood, or fibreboard are screwed onto the chuck plates. These supplementary plates are provided by the turner. They require an annular recess to be preturned, which mates with an annular rib on the chuck plates. This rib ensures positive location under various radial stress conditions. The supplementary plates may be of several thicknesses of material glued together and may have a radius greater than that of the chuck plates. The limiting factor will be the ability of the chuck to safely withstand the centripetal forces generated, which, in turn, will depend on the weights of combined plates, the lathe speed, and the compression of the workpiece. Steel chuck bodies are therefore preferred to cast-iron ones.

The chuck plate system can be used for either outside-gripping or inside-gripping. With outside-gripping (see Figure 4.11), an annular recess having the same diameter as the workpiece perimeter is turned in the supplementary plates. The chuck is then opened slightly, the workpiece inserted, and the jaws tightened. This method allows bowls to be held by their rims so that their bottoms may be finish-turned (see Section 10.7).

Inside-gripping requires a spigot composed of sectors, each of which is fixed onto a supplementary plate. Opening the chuck jaws will cause the outside of the spigot to grip the perimeter of the hole or recess in the workpiece (see Figure 4.12).

The disadvantages of engineer's scroll chucks—their high costs, weights and low gripping areas have been largely overcome by lightweight, steel, four-jaw scroll chucks made specially for woodturners (Figure 4.13). They are operated by two C-spanners or similar rather than by one key, so that a third hand would be useful. Most brands have a wide variety of special-purpose jaws including internal and external dovetail gripping, screwchuck, cupchuck, and chuck plate type.

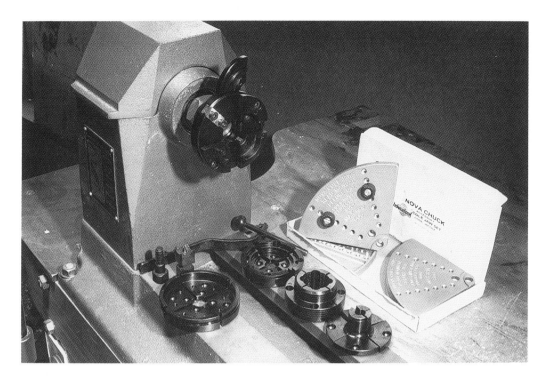

Figure 4.13 A woodturner's Nova scroll chuck. The accessory jaws include: Cole jaws for gripping bowl rims, spigot jaws for cupchucking, and dovetailed jaws for gripping short spigots or into recesses. The chuck can readily be converted into a screwchuck or drive centre.

Figure 4.14 The Craft Supplies Maxie-Grip 2000 operates in both expansion and contraction. Its accessories permit it to grip by pin chucking, cupchucking, dovetailed jaws, a screwchuck, a drive centre, and homemade wood jaw plates.

4.8   COLLET CHUCKS

A collet is a split tube with a uniform internal diameter and a tapered external surface. To reduce the internal diameter of the collet and to thereby grip the work, the collet is either pushed or pulled down an outer casing with a matching internal taper. The collet chucks used for metal turning grip tightly and accurately, albeit over a very small diameter range above and below the nominal size of the collet.

The collet principle is utilised in many brands of woodturning chuck (Figure 4.14), but has been adapted to allow larger radial adjustment, and gripping by both expansion and contraction. As with woodturning scroll chucks, a wide range of differently sized collets, dovetail jaws, loose rings, segmented plate jaws, etc. are available.

Figure 4.15   Wooden split chucks with hose clip adjustment. That on the left is mounted in a 6-in-1 collet chuck (now superseded); that on the right is mounted on a faceplate.

4.9   HOMEMADE CHUCKS

The woodturner who does a variety of work will occasionally wish to produce his own special-purpose chucks. They should preferably act by compressing the work. If, for instance, you wish to hold a turned box by its open end and expand jaws to grip it by its inside, it is likely to be split during the chucking, or if not, by the stresses imposed during turning.

Usually the special-purpose chucks will be made from wood. Occasionally, when the design is successful, it may be worthwhile having the chuck made up in steel. Wooden homemade chucks are usually mounted on faceplates or in a proprietary chuck—in fact in any way which will give consistency of centring and alignment. Two of the most common homemade chucks are described below.

Split Chuck with Hose Clip Adjustment

Shown in Figure 4.15, the split chuck is commonly used to hold small boxes for finishing off their bases. By turning a slight hollow just inside the right-hand end of the chuck, spherical or similarly shaped work can be held. The possible adjustment in diameter is generally about $^3/_{16}$ inch (5 mm). The adjustment may be increased by lengthening the chuck, but its concentricity with the lathe axis may then be adversely effected. Take care to keep clear of the rotating hose clip.

Press Fit Chuck

The press fit (or jam) chuck is a nonadjustable, almost primitive chuck (Figure 4.16) which is surprisingly useful and effective. It is merely a disk of wood or similar, with its grain either parallel or at right angles to the lathe axis, which is mounted on a faceplate or in a chuck. The face is flushed flat and a shallow, parallel-sided recess turned, into which the work fits tightly. The work will need a parallel-sided section or spigot (solid or hollow), preferably with a slight lead-in bevel, and perfect alignment is best obtained by the base or shoulder from which the spigot projects bearing against the face of the chuck. Press fit chucks are much used in bowl turning (see Section 10.7).

Sizing of the recess is critical if sufficient friction is to be able to be generated to prevent the work coming out. The diameter of the recess is marked with dividers and turned out with a detail gouge. It is then trimmed with a gouge, side-cutting scraper, or a skew chisel on its side used as a scraper. It is wise to turn the recess a touch small and carefully enlarge it, frequently stopping the lathe to monitor progress. For a secure hold, the work should need to be forced in with the heel of the palm. If the recess is turned a whisker oversize, wetting to expand the cells of the recess wall or lining the wall with paper may save starting anew, but any undue stress or a dig-in may pull the work partially or fully out of the chuck.

4.10   VACUUM CHUCKS

Vacuum chucks are primarily used for holding workpieces with flat bottoms during faceplate turning. Breadboards, bowls, and lamp bases are commonly held by vacuum chucks during large-volume turning on both hand and automatic lathes. Vacuum chucking is increasingly being used when turning the waste from the bottoms of bowls and boxes, and during the turning of spheres.

The vacuum pump, protected from wood dust by a filter, is connected to the hollow headstock spindle via hoses, a valve (often foot-operated), and a union.

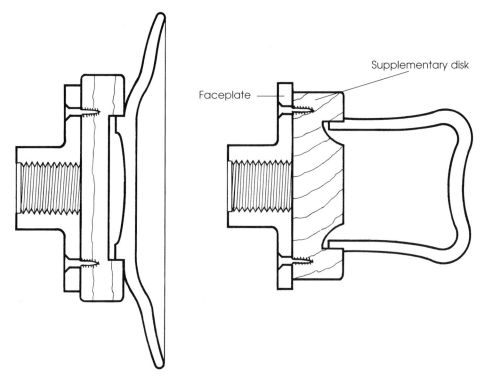

Figure 4.16   Press fit chucks: used to hold a platter by a square shoulder on its base, and a box bottom by the spigot which locates the lid.

A hose connects the pump's filter to the valve which allows the vacuum to be released and workpiece thus mounted or removed. The hose from the valve to the lathe ends at a union, a rotating seal system screwed onto one end of the headstock spindle. The union enables the headstock spindle to rotate without coiling and tearing the hose. At the far end of the lathe spindle a special faceplate is mounted. It will have a perforated face to allow air extraction from the space between the faceplate and the workpiece. Sealing is generally provided by a rubber or butyl sealing ring, and a sprung centre pin is often used to aid axial workpiece mounting.

A press fit chuck can be augmented with vacuum, even that from a domestic vacuum cleaner, for turning-off waste from the bottoms of bowls or boxes.

4.11 CHUCK CHOICE

The choice of chuck types and brands is almost overwhelming, and is complicated by frequent developments and modifications to existing chucks and by the introduction of new ones. As a minimum you will need faceplates, a screw chuck, and a Jacobs chuck. If cost is a major consideration, by just adding a cupchuck you will be able to chuck almost anything. The more expensive engineer's and woodturner's scroll chucks and collet chucks do not make anything new possible, but their convenience and quickness make at least one of them a 'must' for the serious turner. The choice of type, brand, and accessories may be determined by the type and size of work you intend, by the compactness of collet-type chucks, or by the greater range of adjustment of scroll-type chucks. The strength of gripping of a chuck is related to the contact area between the compressible wood of the workpiece and the chuck. The mating chuck material may be relatively non-compressible like steel, or may be as compressible as wood or even turnable like wood. Workpiece preparation prior to gripping with a collet- or scroll-type chuck may include:

1. Drilling for a screw chuck. The hole will usually be ¼ inch (6 mm).
2. Drilling a larger diameter hole for a pin chuck or into which jaws can expand.
3. Turning a shallow recess (often dovetailed) or drilling a shallow recess into which jaws expand.
4. Screwing on a supplementary steel ring into which a chuck's expanding dovetail jaws fit.
5. Prior to cupchuck turning in a collet chuck, turning down the bulk of a workpiece to a cylinder leaving a larger diameter shoulder at one end which is held against the face of the chuck by the chuck's outside collar.
6. An arrangement similar to point 5 above in which a radially split ring housed within a groove turned at the waste end of the workpiece acts as the shoulder.
7. Turning a shallow spigot which will be gripped within contracting dovetail jaws. The spigot itself may be within a recess.
8. Turning a long, constant-diameter spigot which will be gripped within jaws or within the length of a collet.
9. Some brands of chuck have chuck plates similar to those shown in Figure 4.10. Fitting and perhaps preliminary turning of the supplementary plates may be required to enable chucking.

To maximise gripping, the diameter of the workpiece holding feature and that of the chuck jaws or similar should accord. Ideally also, some truly turned part of the workpiece, such as a shoulder, should bear against a part of the chuck which remains truly radial.

4.12 MANDRELS

A mandrel is an axially mounted shaft or spigot which holds bored workpieces by their inside surfaces, thereby allowing their external surfaces to be turned. Mandrels are usually chucked on the right-hand side of the headstock. They may also be held between centres (Figure 4.17).

Figure 4.18 shows the most common situation in which the mandrel has a very slight taper. If the mandrel is correctly sized, the outside of the workpiece can be turned, and both the outside and half of the inside sanded. The workpiece then merely needs revers-

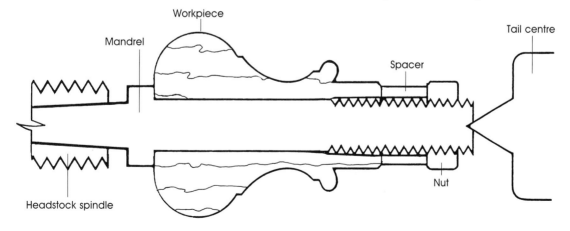

Figure 4.17 A threaded mandrel in use

Figure 4.18   A tapered mandrel mounted in a 6-in-1 ring chuck.

Figure 4.19   An expanding mandrel. By pulling the knob on the left-hand end of the headstock sharply to the left, the split part of the chuck is forced open to grip the inside of the workpiece. A simple but effective application of the expanding collet principle.

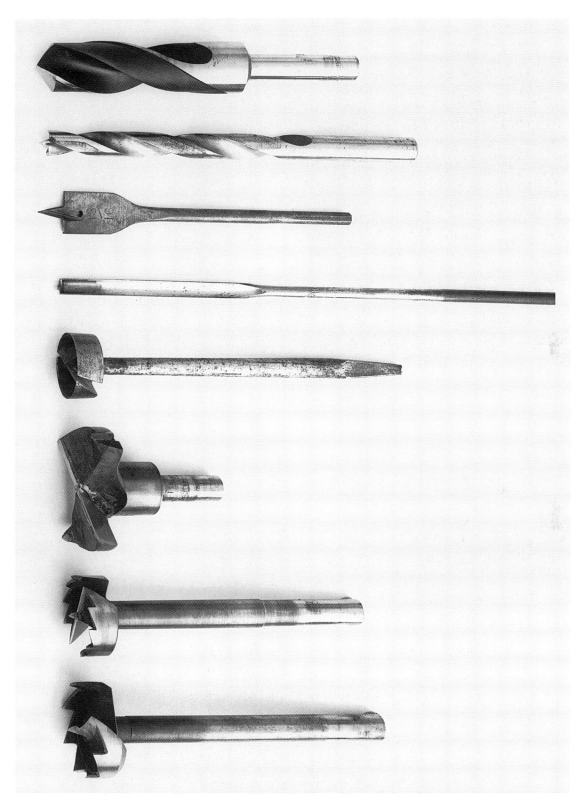

Figure 4.20 Drill bits used in woodturning. *Top to bottom:* twist drill, brad point drill, spade bit, lamp standard auger, Forstner bit, boring bit with tungsten carbide cutters and spurs, and sawtooth bits. Sawtooth bits with only one radial cutter will tend to wander at the commencement of drilling.

ing on the mandrel to enable the remainder of the inside to be sanded.

A mandrel may be made adjustable by applying the expanding collet principle. Figure 4.19 shows the arrangement. If the sanding of the inside surface of a workpiece as described in the previous paragraph has had to be heavy, then on reversing, the workpiece may slide too far along the mandrel to permit access to the unsanded part. The expanding mandrel overcomes this. An expanding mandrel can also be expanded by forcing in the tail centre to wedge the chuck sectors radially apart.

4.13 DRILL BITS

Provided that your lathe's headstock and tailstock axes align properly, you can mount drill bits (Figure 4.20) in either the headstock or the tailstock and drill axial holes in work held by or against the other. It is more usual for the work to be held on the headstock, with the drill bit held in a Jacobs chuck, itself held in the tailstock. Note that larger sizes in engineer's twist drills are also available with Morse taper shanks, eliminating the need to use a Jacobs chuck.

Short work can be held just in a chuck or by a faceplate; longer work also needs location at its free end. To some extent, this is provided by the drill bit itself and your hand can also be used if the rotational speed is kept low. However, it is safer and more satisfactory to locate the free end in a steady or preferably in a special drilling tailstock (see Section 3.8). When drilling, withdraw the bit frequently so that a build-up of shavings will not cause it to jam. A piece of adhesive tape around the drill shank can be used as a

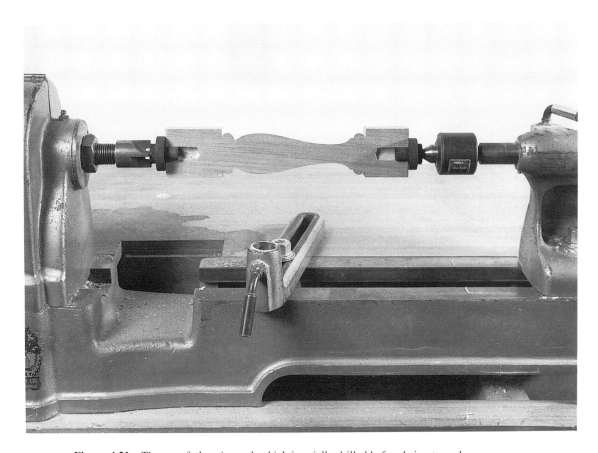

Figure 4.21   The use of plugs in work which is axially drilled before being turned.

depth guide. You can often avoid drilling in the lathe by drilling by hand, or in a pedestal drilling machine or horizontal borer.

Where a workpiece such as a lamp stem needs a truly axial through hole, it is best to bore before finish-turning. After boring, the axial hole can be temporarily plugged so that the work can be turned. For this, a piece of hard wood is turned between centres to a dumbbell shape. The dumbbell is then cut in half into two plugs (Figure 4.21). To give a more positive drive, a couple of brads may be driven into the annular face of the head-stock plug and pinched off, leaving a small amount protruding. For small-diameter axial holes, a rose countersink held in a Jacobs chuck can be used as a driving centre. Special drive centres with accurately sized cylindrical centre pins are made for holding the left-hand ends of pre-bored workpieces such as lamp stems. The nose of a cone live centre is used to locate such a workpiece's right-hand end.

TABLE 4.2   DRILL BIT DETAILS

Bit Type	Diameter, inches	Diameter, mm	Recommended Speed, rpm
Spade	All sizes	All sizes	2500
Lamp standard auger	$^1/_4$-$^1/_2$	6-13	1000
Twist drills and	$^1/_8$-$^1/_4$	3-6	3000
Brad point drills	$^3/_8$	10	3000
	$^1/_2$	13	2300
	$^3/_4$	19	1550
	1	25	1150
Sawtooth and Forstner	$^3/_8$	10	1000
	$^1/_2$	13	750
	$^3/_4$	19	500
	1	25	400
	$1^1/_2$	37	250
	2	50	200

Five main types of wood-boring bits are available (see Table 4.2). Many more types have been made in the past, but most have shanks suitable only for hand braces.

Spade bits are not recommended. Despite slow, careful feeding, spade bits tend to jam, often with dire consequences. Note that spade bits should never be retracted until the rotation of the bit or workpiece has stopped.

Lamp standard augers have an eye or spike so that a wooden handle can be fitted. These augers used to be available in a large range of sizes, but now other than $^1/_2$, $^3/_8$, and $^5/_{16}$ inch (13, 10, and 8 mm) are rare. A superior and far more expensive alternative is the gun drill. These are available through specialist suppliers and compressed air is needed to blow out the chips. Both these bits are maintained in alignment by being a tight fit within the left-hand end of the hole that they are drilling. A long twist drill or a two-fluted carpenter's auger with the screw point and any spurs ground off make only a passable stand-in due to the tendency for there to be a significant component of tip steerage.

For the repetitive cutting of holes which do not have constant diameter longitudinal sections, it is possible to have special cutters made or to grind large twist drills to shape.

5
Turning Theory and Tools

Cutting wood with a sharp chisel and crudely bashing it with a hammer are basically the same process, the application of force to an area resulting in deformation and perhaps even failure. In cutting, the force is concentrated over a very small area, so that the force per unit area, or stress, exerted on the wood causes an opposing stress pattern in the wood

Figure 5.1   Peeling an upstanding rib on a spindle.

whose magnitude is high enough to cause local failure. Also implicit in cutting is that the severed wood can escape so as not to obstruct the path of the cutting tool.

A knowledge of cutting theory is important if you are to understand why certain practices are recommended even though they have grown up empirically. It also helps you to maximise efficiency by enabling you to select the optimum conditions for a particular turning situation. In any situation the optimum conditions of lathe speed, tool selection, sharpening, and presentation are determined by the wood, tool access, and the intended surface contours and finish. These optimum conditions should be the same for all turners. That different turners use different methods in the same turning situation is a reflection of incomplete knowledge or subjective, not objective, preference.

5.1   CUTTING THEORY

Little serious investigation seems to have been undertaken into the various cutting situations occurring during woodturning. I have therefore had to develop much of the theory in this section, starting from research into metal turning and wood planing.

Peeling

Classical cutting theory is based upon cutting away an outstanding rib of a homogeneous and isotropic material, such as metal, with a tool wider than the rib so that side effects are

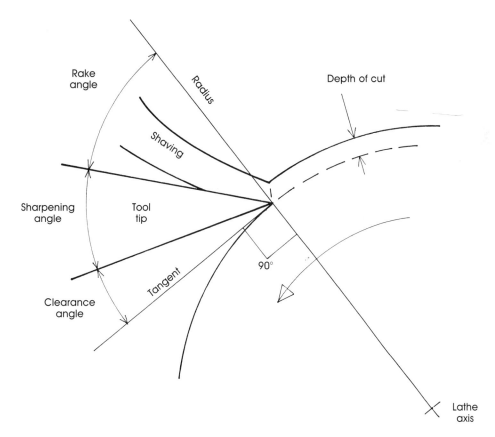

Figure 5.2   A vertical cross-section perpendicular to the lathe axis through the upstanding rib in Figure 5.1. The three defined angles—clearance, sharpening, and rake—will be referred to frequently in the text.

eliminated (see Figure 5.1). Figure 5.2 shows a vertical section through Figure 5.1 viewed from the lathe tailstock.

In Figure 5.2, the shaving expands after severance. The frictional force applied by the top of the tool tip to the underside of the shaving slows the shaving; hence the force which the turner needs to apply can be reduced if the top of the tool tip is smooth. Obviously energy-requiring slowing and expansion of the shaving is further reduced if the rake angle can be enlarged. This can be done by using a tool with a smaller sharpening angle, and by reducing the clearance angle. In practice a sharpening angle much below 25° lacks durability and the minimum long-term clearance angle is 0°, so that the maximum practical rake angle is about 65°. This large rake angle presentation is commonly called *cutting*.

The other common presentation is at a rake angle of about 0° and is commonly called *scraping* (see Figure 5.8). When 'cutting' and 'scraping' are used to signify cutting with large and near-zero rake angles respectively, they will be italicised.

The speed of the wood relative to the cutting edge influences the efficiency of cutting. At higher speeds there is less expansion of the chips and therefore less turner's energy is wasted. Higher chip inertia gives the effect of greater rigidity thereby assisting in chip severance. Higher cutting speeds also lead to higher temperatures at the tool tip, and as wood loses strength at even moderately elevated temperatures (10 to 50 percent loss at 160°F (71°C)), severance is further assisted at higher speeds. The penalty may be unduly rapid blunting of the cutting edge.

Figures 5.3 and 5.4 are close-up views similar to Figure 5.2. They show that after severance the shaving is compressed and deflected by the top surface of the tool tip. Therefore the top surface must exert an upward force on the shaving, and the shaving an equal and opposite force on the top surface. This downward force onto the tool tip I call

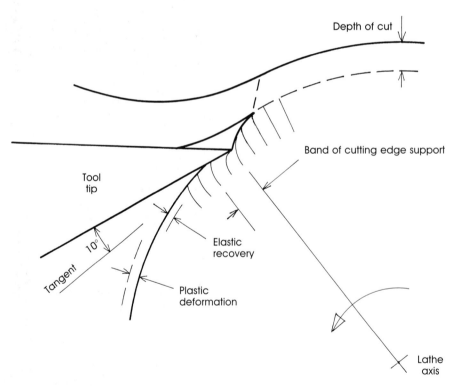

Figure 5.3 Cutting with a positive (here 10°) clearance angle. Severance occurs a little ahead of the cutting edge. There is still cutting edge support despite the clearance angle. The deformations which take place near the just-cut surface are indicated by the short radial lines. After providing support the just-cut surface does not spring back completely.

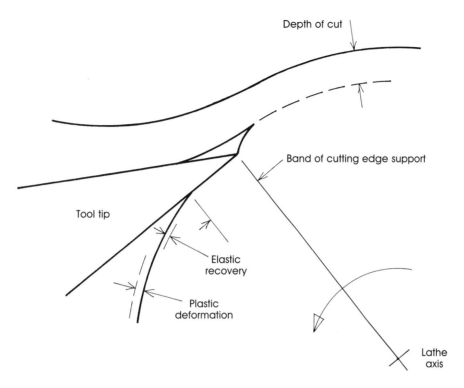

Figure 5.4 Cutting with zero clearance. As in Figure 5.3, the just-cut surface does not spring back entirely, but if cutting edge support is very light it can.

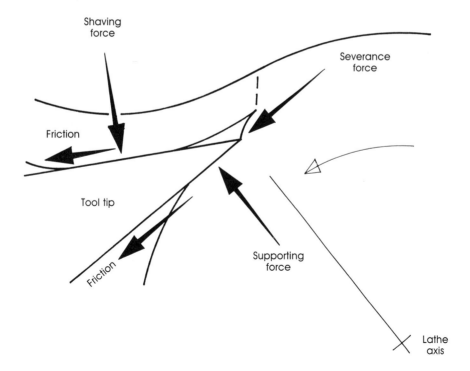

Figure 5.5 The forces applied by the rotating wood to a tool tip cutting at a large rake angle.

the shaving force.

After the shaving is severed, the just-cut surface exposed on the workpiece is, like the shaving, compressed, but by the underside of the tool tip. Hence the just-cut surface applies a supporting force to the tip's underside (Figure 5.5). If the supporting force is light the compression of the just-cut surface will be light and there will be full elastic recovery. If the supporting force is high the compression of the just-cut surface will be large and result in permanent, plastic, and undesirable crushing damage to the just-cut surface.

Cutting Edge Support

In Figures 5.3 and 5.4, the width of the band over which the just-cut surface exerts support is very narrow, in the order of $1/12$ inch (2 mm) or less. This band runs along the cutting edge for a maximum distance equal to the width of the shaving being taken. I term this band the band of cutting edge support. It is commonly termed bevel support, but this term wrongly implies that the full length of the bevel, from the cutting edge to the heel, is being supported by the just-cut surface.

Figure 5.5 shows the forces on a *cutting* tool tip. Figure 5.6 shows the forces on the whole tool. If the turner increases his axial thrust along the tool handle, the tool tip will rise up the just-cut surface and a cut will be able to be taken without there being any support required from the toolrest. In this situation the shaving force is exactly balanced by the opposing supporting force. Theoretically the tool tip will be in equilibrium and can therefore be maintained in this position indefinitely by just applying the appropriate strong, constant, axial thrust. In practice the equilibrium is not stable, but by slightly reducing the axial thrust and thereby inducing a small toolrest support force, a stable equilibrium is achieved. This is the essence of *cutting*: exerting a strong axial thrust on a tool with a small sharpening angle to give a stable tool tip with zero clearance angle.

How does decreasing the rake angle affect the turning process? Consider the 30° rake angle presentation in Figure 5.7. At these smaller rake angles the shavings are slowed and expanded more. The shaving force is therefore higher, as is the severance force. The supporting force is smaller, and especially if there is a significant clearance angle; more importantly the supporting force is angled lower and so is less efficient in balancing the shaving force. To compensate the turner must exert more leverage. Therefore at smaller positive rake angles any changes in the shaving force or the tool overhang must be compensated for by the turner altering his downward leverage. Hence as the rake angle lessens, maximum tool tip overhang must be reduced if control is to be maintained.

What happens if you lose control? When *cutting* you can lose control by lessening your axial thrust which allows the tool tip to be pushed back and down. The shaving force thus increases, a clearance angle opens up, and the balancing supporting force effective-

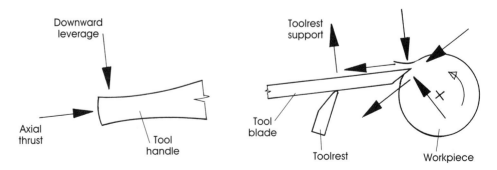

Figure 5.6   The forces which are applied to a turning tool presented at a large rake angle.

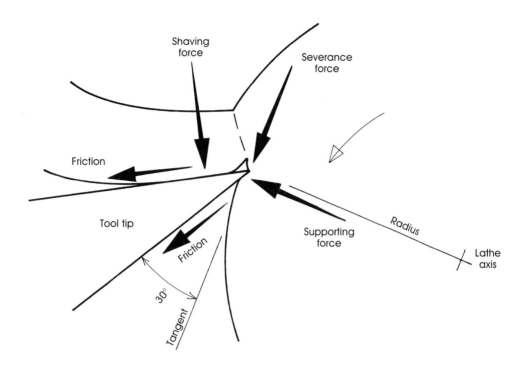

Figure 5.7   The forces on the tip of a turning tool presented with considerable (30°) clearance.

ly declines. In practice, this is relatively gradual, so that there is usually time to react and increase your axial thrust. This is unless the tool tip is presented far too low on the wood at the start of a cut.

In the about 30° rake angle situation where there is no appreciable upward supporting force, any increase in the shaving force must be instantly matched by the turner increasing his leverage. Failure to react in time leads to the tip being pushed down and a rapid increase in the shaving force as the shaving thickens. The worsening situation continues to build on itself and a dig-in results. Although the total loss of control in both large and small rake angle presentations has similar causes and results, the large rake angle loss of control has to pass through the small rake angle stage on the way to disaster.

The inescapable conclusion from the above arguments is that *cutting* is usually the preferred presentation. It has five advantages over lower rake angle methods:

1. Longer safe tool overhang.
2. Longer cutting edge life.
3. Better surface finish.
4. Lower turner energy requirement.
5. Increased rate of wood removal.

Scraping

Restricted tool access can prevent large rake angle *cutting* with gouges or chisels; uncooperative grain directions may cause unacceptable tear-out. In such situations the preferred technique with a horizontal cutting edge can be *scraping* in which a zero or slightly negative rake angle presentation is used (Figure 5.8). In flat *scraping* the major turner-applied force is downward leverage. Flat *scraping's* advantage over positive rake angle presentations is that if control is lost the tool tip tilts down and comes free. *Scraping* is therefore a relatively safe presentation. However, the surface finish in most woods can be extremely poor. But by grinding (without subsequent honing or buffing) a bevel with about a 70° sharpening angle, a tiny vertical cutting edge called a burr is produced. Although not long-lasting, this burr edge does enable a reasonable surface finish to be obtained, especially on harder, crisper-cutting woods except when cutting across or against long grain.

There is an alternative to scraping. Hook and similar tools (Figure 5.37) have a conventional cutting edge like gouges and skews (Figure 5.24). But like scrapers, the hook tool's cutting edge lies approximately perpendicular to the tool's axis. Except when cutting against the grain, such tools leave a less damaged surface than that left by scrapers. Perhaps the unfortunate neglect of such tools in countries dominated by British turning practices is due to: the loss of blacksmiths and the tradition of turners making their own tools; the need for a range of hook tools to cut deeper hollows rather than, say, one scraper; the greater, but hardly excessive, skill required to properly use hook tools; and the slightly greater difficulty of achieving a surface which flows smoothly without ridges or furrows.

Because of the limited number of resharpenings possible without remaking hook and ring tools, I suggest that they be regarded as finishing tools to be used after turning the basic shape with gouges.

Sharpness

If you ignore the quality of the steel, the quality of an edge is determined by the sharpening angle and how the two surfaces meet to form the edge.

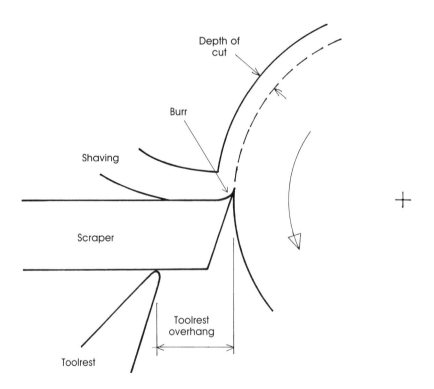

Figure 5.8   Scraping with the top face of the cutting edge at about 0° rake angle.

Figure 5.9 Presentation of an edge with side rake, here 45°.

You tend to think of two smooth faces intersecting to form a perfect edge which after prolonged use becomes rounded and therefore blunt. However, under magnification the faces resemble untidily ploughed fields and the cutting edge a comb with its teeth irregularly broken off. Honing or buffing the two faces improves the cutting efficiency and durability of the edge by evening the jagged projections at the cutting edge. A just-ground edge tends to appear sharp initially, but the surface finish left on the wood is inferior and the edge's apparent sharpness is rapidly lost as the longer vulnerable projections are broken off.

An unhoned edge is sometimes sensible in large rake angle *cutting*. If the wood is very high in silica, it may pay to keep your grinder running and regrind after every couple of cuts. An unhoned edge is also said to deal better with woods of a noticeably fibrous nature.

Presentation with Side Rake

Even with a 65° rake angle, a horizontal cutting edge leaves a surface which is only moderate. This surface can be improved by skewing the tool, by applying the cutting edge with side rake (Figure 5.9). But as you move a tool laterally along the tool rest taking a cut, if you increase the side rake there is less tear-out but the surface tends to become more rippled. Achieving your desired surface finish is therefore not a matter of maximising one factor, but of optimising several.

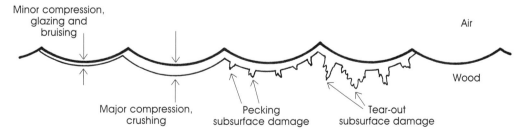

Figure 5.10 A longitudinal and magnified section through a turned surface. The upper scalloped line represents the macro cut surface. The spaces between it and the lower line represent the various types of subsurface damage. The lower line represents the wood surface left by the turning.

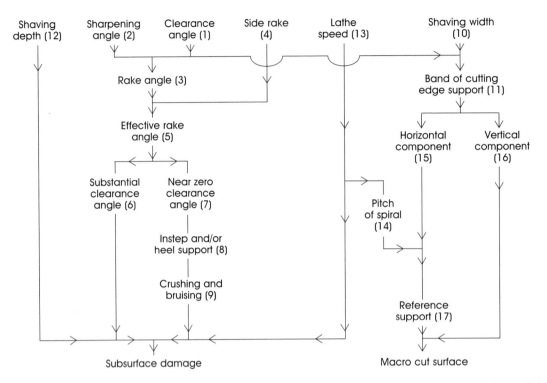

Figure 5.11   A diagram showing how various factors interact to affect both the macro cut surface and the types and degree of subsurface damage.

Surface Finish

There are two aspects to surface finish: the unevenness or rippling of the macro cut surface, and subsurface damage below the macro cut surface such as tear-out, pecking, bruising, etc. I use the term macro cut surface for the surface which would have been left had the cutting edge been perfectly sharp and perfectly presented. The actual surface resulting from the passage of the wood past the tool is often lower due to compression and tear-out. The differences between the two types of surface defect are illustrated in Figure 5.10. Figure 5.11 shows the interaction of the factors which affect both the macro cut surface and subsurface damage during *cutting*. These interactions are somewhat complicated. Although some readers may care to skip to the summary, an understanding of the factors will enable you to become a better and a more fulfilled turner. Note that in the discussions below, the factors are correspondingly numbered both in Figure 5.11 and the text.

As was described earlier in this chapter, in *cutting* the clearance and sharpening angles, (1) and (2), should both be small (0°, and 25° to 30° respectively) to achieve the desirable large rake angle of 60° to 65° (3). When an edge at a particular rake angle is applied with side rake (4), the wood approaching the skewed cutting edge 'sees' an effectively sharper cutting edge, that is an edge presented at an effectively larger rake angle (5) as shown in Figure 5.12. This effective rake angle can be calculated, or obtained graphically as in Figure 5.13.

Not only is an edge applied with side rake effectively sharper, but the severance is gentler and more effective, in part because of a more complex severance of the shaving. The result is less subsurface damage even when the clearance angle is substantial (6).

When you apply an edge at a near zero clearance angle (7) and with side rake (4), you will find that the tool tip can start to bounce. This is because the tip is receiving sup-

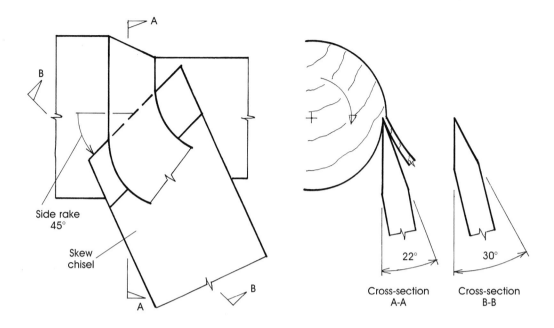

Figure 5.12 Demonstrating how a rake angle of 60° is converted into a larger one of 68° by skewing the cutting edge 45°, that is by applying it with a side rake of 45°.

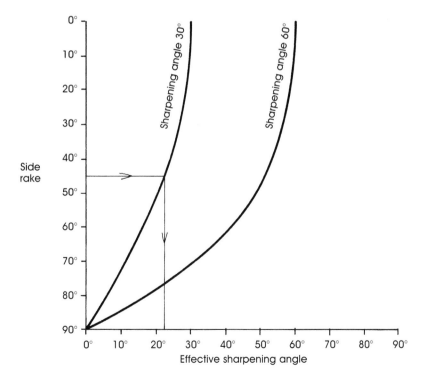

Figure 5.13 A graph for determining the effective rake angle of an edge applied with side rake. The sharpening angle is measured perpendicularly to the cutting edge. The effective sharpening angle is measured parallel to the velocity of the wood. Assuming a zero clearance angle, the effective rake angle is 90° minus the effective sharpening angle.

Figure 5.14 The right-hand half of a bead showing a rippled macro cut surface and glazing due to too much bevel support.

port from possibly the instep, or more likely the heel, of the bevel (8). Such a situation commonly occurs when turning from the walls into the bottom of the inside of a bowl, when cutting the end of a square, and when rolling beads with the tool very high on the wood. The result of such situations is a glazed and bruised surface (9) with increasingly large ripples (Figure 5.14). Such a result is both undesirable and seems to contradict the long held canon that you cannot have too much bevel support. The canon is based upon the assumption that a hand-held turning tool cuts a truly circular surface. Alas it does not, but although the deviations from the truly circular are usually less than $^1/_{250}$ inch (0.1 mm), the high rotational speed of the workpiece means that these deviations can build rapidly if the tool presentation is conducive. And a conducive presentation is one in which the bevel receives substantial support from the workpiece surface cut during earlier rotations. This earlier-cut surface will not be perfectly round, nor will it be of uniform compressibility. The bevel surface supported by this earlier-cut surface will tend to follow it and may also bounce. These deviations are transmitted forward to the cutting edge and magnified there, in part because the cutting edge is further from the contact point between the tool blade and toolrest. The result is the type of increasingly uneven macro cut surface shown in Figure 5.14. However this does not mean that no support from workpiece surface cut during earlier rotations should be sought.

Figure 5.15 shows planing with a skew at different side rakes. For a given width of shaving measured across (along) the cutting edge ((10) in Figure 5.11), larger side rakes (4) yield narrower horizontal components of shaving width and greater shaving depths (12). The lathe speed (13) is also important because if you consider a prolonged cut as producing a spirally grooved surface (Figure 5.16), that spiral has a fairly uniform pitch. If you traverse a tool slowly along a cylindrical workpiece rotating at 1800 rpm at $^1/_4$ inch

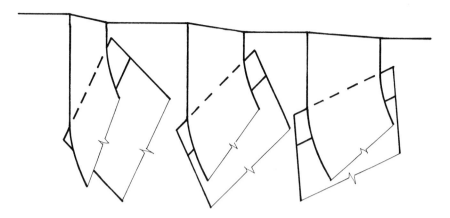

Figure 5.15 Planing with a skew (Section 7.8) at different side rakes. *Left to right*: 65°, 45°, and 25°.

(6 mm) per second, the pitch of the spiral is $^1/_{120}$ inch or about 0.2 mm—quite small in comparison to a typical width of shaving. Therefore traversing slowly gives considerable overlap between each 'cut'. Further, the pitch of that spiral (14) together with the shaving width (10) and depth (12) in part determine the unevenness of the macro cut surface. I say in part because although the lengths of the horizontal and vertical components of shaving width are related to the same components of cutting edge support (11), (15) and (16), they are not necessarily the same. Consider Figure 5.17. It shows that only the upper part of the cutting edge is supported. The unsupported lower length of edge is therefore free to pivot about an axis running from the supported part of the cutting edge to the contact point between the tool and the toolrest. Obviously the deeper the cut at a given side rake, the longer the length of unsupported edge and the greater the tendency of a skew to stutter when taking thick cuts during planing.

I indicated at the end of the last but one paragraph that some support to the cutting edge from a surface cut during an earlier rotation may be desirable. Figure 5.18 shows an uneven surface resulting from unreferenced 'cuts'. Although cutting edge support gives stability to the tool tip, greater control would be achieved if the cutting during a rotation

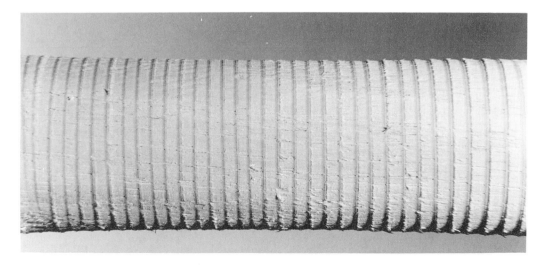

Figure 5.16 A spirally grooved spindle resulting from a low lathe speed and rapid movement of the gouge along the toolrest.

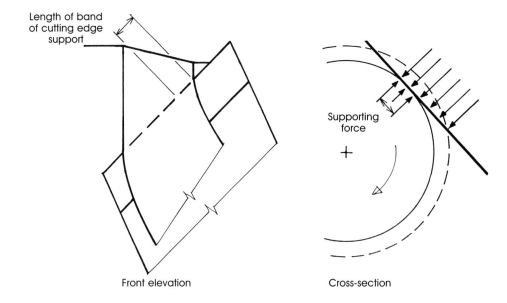

Figure 5.17 Planing a spindle. The cross-section shows that cutting edge support is only present towards the top of the length of the cutting edge cutting.

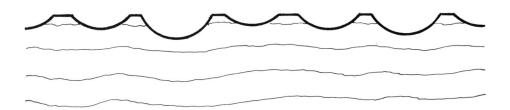

Figure 5.18 If the cut during a single workpiece rotation is barely referenced to the cut made during the previous rotation, there is little likelihood of the bottoms of such cuts being at a consistent radius from the lathe axis and a probability that the macro cut surface will be uneven.

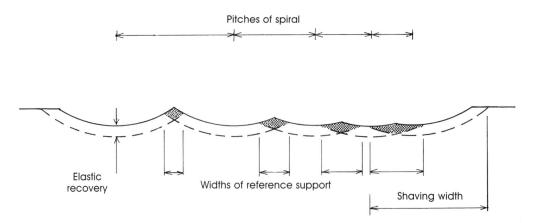

Figure 5.19 A longitudinal section through the surface of a turned spindle. The reference or overlapping support (shaded) varies according to the pitch of the spiral (Figure 5.16); other factors including the tool's flute radius.

could be referenced to the surface cut during the previous rotation. Figure 5.19 shows this reference support, (17) in Figure 5.11. Greater reference support can be achieved by using a tool of larger flute radius (the skew has an infinitely large flute radius), by decreasing the side rake (which increases the subsurface damage), by increasing the lathe speed, or by decreasing the tool's speed along the toolrest so as to enlarge the overlap.

Reference support should also be used at the large side rakes best for finishing cuts in bowl and faceplate turning. However in order to avoid the sort of rippled and glazed surface in Figure 5.14, it is important that the contact between the instep or heel and the earlier cut surface be very gentle. Indeed a critical skill in bowl turning is to so present the tool that this potentially undesirable instep or heel support is little more than a whisper or a caress.

Summary

The preceding paragraphs discussed the factors which influence surface finish. From a knowledge of how these factors interrelate you can select the appropriate *cutting* tool, and its optimum sharpening and presentation. When your objective is to achieve the best conventional finish (a surface without overt tooling, ready for sanding), the following factors are relevant:

1. The sharpening angle should be small and the edge should be honed.
2. The swings and roundabouts nature of side rake means that you need to seek the best compromise between increasing subsurface damage and decreasing rippling of the macro cut surface. Typically for spindle turning about 45° gives the optimum; for faceplate and bowl turning where the grain is less cooperative, 70° to 80° is preferred.
3. Using the smallest suitable curvature of cutting edge (flute) enables the width of shaving and therefore the reference guidance to be increased without thickening the shaving (Figure 5.19).

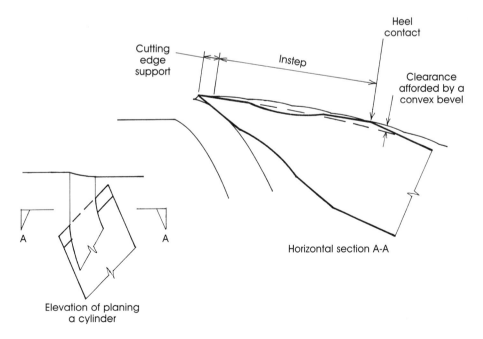

Figure 5.20 Showing how undesirable instep and heel support occurs. A convex bevel avoids the risk.

4. A thicker shaving is stronger and more able to cause subsurface damage by tearing out contrary fibres below the macro cut surface. It also requires the turner to apply greater and perhaps unsustainable forces.
5. The lathe speed should be high. How high is discussed later in this chapter.
6. A near-zero clearance angle presentation is vital for a good surface finish. The choice of bevel longitudinal profile is dealt with next.

Bevel Profile

The difference between bevel support and cutting edge support when a tool is *cutting* has been explained. To promote cutting edge support, a bevel profile which enables a zero clearance angle while giving bevel instep and heel clearance is desirable. This is irrespective of the horizontal and vertical curvatures of the surface being cut. It follows therefore that a convex bevel profile is ideal for any *cutting* situation (Figure 5.20). However to grind a convex bevel on most tools is difficult, and especially so if you want a particular sharpening angle and plan shape of cutting edge. Further, in some cuts it is necessary to accurately visually align the supporting part of the bevel so that the cut can be started and continued with precision. Squaring a shoulder is such a cut (Section 7.12). In such cuts, hollow grinding with honing to produce an effectively flat bevel is frequently and sensibly used as it:

1. Is easy to achieve.
2. Gives a clear line of sight (Figure 5.31).
3. Rarely promotes excessive bevel heel support in use.

The situations where a concave and honed bevel commonly causes undesirable instep and/or heel support are:

1. The insides of bowls.
2. 'Saddles' where the vertical curvature is convex, but the horizontal curvature is concave. Even here, in many cases, undesirable support can be avoided by using a favourable tool presentation such as when cutting a hollow with a spindle detail gouge. The gouge presentations shown in Section 7.14 avoid the problem, but were the gouge to be used in a presentation where its handle was much further from square to the lathe axis in plan while cutting with the tip at a large side rake, then the bevel would need to be convex. As will be shown in Section 5.5, this can be achieved.

Selection of Cutting Speed

Although some factors suggest that very high cutting speeds are preferred, in practice you should try to select cutting speeds which give the optimum compromise between a large number of often conflicting criteria. However, speed selection is not particularly critical, and it is often wiser to err below the recommended maximum. Also, when you are turning a particular piece of work, the tool usually works over a range of diameters so that theoretically exact speed selection based on the work's maximum diameter is rendered somewhat futile.

Some discourses on turning recommend that three speeds be used to turn a piece of a certain maximum diameter—one for roughing, a somewhat faster one for finish-turning, and a faster one again for sanding. A turner's time is much too precious to engage in such pedantry.

The factors which do influence selection of the lathe speed are:

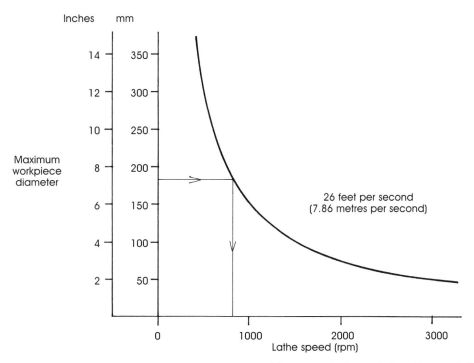

Figure 5.21   The maximum recommended lathe speed for any particular workpiece diameter. It is based on a 3 inch (75 mm) workpiece diameter being rotated at 2000 rpm. This is equivalent to a peripheral velocity of the wood of 26 feet per second or 7.86 metres per second.

1. *Maximum diameter of the workpiece.* Figure 5.21 gives a graph of maximum lathe speed versus maximum diameter for average conditions and high-speed steel tools. No appreciable disadvantage will be experienced if you are 20 to 30 percent down from the recommended speed.
2. *Wood hardness.* The speed could be reduced somewhat because harder wood is heavier, therefore accentuating vibration. Also, for a given speed and depth of cut, hard wood results in higher temperatures at the cutting edge and therefore earlier tool blunting due to abrasion and softening.
3. *High silica content.* Some woods contain silica which is noticeably abrasive to tools when above 0.5 percent. Low speeds and deep cuts will minimise resharpening.
4. *Workpiece slenderness.* When the workpiece is slender, the lathe speed should be reduced to lessen the whipping that will occur. For such workpieces the speed could be reduced to as little as one sixth of normal.
5. *Tool steel used.* With high-speed steel, the high speeds in Figure 5.21 may be used because of the material's greater resistance to abrasion and its ability to withstand very high temperatures without softening. Carbon tool steel, however, softens as its temperature is raised above 445°F (230°C), so that speeds should be selected which prevent this critical temperature being exceeded at the cutting edge.
6. *Weight and rigidity of the lathe.* Wood is hardly ever of exactly uniform density, so that the rotating workpiece will be dynamically unbalanced and cause the lathe to vibrate. Vibration may cause fixings to loosen, and will increase the risk of the workpiece flying out. Light lathes will therefore need to be run more slowly than heavy lathes for a given size of workpiece.
7. *Tendency to split.* If the workpiece is laminated, it is sensible to reduce the lathe speed and use a live, cup tail centre.

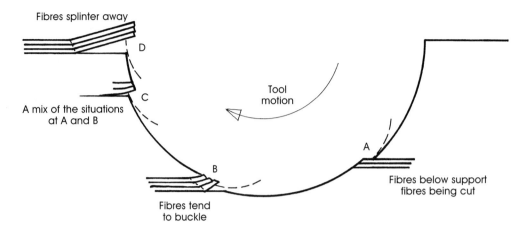

Figure 5.22 *Downhill* and *uphill cutting* in cutting a hollow in a spindle.

Although running the lathe too slowly has no attendant dangers, turning is more difficult. The chips are reluctant to part from the workpiece, the surface finish is rough, and the tool will leave a spiralled surface necessitating prolonged sanding unless its speed of movement along the toolrest is greatly reduced. However, when sanding woods with high resin contents, slowing the lathe will decrease the tendency of such woods to glaze and develop fine surface cracking.

Uphill and Downhill Cutting

When hand planing, you take care to plane with the grain, as this produces a good surface finish. If you plane against the grain, the wood tears out. The synonymous terms in woodturning are *downhill* for with the grain and *uphill* for against the grain. Consider cutting a hollow with a gouge (Figure 5.22). When the tool is cutting *downhill* as at *A*, the fibres being cut are supported by the fibres below and therefore the cutting is clean. If the gouge is taken on past the bottom of the hollow and *uphill* cutting is attempted, the fibres being cut at *B* are put into compression and will tend to buckle. Further these fibres receive only limited support from the fibres above. At *C* the fibres bunch together in order to offer sufficient resistance to allow severance. At *D* the absence of support results in the peripheral fibres being splintered away.

It is therefore important that wherever possible you do not cut *uphill*. This is almost always possible in spindle and cupchuck turning. However in faceplate turning it is impossible not to cut *uphill* twice per rotation with respect to the plane perpendicular to the lathe axis (page 235). Nevertheless, you should still ensure that you cut *downhill* with respect to the vertical plane running through the lathe axis parallel to the workpiece grain direction (Figure 5.23).

5.2   TOOL STEELS

For turning tools, you require a material which is hard enough to take a sharp edge and to hold it under conditions of high temperature and abrasion, and yet tough enough to take the bending and shock stresses experienced during turning. The most suitable materials to meet these conditions are certain types of steel.

Steels are alloys of iron with small percentages of carbon; other elements are also included in these alloys to tailor particular steels to particular working situations. Turning

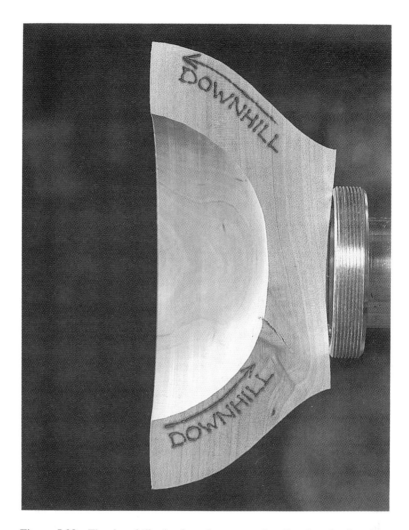

Figure 5.23 The *downhill*—that is optimum—cutting directions for faceplate and bowl turning. That their directions are optimum can be verified by comparing the cutting arrows with the grain direction which is vertical.

tools are made from 'tool steels' which are high-quality steels with high carbon contents of about 1 percent. The ways in which iron and carbon combine depend mainly upon the percentage of carbon, the temperature to which the steel has been raised, the rate of cooling, and the lowest temperature reached in the cooling process. These various states of combination (that is different crystalline structures) are described in metallurgical textbooks by the iron-carbon diagram.

Two classifications of tool steel are used in turning tools: carbon tool steel, and high-speed steel (HSS). These two classes of steels not only have different properties, but their raw material costs and their ease and costs of forging, machining, and abrading also differ. The basic differences between the two steels are that high-speed steel is:

1. Considerably more expensive as it contains large percentages of rare elements such as tungsten and molybdenum.
2. Harder and more brittle. It retains its properties to a considerable degree even at red heat.
3. More resistant to abrasion.

4. Much more expensive to make into tools because of its considerable hardness even when annealed.

5. Heat-treated at much higher temperatures. Carbon tool steel is tempered at about 445°F (230°C), whereas HSS is tempered at about 1050°F (565°C). Note however that raising carbon tool steel above its tempering temperature does not instantly cause softening because the changes to the steel's internal structure take time. So if you overheat carbon tool steel, the surface oxides which form will go darker than light straw, but quick quenching in cold water will minimise loss of temper.

There are a large number of tool steels and one method of classification is that of the American Iron and Steel Institute. Because the tools must possess some toughness, the steels generally used are L2 among the carbon tool steels and M2 or T2 among the true high-speed steels. Note that tungsten carbide is unsuitable for cutting tools such as gouges and skews because it is too brittle. It could be used in scrapers, but it does not burr and so cannot give the fine vertical cutting edge produced on tool steels straight from the grinder (see Figure 5.8).

A recent development is Crucible Particle Metallurgy which enables tougher, harder, and more wear resistant steels to be produced which have improved grindability. The Glaser range of turning tools uses A11 crucible steel.

It is occasionally appropriate to make your own turning tools from new carbon tool steel. Its heat treatment is relatively simple. Annealed steel can be purchased from suppliers and cold shaped and/or heated to a bright red heat and forged. Once shaping is complete, harden by heating to bright red (1480°F, 805°C), holding it there for 30 seconds, and quenching it by plunging and stirring it in cold water. The nose is then emery-papered to a bright surface, and the tool is heated until a light straw coloured oxide film forms at 445°F (230°C). It is then immediately quenched again to temper it. Note that hardening and tempering need be applied only to the working end of tools. Worn files should not be used for turning tools in their hard state as they may shatter explosively. They can be used as a source of tool steel after annealing and grinding-off the serrations, but this is not recommended due to the possibility of unseen cracks.

5.3   THE ROUGHING GOUGE

The job of the roughing gouge (Figure 5.24) is to bring axially-grained wood from a square cross-section down to a cylindrical one. It is also used for turning shallow curves and cutting rough shoulders. If sharp and used correctly it will give a good finish, and hence is rather misnamed. It should therefore normally have a sharpening angle of 30° and a hollow ground and honed edge. For very arduous conditions the sharpening angle can be increased to 35°.

The roughing gouge in cross-section is a sector of an annulus. As it is easier to cut parallel to the grain than to cross-cut it, a wide, shallow shaving is easier to take than a narrow, deep one of the same cross-sectional area. Against that, a large radius of flute curvature can only be confidently used to cut gently varying near-horizontal profiles. It is popular for the sector of the annulus to be a full semicircle; it should not be. It should subtend no more than 170°, or when roughing away from a square (Section 7.7), the upper corner of the gouge is likely to damage the exposed corners of the square. Nor should the cross-section be 'U' or 'V' shaped—there is already a planing tool with a straight cutting edge called a skew chisel.

The longer the cutting edge, the longer between sharpenings as the whole length of the cutting edge can be used. However, to prevent the tool becoming too heavy and clumsy for most normal work, a cutting-edge length of about 2 inches (50 mm) is generally

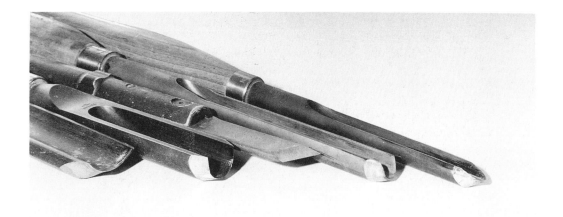

Figure 5.24 *Left to right:* 2 inch (50 mm) roughing gouge, 1¼ inch (30 mm) roughing gouge, 1 inch (25 mm) Glaser skew, ¾ inch (19 mm) bowl gouge, ¾ inch (19 mm) P&N spindle detail gouge.

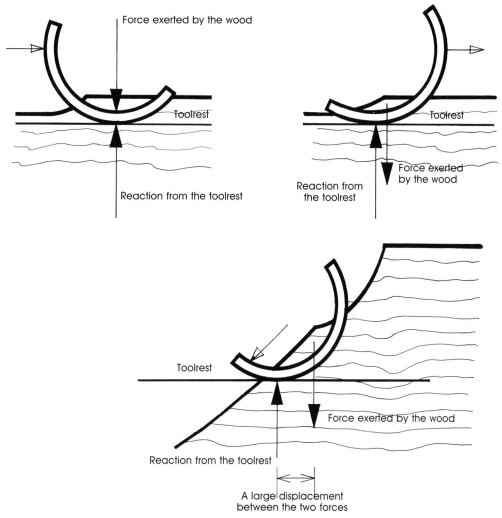

Figure 5.25 The rotational stability of the roughing gouge. As the displacement between the two forces increases, control of the gouge becomes more critical.

used. The radius of curvature of the flute is generally between ¹/₂ and 1¹/₄ inches (13 and 32 mm), with the larger radius being favoured for long work.

In normal use, the roughing gouge is stable because the supporting upward force on the gouge exerted by the toolrest is almost vertically in line with the downward force exerted by the wood (Figure 5.25). However, the gouge cannot safely be used to cut curves which are steep or whose radiuses are near to that of its flute radius. If this is attempted without full cutting edge support, the gouge will tend to catch and flip because of the rotational force (moment) resulting from the large displacement between the two forces. Also, the cutting (severance) force required to cut a long arc of end grain may be unexpectedly large, pushing the gouge back towards the turner and then flipping it over as cutting edge support is lost.

There is some disagreement as to the best plan profile for the nose of a roughing gouge. They are often supplied slightly convex. I recommend that they be ground straight-across. In Figure 5.26, Section A-A shows that when there is zero clearance angle and the gouge is ground straight-across and its blade is at right angles to the lathe axis in plan, then the cut is somewhat blocked by the leading bevel. To prevent this blocking, albeit minor, the tool should be angled slightly in the direction of travel. Figure 5.26 also shows that the sides of the shaving are cut before the bottom is rived. This is desirable in order to achieve a good finish. If the gouge nose were convex, then the shaving severance would be more akin to that with the parting tool; that is, the bottom would be rived and the shaving then levered and torn out upwards, leaving a poorer surface finish.

The usually quoted reason for having the square nose is to facilitate roughing up to or away from a square section. This can be done using a convex-nosed gouge, but it is marginally less straightforward. (For this, the junction between the flute and the edges should be sharp in cross-section, and at just less than 90°). A supposed advantage of the

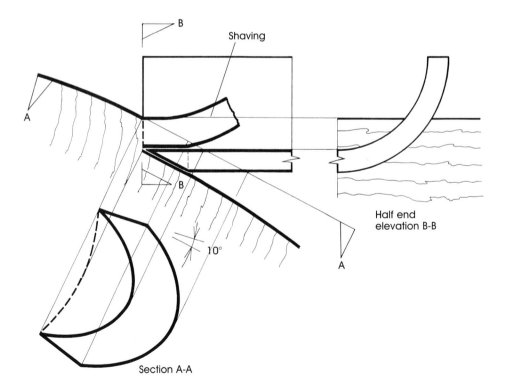

Figure 5.26 Cutting with the roughing gouge. Showing how lateral movement of the gouge is blocked by the bevel if the tool axis is at right angles to the lathe axis.

convex-nosed gouge is that its cuts are slightly skewed. This more slicing type of cut is easily achieved with the proper straight-across nose merely by angling the tool more than is necessary to eliminate the bevel blocking described in the previous paragraph.

The minimum wall thickness of a roughing gouge should be $^3/_{16}$ inch (5 mm). However, many brands of roughing gouges tend to snap off at the point where the fluted section is reduced into the tang, so take care when purchasing that this area is not too thin.

Besides the properly shaped roughing gouge just described, very shallow convex-nosed roughing gouges are sold. I call them 'hybrid' gouges (Figure 4.9). They are largely redundant. They cannot, despite what their manufacturers believe, be used as detail gouges to safely cut deeper hollows with confidence (see Figure 5.36). They can, how-

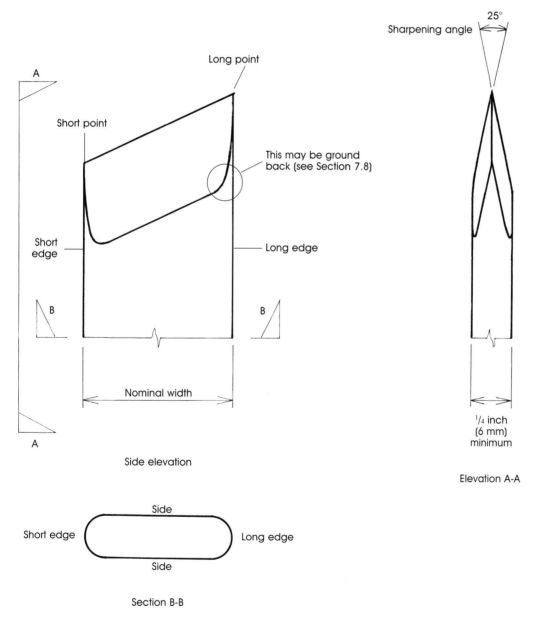

Figure 5.27 The geometry of the skew chisel. The angle at the long point between the cutting edge and the long edge is known as the angle of skewness and is typically 70°.

ever, be used to rough and cut shallow curves in work with interlocked or non-axial grain.

A specialised modification to the nose shape of one of these shallow hybrid gouges is shown in Figure 4.9 where it is used for roughing small work whose left-hand end is held in a chuck.

5.4   THE SKEW CHISEL

The skew chisel (Figure 5.24) is the most precise and the most versatile tool in a turner's kit. It also has a justified reputation for being the most unforgiving and an unjustified reputation for being unpredictable. Therefore cuts which require the skew are deliberately avoided by many turners. This section aims to describe the proper shaping and the varied uses of the skew in the hope that confidence will be restored in this most responsive of turning tools.

Most skews are basically rectangular in cross-section. At the very least their square corners should be arrised round. Regrettably some manufacturers do not even do this, let alone provide the fully semicircular long and short edges which are preferred (Figure 5.27, Section B-B). Such edges do not cause nicks in the tops of toolrests and slide readily. More importantly, when axially rotating a skew 90° from having its sides horizontal to having them vertical, the long or short point moves forward laterally less with the semicircular edges (see Figure 5.28). This aids cutting smaller beads.

Skews of oval cross-section are available. They make for greater tool stability when planing and less when cutting beads and using a skew for peeling cuts. Round cross-section skews are also manufactured.

The skew chisel's skewed cutting edge (Figure 5.27, Side Elevation) has four properties:

1. There is an extra-penetrating long point which is used for V-cutting. 70° gives about the right compromise between penetration and durability
2. A short point is created which is used to cut *downhill* with considerable side rake even when the blade is fairly square in plan to the lathe axis. Its main use is for rolling beads.
3. There is a long cutting edge for planing. The desirable 45° side rake preferred for planing means that the tool axis can be squarer to the lathe axis than can the tool axis of the once-popular, square-across chisels.

   Square-across chisels are still used. The beading-and-parting tool is about $^3/_8$ inch (10 mm) square in cross-section, and is sometimes recommended for both roles—it is inferior in both, like most compromise tools. Normally-narrower versions called parting tools are an essential tool (see Section 5.6).

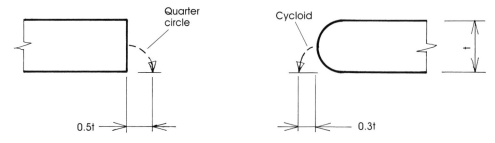

Figure 5.28   A 90° roll with a square short edge causes the short point to move horizontally half the blade thickness. With a semicircular short edge, the short point describes a cycloid and the horizontal movement is only 0.6 of that with a square short edge—this helps when cutting small beads.

Figure 5.29 Squaring a shoulder showing the full clearance angle. The skew is flat on its long edge and has its left-hand bevel perpendicular to the lathe axis in plan. In practice the clearance angle should be minimised when performing this cut.

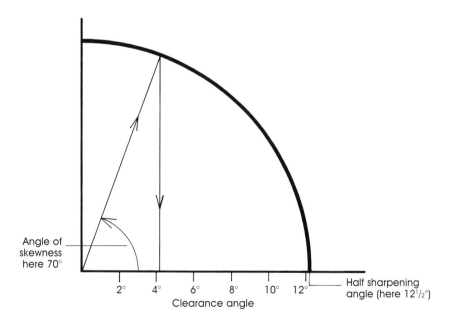

Figure 5.30 The relationship between the angle of skewness and the clearance angle. For a 25° sharpening angle and a 70° angle of skewness, the clearance angle is 4.5°.

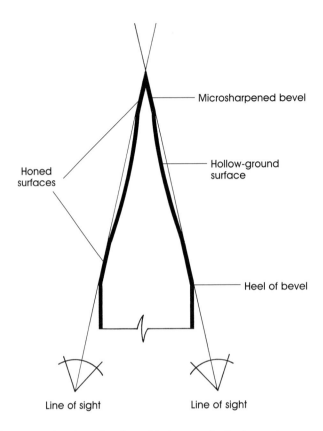

Microsharpened bevel

Honed
surfaces

Hollow-ground
surface

Heel of bevel

Line of sight   Line of sight

Figure 5.31   A cross-section through a skew chisel perpendicular to an edge.

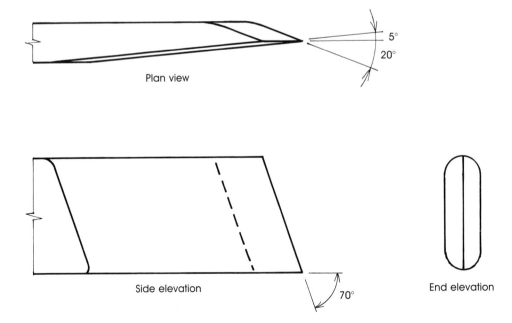

Plan view

5°
20°

Side elevation

70°

End elevation

Figure 5.32   The offset skew used for parting-off close to the front faces of large-diameter chucks.

4. It gives rise to a clearance angle. Consider the correctly sharpened skew in Figure 5.29. It has flat edges for clarity. When squaring a vertical shoulder with the long point, with its nearside bevel at right angles to the lathe axis in plan, and with its long edge flat on the toolrest, the cutting edge leans away from the shoulder by an angle known as the clearance angle. This angle is readily determined graphically (Figure 5.30) and is typically 4° to 5°. If the same cut were attempted with the tool flat on its short edge, the clearance angle would become an interference angle and the tool would dig in. In practice a clearance angle of 1° to 2° is preferred for cuts such as squaring a shoulder with the long point. To obtain this the skew cannot be presented flat on its long edge, but must be axially tilted towards the vertical face.

When you are using the skew, it is often necessary to sight along the bevel to ensure that the tool is presented correctly. The skew's bevels are therefore usually hollow ground and honed with both the heel and toe of the bevel in contact with a flat stone. This ensures that the lines of sight are retained (Figure 5.31).

The width of the sides defines the nominal size of the skew, and sizes vary between $^1/_4$ and 2 inches (6 and 50 mm). Where a skew narrower than $^1/_4$ inch (6 mm) is required, it is preferable to grind the short edge of a wider skew down locally at the end in order to preserve reasonable stiffness, or to skew-grind a parting tool. The minimum thickness of a skew should be $^1/_4$ inch (6 mm), or else the tool is flexible and dangerous, but I prefer $^5/_{16}$ inch (8 mm).

With an engineer's chuck, a cupchuck, or similar, it is desirable to be able to part-off close to the right-hand end of the chuck. The offset skew (Figure 5.32) allows this because its right-hand bevel is ground at 5° instead of at 12.5° to the axis of the tool. An alternative is a parting-off tool (see Section 5.6)

To aid in undercutting (see Section 8.3) the left-hand end of a workpiece being parted-off, the 5° bevel of an offset skew can be ground slightly convex. A cutting edge convex in side elevation is also often recommended for normal skews, notably by Richard Raffan. There is little to choose between the straight and convex cutting edges, although my preference is for the former. Grinding of a convex edge should leave the 70° angle at the long point unchanged, and increase the angle between the short edge and the cutting edge to about 130°.

5.5   THE DETAIL GOUGE

As explained in Section 5.3, it is risky to cut other than near-horizontal gradients with a roughing gouge. In addition the cutting would be at near-zero side rakes and thus leave subsurface damage. A properly shaped and sharpened spindle detail gouge (Figure 5.24) overcomes both these problems. The essence of the detail gouge is that its cross-section should be designed so that there cannot be significant horizontal displacement between the downward force exerted by the wood and the upward reaction from the toolrest.

In designing a particular detail gouge, the flute radius r_f (see Figure 5.33), obviously defines the minimum radius of hollow which can be cut. Although a given detail gouge will cut hollows of radiuses substantially greater than its r_f, plus of course straight and convex profiles, as the hollows' radiuses increase the stock removal rate becomes suboptimum and there is an increasing tendency to leave a corrugated surface finish. Hence, a range of sizes of detail gouge is produced.

A further variable associated with the flute is the shape of the cutting edge. It is not ground straight-across because the freedom to use any part of the cutting edge is one too many variables, and so prohibits the design of a stable gouge. Theoretically, therefore, the

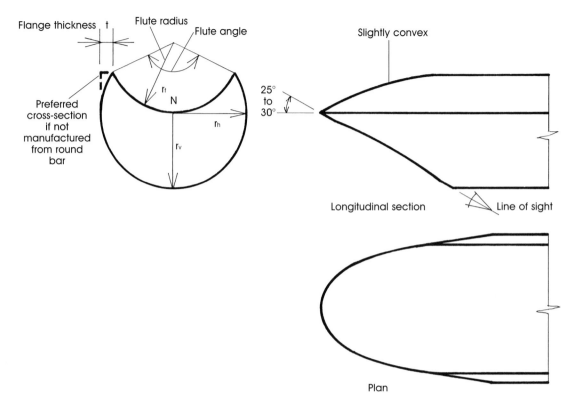

Figure 5.33 The geometry of a detail gouge sharpened with a ladyfinger nose. Although the hollow-ground bevel is recommended for normal use, a convex bevel is preferred for cutting surfaces which are concave in both horizontal and vertical section (see Section 8.4). The production of convex bevels is described in Section 10.9.

cutting edge should be pointed with only the tip being used for cutting. However, reference support would be very small and the tool would tend to produce a corrugated surface finish. So, you compromise by curving the cutting edge rather than pointing it. Figure 5.33 shows the normal shape, known as a ladyfinger nose for obvious reasons, although this is occasionally modified for special situations. The ladyfinger nose:

1. Concentrates cutting around the base of the flute, thereby ensuring rotational tool stability.
2. Enables cutting with about 45° side rake even when the tool is square to the lathe axis in plan—this is provided that the cutting takes place on the sides of the nose as happens if the tool is rotated more 'into' the cut (see Figure 7.58).
3. Being somewhat pointed, allows access to cut detail.
4. Gives long, slightly convex, cutting edges along the sides of the nose which are used especially in faceplate turning.

As gouges are used to cut both the left-hand and the right-hand sides of hollows, the tip of the nose should be positioned centrally in the flute. Assuming that it is the tip of the nose at N which cuts, the two extreme situations are when the cutting is firstly parallel to, and secondly perpendicularly to, the lathe axis (Figure 5.34). In both cases, for stability the blade's outside surface should be in contact with the toolrest vertically below N. In addition, the tangents to the outside surface at these contact points should be at 90° to r_v and r_h respectively. If you widen these circumstances to include cutting any part of a hollow, it is apparent that r_h should equal r_v and that the outer surface of the gouge's cross-section should be semicircular below the level of N. Note that the gouge axial rotations

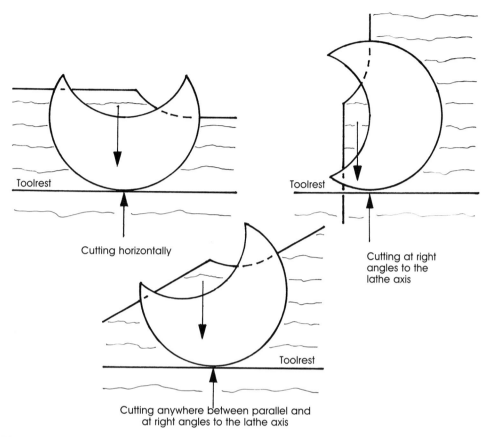

Cutting horizontally

Cutting at right
angles to the
lathe axis

Cutting anywhere between parallel and
at right angles to the lathe axis

Figure 5.34 Showing cutting with a detail gouge having a correct cross-section. The downward force applied by the wood to the gouge is closely in-line with the upward reactional force applied by the toolrest to the gouge.

in Figure 5.34 for *cutting* horizontally and at a gradient have the base of the flute parallel to the surface being cut. In practice the gouge is rotated more 'into' the cut to achieve near 45° side rake cutting on the side of the tip (Figure 7.58).

You frequently want to cut into the wood perpendicularly to the lathe axis. To simplify setting and holding the cutting edge at N in a vertical position, the perimeter of the gouge cross-section at the end of r_h is better continued straight up at right angles to r_h (see Figure 5.33). But since the widespread introduction of HSS for turning tools, detail gouges have been machined from round stock.

Two further variables influence detail gouge design: the flute angle, and the flange thickness t. These variables in turn are dependent on the required blade stiffness and the dimensions of the hollows to be cut.

The flute angle should not be greater than 180° or access for honing is impeded. Practically it has been found that a value of 130° for the flute angle is sufficient even when cutting well back from the tip of the nose.

As r_f increases, the potential size of the shavings which can be taken also increases so that extra blade stiffness is desirable. However, it is for small values of r_f that ready-made gouges are often too weak and flex in use. This results from the regrettable convention manufacturers follow of continuing to reduce the blade width as the flute radius is reduced. The type of cross-section shown in Figure 5.35 achieves a small flute with safe stiffness and tool stability. If necessary a long slim nose can be ground to improve access. Until properly-stiff detail gouges with small flutes are manufactured, the stiffness prob-

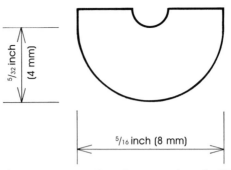

Figure 5.35   A detail gouge with a $^{1}/_{16}$ inch (1.5 mm) flute diameter and good stiffness.

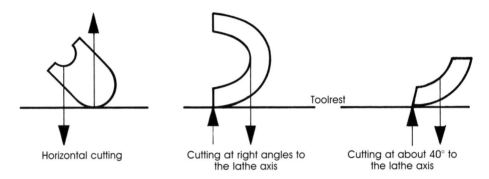

Horizontal cutting

Cutting at right angles to the lathe axis

Cutting at about 40° to the lathe axis

Figure 5.36   Showing how a gouge's stability is affected by its cross-section. The downward force is applied by the wood being cut. The upward force is applied by the toolrest. The larger the horizontal displacement between these two forces, the greater the moment tending to rotate the tool and cause a dig-in if full cutting edge support is lost.

lem can be overcome by grinding the nose of a bowl gouge to the shape of a small detail gouge nose. This is satisfactory because the flute radius r_f at the base of the flute of most bowl gouges is very small while their blades are stiff.

The manufacture of flexible gouges seems to be based upon the assumptions that the flange thickness t (or its equivalent) should be a maximum of $^{1}/_{32}$ inch (0.8 mm) and, sometimes, that stiffness can be increased by making r_v larger than r_h. This latter assumption results in a gouge which is undesirably flexible in a sideways direction, and which requires excessive upward movement of its handle as a hollow is being cut. Conversely, for large values of r_f, to minimise the volume of expensive tool steel, r_v is often reduced. The effects of these departures from the proper profile are shown in Figure 5.36.

In designing the shape of the detail gouge, I first assumed that cutting took place right on the point at N in Figure 5.33. However, you almost always cut just off the point on the side of the nose. In fact, the detail gouge is not a gouge at all in the same sense that roughing or woodcarving gouges are. It should be thought of as two skew chisels welded together along their long edges and then forged into a semicircular cross-section.

In common with roughing and bowl gouges, the surface of the flute forms the cutting edge. Obviously, therefore, to achieve real sharpness, the surface of the flute must have a mirror finish. Be prepared to hone or buff the flute to the proper finish before you use it.

Finally a word about nomenclature. Gouge sizes are traditionally named according to their total width. Obviously, this is almost irrelevant because the gouge width has little bearing on the minimum radius of hollow which can be cut. Calling gouges according to their flute radiuses is much more logical, but I suspect that this proposal is doomed to failure.

5.6   THE PARTING TOOL

The purpose of the parting tool (Figure 5.37) is to cut narrow, vertically-sided grooves with flat bottoms. It is used for removing waste, setting diameters, and cutting short cylindrical surfaces. It is rarely used for parting-off because its crude cutting action makes the process unpredictable.

The tool is somewhat crude in its action. The horizontal cutting edge rives the base of the shaving, while the ends of the shaving are severed by the 90 corners just behind the cutting edge. This latter action is an uphill tearing one and accounts for the very rough finish left on the sides of the groove.

The cutting action causes high downward forces to be exerted on the top of the cutting edge, and the rough groove sides will also tend to grab the tool. If the tool is used in a true *cutting* position, these forces will tend to be resisted by the supporting force exerted by the wood on the underside of the bevel. However, the tool is often used one-handed so that presentation and control are not always ideal. Therefore, the tool should be narrow in width, deep in cross-section to absorb the shocks, with a strong tang, and preferably with a cross-section which tends not to be grabbed by the groove sides.

Various tool shapes are commercially available and are shown in Figure 5.38. Care should be taken with the trapezoidal-like cross-section parting tool to grind the cutting edge where the blade width is at its maximum.

The likelihood of a parting tool being grabbed can be reduced by tapering the blade width towards the tang. Rocking the tool during parting is also used to widen the groove, hence the cutting edge is central rather than being at the end of a bottom edge.

The Roy Child parting tool (Figure 5.38) is for parting-off and leaves a clean-sided groove with a convex bottom. It can even part-off well in faceplate turning. A similar effect can be achieved by grinding the cutting edge of a conventional parting tool into a vee to leave two chisel points (Figures 5.37 and 5.39). This tool is best used with the bevel into which the groove is ground facing down.

The recommended maximum widths of parting tools are $^1/_2$ inch (13 mm) for soft woods and $^1/_4$ inch (6 mm) for very hard woods. Very narrow parting tools are manufactured for use when it is desirable to minimise waste; you can also grind them out of used industrial hacksaw blades.

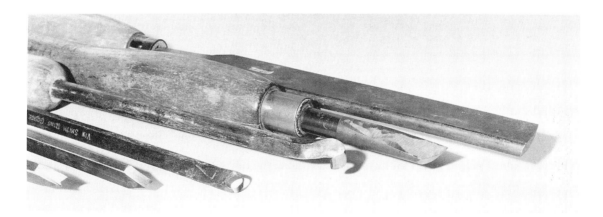

Figure 5.37 *Left to right:* parting-off tool, parting tool, Vin Smith ring tool, Kurt Johansson hook tool, homemade semicircular shear-scraper ground from the stub of a worn-out gouge, flat scraper.

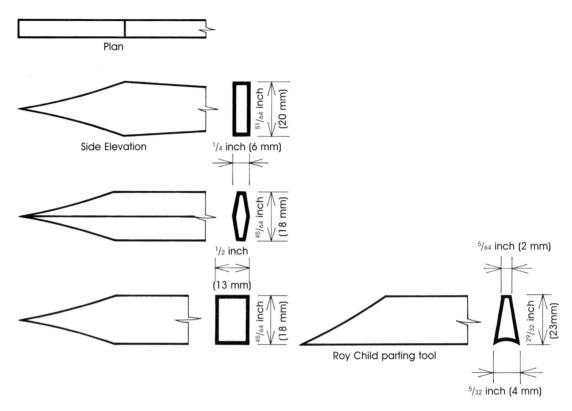

Figure 5.38 A selection of commercially available parting tools.

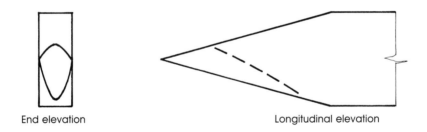

Figure 5.39 A parting-off tool, made by grinding a groove with the corner of the grinding wheel at the end of one bevel.

5.7 SCRAPERS

That scrapers (Figure 5.37) are overused and abused does not destroy the fact that they have proper roles to play in spindle, cupchuck, and bowl turning. A useful range is shown in Figure 5.40. They are mainly used in two special situations: when it is impossible to obtain or maintain proper bevel support, and when the desired profile would be less efficiently produced by *cutting* tools.

Scraping tools are used almost exclusively in metal turning to push the metal off. In woodturning, it is preferable to somehow *cut* the wood away and it is found that the burr left after grinding is effective, giving an edge similar to a cabinet scraper. To relieve the edge slightly and give a good burr, the sharpening angle should be about 70°. High-speed steel gives a burr which is longer lasting than that produced on carbon tool steel scrapers. The burrs on both steels can be ticketed, but most turners prefer to just regrind when the edge becomes blunt.

Scrapers should be thick, between $^{1}/_{4}$ and $^{1}/_{2}$ inch (6 and 13 mm) depending on the overhang anticipated. Widths and nose shapes will vary according to usage. Scrapers may be solid carbon tool steel, solid HSS, or HSS-tipped. The top face should be polished so that the burr will be even and to enable shavings to escape easily. The bottom face should also be smooth so that it slides easily on the toolrest, and the corners where it joins the edges should be finely arrised. Note that flat scrapers should always be used with their

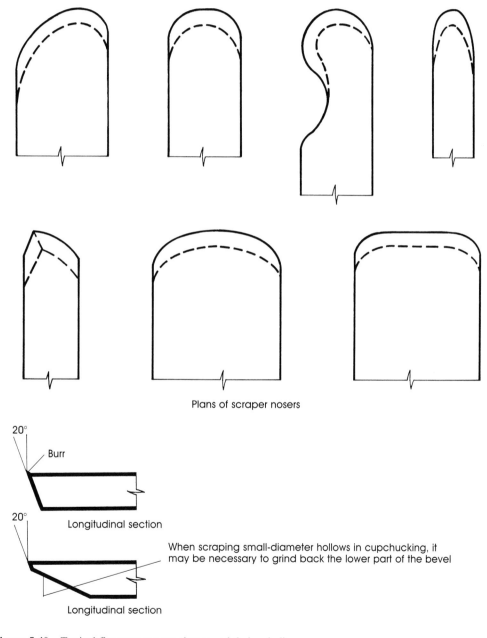

Plans of scraper nosers

20°
Burr
Longitudinal section

20°
Longitudinal section

When scraping small-diameter hollows in cupchucking, it may be necessary to grind back the lower part of the bevel

Figure 5.40 Typical flat scraper nose shapes and their grindings.

bottom faces flat on the toolrest.

Scrapers are generally used taking shavings at axis height. They should normally be used pointing slightly downwards so that if grabbed by the wood there is no possibility of a serious dig-in. To obtain the best possible surface finish, always cut *downhill*. The surface finish can be improved by presenting a scraper with side rake (shear scraping). The cross-section should then be triangular or semicircular (Figure 5.37) to aid rotational stability. The bevel on shear scrapers is sharpened similarly to that on flat scrapers.

5.8   RECOMMENDED SET OF TOOLS

The recommended list of tools below is a minimum. Others can be added as the need arises.

The problem in buying tools, especially gouges, is not usually to obtain the types, but to obtain the proper cross-sections. Always buy 'long-and-strong' in preference to normal strength. Boxed sets are not always good value for they sometimes contain redundant tools such as the diamond-point scraper.

Carbon tool steel tools are satisfactory for the hobby turner, but have been largely replaced by the superior high-speed steel.

For spindle turning:
Roughing gouge, $1^{1}/_{4}$ inches (32 mm)
Skew chisel, 1 inch (25 mm)
Detail gouge, $^{1}/_{2}$ inch (13 mm)
Parting tool, $^{1}/_{4}$ inch (6 mm)

For cupchuck work (in addition to spindle tools):
Round-nosed scraper, 1 inch (25 mm)

For bowl turning (in addition to spindle and cupchuck tools):
Bowl turning gouge, $^{1}/_{2}$ inch (13 mm) or $^{5}/_{8}$ inch (16 mm)

5.9   TOOL HANDLES

Woodturning tools are generally used with wooden handles (Figure 5.41). These handles avoid the need to greatly extend the lengths of the steel blades, themselves made of expensive tool steel. They also provide a comfortable grip; enable axial, rotational, and levering forces to be exerted; and give the tools some sort of balance.

Carbon tool steel tools are usually produced with tapered tangs, usually square-sectioned so that they will not twist in the wooden handle. For these tangs to hold well in the handles, their taper should be less than 1 in 10 and the minimum length of tang in the handle should be about $1^{1}/_{2}$ inches (37 mm).

High-speed steel tools often have circular cross-section tangs of uniform diameter. If they work loose and rotate within their drilled tang holes they can be removed and epoxied back in. You may need to groove the side of the tang hole or drill a tiny hole into its bottom from the outside of the handle to prevent a piston effect pushing the tang out (Figure 5.42).

Turning tools are often bought unhandled, and the natural temptation is then to make a set of matched handles as supplied on ready-handled tools. However, it is preferable to have your handles all different, that is, in various shapes and in different woods. Further differences can be provided by V-cuts and other decorations. The reason for having dis-

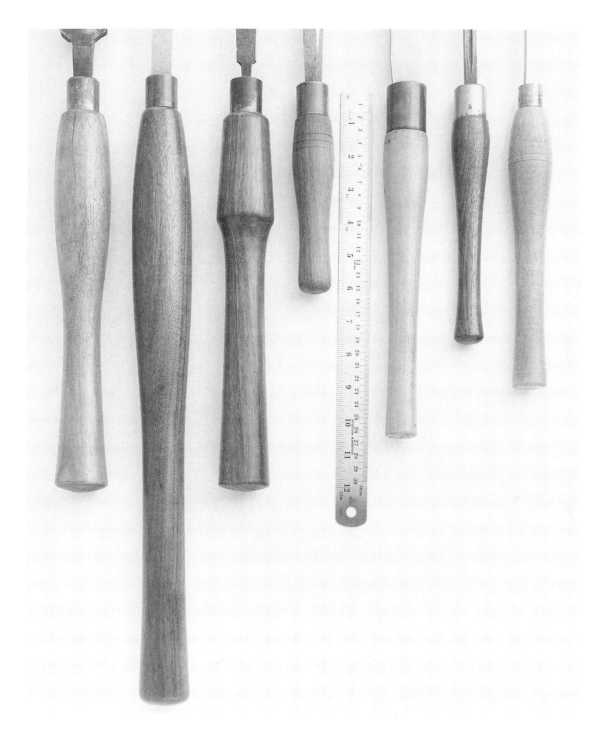

Figure 5.41 Tool handles. From left to right the handles are for a scraper, a scraper, a scraper, a bowl gouge, a skew, a small-fluted detail gouge, and a skew.

similar handles is so that individual tools may be more quickly selected. In addition, different tools and different usages of the same tool ideally demand different handles. Some turners change handles on a tool according to whether it is being used for large or small work.

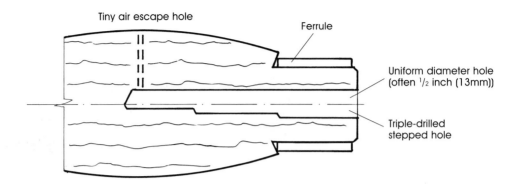

Figure 5.42   A longitudinal section through a handle.

Average-sized handles are about 13 inches (330 mm) long; have brass or steel ferrules with outside diameters between $^3/_4$ and $1^1/_2$ inch (19 and 37 mm); and are about 1 inch (25 mm) in diameter where usually gripped by the hand. Heavier or longer handles may be preferred for roughing bowls and for scrapers; and short, light handles for small spindle work and smaller tools.

5.10 MAKING HANDLES

First prepare the ferrule. It should be between $^3/_4$ and 1 inch (19 and 25 mm) long and will usually be cut from a length of tube. Take care to keep the ends square. File or scrape away any burrs left after the cutting.

The tough-hardwood blank should be about 1 inch (25 mm) longer than the required finished length of the handle. The tang hole may be drilled outside the lathe or drilled in the lathe after the turning. For tapered tangs a series of holes deepening in length and reducing in diameter should be drilled which approximate to the tang profile (Figure 5.42). Alternatively, a tapered drill bit could be used.

Centre the wood in the lathe with the ferrule end held by the tailstock. If the tang hole has been predrilled, locate the tail centre in it. Rough the general shape, turn the pin for the ferrule using a parting tool and callipers, and cut a small bevel on the end of the pin. The pin diameter should be such that the ferrule is a tight fit and the pin's length should be slightly longer than the ferrule to allow for the lead-in bevel. After turning the pin and, if required, trying the ferrule for size, finish-turn the rest of the handle with a skew. Slightly undercut the handle at the inside end of the ferrule pin (Figure 5.42). Hammer on the ferrule using another piece of tube to drive it home fully. Recentre and sand both the wood and the ferrule. Then, unless the tang hole is to be drilled in the lathe, part-off with the skew at the headstock end.

If the tang hole is to be drilled in the lathe, leave a waste peg at least $^1/_2$ inch (13 mm) in diameter at the headstock end of the handle. Remove the handle from the lathe, mount a Jacobs chuck holding the appropriate drill bit in the headstock swallow, and remount the handle in the lathe, but the opposite way round. What was the tailstock end should be positioned by your left hand just short of the end of the drill bit. Lower the lathe speed. Switch on, and by gently winding in the tail centre while locating the left-hand end of the handle, an axial hole can be bored. Clear the shavings frequently so that the bit does not jam. After the drilling is completed (using several bits if required to achieve the desired hole profile), replace the Jacobs chuck by the driving centre, remount the wood in the lathe, again with the ferrule end on the right, and part-off neatly with the long point of a skew.

If necessary, ream the tang hole either with the tang itself or with a suitable reamer, and force the tool into the handle. Do this by inserting the tang into the tang hole and by banging the other end of the handle sharply and vertically down onto a rigid surface. The momentum of the steel blade will force it down firmly into the handle. Obviously, the blade and handle should be in line.

The projecting blade can then be used to hold the handle during finishing, for which polyurethane is recommended.

When it is required to remove a handle, hold the blade at its nose end and accelerate a heavy scraper or a roughing gouge flute-downward sharply along the blade to hit the ferrule end of the handle.

5.11 OTHER TOOLS

As stated elsewhere in this book, efficient turning depends on using the minimum number of tools the minimum number of times. Some of the tools described in this section work perfectly well, but merely duplicate the roles of the usual tools. Others are obsolete, and yet others are highly specialised.

The Bruzze

The bruzze is an obsolete tool of V-shaped cross-section used for decorative V-cuts.

Sizers

Sizers (Figure 5.43) are used in repetition turning for setting diameters and particularly for turning pins. There are two styles. In the first, a parting tool is used with a curved metal extension piece. In the second, a short tool bit, preferably of HSS, is clamped to a tool shaped like a question mark.

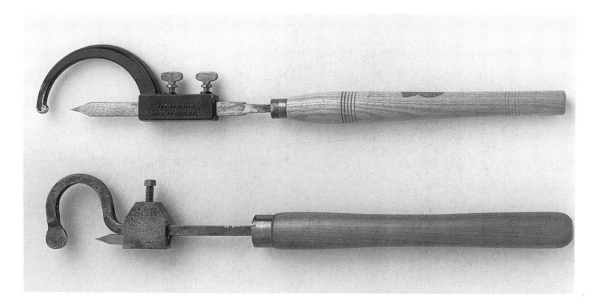

Figure 5.43   The two types of sizer. The extension piece on the top sizer is available from Craft Supplies.

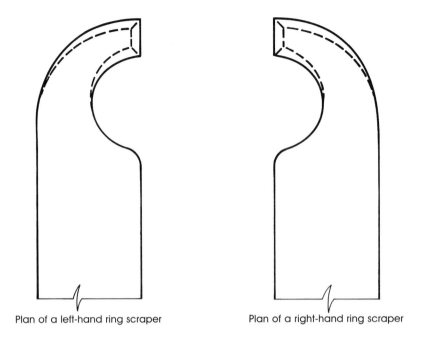

Plan of a left-hand ring scraper   Plan of a right-hand ring scraper

Figure 5.44 Ring scrapers.

To use, the required diameter is set between the cutting edge and the inside of the rounded end facing the cutting edge. The work is brought down to within $1/4$ inch (6 mm) or less of the required diameter before switching to the sizer to finish. This is because the cut is a scraping one. In use, the sizer is held as described in Section 6.4 and is forced down over the pin. Be careful not to push forward and hence cut the pin undersize. Similarly, when levering the sizer up after having cut the pin, exert an axial backwards pull on the tool so as not to accidentally reduce the finished pin diameter.

Ring Scrapers

Loose rings are a feature of one design of a child's wooden rattle. They were also a feature of some very ornate 'thrown' chairs. Ring scrapers (Figure 5.44) are particularly used where the rings are required to have circular cross-sections and where they have to be turned in a comparatively narrow hollow. Their use is straightforward. After turning as much as possible of the ring profile and deepening the hollow with conventional tools, use the left-hand and right-hand scrapers to turn the inside of the ring and part it off. Note that the outside surface of a ring is sanded before it is parted-off. Its inside surface can be sanded by taping abrasive paper in the hollow in the workpiece and then running the lathe.

English turner David Regester has developed small curved skews which *cut* the insides of rings and thus leave a better surface finish.

Hook and Ring Tools

Neglected until recently in English-speaking countries, hook and ring tools (Figure 5.37) enable *cutting* with side rake in areas where access for the proper presentation of gouges is restricted. In use the main axis of these tools is approximately perpendicular to the surface being cut. Many turners make their own from carbon tool steel and produce cranked and canted versions for particular access situations. A development of the hook tool is the ring tool invented by Vin Smith in Tasmania. A ring tool which an adjustable frog to limit shaving thickness has been developed by Ken Port in New Zealand.

Although the bevel which is ground and honed to maintain sharpness is inside the hook or ring, cutting edge support is obtained from the just-cut surface of the wood pressing on the outside of the hook or ring. The curvatures of the outside of the hook or ring in both the vertical and horizontal planes should therefore suit the intended usage.

Chatter Tools

To the uninitiated they produce ornamental turning effects on end-grain hard woods.

Bead Forming Tools

Basically scrapers with a semicircular hollow end. I do not agree with their promoted use for forming beads on spindles of common woods. Not only will they leave a poor finish, but their existence will be used by some to further delay learning to turn properly.

5.12 TOOL GRINDING

Tool grinding is much more frequent in woodturning than it is in cabinetmaking. Turning tools may need to be ground as little as once per working day; on siliceous woods they may need grinding after two or three cuts. But although freehand grinding is the quickest and most versatile, it is difficult to master. Amateurs and most professionals could therefore benefit from the use of sharpening jigs.

It was explained in Section 5.1 that for proper cutting edge support a hollow-ground bevel is neither necessary nor always desirable. However for many tools the hollow-ground bevel is relatively easy to achieve; and aids honing, the preservation of a clear line of sight, and the maintenance of the chosen sharpening angle. If the hollow grind is of too small a radius, the cutting edge is weakened; if too large, grinding is made more difficult and only one honing may be practical before a regrind is necessary. A double-ended dry grinder with wheels 8 inches (200 mm) in diameter and 1 inch (25 mm) wide or wider is therefore the most suitable for our purposes. Wheels should be properly guarded and transparent eye shields are a sensible fitment if available. When you use the grinder, goggles or a face shield should be worn to prevent spark damage to your eyes or spectacles, and also to prevent eye injury in the unlikely but possible event of a grinding wheel disintegrating.

The quality of toolrests has in general suffered so as to make grinders more affordable. You are likely therefore to need a separate adjustable toolrest. So why not obtain a sharpening jig of the type shown in Figure 5.45. It will enable you to:

1. Dress the wheel. Some brands have a sliding fence which assists if you are using a single point diamond dresser.
2. Tilt the toolrest platform to the different angles needed for gouges, skews and scrapers.
3. More easily grind scrapers, skews and bowl gouges due to the substantial width of the platform.

There is also grinding jig designed by Californian Jerry Glaser which was released in 1994 which is excellent for gouges.

The abrasive wheels normally supplied on a grinder are usually too hard. It is a para-

Figure 5.45   An adjustable grinding jig. One of many similar brands, this Canadian Sabre Sharpening Centre has accessories which slide in the groove to jig plane blades, skews, and wheel dressing.

dox that as the hardness of the steel increases, so the bond of the grinding wheel should be weaker.

Grinding wheels are manufactured of abrasive grains together with a material which supports and binds the grains. There are several variables which determine a grinding wheel's ideal usage: the kind of abrasive, the grain size, the grade or strength of bonding, the bonding material, and the wheel geometry. Manufacturers of abrasive wheels will be willing to advise on the best wheel to use, and they often produce informative booklets. (An excellent general book on sharpening is Leonard Lee's *The Complete Guide to Sharpening* (The Taunton Press)). Grinding wheel technology is continuing to advance with new wheels in attractive pastel colours being introduced, but the optimum widely available wheel type is probably a 38A 80 JVBE. This coding translates as follows:

38A is a white, more friable type of aluminium oxide.
80 is a fairly fine grain size. A compromise between the fast metal removal of a coarser wheel and the less scored surface left by a finer wheel. For tools which will be left unhoned the 120 grit size may be preferred.
J is a weakish bond which will allow worn grains to escape more readily and therefore grind more quickly and coolly. Leonard Lee recommends H bond.
VBE refers to a vitrified bond.

Abrasive wheels are brittle and hence care must be taken to avoid damage which may lead to the wheel disintegrating in use. Before mounting a wheel, inspect it visually. As an additional check, suspend the wheel on your forefinger and tap lightly in several places. A vitrified wheel should give a clear metallic ring; if it does not, reject it.

The wheel should fit neatly onto the spindle and be gripped between flange facings of compressible material such as blotting paper, leather, or thin rubber sheet, slightly larger than the flanges. When a new wheel has been fitted, stand aside and run the grinder for a couple of minutes to ensure that the wheels are sound and properly fitted.

Figure 5.46 Using a mechanical wheel dresser on a Carba-Tec grinding jig. The projections at the front of the dresser are hooked over the front edge of the rest. A much used dressing stick is shown at the bottom of the photograph.

In use, wheels should not be run at above the recommended peripheral speed, usually about 5500 feet per minute (27 meters per second).

In order to remove metal as quickly as possible while keeping the cutting edge as cool as possible, it is important that the wheel surface be dressed once the outer grains have become worn and steel particles have become embedded in the pores of the wheel. Abrasive sticks (Figure 5.46) are the cheapest form of dresser and are ideal if you want to hollow the grinding wheel rim (Section 10.9). There are also mechanical star-wheel dressers (Figure 5.46) and diamond dressers. Unless you are using a sliding fence to guide a single point diamond dresser, wide-faced diamond dressers enable you to achieve

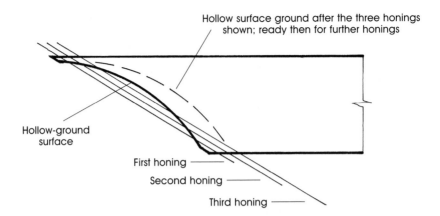

Figure 5.47 A longitudinal section through a tool tip showing the principles of regrinding and honing. (The curvature of the hollow grind is exaggerated for clarity). Ideally, regrinding should leave very narrow honed bands at the cutting edge and bevel heel, thus maximising tool life.

a flatter grinding wheel rim. The dresser should be rested on, and if possible be hooked over the grinder's toolrest, and be moved to-and-fro sideways as required (Figure 5.46), concentrating on any high spots.

The required bevel and cutting edge shapes have been described earlier. In order to achieve these, the various tool categories require their own specific grinding techniques. First, however, some general points:

1. Tools being ground may be entirely or partially supported by the jig or toolrest; they can also be supported in both hands. During regrinding the pressure of the tool on the wheel should be light as only a very thin layer of metal needs to be removed (see Figure 5.47).
2. Always wear eye protection.
3. If during grinding carbon tool steel tools the steel is burned (that is, a dark-coloured oxide film forms), quench immediately to prevent softening of the steel developing further. It may not then be necessary to grind the burnt steel away.
4. Carbon tool steel tools should be stirred frequently in a large container of water to prevent the temperature of the cutting edge exceeding the tempering temperature of 445°F (230°C). High-speed steel tools should not be water-cooled as there is a danger of micro-cracking.
5. Ensure that you have a good light over the grinder.
6. Typically, cutting tools are freehand ground by placing the heel of the bevel on the wheel and by then gently raising the handle until the whole bevel is felt to be in contact.

Grinding Skew Chisels and Parting Tools

The skew is ground with its cutting edge parallel to the grinder's axis. The grinding of skews is greatly aided if you use a jig (Figure 5.45). For freehand grinding, place the heel of one of the bevels on the rotating wheel and gently raise the handle with the right hand (see Figure 5.48) until the whole of the bevel is felt to be in contact. Move the skew slowly from side to side until the two shiny honed sections are almost ground away; at this stage sparks will start to climb over the end of the cutting edge. The other bevel is then ground in a similar way.

Unfortunately, freehand grinding a skew does not always go quite as smoothly as the above implies. Often the angle of skewness is wrong or the cutting edge is not central; in

Figure 5.48   Freehand grinding a skew chisel. The cutting edge is held parallel to the grinder's axis.

Figure 5.49   Grinding a roughing gouge on a sharpening jig.

either case, hold the skew on the toolrest at the required angle of skewness and in a plane radial through the grinder's axis. Then push the tool against the wheel until the cutting edge is ground back sufficiently to permit proper regrinding and is at the correct angle of skewness.

The heel of each bevel should be parallel to the cutting edge. If not, then slight pressure should be applied to the appropriate side of the skew during grinding.

Parting tools are sharpened in the same way as skews except that the angle of skewness is 90°.

Grinding Gouges

In this section I shall only describe the grinding of roughing and detail gouges; the grinding of bowl gouges, including those with convex bevels, being left to Section 10.9.

When grinding was done on wide, natural-stone wheels, professionals ground their gouges in the grooves which tended to form in the wheel rim; it being easier to grind a smooth bevel of convex cross-section in a round groove than on a flat trued rim. It is for you to decide whether to dedicate one of your grinding wheels for gouges only. If so, for a 1 inch (25 mm) wide wheel, dress the rim to a hollow of about 1 inch (25 mm) radius with a dressing stick.

Grinding Roughing Gouges

Roughing gouges are the easiest gouges to grind. If you have a jig, merely set the sharpening angle using a template or the gouge bevel itself, and axially rotate the gouge alternately clockwise then anticlockwise while keeping the sharpening angle unchanged (Figure 5.49). The axis of the gouge should remain at right angles to the grinder's axis.

In freehand grinding place the bevel heel-first on the stone, lift the handle until you

Figure 5.50 The starting position for freehand grinding a detail gouge.

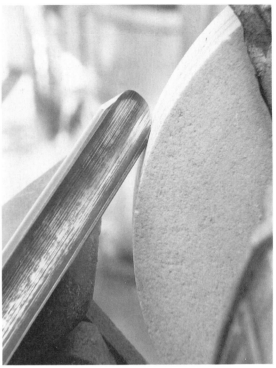

Figure 5.51 The completion of a fanning action to the right. The tool axis is at about 20° below the horizontal when viewed looking towards the front of the grinder. The fanning sharpening method can only be used with a flat-rimmed grinding wheel.

Figure 5.52 The completion of a clockwise rotation with the rotate-and-push method. Compare this photograph with Figure 5.50 to see how the gouge has been pushed up the wheel.

feel full bevel contact, then start the rotations, keeping the sharpening angle unchanged throughout.

Grinding Spindle Detail Gouges

The Glaser jig mentioned earlier is the only jig which currently de-skills this process. It mimics the *fanning* detail gouge sharpening method described in Dale Nish's *Creative Woodturning*. In this method the gouge is first positioned flute up as you would a roughing gouge (Figure 5.50). The handle is then slowly fanned, say first to your right. As this fan proceeds, the gouge will need to be axially rotated, typically clockwise about 10°, and the handle lifted. Figure 5.51 shows the completion for a right-hand fanning movement. The movements are then reversed until the tool is in a position identical to Figure 5.51 transposed. Fanning then continues to alternate until the bevel is ready for honing.

Figure 5.53 For freehand grinding, tools should be held in your fingers so that tool rotations are not impeded. Note the paint tin holding cooling water for carbon tool steel tools.

The *rotate-and-push* sharpening method is, I believe, easier to master. Again the gouge should be positioned as in Figure 5.50 at the start. The gouge is then slowly axially rotated, say first clockwise between 70° and 90°, and towards the end of the rotation the gouge nose is pushed forward, higher up the grinding wheel (Figure 5.52). The procedure is the reversed until the Figure 5.52 transposed position is reached, and then continued. Throughout this and other freehand grinding operations the tool should be held in the fingers.

The rotate-and-push method can be used with minor fanning, but whichever method you adopt, freehand detail gouge grinding will take practice to master. Note the importance of creating a ladyfinger nose which has the cutting edge slightly convex in profile and convex, without hollowed sides, in plan (Figure 5.33).

Grinding Scrapers

The noses of flat scrapers are ground while resting flat on the grinder's toolrest. The angle of the tool should be such that the correct sharpening angle of 70° is maintained. The grinding pressure should not be too heavy. Shear scrapers are ground similarly. Reg Sherwin in *Pleasure and Profit from Woodturning* recommends grinding scrapers upside down, but this does not seem to leave a better burr.

5.13 HONING

Scrapers are not usually honed because the burr forms a short vertical cutting edge (Figure 5.40)—this means that the wood is really removed by a *cutting* process, as opposed to a *scraping* process which would be the case were the burr to be honed off. However, with gouges, skews, and parting tools, the burr left after grinding is approximately perpendicular to the tool axis. It therefore effectively blunts the cutting edge. When this burr is worn or broken off by the rotating wood, a jagged edge is left which, like a serrated fruit knife, gives the illusion of sharpness. Many turners advocate that you do not hone. I am not one of them. A properly honed edge will be without a burr, sharper, and smoother; it will retain its sharpness longer and leave a better surface finish on the wood. Further, honing takes no longer than regrinding and gives a much longer tool life. It is usual to be able to hone about three times before regrinding (Figure 5.47). Of course, you can hone more times between regrinding, but the amount of metal which has to be stoned away means that honing would take too long.

The stones used for honing should be fine grained. Oilstones are most commonly used. Stones using diamonds as the abrasive cut especially quickly.

Kerosene is a perfectly adequate lubricating medium for oilstones, and your stones can be kept immersed in a shallow lidded tray (I use an aluminium freezer tray with a wooden lid) kept handy to the lathe.

Skew and parting tools are honed on a normal bench stone which is held stationary. The heel of the bevel is placed on the stone, and the handle is then gently raised until the toe of the bevel is felt to contact the stone (Figure 5.54). The tool is kept at that angle and rubbed backwards and forwards a few times. The movements should be kept small, about an inch (25 mm), so that there is little danger of altering the angle of the tool. The other bevel is then similarly honed. Both of the bevels should be honed again if necessary. Stropping is usually not advantageous.

The technique of honing gouges is somewhat different (Figure 5.55). A suitable slipstone is used and moved up-and-down while the gouge is axially rotated. The gouge is held nearly vertical about halfway along the blade in your left hand, with the end of the handle in the hollow at your left hip. The slipstone is held in your right hand by its two long edges and top, and the flat face is brought into contact with the heel of the bevel. The slipstone is then tilted forward so that it is in contact with both the heel and the toe. It may then be rubbed up-and-down as the gouge is rotated by the left hand, first one way then the other. To hone the surface of the flute, the slipstone is repositioned in the right hand so that the appropriately curved edge can be held into the flute. As before, the gouge is rotated while the slipstone is moved up-and-down. Care should be taken that the end of the flute is not dubbed over, and it is therefore wise if at least two-thirds of the length of the slipstone's edge remains in contact with the flute.

Figure 5.54 When honing a skew chisel, both the heel and the toe of the bevel remain in contact with the stone during the short to-and-fro strokes.

Figure 5.55   Honing the bevel of a gouge. The slipstone is held so that it can be maintained in contact with both the heel and the toe of the bevel while it is moved up-and-down.

An alternative to honing is buffing. Use a hard felt wheel of the same nominal diameter as your grinding wheel. In buffing, the top of the wheel turns away from you—the opposite to grinding. Buffing compound (fine abrasive in a wax matrix) is used on the wheel, and great care must be taken not to dub over the cutting edge.

Sharpening Hook and Ring Tools

The bevels are 'inside' and may be ground using a small conical or cylindrical stone held in a Jacobs chuck in the lathe headstock, in a drilling machine, or in an electric chainsaw sharpener.

Hook tool bevels are honed with a slipstone. Ring tools can be honed using a rotating hardwood cone dressed with buffing compound.

Traditionally, once a hook was worn away, the turner or the blacksmith next door just reforged, hardened, and tempered a new hook on the same blade.

6

Workshop Procedures

Chapters 7, 8, 9 and 10 consider turning procedures in detail. This chapter is largely concerned with procedures which, although not specific to spindle, cupchuck, or faceplate turning, are of equal importance.

6.1 WORKSHOP SAFETY

Safe working is largely a matter of common sense and concentration. However, it is important to ensure that working conditions are conducive to safety and that they conform to the appropriate regulations.

Personal Safety

For personal safety observe these rules:

1. Do not wear loose clothing which may become caught.
2. Wear sturdy shoes or boots. Tools sometimes fall from the lathe and spear down towards the floor.
3. How far you should go with protective clothing is a matter for you to decide. A dust coat is commonly worn but chips always enter through the collar. A smock or other garment that fits closely around the neck is more suitable, but may be too warm. Eye and face protection is best provided by a face shield or similar.
4. Wood is not generally considered to be a highly toxic material. However exposure, particularly to wood dust, can cause irritation, allergies, and respiratory ailments. Some species, mainly tropical, are especially irritant due to the particular extractives they contain. Exposure to wood dust will often cause coughing, wheezing, and tightness. Although the effects of such exposure vary enormously

from person to person, they seem to be cumulative so that susceptibility increases with exposure.

Long-term heavy exposure can cause permanent health damage. To at least lessen or prevent dust intake, wear a well-fitting dust mask or a ventilated face shield—these have a pump and filter, either helmet or waist mounted, which supply clean filtered air. Popular brands include Racal and Record. Your workshop should also be equipped with proper ventilation and dust-extraction equipment. Wood dust may also be a very low level carcinogen. Wood induced dermatitis is comparatively rare, but if you are susceptible, avoid contact with the offending species.

Workshop Safety

For workshop safety observe these rules:

1. Ensure that the workshop is kept clean and tidy and that the floor is clear of debris.
2. Ensure that the floor is not slippery.
3. Provide sufficient working area around individual machines.
4. Ensure that all machines are properly guarded.
5. Stack materials safely.
6. Electrical installations should be performed by a professional electrician and should be maintained in a safe condition.
7. When working inside machinery, ensure that the power is disconnected first.
8. Maintain and know how to use a first-aid kit.
9. Keep details of the nearest doctor and hospital in a prominent place.

Safe Procedures

Throughout this book, proper and therefore safe practices are described. This section emphasises the most obvious:

1. Ensure that the wood is free of defects which could cause it to tear apart during the turning. Wood that is safe to turn will give a clear sound when tapped, whereas cracked wood will sound dead.
2. Check the lathe speed, that the wood is securely held, and that the work clears the toolrest.
3. Stand aside when switching the lathe on.
4. Tools should always be in contact with the rest before being brought into contact with the wood.
5. Keep your hands away from the rotating wood.
6. Ensure that wood being bandsawed cannot tip over or be grabbed and rotated by the blade.

6.2   LIGHTING

Twin fluorescent fittings somewhat longer than the full length of the lathe will be found ideal. They should be suspended about 3 feet (1 metre) vertically above the lathe axis. If there is provision for outboard turning, the fluorescent fittings should run well to the left of the headstock. An adjustable light is very useful for close examination of bowl surfaces and for illuminating the insides when doing hollow cupchuck work.

The whole workshop area should be well lighted with the bandsaw table and grinder receiving special attention.

Figure 6.1 The stance for turning. The right arm is comfortably close to the body to give both freedom and control. The left upper arm hangs down. The left elbow should not be raised as is commonly seen.

6.3   THE STANCE

A proper stance (Figure 6.1) is important if you are to be able to spend any length of time at the lathe. For spindle turning, stand upright with your feet and hips parallel to the lathe and at a comfortable distance away from it. Many turners stand too far away from the lathe. The feet should be about shoulder width apart. During spindle turning, considerable lateral movements of the tools need to take place and you will need to be continually shuffling and swaying to your left and right. If you adopt the more natural stance with your right foot back, you will be unable to move easily to accommodate the required tool movements. Therefore, in turning as in many other activities, footwork is all-important. Poor footwork and body positioning will cause the right arm to be cramped against the body or be too remote from it, and therefore unsteady. In turn, this will result in the tool being improperly presented to the wood with the attendant risks of dig-ins and slips.

In bowl turning the stance is more flexible. However, the right arm should be reasonably close to the body. If long handles are used, they can be braced against the side of the body. They should not be braced into the front of the body, for if they are grabbed by the work an injury could result.

In scraping and cupchuck hollowing, the toolrest height is governed by the work and is the same for all turners. However, when spindle turning, the optimum toolrest height may vary somewhat depending on the relative heights of the turner and the lathe axis, on the diameter of the work, and also on the average blade thickness of the tools used. For example, thick, heavy tools will require the toolrest to be a little lower than light tools in order to have the same angle of presentation to the wood. The essential point is that you stand up and feel comfortable and unrestricted in your movements. Typically the top of the toolrest will be about $1/8$ inch (3 mm) below the lathe axis.

6.4   TURNING GRIPS

This section describes both the usual overhand turning grip and the preferred grip for detailed turning, the tied-underhand grip. Although the emphasis is on the left hand, the simpler, but no less important, role of the right hand is also examined. Those who turn left-handed will be well used to converting descriptions such as those in this book for their own use. They should also give consideration to turning right-handed. As I recommend a dominant left hand for most detailed turning, left handers who change will not be disadvantaged. They will also thereby avoid the problems inevitable with left-handed cupchuck hollowing. (This can be avoided by those who turn left-handed using lathes with swivelling headstocks).

Ambidextrous turning has some followers, although I have not found any need for it.

Overhand Turning

The overhand grip is the one most commonly illustrated in woodturning books and articles. Its characteristic is that the left hand rides on the tool but is not necessarily in contact with the toolrest. Generally this method is preferred for roughing and planing (see Figure 6.2) where considerable lateral tool movements along the toolrest are necessary. It can also be used when scraping, and for faceplate and bowl work.

Invariably in other publications the toolrest is illustrated almost touching the work. As described in the section below on the tied-underhand grip, this is not only unnecessary but undesirable for much work. The main exception is when you are turning concave bowl surfaces with the tool in a near-vertical presentation (Section 10.10).

It is preferable that the thumb lie above rather than below the tool blade, otherwise

Figure 6.2 One version of the overhand grip. The fingers are frequently straightened to deflect chips away from the turner (see Figure 7.14).

Figure 6.3 A side view of the tied-underhand grip. Some turners have a tendency to push the left forefinger too far up the back of the toolrest during some cuts and thereby restrict free movement of the left hand. During some cuts, for example, the tip of the forefinger might be in contact with only the bottom edge of the toolrest.

in some cuts it can become trapped between the tool and the toolrest. Also the left hand should not exert any appreciable downward force which will increase friction between the tool blade and the toolrest or else tool movements are impeded.

Underhand Turning

The essential feature of the tied-underhand turning grip is that the forefinger of the left hand passes beneath the toolrest to grip the far side (see Figure 6.3). The blade of the tool is gripped into the palm with the thumb and remaining three fingers (Figure 6.4). Therefore, not only is the blade securely held in the left hand, but they in turn are both tied in with the toolrest. Thus the role of the left hand can be much more positive and, for instance, it provides most of the power and control in bead rolling cuts.

The tied-underhand grip became possible with the introduction of steel toolrests, wooden rests being much too bulky in cross-section. The grip seems to have been developed in the 1920s in New Zealand or in Sydney, Australia, and although spreading rapidly, many current toolrests are incompatible with its use. They are either too deep, vary in cross-section along their lengths, or have a large boss where the stem meets the top section of the toolrest. Figure 3.13 shows a suitable cross-section which you will probably have to have specially made unless you can reshape your existing ones.

There is an understandable fear that the forefinger will become trapped and crushed between the rest and the work. However, there is no danger of this as the finger would be knocked downwards out of harm's way. In practice, accidental contact between the fore-

Figure 6.4   The turner's view of the tied-underhand grip. Three fingers grip the blade securely, but not rigidly, into the palm. The forefinger passes beneath and grips the far side of the toolrest.

finger and the work is almost unknown as a turner very quickly learns to have a minimum gap of about $^{1}/_{2}$ inch (13 mm) between the toolrest and the work. This gap is in itself of benefit because:

1. It encourages use of proper long-and-strong turning tools.
2. Both the top and the bottom surfaces of the work can be viewed simultaneously which greatly aids eyeing diameters and tapers.
3. There is no feeling of constriction. The tool has plenty of working room and there is no chance of having the bevel instead of the uniform section of the blade in contact with the toolrest.
4. There is no necessity to move the toolrest when sanding, although it is both safer and recommended that you do.
5. Movement of the toolrest is minimised. When starting from, say, a square up to 3 inches by 3 inches (75 mm × 75 mm), the toolrest is positioned so that it just clears the corners. The wood is then roughed using the overhand grip, leaving the toolrest ideally positioned to start detailed turning using the tied-underhand grip.
6. Movements of the right hand during detailed turning are reduced in magnitude because the fulcrum formed by the toolrest is farther from the work.

The forefinger is not merely passively gripping the rest, it powers lateral tool movements and can also exert a strong pull towards the workpiece when very heavy cuts are being taken. Its close, yet safe, position means that it can, in addition, act as a steady for very fine work (see Section 7.17), and can be used to remove the ring shavings often produced during bead rolling with the skew chisel. It is also handy for feeling whether a

Figure 6.5   The best-known but inferior form of the underhand grip. Many turners who prefer the tied-underhand grip to this one, rather than use their wrists and forearms actively, allow their tied-underhand grips to slacken into a similar open thumb and fingers version, but with the forefinger passing beneath the toolrest.

square has been roughed down to a true cylinder, and for checking that the wood's surface is unmarred by any splitting out.

The left hand is, of course, an extension of the forearm and wrist. In the rolling cuts performed with the skew, the forearm and wrist must work to rotate the tool or else the hand tends to open and control is lost. The tied-underhand grip is hence recommended for almost all cuts except where large lateral movements are required, or where the need to minimise tool overhang means that the toolrest must be positioned very close to the work.

Note that there is a commonly illustrated type of underhand grip (Figure 6.5) in which the tool is held between the left-hand thumb and the fingertips. The hand merely rests against the toolrest. This grip is therefore inferior.

Under some circumstances, the left hand is not taking much or indeed any part in controlling the tool. In slender turning, the left hand may be acting as a steady and you may have to work cross-armed (Section 7.17). When you are callipering, the left hand will be holding the callipers (Figure 6.6), and when you are parting-off, the left arm will cross over ready to catch the work as it comes free (Section 7.15).

The Right Hand

The previous section rather neglects the right hand which provides some of the power and 'steering' during turning. Correct right-hand gripping also leads to surer turning techniques. Extending the forefinger along the handle gives a greater feeling of control and 'oneness' with the tool.

When you are doing a series of cuts with a particular tool, it is natural to regrip for each cut so that the right hand is comfortable during that cut. When, however, the cut is a rotational one, it is best to grip the tool so that the right hand reaches the natural, com-

Figure 6.6 Callipering with a parting tool. The tool handle is safely held beneath the forefinger and the forearm—the latter ensuring that if the tool tip is grabbed the tool handle cannot be jerked upward and hit you on the chin. The right hand should be fairly close to the tip of the tool.

fortable position at the completion of the cut (see Section 7.9). This makes the cut almost automatic because of the right hand's natural desire to rotate into an unstrained position.

When you are callipering or parting-off or using the sizer, the tool is held by the right hand only. Control can be improved by having the tool in reasonable balance (therefore the handle should be fairly light in weight), by holding the tool so that the handle is braced under the forearm, and by extending the forefinger along the top of the blade (Figure 6.6).

6.5   SMALL-SCALE TURNING

The purpose of this section is to correct certain misconceptions which are prevalent. Small-scale turning is exactly what it says; it is the turning of pieces which may be, but are not necessarily, small-scale replicas of the full-size originals. However, many items are small in their own right.

Small-scale turning, contrary to popular opinion, requires proper cutting techniques, and scraping should be used only when it is the superior technique to use, which is infrequently. *Cutting* gives a better finish, more quickly, and perhaps most importantly, imposes smaller forces on the delicate work.

Small-scale turning requires higher lathe speeds, but not necessarily small lathes. The rigidity of the lathe is important because fine work requires freedom from vibration.

Obviously small-scale turning may require small tools. However, most can be performed with normal long-and-strong tools. When small tools are required, ensure that they are not weak and flappy and therefore dangerous and unpredictable. Miniature tools are available, but you can locally grind down the ends of long-and-strong tools. Some turners make their own for special situations.

6.6   TURNING OTHER MATERIALS

Besides wood, you can use woodturning techniques to turn:

> Soft metals
> Bone
> Ivory
> Rubber
> Some plastics
> Fibreboard

Soft metals are scraped. The other materials are preferably cut but, except for rubber, can be scraped.

Readers may question the turning of rubber and be relieved to read that I turn rubber rings which are half recessed into the bases of objects which are required to have nonslip bases. The rubber or butyl sheet is tacked onto a disk of plywood mounted on a faceplate or screwchuck, and the required size of ring cut out with the long point of a skew. If necessary, further support can be provided by sandwiching the rubber between the plywood on the faceplate or screwchuck and a further plywood disk.

Fibreboard (MDF) turns quite well, particularly on the faceplate. It is, however, very dusty to turn and gives off a rather unpleasant vapour. Fibreboard is completely stable and therefore often laminated. It can even be turned between centres with the laminations parallel to the lathe axis, the finishing cuts being made with a skew or a detail gouge presented with plenty of side rake.

6.7 TURNING FOR FURNITURE RESTORATION

Restoration turning is certainly the most varied aspect of woodturning and also one of the most enjoyable. The turner has continual contact with interesting people, unusual pieces of furniture and treen, taxing turning situations, and unfamiliar woods.

Because of the transportation and export/import of furniture which has occurred over the years, the turner will be in contact with pieces both locally and distantly made. Hence, besides the indigenous species which are used, the restoration turner will need a stock of mahoganies, walnuts, oaks, ashes, elms, satinwoods, ebonies, rosewoods, birches, maples, cedars, certain softwoods, etc. Obviously, acquiring these woods will be both time consuming and expensive so that the turner should not be afraid to include the proper price for them in quotations and charges.

Wood matching is a continual problem. Species were used which may now be rare or unobtainable. Certainly the large sizes used in legs, pedestals, and urns may have to be laminated.

Suitable species may be purchased from specialist timber suppliers or gleaned from old furniture and buildings. Indigenous woods may be harvested or bought locally. A further possible source of wood for a particular job is the client—many dealers acquire stocks of useful wood. For less critical restoration, alternative species may be able to be substituted. You will quickly become an expert at wood identification, as you will not only be working with raw wood and conversing with others knowledgeable on the subject, but will be continually coming into contact with items which, being broken, show both the raw wood and areas covered with old finish.

The restoration turner should be knowledgeable about the styles and construction of furniture and treen. Much of this knowledge will be acquired during the course of the work, but the turner should also study and have a reference library. A library will be valuable when he has to produce a replacement for which no original still exists.

Spindle and cupchuck turning will comprise the majority of the work, with the proportion of the latter being particularly high due to the vulnerability of knobs and finials. Because of the unusual and peculiar situations which arise, a good range of chucks is essential. The restoration turner will need to be able to design special chucking arrangements, and to develop unusual procedures and special-purpose turning tools.

The turning required will usually be highly detailed and require really sound turning techniques. Because of the sometimes irreplaceable nature or cost of the wood which the turner is using, this is not a field for the beginner.

Many clients are vague about what is required so that it can be up to the turner to define the particular job, and the following points should be noted:

1. Will the turner have to go and see the broken item or can it be brought in? The latter is preferable, but may be impractical with case furniture. When going out to see a job, be sure to take sufficient equipment, etc., so that the job can be measured up on the spot.
2. Agree on the wood species and decide who will supply the wood.
3. How will the replacement be held in the piece of furniture? Be sure to measure maximum socket or pin diameters and lengths. If necessary, turn pins oversize so that they can be trimmed by the restorer.
4. If there are sections of the work which are threaded, can these be matched or will plain pins or sockets with suitable gap-filling glues suffice?
5. If the turning is to be carved, fluted, or reeded, who will do this? Should the turner leave extra waste so that the turning can be held securely to facilitate these later operations?
6. Old items will tend to be neither straight, square, nor round due to the wood warp-

ing and shrinking. Where necessary, allow fullness in the turning so that the new piece can be carved-in to meet the original.

7. As a general principal, preserve as much of the original item and finish as possible.
8. When joining a replacement onto a section of the original turning, the joint should be at a discontinuity in the original design, such as a V-cut, the junction of a bead with a fillet, or a turned section with a square section.
9. Who will polish the replacement? Should the turner supply a wood sample so that the polisher can experiment to achieve a colour match?
10. Who will supply any fittings required? How much liaison will be required with the client and others involved in the restoration process? Who will arrange and pay for transport and deliveries?
11. Is a fixed or approximate quote required or can it be arranged as a 'do and charge'? Agree on a completion date and how and when payment will be made.

6.8   SANDING

You sand for two reasons:

1. To remove any surface defects left after turning—ridges, small hollows, ribbing, bruising, burnishing, pecking, etc.
2. To prepare the surface for any subsequent application of finishes by eliminating the scratches left after point 1 above, and by creating a surface with, as far as possible, uniformity of absorption.

Sandpaper is now obsolete, and only two types of abrasive paper need be considered. The most commonly used has aluminium oxide as its abrasive, a pale brown-coloured metal material with a hardness of 9.5 on Mohs' scale. The second has silicon carbide as its abrasive, a blue-black grit slightly harder and more brittle than aluminium oxide. Silicon carbide paper uses waterproof glues and paper, and is sold as wet and dry paper.

The abrasive grits are graded to size so that, for example, 100 grit abrasive will pass through a screen having a mesh of 100 threads per linear inch (25 mm), but will be retained on the next finest mesh which has 120 threads per linear inch (25 mm).

Abrasive papers are made by depositing the particular-sized grains onto glued backing paper. The grains may be deposited tightly together (*close coat*) or with space between (*open coat*). The latter is more suitable for turning, being cheaper and less liable to clog. In addition to being glued to the backing, the abrasive is often surface coated to further reduce the tendency to clog. Stearate is frequently used, and therefore open coat, stearate-coated, aluminium oxide papers are recommended. Various weights of papers are used, with the finer grits being deposited on the lightest paper (A weight). Coarse grits are usually deposited on C weight paper. Cloth is also frequently used as a backing material, and the lightest Jeans (J) weight cloth is particularly good for really coarse, heavy sanding. There are now some even lighter cloth backings available, which although more costly than paper, because of their durability, thinness and flexibility provide a real alternative to paper.

The sequence of grits normally available is 60, 80, 100, 120, 150, 180, 220, 240, 280, 320, 360, 400, 500, and 600.

In the sanding of turnings, the paper or cloth has to be curved to follow the curves in the work. Obviously, the lighter the weight of the backing, the more easily and more tightly it can be curved. However, the atmospheric relative humidity can significantly affect this quality. Papers which are too dry may be brittle (although modern glues have greatly reduced this problem), and damp papers are limp and lifeless. To improve the flexibility of papers, pull them over an arrised edge such as that of the workbench or lathe bed (Figure 6.7). If your workshop is too damp, it may be advisable to keep your abrasive papers in a heated cupboard (a low-wattage light bulb could be used) which is designed to allow good internal air circulation. Papers should be kept flat and if necessary weighted, although modern papers have little tendency to curl.

Sanding is slow, boring, and dusty, and abrasive paper is expensive. It is therefore a process which should be minimised. Furthermore, it is a process which is quite efficient at removing projecting defects, but not at removing subsurface defects such as bruising and pecking in which a substantial thickness of wood covering a large area has to be abraded away. Finally, the rate of abrasion varies according to the apparent hardness. So, side grain is abraded more rapidly than end grain, knots are abraded less than the surrounding wood, quartersawn faces may be abraded more than plainsawn (backcut) faces depending on the hardness and spacing of the medullary rays, and woods with soft spring growth and much harder summer and autumn tissue will be abraded to produce a wavy surface. Hence, sanding will tend to destroy the almost true circularity left by your turning tools.

The most important way to minimise undesirable sanding is to produce the best possible off-the-tool finish. The second way is to sand only as necessary. For instance, if you

Figure 6.7   The flexibility of abrasive paper being improved by pulling it over an edge.

are turning a veranda post which will be painted, a quick sand with 60 grit and 100 grit will be sufficient. For a small objet virtu which will be handled and closely examined, you should sand to, say, 400 grit, but you may be able to start sanding with 180 grit. If the wood is to be stained, sand to at least 320 grit.

The selection of the grit which you use to start sanding with is also important. Too coarse, and you make the surface worse before you start to improve it with finer grits. Too fine, and you take longer than necessary and may even have to switch to a coarser grit when you realise the futility of your initial choice.

If insect holes or other defects are suspected in the wood or if there are areas of cranky grain, it is usual to inspect for and fill any such defects before commencing sanding. If the stopping used is slow drying, the wood may have to be temporarily removed from the lathe so that other work can continue. Care should be taken that metal tools used to mix or apply stoppings do not cause dark staining. Apply them slightly proud to allow for any shrinkage. If colour matching is important, try the procedure on a waste sample of the wood and note the effect of polishing. If the defects are small, it may be quicker to stop and hand sand either during or after the in-lathe operations.

Abrasive cloth is generally supplied in rolls or belts, and you will have to tear off suitable lengths as required. Abrasive papers are available in rolls or sheets, and are often bought in packs of standard sheets 11 inches × 9 inches (280 mm × 230 mm). Buy A weight papers for small and medium-sized work. Coated aluminium oxide papers are cheaper and longer lasting than silicon carbide papers and are therefore preferred for general sanding. However, as silicon carbide grains are and fracture sharper, they leave a better surface than aluminium oxide grits and so are preferred for the final sanding of objets virtu.

If the abrasive paper is not sufficiently flexible, pull it in both length and breadth over an arris to improve flexibility. Then fold and tear into four and fold each piece into three (see Figure 6.8). The folded quarter sheet gives three sanding faces and two sanding edges. Furthermore, the three thicknesses of paper insulate the fingers from heat and do not slip because each uncoated face is in contact with a coated face. When first folded, only two faces are exposed. After they are both worn, refold to expose the fresh face. Finally, when a piece of abrasive paper is too worn, throw it away; worn 100 grit is not equivalent to fresh 150 grit!

The lathe speed is generally not altered for sanding, though a lowered speed is better for woods with a high resin content. It is safer to stop the lathe and remove the tool-rest before starting sanding.

To prevent the classic accident in which the hand is dragged down between the rest and the work, two sanding methods are used. In the first (Figure 6.9), which is used for long spindle turnings, the turner faces the headstock and sands towards it from the tailstock end. The paper is held in both hands, but mainly by the right. The faces are used to sand the straight sections and long curves; the edges to sand fillets and the intersections of curves. To sand hollows, the paper is sprung into a curve (Figure 6.10). In the second sanding method (Figure 6.11), the paper is held mainly by the right hand which is beneath the work and loosely by the left hand which reaches over the rotating work. The roles of the hands may also be reversed. The stance for this method is parallel to the lathe.

The essence of the hand-turned piece is really crisp detail. Having taken care to turn it well, you will appreciate how important it is that the sharp detail is not destroyed by careless sanding. Note that faces perpendicular to the lathe axis at the ends of square sections cannot be sanded or their leading edges will be dubbed over.

When sanding, proceed through the full series of grit grades. Do not miss grades, for each grade is sized so as to efficiently eliminate the scratching left by the preceding grade. Many professional turners do omit grades, but the surface will generally suffer somewhat. If you are using a large series of papers, set up a rack so that they can be kept in order.

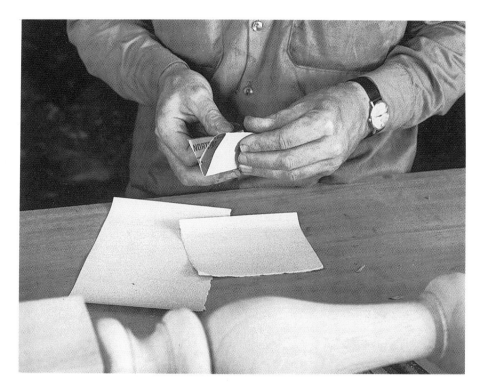

Figure 6.8   A standard-sized sheet of aluminium oxide, stearate-coated, abrasive paper has been folded and torn into four. One of these quarter sheets is being folded into three.

Figure 6.9   The first spindle turning sanding method. The right hand is actively resisting the frictional force that the wood applies to the paper.

Perhaps one day abrasive papers will be made with each grit on a different-coloured paper so that they are easier to distinguish.

Where a really high-quality finish is required or where a stain or grain-raising polish will be applied after sanding, you can dampen the surface to raise the grain, dry (say with a hair drier or heat gun), and sand again. Also, before parting-off or sawing off the waste, consider whether this might be better delayed to facilitate finishing.

6.9   FINISHING

Wood finishing is a major subject in its own right with a literature as extensive as that of woodturning. It is not the aim of this section to be totally comprehensive, but to provide thoughts and information of special relevance to woodturning.

In finishing, there are two main decisions: the choice of the most suitable finish, and the finishing procedure. The two decisions obviously cannot be made in isolation. In selecting the finish, you may find the following points relevant:

1. What is the degree of protection required? Oils and waxes give little protection, attract dirt, and will in use aid the development of a patina which may or may not be desirable. Some finishes are affected by oil, alcohol, and even water. Will the

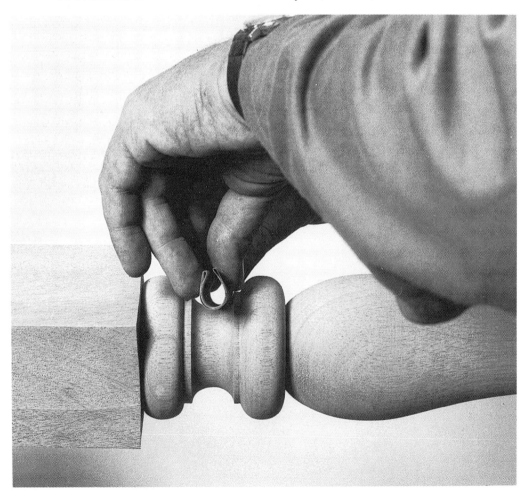

Figure 6.10   Sanding a hollow. The abrasive paper is held by both hands.

Figure 6.11 The second sanding method. The frictional pull on the paper is being resisted by the right hand.

finish have to stand up to the weather?

2. What appearance is required? Is an opaque finish such as paint suitable, or must the finish be basically clear? Among the clear finishes, almost all will yellow in time and most have a yellow or brown tinge to start with. However, some totally clear finishes are available. Some finishes contain ultraviolet inhibitors which slow down the yellowing of the finish and delay colour changes in the wood itself.

3. Is it required to stick adhesive labels onto the finished object? If so, oils and waxes are generally unsuitable.

4. Will the work be used to contain food? Obviously toxic, soluble, or smelly finishes cannot be used.

5. Does the finish have to match that on an existing item?

6. If the wood contains any unusual extractives or if chemical stabilisation has been used, will the finish be compatible?

7. Should the finish be glossy, satin, or matt? The gloss level, the depth of penetration of the finish into the wood, and the thickness of the on-surface coating can

be varied by thinning and by the particular method of application.

8. What equipment do you have? Some finishes require spraying or heating equipment. Most give off vapours which need to be exhausted.
9. Should you do the finishing yourself or send it to a specialist contractor?
10. How critical is the standard of finish, and is this requirement compatible with the time and cost of finishing and the number of items to be finished?
11. Does the proposed finish require any in-lathe time, and is this compatible with other production requirements? Does this dictate a finish which hardens rapidly?
12. Finishes vary in their toxicity, both in their liquid and vaporous states, and after application. Regulations are continually being tightened and water-based products are replacing organic-solvent-based ones. Read the manufacturer's warnings and instructions.
13. Is the hardness or the toughness of the finish important?
14. Friction French polishes are available for turners. They are applied to the workpiece while it is in the lathe. Although they give an excellent and easy finish for small items. they do not all seem to truly harden unless buffed vigorously. If you get the polish on your fingers it will cause deep cracking in your skin, so wear vinyl gloves.

Finishes which set hard are almost essential on open-grained or soft woods which look very hungry when given a penetrating type of finish. However, finishes which set hard require a high standard of surface preparation and are traditionally preceded by filling and staining. The fashion now is for a more natural appearance, so that these two preliminaries are often ignored.

Perhaps I might end this section by giving my own personal preference for a hand-applied finish. Dilute four volumes of gloss one-part polyurethane with one volume of mineral turpentine, and apply liberally with a nonlinting rag or brush. When no further absorption takes place, buff off quickly with a rag just moist with polish and allow to dry. For some fine-grained hardwoods, one coat is sufficient and does not raise the grain perceptibly. Otherwise, flat with 400 grit or, less satisfactorily but more easily done, fine steel wool and recoat in the same way. Under average conditions the second coat should be applied within six hours so that it bonds properly to the first. If a heavier build-up of polish is required, the polyurethane/turpentine solution can be applied with a fine-bristled brush and not wiped off.

Occasionally a finished piece will be accidentally dented. If the damaged wood is steamed, the cells can usually be restored to almost their earlier form. A little light sanding is then used to flat the grain raised by the steam, and local refinishing is then all that is necessary to restore the piece.

7

Spindle Turning

In spindle turning, the wood is mounted between the lathe centres and is rotated forwards against turning tools. It remains by far the most common form of turning despite an increase in the proportions of bowl and cupchuck turning since the recent rise in the popularity of craft turning. It furthermore remains, to my mind, the most enjoyable once the skew chisel is mastered. Although it may strike the uninitiated as boring, there is something uniquely satisfying about turning a set of 50 identical legs or stair balusters after the relative freedom of a period of bowl turning.

This chapter attempts to describe the various fundamental procedures and techniques used in spindle turning before explaining specialised methods which are generally used less frequently. However, certain techniques associated with woodturning such as precision sawing, routing, and carving are not dealt with in detail because they are essentially adjuncts to woodturning.

7.1 PENCIL AND PIN GAUGES

Most spindle work is repetitive so that varying numbers of identical turnings are required. To achieve acceptably close agreement to a design or between turnings, you usually use gauges and other aids to set out the wood, to measure diameters, and occasionally to compare curves during the turning process.

Aids which you could use during repetitive turning include:

1. Pencil gauges.
2. Pin gauges.
3. Callipers and other diameter gauges with parting tools or gouges.
4. Sizers.
5. Swing arm diameter setters.
6. Profile curves, templates, or a Mimic.

Pencil Gauges

Before preparing your pencil or other gauges, you must decide which will be the headstock and tailstock ends of the turning. In many cases it will not matter, but the following points may influence the decision:

1. If one end of the turning is to be narrower than the diameter of the driving centre, as in a toupie foot, then that end will be held by the tailstock.
2. If the work is to be parted-off, then that must be done at the headstock end.
3. If the turning is slender and one end of the workpiece is to be held in a chuck to increase effective stiffness, then the weakest sections in the finished turning should be at the headstock end and you work from right to left.

A pencil gauge consists of a piece of wood or plywood $^1/_4$ to $^3/_8$ inch (6 to 10 mm) thick, 3 inches (75 mm) or more wide, and about 1 inch (25 mm) longer than the spindle if the latter is to be fully turned. The spindle to be turned is drawn full size, and the important reference points are projected with a try square to the top edge. A three-cornered file is then used to form grooves in the top face of the gauge at the ends of these projected lines (Figure 7.1). The gauge is used after roughing, and planing if relevant, by holding it onto the toolrest with its reference edge just against the rotating work. A pencil point is then pushed along the grooves to mark the wood (Figure 7.2).

The reference points chosen for projection are the intersections of beads with fillets or rings with straightish sections, bases of V-cuts, maximum and minimum diameters, etc. Fillet widths are eyed, and there is no need to use the intersections of fillets with hollows as reference points.

You may wish to modify the pencil gauge for certain situations:

1. *When squares (that is, unturned sections) are to be left at each end of the work.* Use a gauge a little shorter than the turned section (Figure 7.2). The reference points in the left-hand half of the turned section are marked with the gauge abutting the rotating left-hand square and vice versa.
2. *When a turned section lies outside a square section.* The pencil gauge is pushed lightly against the adjacent end of the rotating square section and the reference lines then marked (Figure 7.3).
3. *When there are major sections of the spindle with different diameters.* In this case, the spindle is roughed to two or more diameters and a gauge with a stepped top edge is used (Figure 7.4).
4. *For faceplate work.* Here a gauge with reference marks running to two edges is used (Figure 9.9).

Diameters to be callipered, size of wood required, turning time, etc. can be recorded on both pencil and pin gauges.

Pin Gauges

For large numbers of repetitive turnings, the pencil grooves can be replaced with brads $^3/_4$ inch (19 mm) long which are hammered into the top edge of the gauge until about $^1/_4$ inch (6 mm) projects. The heads are then pinched off and the resulting projections filed into small cutting edges at right angles to the top face of the gauge (Figure 7.1).

The pin gauge is used in a similar way to the pencil gauge, but while being supported on the toolrest, its top edge is lightly pressed towards the revolving wood so that the chisel points make fine cuts in the workpiece.

In some instances, it is useful to have a locating bearing point so that the set-out is always exactly the same distance from the tailstock end of the work. Use a heavier-gauge brad or jolt-head nail projecting about $^3/_8$ inch (10 mm), located $^1/_2$ inch (13 mm) in from the right-hand end of the gauge (Figure 7.1).

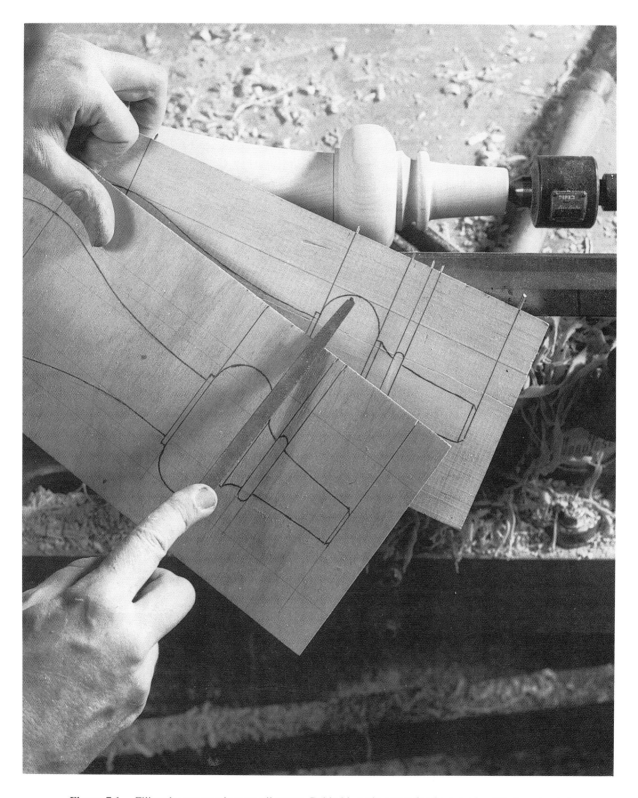

Figure 7.1   Filing the grooves in a pencil gauge. Behind is a pin gauge for the same leg. The long brad at the right-hand end of the pin gauge bears against the right-hand end of the rotating workpiece after roughing and ensures that the reference points then marked by the sharpened brads are accurately positioned.

Figure 7.2 Marking out a baluster. The reference points at the left-hand end of the round section are being marked with the left-hand end of the gauge abutting the end of the left-hand rotating square section. Prior to the marking of reference points at the right-hand end of the turned section, the pencil gauge will be moved to the right until it abuts the far square section.

Figure 7.3 Using a pencil gauge to mark out a turned section adjacent to a square section. The pencil point is guided by the grooves in the top of the gauge.

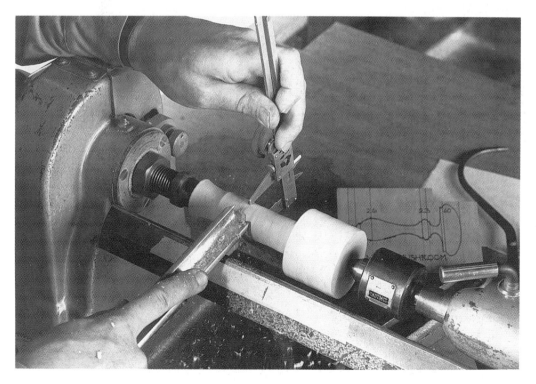

Figure 7.4 Roughing for a darning mushroom. The top edge of the pencil gauge visible behind the tail centre is stepped to correspond with the two diameters left after roughing. A pencil mark on masking tape on the toolrest indicates where to step the diameter.

Other Aids to Accurate Turning

Callipers and other diameter gauges are considered in Section 4.1, sizers in Section 5.11. Swing arm diameter setters, profile curves, and templates are usually more of a hindrance than a help, whereas accurate marking out with a pencil or pin gauge, selective callipering of diameters, and full use of your eyesight are usually both quick and efficient. By actively judging diameters and depths, and by comparing diameters being cut with other diameters already cut, the need to calliper can be greatly reduced. You can even use the diameters of parts of your driving and tail centres for reference. It can help to have a strip of masking tape pressed onto the toolrest upon which to mark information, for example, where a roughed workpiece should change in diameter (see Figure 7.4).

7.2   PREPARATION OF WOOD FOR TURNING

The wood used for spindle turning should be straight and axially grained and free of splits and large knots. You can check the workpiece by tapping it on the lathe bed—flawed wood makes a dead sound. Less than ideal wood can be turned to a good finish, but it can take longer. Also, of course, nonaxial grain produces a weaker finished product and therefore should not be used for highly stressed items like chair legs.

The wood is normally used in the form of sawn square sections about $1/4$ inch (6 mm) thicker than the maximum diameter of the turning. Sound rived sections are also suitable. There is no need to dress off the corners of the blanks prior to roughing as recommended by some writers. The sawn blanks need not be dressed unless square sections are to be left in the finished turning.

Figure 7.5   Using a marking gauge to mark the centres is quicker and more accurate than trying to draw diagonals.

After any required dressing, the wood is cross-cut into the required lengths which will need to be longer than the finished length of the turning if the work is to be parted-off, or if one or both ends are to be hand finished outside the lathe. Where the item is to have square sections, centres need to be precisely marked (Figure 7.5) and preferably punched. The extents of the squares are pencilled (on one side is usually sufficient) using a try square, and often then marked with a cross (Figure 7.6).

Holes are sometimes required in a finished turning. Those into the side of a turning can be drilled before or after turning. If before, there is a slight possibility that the sides of the holes may split out during the turning process. Axial holes can be prebored, and if necessary, plugs are used to enable the work to be held in the lathe (see Section 4.13). Long-hole boring is described in Section 3.8. Alternatively, but less satisfactorily, axial holes can be drilled after turning.

For mounting the wood in the lathe correctly centred, the centres can be:

1. Judged by eye as the wood is put in.
2. Marked by drawing the diagonals, or better by using a marking gauge set at about half the wood's thickness.
3. Punched after marking as in point 2 above. Only for very hard woods should there be any need to drill holes for the driving and tail centres.
4. Punched using a purpose-made centre punch (Figure 7.7).

Figure 7.6 Marking the extents of square sections.

Figure 7.7 A self-centring centre punch. The upstanding square frame is a little oversize. To use the punch, the end of the workpiece is held vertically inside the frame, twisted until it jams against the frame sides, and then tapped down onto the centre pin. Professional spindle turners should make steel versions.

7.3   MOUNTING THE WOOD BETWEEN CENTRES

Amateur turners should mount and remove spindle turnings with the lathe switched off. The tailstock should be locked onto the bed in such a position that the tailstock spindle does not project too far from the tailstock body.

Once the wood is correctly positioned between the driving and tail centres (Figures 7.8 and 7.9), wind the tail centre in sufficiently hard so that the driving centre's prongs engage properly. Retract the tail centre a little, wind it back in fairly firmly but not too hard, and then tighten the tailstock spindle locking lever. When the wood has annual rings with spring growth which is very much softer than the summer and autumn tissue, the short pin of a ring centre is less liable to be deflected off centre than the standard tail centre's cone-shaped nose.

The banjo should, if possible, be secured with its neck is at right angles to the bed so that there is little chance of hitting it with the points of your turning tools when swapping

Figure 7.8   Mounting the wood in the lathe for spindle turning. The turner stands facing the headstock with his head over the driving centre. The workpiece is held with its sides roughly horizontal and vertical. If the centre has not been punched, you will have to push the workpiece's end lightly and centrally onto the driving centre's centre pin. Then axially rotate the workpiece 90° and check that the driving centre's pin is still central. If not, adjust and then do a further check rotation.

Figure 7.9   To centre the tailstock end of the workpiece, move backwards and sight along the tailstock. Wind the tail centre into the centre of the right-hand end of the workpiece. If necessary, do a check 90° rotation and make any adjustments.

one tool for another. With wood about 3 inches (75 mm) in side width, the toolrest is set so that the corners of the square clear it by about ¹/₄ inch (6 mm). There is then usually no need to move the rest forwards once roughing is accomplished. Use a rest of the appropriate length a little longer than the workpiece—it is much better than moving a rest which is too short to- and-fro along the bed. The top of the toolrest is usually positioned about ¹/₈ inch (3 mm) below the lathe axis and a little higher with larger diameters.

The wood should now be correctly mounted with the tailstock locked to the bed, the tailstock spindle locking lever tight, and the corners of the workpiece clear of the toolrest. It remains only to check that the lathe speed is not too high.

When switching the lathe on, be in the habit of standing to the side so that if the wood does fly out, you will not be hit. Stopping the lathe and winding the tailstock spindle further to the left will usually prevent the wood flying out if that seems likely. However, ensure that you do not have to move through the danger zone in order to switch off.

Professional turners doing repetition work usually centre the wood with the lathe running (Figures 7.10 to 7.13). However, this method should be used only by experienced turners, and then only with small work.

In restoration turning, it is sometimes necessary to re-turn a piece of work for which it will not be possible to accurately premark the centres. To overcome this problem, centre the work by eye without embedding the centres too deeply, and switch on the lathe.

With the long point of a skew, just nick the corners in a waste part of a left square section, stop the lathe, loosen the tailstock a little, tap the work so that it is centred correctly using the depths of the nicks as a guide, retighten the tailstock, and repeat if necessary.
If there is no suitable square section, use a pencil supported on the toolrest to mark on the
circular periphery in lieu of the nicks with the long point.

7.4   PRINCIPLES OF SPINDLE TURNING

Turning is a type of carving. The major reason for its continued existence is that it allows
circular cross-sectioned shapes to be carved more quickly than could be done by hand.
Hence, speed and efficiency are two essential characteristics of good turning. Proper initial conditions such as good equipment, really sharp tools, and correct lathe speed assist
in the minimisation of turning time, but the order in which tools are used can also have a
significant effect. To put down one tool, select another, and pick it up takes precious seconds. By forethought and by having sufficient expertise so that one tool can perform a
whole range of cuts, you can eliminate needless steps. The basic order of tool usage is:

1. Rough
2. Mark out
3. Skew chisel
4. Detail gouge

Some simple turnings may require fewer steps, some the four, and others more than
four. You can, of course, take things too far and turn a veranda post using only a small
skew chisel, but the principle nevertheless remains valid.

In selecting the tools to use for a particular job, choose the largest which will be comfortable. Where there is a large range of sizes in the detailing of a job, it may be better to
use more than one of any particular tool type. However, by rationalising design (see
Section 2.7), some reduction in the number of individual tool usages and calliperings can
often be made.

Nine further points should be noted:

1. The tool must always be in contact with the toolrest before contact is made with
   the wood. If not, the wood will grab the end of the tool and bang the blade down
   onto the rest.
2. Whenever possible, use the tied-underhand grip because of the greater control
   which it ensures. Use of the overhand grip is therefore restricted to cuts with
   large, lateral tool movements, such as roughing and planing, or where large tool
   overhangs require the rest to be positioned very close to the work.
3. Always cut *downhill*, that is in spindle work from larger to smaller diameter. Only
   in faceplate work do you cut *uphill*, and only then because it is unavoidable
   (Figure 9.1). In the *downhill* cutting situation, there is full support from the wood
   below so that the fibres are cut cleanly and the cut surface is then lightly bur-
   nished by the underside of the cutting edge.
4. In turning, it is critical that the tool be positioned correctly before a cut is started.
   If a cut starts off wrongly, it will be difficult to correct it. So, position the tool,
   pause to check that its presentation is correct, and then start the cut.
5. Ensure that tools are properly shaped and sharpened.
6. When you are taking cuts, it is preferable if they are of even thickness and of perceptible thickness. The cutting force required for a shaving of even thickness is
   predictable and the tool will tend to follow the existing profile. So take care with

Figure 7.10   The lathe is running at a suitable speed, and the banjo and tailstock are locked in position. Your eyes are over the driving centre and the wood is held by both hands. The left hand holds the wood's left-hand end with the palm upward and passing below the toolrest and with the thumb passing over the toolrest. The right hand holds the wood palm-downward with the forearm over the tailstock. Push the wood centrally onto the centre pin of the rotating driving centre, but not so far that the prongs engage. If the workpiece's centre has not been punched, rotate the wood 90° and adjust the centring if necessary.

Figure 7.11 Once the left-hand end of the work is satisfactorily centred, transfer the left hand to the tailstock end of the wood and regrip in the same way as in Figure 7.10.

Figure 7.12 Remove the right hand from the wood and gently start to wind the tailstock spindle to the left.

Figure 7.13   As the driving centre prongs start to engage, initially restrain the wood from rotating with the fingers of the left hand. When the centres are in far enough so that the wood will not fly out if released, bring the left thumb back onto the nearside of the toolrest out of harm's way and release the wood by straightening the fingers. Continue to wind the tail centre in until the prongs are firmly embedded in the left-hand end of the wood and then lock the tailstock shaft with the locking lever.

the preliminary cuts and the final finishing cuts will be all the easier. It is also best if cuts are definite. Very fine skimming cuts require ultra-sharp tools, or else the edge will merely burnish the surface of the wood, making further cutting edge penetration much more difficult, with the result that you force the tool and it then tends to penetrate too deeply.

7. A heavy cut removes as much wood as two or three light cuts, yet takes less time and blunts the tool less. Therefore, heavy cuts are preferred unless, for instance, the grain is nonaxial, the work is slender, or the cut is a finishing one. However, as explained in point 6 above, even finishing cuts should be positive.

8. Turning should be rhythmic. Take sure, steady cuts, not a greater number of rushed ones with the attendant risk of slips or dig-ins. Once correct tool penetration has been made, watch the profile being cut rather than the cutting edge of the tool. Correct tool action gives properly shaped curves which flow smoothly and are free from bumps, dents, and unintentional straight sections. Surface finish is good with freedom from bruising caused by high bevel heel pressure resulting from improper tool presentation, and sanding time is minimised.

9. During the spindle turning process, tools rest with their handles under the bed or on the bed with their blades on the bench behind. They should lie at right angles to the lathe bed so that their points will not knock against the banjo, which should be similarly directed. The tools may be grouped to either the left or right of the tailstock depending on the length of the work. For some lathes, it may be wise to have a moveable wooden tray which will hold both tools and abrasive papers.

7.5 ROUGHING

Unless square sections are to be left (see Section 7.7), roughing will be the first turning operation. The tool is held in the overhand grip because of the long, lateral tool movements required. The left hand is on top of the gouge, which is in turn on its back and in contact with the toolrest. The fingers are usually straight and together, and thereby act as a shield preventing the turner being smothered in shavings (Figure 7.14). When roughing a slender spindle you should use the hand positionings described in Section 7.17. The gouge should be *cutting*.

The first objective is to cut away the corners of the square without splitting off long, dangerous splinters. To do this (see Figures 7.14 and 7.15), take a series of biting cuts starting at the tailstock end, each successive cut starting about 1⁵/₈ inches (40 mm) to the left of the previous one. For these biting cuts, the tool is pointed somewhat to the turners right (10° to 20°) so that the shavings will tend to be directed away. After each bite is taken, the tool is pushed through to the right-hand end of the work so that the diameter of the work is being continually reduced. Alternatively the biting cuts can be kept short and rapid without the gouge being pushed through to the workpiece's right- hand end.

If the series of biting cuts are continued, the final one would come into the left-hand end of the square from its left. The gouge would therefore tend to be jerked clockwise as the corners of the square contact the right-hand corner of the gouge. To avoid this, the last couple of biting cuts should be identical to the first couple, but transposed. The first of these cuts should therefore contact the wood about 1⁵/₈ inches (40 mm) from its left-hand end, and progress to the left.

Although it is more convenient for a right-handed turner to commence roughing at the right-hand end of the workpiece, the roughing can equally be commenced from the left-hand end.

After the corners have been cut off, take a series of full length lateral cuts alternately to the left and then to the right in order to bring the wood down to a cylinder. For these

Figure 7.14 Starting the third of a series of biting cuts. The angle of the gouge ensures that the bevel does not block the cut and deflects the chips to the turner's right. The overhand grip is used because of the long lateral tool movements and the straightened fingers also deflect the chips away from the turner. Roughing cuts should usually be forceful—you are trying to remove waste wood rapidly.

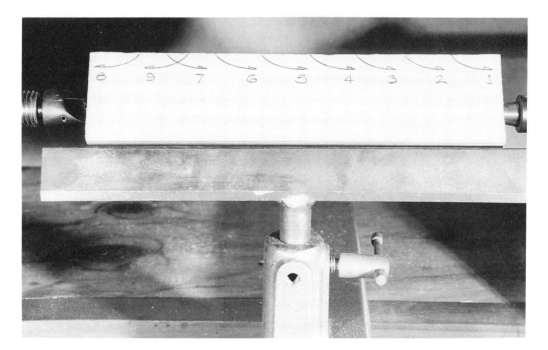

Figure 7.15 The recommended sequence for biting cuts. For a $1^{1}/_{4}$ inch (30 mm) half-round roughing gouge, the spacing of the cut starts is about $1^{5}/_{8}$ inches (40 mm). This spacing will vary according to the gouge's flute radius.

lateral cuts, the tool should again be pointed 10° to 20° off square (see Figures 5.5 and 7.16) in the direction of cutting. These cuts should not be started into the end of the workpiece as the wood will splinter and the gouge will tend to be grabbed. To equalise wear on the gouge's cutting edge, rotate the tool during each cut, or preferably use the cutting edge at the base of the flute to remove the corners, and reserve the cutting edges at the ends of the left- and right-hand flanges for finishing cuts (Figure 7.17).

As the work approaches a true cylinder, its outline will become less blurred, particularly that of the underside (a further reason for not having the toolrest too close to the work). You can feel to determine whether any flats remain. This is done using the left hand, which is held palm-up underneath the rest and the work. The fingers may then be brought quite safely into contact with the back of the rotating wood (Figure 7.18). On no account should the hand be on top of the wood or there is the risk of your thumb being pulled down between the toolrest and the wood. At the stage where you just cease to see a blur, the wood may not yet be quite round and it may be necessary to reduce its diameter by about another $^1/_8$ to $^1/_4$ inch (3 to 6 mm) depending on the wood diameter.

In many instances, you just wish to rough the workpiece down to the largest possible true cylinder. In other cases you may wish to rough to a definite diameter, and do this by holding the roughing gouge in the right hand, palm-down roughly over the ferrule so that the tool is in reasonable balance. The forefinger is extended down the flute and the handle is located beneath the forearm (see Figures 6.6 and 7.19). The tool is thus held safely and firmly. The callipers are set to the desired diameter, and once the wood is reasonably close to diameter—within about $^1/_4$ inch (6 mm), which can be gauged by eye the callipers are pressed lightly against the back of the wood at the location to be callipered.

Figure 7.16 Roughing from right to left. Note that the tool is angled slightly in the direction of travel so that the bevel does not block the cut. The striking part of the hand is against the toolrest which thus acts like a fence to aid in achieving a constant diameter.

Figure 7.17   Taking a fine finishing cut with the cutting edge at the end of a flange applied with about 45° side rake. To further improve the macro cut surface, traverse the tool slowly along the toolrest.

Figure 7.18   Safely feeling whether the workpiece has been brought down to a cylinder. The thumb is safely on the nearside of the toolrest. The crisp line along the underside of the work shows that the wood is truly round or very close to it.

To bring the wood down to diameter, push the gouge *downhill* alternatively in from the left and then from the right, each time reducing the diameter slightly, until the callipers gently slip over the wood. Take care not to try to cut too steep-sided a hollow or the roughing gouge can be flipped over. To achieve a good surface finish in the bottom of the hollow, present the gouge with side rake as shown in Figure 7.19. (I point the gouge to the left both for cuts from the left and from the right). Surface damage will be caused if the callipers are pressed firmly onto the wood.

If a particular diameter is desired after sanding it is necessary to calliper fractionally oversize. The work is callipered in as many spots as necessary and the remaining oversize wood cut away with lateral cuts of the roughing gouge. To improve surface finish, the gouge should be skewed so that the cutting edges at the ends of the flanges are presented with 30° to 45° of side rake (Figure 7.17). This will necessitate the cut being taken a

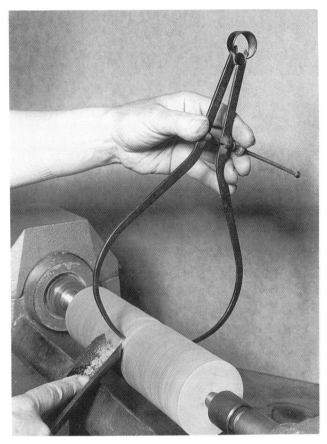

Figure 7.19 Callipering to diameter with the roughing gouge. The callipers are held so that the adjusting knob cannot loosen, and so that the calliper ends are at the back of the wood rather than on top and are thereby well clear of the tool tip.

little lower on the workpiece with the bevel heel just clear of the wood. If the workpiece's grain is not straight and axial or its diameter is large for the skews that you have, this finishing cut with the roughing gouge should be used instead of planing with a skew.

In addition to bringing the wood down to a cylinder, the roughing gouge will often be used for removing the bulk of the waste before and after marking out. It is also used for shaping long curves, either ready for sanding or, more usually, ready for final planing with a wide skew.

In Section 5.1 the differences between *cutting* and *scraping* were explained. It seems appropriate here that beginners should demonstrate for themselves proper *cutting* with a zero clearance angle. This desirable *cutting* action is frequently referred to as 'cutting with the bevel rubbing', a term which as explained earlier is convenient rather than accurate.

Begin by holding the roughing gouge on the toolrest with its flute facing upward and its blade at right angles to the wood. The tool handle should start low and then be raised slowly so that the back of the blade below the bevel starts to bounce on the rotating wood. Gradually draw the gouge axially backwards, keeping the blade in contact with the wood. The contact point between the tool and the wood will thereby be transferred from the uniform section of the blade, along the bevel, and to the cutting edge. When the tool just starts to take a shaving, then that is *cutting* (Figure 7.20), and you will notice that you

Figure 7.20 Shavings are just starting to be taken. This is true *cutting*.

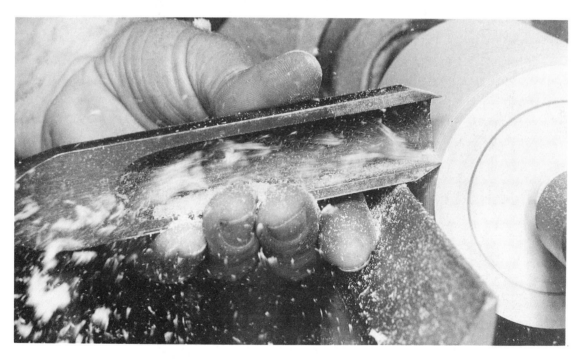

Figure 7.21 There is now a substantial clearance angle between the bevel and the wood surface. However, as there is still a positive rake angle, this is approximately midway between true *cutting* and true *scraping*.

only have to apply an axial push to the tool. Continue to draw the tool slowly backwards, at the same time raising the handle. The cutting will become noisier, the sweet feeling felt through the tool will disappear, and you will have to start to exert leverage as bevel support is lost. This latter sub-optimum form of cutting (Figure 7.21) should be avoided because tool control is more difficult, the wood removal rate is reduced, the surface finish is poorer, and tools blunt more quickly. To take proper heavier cuts, the tool will need to be held at a very slightly shallower angle than in Figure 7.20 and the axial thrust will need to be increased.

When the wood's grain is adverse, to lessen subsurface damage you should traverse the tool more slowly, and take finer cuts with more side rake. You can also use the technique of backcutting in which the tool is presented as if it is to be traversed along the toolrest, say from left to right, but is instead traversed in the opposite direction. The tear-out is reduced with backcutting because the cutting tends to be radially inwards rather than radially outwards.

7.6   V-CUTS

V-cutting is an essential but neglected area of turning practice. Non-decorative V-cuts are usually made to produce a face (as in the face of a shoulder or of a section left square), to create space for other cuts, or to define a point (such as the intersection of a bead and a fillet).

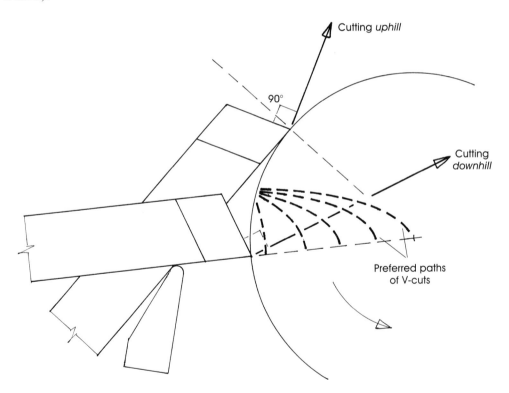

Figure 7.22   V-cutting showing how the skew's inclination affects whether the cutting action is *uphill* or *downhill*. The preferred arcing paths of the long point are shown. With such paths it is easier for the long point to finish exactly at the required point on the radius joining the lathe axis to the top of the toolrest. This is because during the latter part of a cut the band of cutting edge support will act like a skate as it is in line with the path of the long point.

V-cuts are almost always performed using a skew chisel resting on its long edge. The action a should be a crisp, rhythmic, swing-push. Because the cutting is performed with the long point and because the cutting edge faces 'upwards', you might think that the cutting action is to an extent radially outwards or *uphill*. As Figure 7.22 shows, this is only so when the skew's handle is very low. Therefore V-cutting is generally *downhill*, and always so except sometimes at the start.

It may be thought that a chamfer is equivalent to the side of a V-cut. It isn't. The chamfer should be a finished surface and should be cut with the short point.

7.7   LEAVING SQUARES

Unturned, left-square sections (squares) are often left on turnings such as table legs and stair balusters. The skew chisel is used to square-cut the ends of squares, either before or during roughing. A large, square, cross-section workpiece even when symmetrically mounted can cause significant lathe vibration. If so it is wise to do the majority of the roughing first to lessen vibration, then V-cut to form the end(s) of the square(s), then complete the roughing.

The preferred method uses a series of increasingly deeper deepening cuts. The bottoms of the deepening cuts should create a rough cone, its top surface descending at about 35° to the vertical (Figure 7.23). Therefore the first of a series should start about one sixth of the side width of the workpiece to the waste side of the intended end of the square.

You should present the skew on its long edge with its bevel facing the end of the square remaining almost in a plane perpendicular to the lathe axis throughout each cut

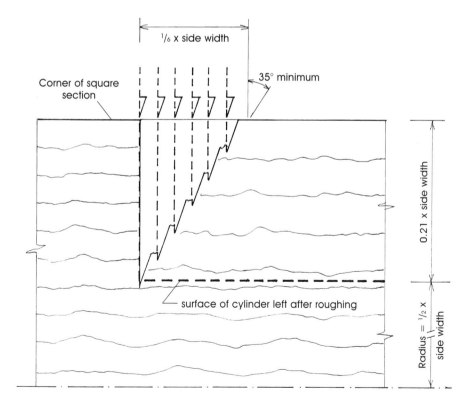

Figure 7.23   A radial longitudinal section through a corner of a square showing the geometry of the deepening cuts used to cut the end of a square.

(Figures 7.25 and 7.26). I say 'almost' because the bevel needs to be tilted away from the vertical by just 1° to 2° to give clearance. Similarly the facing bevel heel adjacent to the long edge should just avoid brushing the vertical face of the cut.

The cuts are swing pushes and should be performed smoothly, crisply, and rhythmically. They should have intent. You should not give up on them. If the action is correct you will not have to force them. The first cut produces little more than a deep nick. Succeeding cuts increase in depth.

You usually want to take the bottom of the last V-cut to just below the surface of the square. As the series of cuts proceeds, the cuts will feel more continuous; also the narrowest diameter of the cone will look less blurred. But particularly with single, larger workpieces, you should stop the lathe and check progress.

To aid in maintaining the skew's presentation throughout each cut, the cut must be basically performed by the left hand. The skew is held in the tied-underhand grip. The left hand should be started well back, and arcs forward and up,

Figure 7.24 V-cutting the end of a square. Towards the end of the final cut. The bevel is almost perpendicular to the lathe axis to allow just the minimum clearance for the left-hand bevel heel and up the cutting edge.

keeping in the plane perpendicular to the lathe axis (Figures 7.27 and 7.28).

The cuts are exacting. Too much bevel clearance and too thick a shaving are frequent causes of trouble. As early in the deepening cuts you are mainly cutting air, the lathe should be run at a safe speed, but one which is not overly slow. Sometimes the corners of the square are splintered away, there being no supporting wood behind the corners. As Figure 7.22 showed, if the handle is too low at the start of a cut the cut is in part radially outwards. Therefore the handle should not start too low before arcing forwards. Typically the long edge will rotate in side elevation through about 30°, but should not be taken past the radius connecting the lathe axis to the top of the toolrest as this will generate unnecessary frictional heat without materially increasing penetration.

If the corners of the square are dubbed over, its vertical face is rippled and even lightly charred, and the tool bounces with increasing severity during the cut, the likely cause is an inactive left hand. An inactive left hand merely allows the right-hand-controlled blade to slide through it, and the critical bevel presentation alters thereby causing increasing bevel heel contact.

After the end of the square is formed, it can be made convex with a skew's long or short point, or with a detail gouge (Section 7.14). The corners of the square can also be decorated with cavettos or ogees (Figure 7.71). A much softer junction between a cylin-

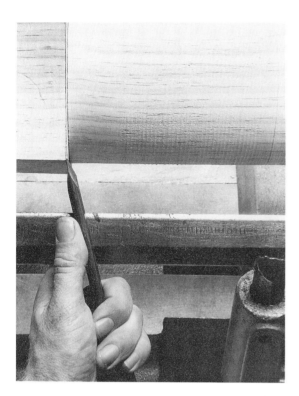

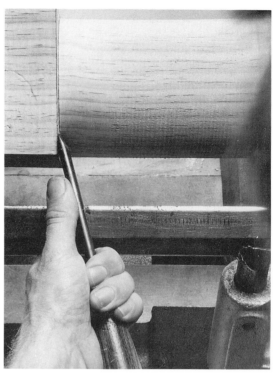

Figure 7.25   The hand and chisel position at the start of a V-cut for forming the end of a square. Note the mark on the toolrest to the right of the skew blade.

Figure 7.26   The completion of the cut started in Figure 7.25. The hand has thrust forwards in a direction square to the lathe axis. This has caused the contact point between the blade and the toolrest to move to the right to the mark on the toolrest (Figure 7.25), and the left-hand bevel to remain in the correct, almost perpendicular, presentation

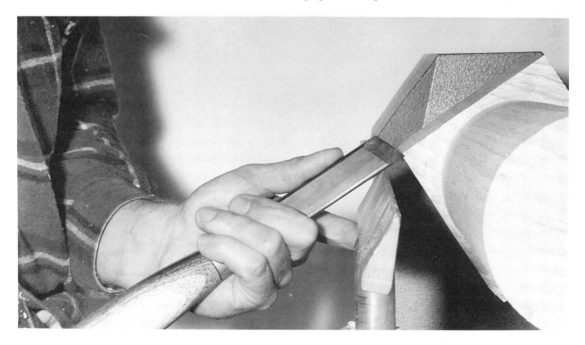

Figure 7.27   The tool and left-hand position at the start of a V-cut. The left hand is well back.

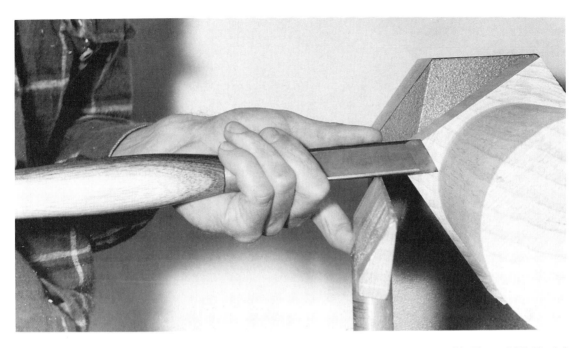

Figure 7.28   The tool and left-hand position at the completion of the V-cut started in Figure 7.27. The left hand has arced forward, keeping in a plane exactly perpendicular to the lathe axis.

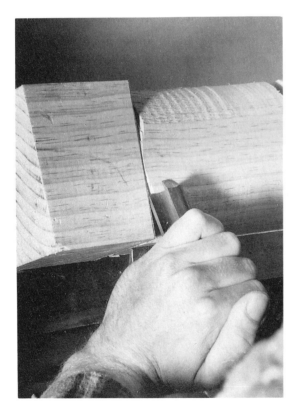

Figure 7.29   Starting a roughing cut adjacent to a square. The tool is perpendicular in plan to the lathe axis and fully on its side.

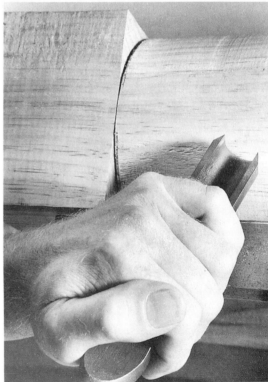

Figure 7.30   The roughing cut started in Figure 7.29 continuing. Once a tool presentation similar to that in Figure 7.16 is reached, it will be retained for the rest of the cut.

der and a square can be made by connecting the two by only a half hollow turned with a detail gouge.

After the end of the square has been cut, you can rough away from it with a roughing gouge (Figures 7.29 and 7.30). When starting to rough away from the face of a square, the gouge should be presented with its flute facing the square, its blade perpendicular in plan to the lathe axis, the top edge of its lower flange in light contact with the square, and the end of the cutting edge adjacent to the square lying horizontal. The gouge is then axially rotated away from the square and moved laterally along the toolrest while being adjusted into the normal roughing gouge roughing presentation.

7.8   THE PLANING CUT

The planing cut is used in two main situations. The first and less important situation is to true and plane the surface of a cylinder after roughing but before marking out. Because of the tear-out caused by nonaxial grain, this cut is sometimes dispensed with; also, full-diameter sections can be individually skimmed during the detailed turning. The second and major role of the planing cut is to enable smooth, long curves to be produced. In this role, it is far superior to gouges, and should leave a smooth, even surface. Take care, however, not to cut *uphill*.

Most general turning is done using about a l-inch (25-mm) skew. Where a constricted space dictates using a smaller size, you must decide whether to use a small skew for the whole job or two differently sized skews. Where there is a large proportion of planing in the work, you might favour using two skews, for planing is best done using a wide skew so that both points can easily be kept clear of the wood.

In the planing cut, the skew is used with its supporting bevel almost tangential to the surface of the wood and the cutting edge at about 45° side rake (Figures 7.31 and 7.32). An inferior surface finish will be left on interlocked or nonaxially grained timber unless the cuts happen to be fairly steeply downwards. As in roughing, the overhand grip is used.

Sensitive control, which is one of the joys of using the skew, is affected by slightly varying the presentation of the tool to the work. To take a deeper cut, merely raise the handle. To increase the downhill gradient of the cut, slightly steepen the angle of the cutting edge by rotating the tool. To minimise tearing-out, swing the handle backwards so that the cutting edge is at about 60° side rake and reduce the depth of cut.

The sometimes recommended step of raising the toolrest for the planing cut is unnecessary and time consuming. Merely lower the handle so that the tool is correctly presented with the honed toe of the bevel supporting the cutting edge at zero clearance. Note that the heel of the bevel must be kept just clear of the wood or else the tool will tend to bounce.

The full length of the cutting edge can be used except for the long and short points. If the long point is buried, the shaving is only partially severed and pushes the long point down into the wood resulting in a deep tear, and the blade is banged down onto the toolrest. Cutting within the bottom two thirds of the edge avoids this. If the short point is buried, the action while safe becomes more of a riving one, and splinters, not shavings, will tend to be taken and the surface finish may be inferior.

You should not start planing inwards from the end of a workpiece or a shoulder as the wood will tend to splinter out. The tool will also be grabbed if its presentation is not perfect. So start planing say 2 inches (50 mm) in, and plane the area missed when traversing in the opposite direction.

A cabinetmaker's bench plane can also be used for planing, but only for straight or uniformly tapering sections. The plane blade is used similarly to the skew, namely at 45° side rake and with both blade corners free of the wood.

Figure 7.31 Planing from right to left with a l-inch (25-mm) skew. The overhand grip is used because long lateral tool movements are required. Both the long and short points are kept clear of the wood.

Figure 7.32 Planing from left to right. The heel of the lower bevel is only just clear of the work.

Figure 7.33   Near the completion of the planing cut shown in Figure 7.32 the tool is pushed axially forwards so that the cutting slides down onto the short point by the time that the upstanding fillet is reached.

Surprisingly, hollows can be cut with a skew although firm control is necessary. The lower middle section of the cutting edge is used and it is essential that full cutting edge support be maintained, so exert plenty of axial thrust. In a repetitive situation where the finished surface is marred through contact with the corner where the bevel heel meets the long edge, it may be worthwhile grinding the offending corner away (see Figure 5.27), although it is already softened if you have a semicircular long edge.

Where a long curve is bounded or interrupted by a ring or similar upstanding projection, it is useful to modify the planing cut into what could be termed the *slide cut*. As you approach the projection with the skew planing, gradually slide the tool forwards along its axis so that when the projection is reached, the short point itself is cutting (Figure 7.33).

7.9   BEAD CUTTING

The conventional bead is a convex curve, often semicircular. It is usually, but by no means always, cut solely with the skew chisel. When the bead is limited by a fillet or other discontinuity, the skew is almost always used, the gouge being usually reserved for beads which flow without interruption into other curves.

Bead cutting is usually the next step after marking out from a pencil gauge or pin gauge. The process is twofold (Figure 7.34): first, to establish the width and depths of the bead by V-cuts; and by removing waste, to make room for the second stage, that of cutting the bead by a series of rolling cuts. For a bead with a radius of ½ inch (13 mm) in a medium hardwood, three V-cuts would be needed on each side, followed by three rolling cuts for each half of the bead. It is much easier to shape a bead properly, especially a large one, if both halves are shaped as far as possible together. In practice, the V-cuts would be completed on one side before those on the other side were done, but with the rolling cuts, there could be some alternation so that the overall bead shape could be monitored during its development.

There are two types of V-cutting: symmetrical and offset. Symmetrical V-cuts are used between adjacent beads (Figure 7.34) and often at the edges of isolated beads. Offset V-cuts are used alongside beads, curves or shoulders which are required to spring at right angles to the spindle axis (Figure 7.35), not at 12° to 15° shallower. Offset V-cutting is also used to cut the ends of squares (pommels) as described earlier in Section 7.7.

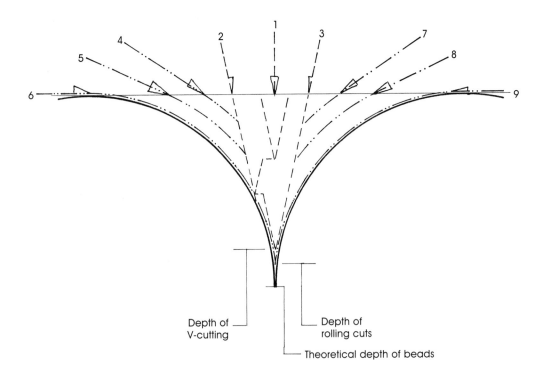

Figure 7.34   The V-cuts and rolling cuts required for a pair of adjacent semicircular beads: 1, 2, and 3 are V-cuts; 4 to 9 are rolling cuts. The inclinations and starting points of the skew's cutting edge at the start of each rolling cut are indicated. Note that the V-cutting finishes a little above the intended base of the beads. The second, left-hand V-cut is shown being started too far to the left, and shows how this leaves rough fillets in the grooves.

Symmetrical V-cutting

Your marking out should have defined the lateral extent of the bead. Your V-cutting must preserve that, plus define the bead depth, plus remove sufficient waste so that there will be room to perform the rolling cuts to follow. It is also important that the sides of your V-cuts are not angled too far apart otherwise they will remain as flat areas beneath the intended surface of the finished bead.

Figure 7.34 illustrates the V-cuts and rolling cuts for two adjacent halves of semicircular beads. Assuming that the edge projection sharpening angle of your skew (Figure 5.22) is 25°, the minimum angle at the cusp formed by the bases of the two beads is also nominally 25°. This cusp angle influences the geometry of the beads in Figure 7.34 which are nominally intended to be semicircular. It also suggests that your V-cutting should ideally stop a touch short of the bottoms of the final rolling cuts in Figures 7.34 and 7.35 so that the whole finished surface of each half bead can be formed in a single, final, rolling cut.

All V-cuts are made using the long point with the skew's long edge supported on the toolrest. For the first in a series of symmetrical V-cuts (Figure 7.36), the tool is at right angles to the lathe axis, the long edge is flat on the toolrest, and the sides are vertical. The long point is positioned above the mark signifying the outer edge of the bead, or the cusp between two beads, and the handle is swung up and forwards smartly so that the point sweeps down into the wood. Typically the long edge overhanging the toolrest will be swung down through about 30° during V-cuts until it points at the lathe axis. (Figures 7.27 and 7.28 show a swing-push cut in elevation). Continuing the cut further will barely increase penetration while creating unneeded heat and crushing.

The number of further V-cuts now required will depend on the depth of the bead and the hardness of the wood, but two is most usual. The first of them may be taken from the

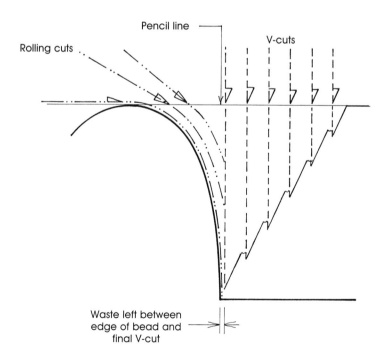

Figure 7.35 The offset V-cuts and rolling cuts for a steep bead. The final V-cut should finish a touch above the base of the bead and leave a small thickness of waste ($^1/_{16}$ inch (1.5 mm) or less) on the side of the bead which will be cut away by the rolling cuts.

Figure 7.36 Completing a first symmetrical V-cut. The cut raises feathering on each side, but does not remove any wood.

Figure 7.37 The second symmetrical V-cut from the left in progress. During the cut the left hand moves very slightly to the right as it arcs forward.

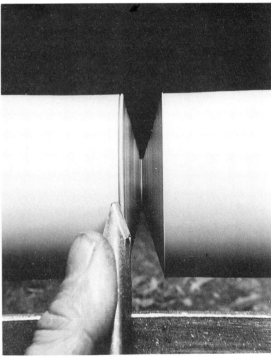

Figure 7.38 The third V-cut in the series shown in Figure 7.36 and 7.37.

Figure 7.39 Starting a deep V-cut from the left.

left or right. Where the bead is isolated this second V-cut is often taken on the side adjacent to the bead as there is then little likelihood of V-cutting below the intended final bead surface if the third V-cut is the final one of the series. Similarly where there will be more than three V-cuts down the side of an isolated bead, the penultimate one should be taken on the bead side of the vee groove.

Assume that the symmetrical V-cuts are being taken on the right-hand side of an isolated bead; the second V-cut of the three should therefore be taken to the left of the first (Figure 7.37). For this cut the skew should again be presented with its blade at right angles in plan to the lathe axis, and should be supported on its long edge. The sides however should not be vertical, but tilted about 5° anticlockwise. The long point should be poised to sweep into the wood immediately to the left of the feathering raised by the first V-cut. As in Figures 7.27 and 7.28, the chisel should be swung and pushed

Figure 7.40 Completing the cut started in Figure 7.39. The presentation of the cutting edge is still the same. The blade has remained square to the lathe axis in plan, therefore the left hand has thrust forwards and to the right.

crisply and rhythmically through an arc of about 30° until the long edge points to the lathe axis. Ideally throughout the cut the blade should remain tilted at about 5° and be at right angles in plan to the lathe axis. The contact point between blade and toolrest should therefore move slightly to the right during this cut.

Assuming that your third V-cut (Figure 7.38) is from the right, it should start a little further outside the feathering than did the second V-cut. It is performed in the same way as the second, except that the blade is axially tilted about 5° clockwise from the vertical. Again the blade should be swung through a vertical arc of about 30° and should remain tilted and at right angles to the lathe axis throughout the cut. As shown in Figure 7.34, the final V-cut should not quite penetrate to the intended base of the bead.

Common V-cutting faults are to be jerky, ponderous, or timid. You should not attempt to lever the shaving out—it will come away cleanly unless you give up before finishing the cut. Neither is there any need to curve the cut. Many turners cut a vee which has an unnecessarily large included angle. This is due to not having the blade at right angles to the axis in plan, but having it pointing say somewhat right-to-left during a V-cut from the right and vice versa.

If required, further V-cuts are performed similarly to the second and third described above (Figures 7.39 and 7.40). If a noticeable fillet or ruff is left towards the bottom of a V-cut at the finished depth of the previous one, it merely signifies that the later cut was a little thick (Figure 7.34).

Offset V-cutting

With deep beads, there is a tendency for symmetrical V-cutting to wander so that the base of the bead as defined by the final V-cut could be displaced either to the left or right of its proper position. To overcome this use offset V-cutting.

The procedure for the deepening cuts used in offset V-cutting is detailed in Section 7.7. If you are offset V-cutting to the right of a bead, the skew's facing (left-hand) bevel should start and remain almost in a plane perpendicular to the lathe axis. The cuts are swing pushes with the left hand doing the work.

If it looks as though your V-cutting will go too deep, merely stop your V-cuts at the appropriate depth. If it looks as though you will not go deep enough, go back and deepen the later cuts on the cone or start another series further away from the face of the bead.

An inferior alternative to the offset V-cutting method detailed in Section 7.7 is to tilt over the symmetrical V-cutting procedure. This involves using vertical deepening cuts down the bead edge, alternating with sloping clearing cuts to remove waste (Figure 7.76).

Rolling Cuts

Beads can be cut with either the long or the short point of a skew, a parting tool, or a detail gouge. Normally, however, the short point of the skew is preferred because:

1. It cuts *downhill* with side rake and therefore leaves an excellent surface finish. The long point tends to cut either *uphill* or with less side rake (Figure 7.22), thereby lifting the ends of the wood fibres and leaving an inferior, porous, surface finish.
2. If the cutting is performed by the short point, the width of the shaving is tiny and only a low severance force is required. But a bead can be planed. For bobbin- or sausage-shaped beads it is preferable to plane at the start and gradually slide the tool forward as the steepness of the cut increases so that you are cutting on the short point towards the end. However, for beads which are not wide in comparison with their heights, rolling cuts performed entirely on the short point are best.
3. To use either the parting tool or a detail gouge requires an unnecessary tool change. The geometry of many parting tools does not facilitate rolling cuts, and the upstanding flanges of a detail gouge require excessive clearance. However, either of these tools, or better a narrow skew, would be needed to roll, say, the right-hand half of a bead immediately to the right of a square section.
4. Rolling with the long point gives greater visibility to the area where cutting is taking place. However once a rolling cut is started, you should be watching the top of the cut and monitoring the profile being cut rather than be watching the cutting point.
5. The straight cutting edge of a skew receives more reference support than can the curved edge of a gouge.

It is the rolling cuts which are the main cause for the skew's ill-deserved notoriety. They require simultaneous lateral, vertical, and rotational movements of the cutting point, plus lateral movement of the blade along the rest. Needless to say, they need to be taken slowly and require considerable practice so that the proper coordination of these individually simple component movements can be consistently achieved.

Consider the three rolling cuts necessary to complete the right-hand half of the bead in Figure 7.34. The objective is to roll three cuts of even thickness. When the profile left after a rolling cut is correct, the next cut is made much simpler because the forces which the turner has to apply increase evenly through the cut and because the tool will tend to follow the profile of the previous cut.

Correct gripping and tool presentation during each rolling cut is critical and is illustrated in Figures 7.41 to 7.44. The tool should first be gripped with the right hand after positioning the tool as it should be at the completion of a final rolling cut, that is, on its short edge with its sides vertical. Use the shaking hands or tennis grip with the vee

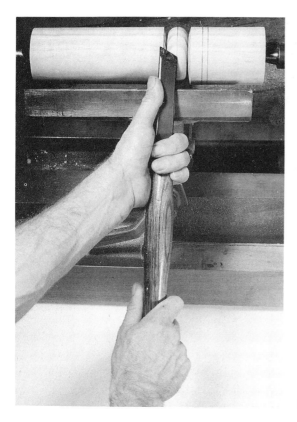

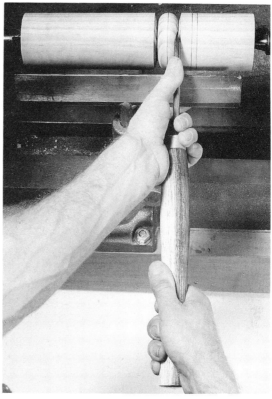

Figure 7.41 Starting a final clockwise rolling cut. The right wrist is strained. The left wrist is fairly straight. In plan the blade is angled slightly behind .

Figure 7.42 Completing a final clockwise rolling cut. The sides of the blade have rotated 90° to become vertical. The right hand has reached its unstrained position and pushed the handle up and forwards. The left wrist has hinged backwards as the left forearm thrusts to the right, thereby also moving the hand along the toolrest.

between the thumb and forefinger on top of the handle (Figure 7.42). This right hand grip should be retained without adjustment throughout a period of bead rolling. Thus when you start a rolling cut your right hand will feel strained (Figures 7.41 and 7.43). It will therefore want to axially rotate the skew into a position in which it is less- or unstrained (Figures 7.42 and 7.44). With an average length of handle, the hand should be positioned towards the handle's rear end.

For clockwise rolling cuts the tied-underhand grip should be as shown in Figure 7.41. The thumb should be slightly arched with only the pad at its tip in contact with the long edge. If the full length of your thumb is in contact with the long edge, the vee between thumb and forefinger tends to become locked under the bottom edge of the tool-rest. The tool should be gripped into the palm with the fingers. Some turners have a tendency to grip the blade entirely between the thumb and fingers, an inferior variant which is less secure, but less demanding of wrist and forearm work (Figure 6.5).

Inevitably when you first start to turn your grip will be far too tight. Once confidence is gained your grip should be an alive one. Imagine holding a little bird. When the bird is quiet your grip should be relaxed. If the bird starts to struggle your grip should tighten perceptibly. Your turning grip should be the same; relaxed, but alive to the need to tighten and exert greater force.

With practice, correct positioning and flexing of the left forefinger will become auto-

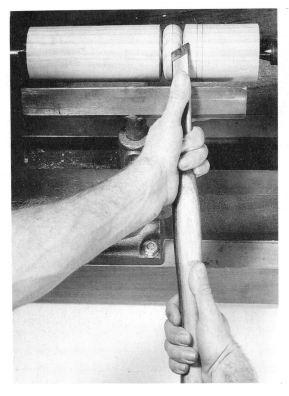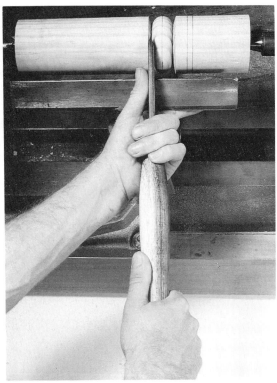

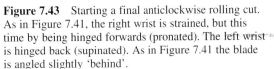

Figure 7.43 Starting a final anticlockwise rolling cut. As in Figure 7.41, the right wrist is strained, but this time by being hinged forwards (pronated). The left wrist is hinged back (supinated). As in Figure 7.41 the blade is angled slightly 'behind'.

Figure 7.44 Completing a final anticlockwise rolling cut. The left wrist has thrust to the left and down so that the back of the left hand now faces the lathe bed. The right hand has reached its unstrained position.

matic. For clockwise rolling it should start fairly straight and its tip should grip low on the far side of the toolrest. During a cut, the forefinger can largely control the movement of your left hand to the right.

The common errors in bead rolling will be discussed in detail later. The two most prevalent are: not to keep rolling through the cut; and to allow a clearance angle, either through lack of axial thrust or through a starting presentation with the short point too low on the wood. Therefore, your presentation of the short point should not be at too steep an inclination, nor be too low on the wood. To be safe, it is better to have the starting inclination of the cutting edge too flat (you can safely steepen it); also if you present the short point too high, you can bring it down until it just starts to cut, at which point it is at the correct height. The starting inclinations for rolling cuts are indicated in Figure 7.34, and those for both clockwise and anticlockwise rolling cuts are shown in Figures 7.45, 7.47, and 7.51.

Another ingredient for a correct starting presentation is to angle the short edge so that it is a little (less than 5°) behind being at right angles to the lathe axis in plan (Figures 7.41 and 7.43). There is no advantage in angling it further back because you will then have to move the blade further along the toolrest during the cut. Where the short point contacts the wood at the starts of rolling cuts are indicated in Figure 7.34, and appear as pencil lines in Figure 7.45.

If your starting presentation has been correct, the cut should proceed without incident provided that:

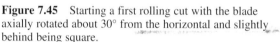

Figure 7.45 Starting a first rolling cut with the blade axially rotated about 30° from the horizontal and slightly behind being square.

Figure 7.46 Completing a first rolling cut. Even with so small a cut the blade has rolled and moved along the toolrest.

1. You take the cut slowly. This allows time for you to coordinate the simple component actions. By watching the top of the bead rather than the short point, you will be able to monitor progress and adjust if necessary.
2. You roll continuously.
3. You keep the short point high on the wood. If you thrust too much, you will feel and hear the bevel bounce and you should then allow the short point to come back towards you a touch. If you exert insufficient axial thrust a clearance angle will start to open, the prelude to one of the dreaded spiral dig-ins.
4. You work particularly your left wrist and forearm. Although both hands must work together, the left hand should dominate and powers the blade rotation and the movement along the toolrest.
5. You steadily move the tool along the toolrest. If the half bead you are cutting is bounded by another, at the end of the final rolling cut the blade should have its sides vertical and be at right angles to the lathe axis in plan. Therefore in plan the blade should be at or near right angles to the lathe axis throughout a rolling cut. If the base of the bead is required to be vertical, at the end of the final rolling cut the skew's blade will need to be rotated past the vertical about 5° because of the interference angle (see Section 5.4), and the handle will need to be taken further along the toolrest until the facing bevel is at right angles to the lathe axis (see Figure 7.50).

The action of the left hand in clockwise rolling bears further elaboration. At the start

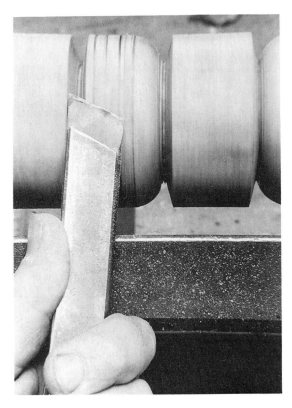

Figure 7.47   The start of the third rolling cut for the right-hand side of a bead. The skew is angled about 5° behind the cut so that the extreme end of the cutting edge is presented to the wood, not the end of the short edge.

Figure 7.48   Halfway through the third rolling cut. The left wrist and thumb are rotating the skew clockwise and moving it laterally along the toolrest. The right hand is playing the minor role, steadying and pushing the handle forwards, upwards and to the right, and not resisting the tool rotation.

of a cut the wrist is approximately straight. To achieve the required axial rotation of the skew the forearm must thrust to the right. This will aid the movement of the skew along the tool rest and cause the wrist to bend back or supinate.

Throughout rolling cuts the left upper arm should hang down comfortably and the left elbow barely moves. Cutting should take place about in line with the right-hand side of your body, so ensure that your body is in the proper position before you start.

The path of the short point and tool when performing anticlockwise rolling cuts should be exactly the same as that for clockwise cuts except transposed. But the gripping and hand actions are somewhat different. The right-hand grip should not have altered since the start of the series of rolling cuts, therefore the right wrist should be pronated at the start of an anticlockwise rolling cut (Figure 7.43). The left hand though will need to regrip (see Figure 7.43) unless the previous cut was anticlockwise roll. The top pad of the thumb should be in contact with the skew's upper side. This will cause the back of your left hand to face approximately horizontally to your left at the start of the cut, and your wrist to be hinged back. A powerful pulling action with the left forearm should then cause the wrist to straighten and then pronate. At the completion of a full roll, the back of the hand should face the lathe bed (Figure 7.44). The left forefinger should be bent at the start of anticlockwise rolling cuts.

Few turners who have attempted bead rolling with the skew will not have experienced the dreaded spiral dig-ins. Some turners have such a problem with them that they

Figure 7.49 The completion of a final (here third) clockwise rolling cut as if it was made between two beads. The left hand has not let go. The skew's blade is perpendicular to the lathe axis and has its sides vertical. The right hand has reverted to its relaxed position.

Figure 7.50 The completion of a final clockwise rolling cut for a bead with a vertical base. Rolling has continued to overcome the interference angle, and the sides have therefore rolled about 5° past the vertical. Also to ensure clearance for the lower, left-hand bevel heel, the handle has continued to move to the right. The extra component of the cut between Figures 7.49 and 7.50 is quite demanding.

become paranoid and will use their skews only for sharpening pencils. Fortunately the causes of dig-ins and other problems with the skew are both understandable and can be overcome. Below I explain the main causes which can occur both singly and in combination:

1. A common error is not to exert sufficient axial thrust on the skew. If the thrust is insufficient the skew is pushed back towards you and a clearance angle starts to open so that cutting edge support lessens. The shaving force then dominates and the skew spirals back up the bead.
2. Allied to point 1 is presenting the short point too low on the wood. You therefore have minimal cutting edge support from the start. To get out of trouble you should thrust forwards which will push the cutting edge up until the shaving and support forces balance. Unfortunately you tend to think that doing this will increase the probability of a dig-in and so don't take the proper corrective action.
3. When presenting a skew too low on the wood there is also the tendency to cut with an appreciable length of cutting edge, not just with the short point. As described earlier, beads can be planed, but high axial thrusts have to be applied because of the greater shaving width and therefore greater severance force

Figure 7.51   The start of a final anticlockwise rolling cut. The left hand has regripped after the clockwise rolling cuts. The pad of the thumb is now on top of the upper side of the blade so that the back of the hand faces to the left.

Figure 7.52   The completion of the cut started in Figure 7.51. During the cut the left wrist thrust down, and the left hand pulled down and under so that the back of the hand finished facing vertically downwards.

required. Furthermore the severance force has to be increased for a given shaving width during a roll because the severance force required for the end grain will be about double that for the cross grain.

4. Many turners have difficulty achieving a full axial tool rotation. To overcome this some have the tool rotated too much at the start and cut bevels rather than arcs and produce Gothic beads. However, if you start the cutting edge too steeply, and sometimes if you don't, you tend to reverse the skew's proper direction of rotation or continue the cut without rotation. In either case the result is the same, a sudden increase in shaving width and an inability to react quickly enough to increase the axial thrust to compensate for the extra severance force required. The tool is therefore forced backwards and the spiral dig-in begins.

5. Insufficient lateral movement of the tool along the toolrest causes the tool to 'pivot'. The short point cannot maintain contact towards the base of the bead and comes free.

6. Cutting edge support can be lost due to sudden excessive rotation of the cutting edge or because of too much lateral movement of the handle. This most commonly happens when rolling a steep face as in Figure 7.50.

Bead Rolling with the Long Point

Bead rolling with the long point leaves an inferior surface finish and is not therefore recommended. It is executed in a similar way to that with the short point, that is, with the

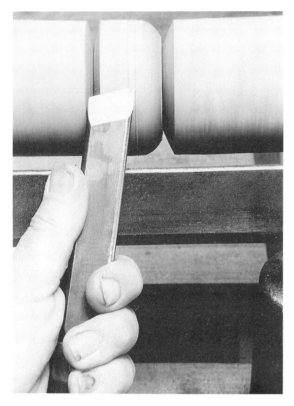 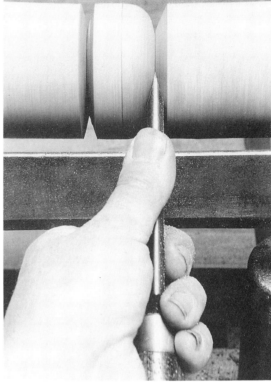

Figure 7.53   The start of a clockwise rolling cut using the long point. The hand grips and actions are virtually identical to those used when cutting with the short point.

Figure 7.54   Towards completion of the rolling cut started in Figure 7.53. For the base of the bead to be perpendicular to the lathe axis, the skew in plan would have to be swung 12.5° past the perpendicular, and the bevel would need clearance in a vertical plane.

cutting edge being rotated through successively increasing arcs, the final one usually being a full 90° roll (Figures 7.51 and 7.52). The cut is sometimes used to roll where a short point roll would cause the long point to foul say the right-hand end of a square section, but it is generally better to use a spindle detail gouge or a very narrow skew.

The long point also has another use in bead cutting—that of cutting out any ragged bits left, such as in the cusp between two adjacent beads.

7.10 CUTTING FILLETS

A common situation is two beads separated by a hollow with fillets separating the three curves. The waste between the two V-cuts can be removed with a parting tool or a detail gouge, but to save a tool change the skew is usually retained. A series of short, sloping slide cuts are taken from both the left and the right with the short point (Figures 7.55, 7.56 and 7.57). The tied-underhand grip is normally used, but for long cuts switch to the overhand grip.

For these cuts the whole tool is moved laterally, not pivoted about its initial contact point with the toolrest. By using a scooping action you will find it possible to cut the fillets horizontal even when the beads are fairly close together. You will need to exert a strong axial thrust on the skew, and support the upper part of the bevel heel on the cut surface to achieve the scoop. You will find it awkward to start the short point into the steep sides of earlier V-cuts, so when this becomes necessary switch direction. If your slide cut

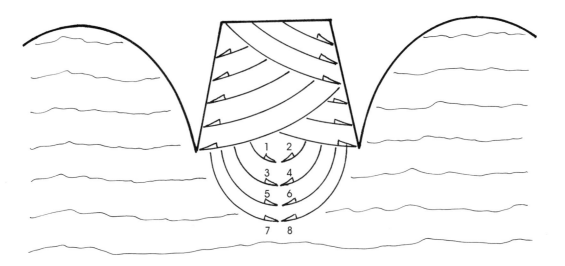

Figure 7.55   The slide cuts for cutting fillets, and the hollowing cuts for cutting a hollow.

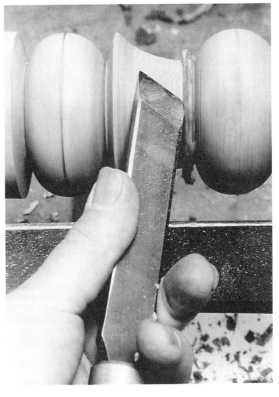

Figure 7.56   Starting a fillet-forming slide cut. The shaving is taken on the short point throughout. The side rake is 45°.

Figure 7.57   The completion of the slide cut started in Figure 7.56. The skew has been rotated anticlockwise, the axial thrust along the skew is strong, and the bevel heel back towards the long point is bearing on the recently cut surface to enable the spooning action.

is deeper than the bottom of the earlier rolling cut, a ruff of fibres will be left which will need to be cut away with a vertical cut with the long or better the short point. Care also needs to be taken not to contact, and hence spoil, the side of the bead above the intended fillet.

7.11 REMOVING WASTE WITH THE SKEW

The elevation of an edge of a skew is similar to the side elevation of a parting tool, and indeed a skew resting flat on one of its sides can be used in a similar way. When you are callipering, the skew is held in the usual one-handed fashion under the forearm with its cutting edge parallel to the lathe axis and in the *cutting* position (Figure 6.6). During the cutting, the skew will tend to move to the right or left in the direction of the long point.

Skew chisels are not specifically designed for the role of parting; they are thinner than parting tools and do not have an antigrab cross-section. Wide skews should therefore not be used at long overhangs or in hard woods, but you could use just part of the width of the cutting edge adjacent to the long point (Figure 8.20).

7.12 SQUARING SHOULDERS

In Section 5.4 the technique of squaring a shoulder with the long point was used to illustrate the concept of the clearance angle. Squaring a shoulder is straightforward if the skew is sharpened and presented correctly. The tool should be supported on its long edge with the bevel facing the shoulder almost perpendicular to the lathe axis. The tool should not be flat on its long edge as the cutting edge will have too much clearance and will then tend to be pushed laterally deeper into the shoulder by the shaving. Therefore axially rotate the skew towards the shoulder to reduce the clearance to 1° to 2°. The long point should describe an arc as shown in Figure 7.22 with the long edge finishing pointing at the lathe axis. These cuts are basically the same as those used in leaving squares (Section 7.7) and offset V-cutting (Section 7.9).

The main problem beginners experience is heel-of-bevel bounce. As the tool arcs forward, a dominant right hand will cause the blade to become squarer to the lathe axis in plan, and this pushes the bevel heel against the shoulder.

Comparing Figures 7.25 and 7.26, you will see that to keep the bevel at right angles to the lathe axis, the contact point between the long edge and the toolrest has to move away from the shoulder during the cut. By starting the cut with the left hand well back from the toolrest (Figure 7.27), the hand and tool can be arced forward as a unit thereby automatically keeping the presentation correct (Figure 7.28).

The squaring can be made slightly convex by pushing the skew along a path curved in plan. If it is desired to undercut the shoulder, clearance must be retained by tilting the skew's cutting edge away from the shoulder and by angling the skew into the cut a little.

At first glance, it would be supposed that the long point cuts *uphill*. The analyses in Figure 7.22 show that the long point cuts *downhill* unless started very high on the wood, and there is hence no tendency to split away the peripheral fibres. The *downhill* cutting also explains the fine finish which this cut should leave.

7.13 PARTING TOOL WORK

The parting tool is used for quickly setting diameters after marking out, for removing waste, and for cutting pins. It is rarely used for parting-off because the finish left on end grain is very poor and because it tends to jerk the finished turning free from the waste rather than sever them gently apart.

When setting diameters, hold the callipers in the left hand (Figure 6.6). The tool is held in the usual one-handed grip with the right hand positioned near to the toolrest and over the blade, the forefinger on top of and pointing along the blade, and the handle beneath the forearm. Keep the tool tip high in the *cutting* position. To ensure that the tool is not grabbed by the sides of the channel being cut, the tool tip is rocked slightly from side to side quite quickly to widen the channel while being pushed up and forwards into the wood. Because the horizontal surface left at the bottom of a parting cut is poor, you may need to set the callipers a little oversize to allow for a later skimming cut and sanding. Also, as the sides of a parting cut tend to be torn out, when parting down alongside what is intended to be a finished surface, allow up to $^1/_8$ inch (3 mm) of waste which will be cut away separately with a finishing cut, usually with the long point.

7.14 USE OF THE DETAIL GOUGE

The detail gouge is often the last tool to be used in the spindle turning process, and is primarily used for cutting hollows (sometimes called coves). It is also used for softening and decorating the corners of squares (Figure 7.73), and for beads and convex profiles— usually those not bounded by fillets or similar.

Generally in spindle turning, you cut with the part of the gouge cutting edge just back from the extreme point, and the base of the flute is approximately tangential to the curve at the point where the cut is being taken at that instant (Figure 7.58). But note I say approximately tangential. The importance of cutting with side rake to improve the surface finish has been stressed. With a detail gouge square to the surface in plan, an axial rota-

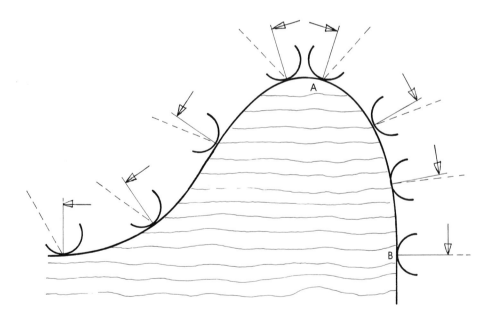

Figure 7.58 Detail gouge axial rotations when cutting curves. In order to cut with side rake and thereby achieve less subsurface damage, the gouge is generally tilted into the cut and *cutting* takes place on the leading edge of the nose. The fine lines are at 90° to tangents to the curve, the dashed lines represent the axial rotations of the detail gouge.

tion of the gouge of about 30° relative to the gradient being cut will achieve a 45° side rake. Therefore when cutting horizontally the gouge is axially tilted about 30°, this tilt being gradually reduced to zero as the surface being cut approaches the vertical.

The size of gouge selected should be the largest which can be used in the particular situation. Smaller gouges may be preferred when the wood is interlocked or slender, in which case the gouge should be used more on its side than usual, giving a more slicing action.

Cutting Hollows

The cutting procedure for hollows is indicated in Figure 7.55. The shape is developed gradually using cuts alternately from the left and right. Each cut is stopped when the bottom of the hollow is reached—carrying on up the other side leaves a poor surface finish (Section 5.1). Alas hollowing is not quite as straightforward as Figure 7.55 suggests, and I shall therefore start by looking at the final cut, say from the left, used to form a U-shaped hollow with a vertical side descending to a semicircular bottom. Figure 7.59 shows the preferred spindle gouge presentation during a long cut starting from the rim of the U, at the point where the vertical side ends and the semicircular bottom begins. At this point:

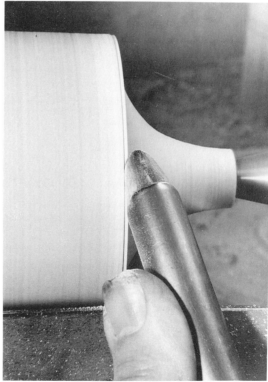

Figure 7.59 The gouge has cut down the vertical leg of half of a U-shaped hollow. The gouge is high on the wood with zero clearance and facing horizontally to the right. Although the cutting is taking place below the gouge tip, the deepest part of the cut is being taken at the very tip.

Figure 7.60 This inverted gouge presentation enables the bit of cutting edge which first contacts the wood to lie in a vertical plane perpendicular to the lathe axis and thus be stable.

Figure 7.61 Possible paths for the gouge tip to follow when cutting half a semicircular hollow. The upper path is preferred. The gouge is in the correct starting presentation for a final cut.

1. The flute is facing horizontally, here to the right.
2. There is zero clearance angle and the 'bottom' of the bevel is perpendicular to the lathe axis in plan.
3. Cutting is taking place on the lower part of the tool tip.

If the gouge presentation shown in Figure 7.59 is desirable when you are about to cut the semicircular bottom of a U-shaped hollow, it is surely equally desirable when starting one of the final cuts for a hollow which is just semicircular. Alas the likelihood is that if you attempt this, the gouge will lurch away from the hollow. This is because the part of the cutting edge which first contacts the cylindrical periphery of the workpiece is not the vertical part at the base of the flute. The part which contacts first is further back on the low side of the nose and will be inclined pointing upwards to the left. Further there will not be full cutting edge support. The edge will therefore act like an ice skate blade and lead the tool out of the cut before that part of the edge which will be used to cut the hollow has penetrated the surface and gained full cutting edge support.

You can overcome the problem by using the gouge starting presentation shown in Figure 7.60. After entry the gouge is then rolled anticlockwise into the Figure 7.59 position, and the cut then continued conventionally as will be described shortly. The problem with this Figure 7.60 presentation is that as the gouge is initially partially inverted, the relevant cutting edge is hidden and you cannot be sure of presenting it correctly. This problem can be overcome by using an alternative radial presentation.

The radial presentation alternative (Figures 7.61 and 7.62) enables you to achieve a certain and stable cutting edge entry for a final cut for a semicircular hollow. Three factors need to be correct:

1. The flute must point horizontally to the side so that the cutting edge at the tip of the gouge is vertical when it touches the wood.
2. That part of the bevel which will be actively used must lie at right angles to the lathe axis in plan.

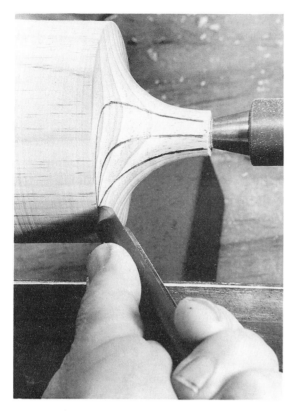

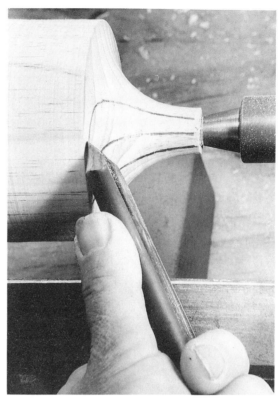

Figure 7.62   The normal and recommended starting presentation for a final cut from the left (cut 7 in Figure 7.55) for a semicircular hollow. The bevel is square to the lathe axis and the flute faces horizontally to the left. Note the position of the left hand and how it changes through the cut in subsequent Figures. The blade is slid forward through the left hand during the cut and rotated within it.

Figure 7.63   Shortly after correct entry. The tool tip has been strongly thrust up and forwards and blade axial rotation has barely started. To ensure that the bevel instep and heel do not crush the wood at the edge of the hollow, the contact point between blade and toolrest has moved to the right much as it should in offset V-cutting.

3. The axis of the gouge must point to the lathe axis. Therefore the handle must be held quite high.

If you do not have all three presentational factors correct, the tool is likely to lurch sideways as it contacts the wood because it will not obtain full cutting edge support, or because the active part of the cutting edge will not be vertically aligned. The most common error is not to raise the gouge handle sufficiently.

There are an infinite number of paths which the gouge tip can follow between the entry in Figure 7.62 and the cut's completion in Figure 7.66. Just three are pencilled onto the wood in Figure 7.61. The cutting action in the lowest path will tend to *scraping*. Many turners use a path similar to the middle one, but it still involves cutting with clearance. The top path is the ideal and has two components, the first flowing smoothly into the second.

The first component of the top path in Figure 7.61 is from entry to achieving a presentation similar to that shown in Figure 7.59. Figures 7.63 and 7.64 show how, and demand that:

1. Plenty of axial thrust is applied to the gouge. If too little thrust is applied, clearance opens and the tip will stutter.

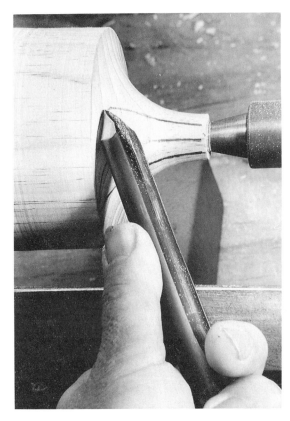

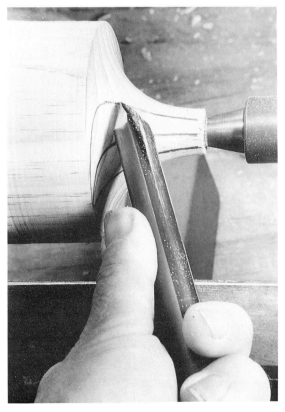

Figure 7.64 This is the highest point on the hollowing path. The tool tip is about to start its descent. Movement of the blade along the toolrest has stopped, but thrust and rotation continue.

Figure 7.65 Halfway down. The axial thrust is strong so that the tip is high on the wood with zero clearance. Anticlockwise axial rotation is continuing.

  2. As the nose is thrust forwards and up, the contact point between tool and toolrest moves here to the right such that the heel of the bevel does not move to the left. If this is allowed, the heel will contact the hollow's rim which becomes used as a fulcrum and is thereby crushed.
  3. As the nose is pushed up, the gouge is axially rotated, but only slightly.

Having thrust the gouge into the correct position from which to start the inward and downward component of the path, most of the battle is over. Figures 7.65 and 7.66 demonstrate the action. Strong thrust is required to maintain a zero clearance angle. A good surface finish is further facilitated by using a side rake presentation—at the completion of the cut (Figure 7.66) the flute is not facing vertically upwards, but is tilted at about 30° from the vertical in the direction of lateral nose movement.

At the completion of a final hollowing cut the blade is perpendicular to the lathe axis in plan. In plan therefore it has to perform an awkward scissor motion with the handle moving in the opposite direction to the nose, that is unless the hollow is wide and the toolrest close.

With intermediate cuts for hollows or final cuts for hollows shallower than semicircular, there is no easily definable starting presentation for the gouge tip. To achieve the stable presentation which has the first contacting bit of cutting edge lying in a vertical plane (that is with 90° side rake) you would have to have the flute facing below horizontal—as in Figure 7.60, but less extreme. The angle alpha in Figure 7.67 should also equal the angle beta. Although this inverted presentation assures a stable entry it is a demanding one to achieve.

The usually preferred method for hollowing cuts in which angle beta in Figure 7.67 is less than 90° has the flute facing above horizontal. There are no rules which will enable you to precisely position your gouge for the starts of such cuts, and even for experienced turners the risk of losing control is small but ever present. This risk is there because the bit of edge which first contacts the cylindrical periphery does not lie in a vertical plane.

Figures 7.62 to 7.66 show gouge tip presentations at reducing workpiece radiuses. These presentations can also be considered to form a spectrum of starting presentations for reducing values of angle beta (defined in Figure 7.67), and are the ones I recommend. In them angle alpha equals angle beta, angle delta is a maximum, and the side rake is always less than 90°. For a first hollowing cut (cut 1 in Figure 7.55) the side rake is typically between 45° and 60° depending on the geometry of the hollow.

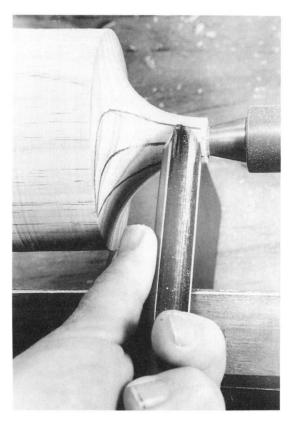

Figure 7.66 Completion of the cut. The blade is square to the lathe axis in plan (a position demanded when the hollow is deep), and rotated into the cut by about 30°.

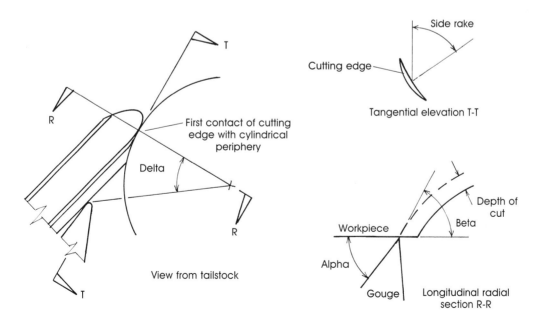

Figure 7.67 The start of a hollowing cut. The angles shown are referred to in the text.

Many turners opt for a lower value of angle delta. This should necessitate large tool movements similar to those in Figures 7.62 to 7.64 to get the tool tip onto the preferred upper cutting path and into a suitable presentation. To assist in such movements many turners lever the bevel off the edge of the hollow, which is not desirable for a final finishing cut as it causes crushing.

Although at the start of most hollowing cuts there is a risk of loss of control, it can be rendered minimal by:

1. Using the tied-underhand grip. The right hand should grip so that it is in the comfortable shaking-hands position when the tool is on its back with the flute facing vertically upwards. There are two choices with the left hand. When the tool is on its back, a neutral tied-underhand grip can be taken on the blade and is retained in much the same position on the blade throughout the hollowing. The more common, less secure but less straining alternative is to still use the neutral tied-underhand grip, but to allow the gouge blade to slide and rotate within the grip, which is however still actively supplying movement of the blade along the toolrest. Figures 7.68, 7.69 and 7.70 show the preferred high starting positions for cuts 1, 4, and 5 in Figure 7.55. Note the starting, second alternative grips and the grip as the gouge tip reaches the bottom of the hollow in Figure 7.71.

2. Being positive with the tool entry. A firm entry will help put the tool tip into the stable hollowing presentation before the unstable presentation at first contact with the cylindrical periphery has time to manifest itself.

3. Align the tool in plan so that your thrust along the tool blade counters the desire of the tool tip to move sideways. Therefore if cutting from the left, the tool han-

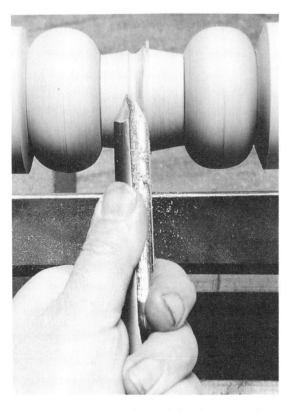

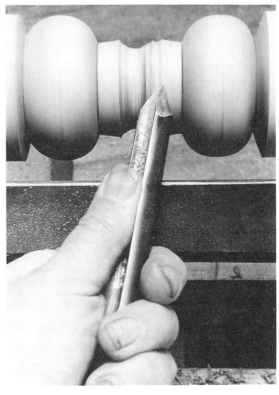

Figure 7.68   The start of a first hollowing cut, cut 1 in Figure 7.55.

Figure 7.69   The start of cut 4 in Figure 7.55.

Figure 7.70   The start of cut 5 in Figure 7.55.

Figure 7.71   The completion of the cut started in Figure 7.70.

dle is positioned further to the left than indicated in Figures 7.63 to 7.66. Such undesirable presentations result in crushing damage at the rim of the hollows.

4. Having your body in a position which assists firm control. Hollowing demands very large body movements to-and-fro along the lathe. Hollowing cuts from the right can even require your body to be positioned to the left of the headstock, so ensure that your feet are positioned as in Figure 6.1.

The details of hollowing have been covered. Overall the procedure is described in Figure 7.55. The first in a series of hollowing cuts (Figure 7.68) is started slightly to the side of the centre of the hollow, say to the left side. The flute should be angled between 40° and 70°, but typically 60°, clockwise from the vertical depending on the size and proportions of the hollow. With the cutting being done by the right-hand side of the nose, the gouge is thrust forwards and upwards into the wood and steadily rotated anticlockwise during the cut until the flute faces about 30° clockwise from the vertical when the intended centre of the hollow is reached (Figure 7.71). Cutting must not continue past the centre of the hollow, or it will be *uphill*.

A similar cut is then performed, but from the right of centre. A sequence of cuts, alternately from the left then from the right, is performed to both deepen and widen the hollow. Each cut is started with the tool rotated a little more onto its side than the one before from the same side. Also the tip is presented lower on the wood, and the blade is angled more across in plan. At the completion of each hollowing cut the flute faces about 30° from the vertical in the direction of tool movement, and the blade is square to the lathe axis.

Figure 7.72 Effectively increasing the flute diameter of a detail gouge to lessen macro surface rippling.

Other uses of the Detail Gouge

Detail gouges are commonly used to cut convex profiles. For this they are less suitable than skews, needing more room, leaving a more rippled macro cut surface, and cutting with less side rake. They are commonly used to roll the fronts of knobs (Figure 8.4, cut 11). At the start of such cuts (Figure 7.58, point A) the blade should be square or a little behind in plan. At completion (Figure 7.58, point B), the gouge must be in the presentation shown in Figures 7.61 and 7.62.

Planing-type cuts are sometimes performed with a detail gouge rather than a skew when the grain is non-axial. The cut is straightforward with the tool in plan approximately perpendicular to the lathe axis while being rotated about 30° from the vertical in the direction of cutting. Another useful technique for planing is to artificially increase the flute diameter by pushing or dragging the gouge with its axis not at right angles in plan but at about 30° to the wood surface (Figure 7.72).

As outlined in Section 7.7, a decorative and practical detail is to turn a cavetto or an ogee curve at the corners of sections left square (Figure 7.73). Take light but firm cuts with the gouge well on its side at the start of the cut. A simple ovolo may also be cut in a similar manner. A spindle gouge well on its side may also be used to round and thereby soften the sharp end of a square, although this is frequently achieved using a skew's short or long point.

There are two details in which the gouge is used with a quasi-scraping action. The first is a half hollow with a projecting shoulder at the bottom; the second is a downhill

Figure 7.73   Using the detail gouge to cut an ogee on the corner of a section left square.

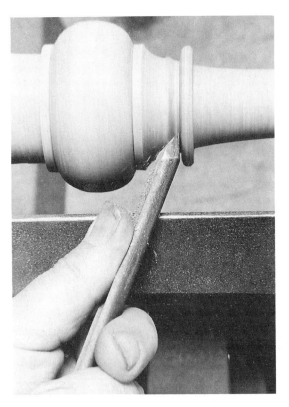

Figure 7.74 Immediately to the left of the ring, cutting is started with the tip of the nose and the flute facing horizontally to the left. As it clears the ring, the gouge is rotated clockwise to give a better cut.

curve starting from the base of a shoulder. In both cases the gouge is used fully on its side with a sort of scraping action using the end of the nose. In the first, you scrape *uphill* initially, (Figure 7.74); in the second, *downhill*. In each case, rotate the gouge into a proper cutting position as soon as possible.

7.15 PARTING-OFF

A spindle may be finish-turned, sanded, and then cut completely through close to its left-hand end with the lathe still running so that it falls free. This process, called parting-off, can be used only for smallish work which has no square at its left-hand end. Parting-off when cupchuck turning is trouble-free. With spindle turning, any axial force exerted by the tailstock can prevent the work falling free cleanly and safely.

If a spindle is to be parted-off, allow a sufficient length of waste (at least $1/2$ inch (13 mm)) at its left-hand end. After the spindle has been sanded, part-off at the right-hand end of the waste section. This can be done with a series of increasingly deeper V-cuts, with a parting-off tool, with a parting tool alone, or better with a parting tool followed by final V-cuts. As you approach severance, to allow the spindle to come free the tailstock is slackened sufficiently so that there is no axial pressure, yet the prongs of the driving centre still engage. A skew (preferably) is then held one-handed and its long point used to make a series of small V-cuts until the wood is fully parted through and can be caught by the left hand, which has to cross over the tool in order to be in position (Figure 7.75).

When you want to part-off solely with a skew leaving a vertical face on the end of the workpiece, a series of special leapfrogging V-cuts is used (Figure 7.76). The normal offset V-cutting procedure described in Figure 7.35 is unsuitable because towards the end, the small diameter of waste left will probably break as you attempt a final, full-depth, deepening cut. The leapfrogging cuts consist of offset deepening V-cuts alternating with clearing V-cuts. The deepening cuts are performed as described in Sections 7.7, 7.9 and 7.12, except that they are all performed down the same vertical plane. The clearing cuts are performed similarly (Figure 7.76), except that the blade is axially rotated away from the vertical face so as to cut a steep cone with the long point. This leapfrogging series can be used in place of normal offset V-cutting prior to cutting steep-sided beads, but is less efficient.

In Section 7.3 the professional method was described for mounting small and medium-sized work in the lathe while it is running. This is, of course, all in vain unless you can also remove work under the same situation. If the work has been parted-off and the waste has not dropped away, it can be nudged off with a tool bevel, taking care to not contact the driving centre prongs (which probably need deburring). When a square section is to be left at the left-hand end, the left hand holds the work loosely just to the right of the

Figure 7.75 Parting-off a small spindle using the long point of a skew chisel. The left thumb is braced onto the toolrest. The skew needs to be angled in plan so that the right-hand bevel heel does not contact the vertical end of the spindle.

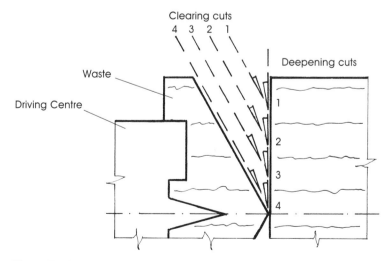

Figure 7.76 Offset parting-off V-cutting. A series of overlapping deepening and clearing V-cuts.

square section and pushes towards the tailstock as the latter is slackened. The procedure is similar with a fully turned workpiece which is not required to be parted-off. The left hand then closes onto the work as it ceases to be rotated by the driving centre. Sometimes, however, the work will not come off the prongs, and if the tailstock is slackened back any appreciable distance, the work can fly out of the lathe. Therefore, watch to see that the work comes free properly as the tailstock is retracted; if it does not, switch off the lathe before you remove the workpiece.

7.16 COPY TURNING

Copy turning is the production of numbers of turnings which are required to be identical. Most copy turning is now done on automatic lathes, but runs of 100 items and more are still quite commonly required from professional hand turners.

Although there are no special techniques involved in copy turning, it is undoubtedly one of the best ways to practice and improve.

If you measure up a set of hand-turned balusters, you will often find surprisingly large variations in diameters, but because they are seen as a whole in a building and not individually, the variations remain unsuspected. However, any variations in a pair of candlesticks would be noticed because they are more visible and people will tend to idly compare them if there is a delay in the meal. In short, make the items as identical as possible, but do not be unnecessarily exact when it is not warranted.

Decide upon the turning method and prepare the wood. Make the pencil or pin gauge and prepare the lathe and tools. Mount the first item turned (assuming it is satisfactory) close behind where the remaining items will be turned so that it can act as reference for comparison during the remaining turning. When turning, watch for and use relationships between adjacent details to aid consistency. Calliper as little as possible and rely on training your eye. Consider whether changes in the order of turning or in your technique can speed up the work.

7.17 SLENDER TURNING

A piece of spindle turning is slender if it tends to deflect when being turned or whips when no tool is in contact. Many blanks will bow during the turning process as internal stresses relax into a new equilibrium (Section 1.7), and this is often more troublesome than deflections due to their slenderness. Obviously, slender work is usually long in relation to its diameter, but short work of large diameter may become effectively slender if deep hollows are turned in it, particularly near the centre of its length. In this latter case, the effective diameter is small even though the average diameter may be large.

The symptoms of slenderness are that the wood may bounce under the tool, giving a rippled or diamond-patterned surface. There will be a tendency for tools to grab and for the wood to climb up over the noses of detail gouges.

Several methods can be used to alleviate the difficulties of turning slender workpieces, either alone or in combination:

1. Modify tool usage.
2. Minimise tailstock pressure.
3. Turn the work in an order which preserves stiffness for as long as possible.
4. Reduce the lathe's speed of rotation.
5. Hold the headstock end of the work rigidly in the line of the lathe axis, thereby effectively reducing slenderness.

6. Use one or more steadies.
7. Turn the work in sections rather than in one piece, or change the design to reduce slenderness.

In slender turning, you try to keep the work rotating as axially as possible. If heavy cuts are taken, the work has more tendency to bounce under the tool. Also, the work will have more tendency to climb up over the end of the tool. This is especially so with the detail gouge, so a skew is preferred where possible. If the use of a detail gouge is unavoidable, rotate it more into the cut so that the cut is being taken farther back on the side of the nose. This has two advantages: the wood has to deflect more to be able to climb over the nose, and the cut will be more of a slicing one, so tending to deflect the work less.

If tailstock pressure is high, the tendency will be for the wood to shorten by bowing, exactly what you are trying to avoid. So when centring, exert sufficient force so that the centres are properly home, and then slacken the tailstock off a little.

It is not always obvious which order of turning would best minimise slenderness problems. However, you generally work from the centre of the work back towards the headstock and the tailstock, and turn the larger diameter sections first. Although it is tempting to defer cutting hollows until the end in order to preserve stiffness, it is during these cuts that the wood is most likely to climb up over the nose of the gouge. Hence, it may be wise to cut central hollows earlier and accept that the work's effective slenderness will thereafter be somewhat reduced.

Reducing the lathe's speed is particularly effective in reducing whip. For a given diameter you may choose to reduce the speed to as low as one sixth of normal. As the speed drops however, the problems attendant with low lathe speeds will become apparent.

Slenderness is only a problem because the work is not restrained from deflecting. Deflections can, however, be restrained by using steadies or by rigidly holding the ends of the work in line with the lathe axis. It is straightforward to do the latter at the headstock end of the work, and you can:

1. Use a four-jaw, self-centring chuck on square sections.
2. Turn the left-hand end of the work to a cylinder before housing it in a scroll, Jacobs, or collet chuck.
3. Preturn the left-hand end with the appropriate Morse taper and force it into the headstock spindle swallow.

The effectiveness of restraining a workpiece's left-hand end in axial alignment is difficult to quantify. Some idea can be given by considering the relative deflections under static vertical loading of a workpiece held just between centres and a similar workpiece of the same exposed length held by a scroll chuck and a tail centre. The deflection can be shown to be 2.4 times greater in the former situation. Also, deflection is proportional to the workpiece length cubed, so that a 10 percent increase in length would lead to a 33 percent increase in deflection. Note that when turning slender work which has its left-hand end chucked, you should tend to work from right to left to preserve stiffness.

As slenderness and workpiece size increase, the means detailed so far cease to be sufficient to counter the problems encountered. You will need to resort to steadying, either manually or mechanically.

Steadies are devices for holding the rotating work in the line of the lathe axis. Their use is not, however, as straightforward as it may first appear, and the following points should be considered:

1. The effectiveness of the restraint provided.
2. Whether the work has to be preturned in any way in order to mount it in or

through the steady.

3. Whether the steady damages the work in any way, and if so how much.
4. The ease of mounting the work in or through the steady.
5. Whether the workpiece has to be later turned off or hand finished where a steady had been located.

By far the best and most common form of steady is your left hand. On very small work such as lace bobbins, the left-hand forefinger can act as a mobile steady when using the tied-underhand grip (Figure 7.77). When the work is somewhat larger, the whole of the left hand is employed. This means, however, that the tool is largely controlled by the right hand, although the left hand does play a very helpful part. Figures 7.78, 7.79, and 7.80 show the uses of the hand as a steady. Once the work becomes larger than 2 inches (50 mm) in diameter, however, the left hand's effectiveness as a steady falls away as the force which needs to be exerted increases rapidly. Wearing a leather glove can help by allowing you to exert greater pressure without burning your hand.

When the steadying effect which can be applied by the left hand becomes insufficient, you will have to resort to mechanical steadies. There are three basic types: friction, planetary, and collar:

1. *Friction steadies*: The traditional type of friction steady most pictured is a wooden wedge of some sort with a notch in and against which the rotating workpiece bears. Figure 7.81 shows a more sophisticated version. Because of the friction between the rotating workpiece and the stationary surfaces of the steady, noticeable damage is caused to the workpiece surface. To limit this the lathe speed is lowered and the bearing surface of the workpiece is often waxed.

   It is obviously necessary that the bearing surface of the workpiece has to be preturned to a cylinder before such a steady can be used.

2. *Planetary steadies*: Such steadies have one, or more commonly two or three wheels which bear against the workpiece. Their radial distance from the lathe axis is adjustable. They cause less damage to the workpiece surface than friction steadies, particularly if they have resilient surfacing. The workpiece can therefore be run at a higher speed than that appropriate for a friction steady. Three-wheeled versions can be used to steady the right-hand ends of long cupchuck turnings.

3. *Collar steadies*: In collar steadies the workpiece is fixed within a collar, and the collar then acts akin to the outer cylindrical surface of the workpiece. The collar can be a short length of steel tube which then runs within a friction or planetary steady. Commonly the collar is the inner race of a ball bearing which is housed concentrically with the lathe axis. With collar steadies the workpiece needs to be fixed axially within the collar or inner race. Wedges (temporarily tacked, taped or hot melt glued in place for security) can be used to hold the round or square workpiece cross-section within the collar. Alternatively the workpiece may be able to be preturned to be a snug fit within.

With the first type of collar steady (such as the steel tube) there are two methods of alignment: house the collar axially within the steady and then centre the workpiece within it, or use the workpiece to centre the collar and its housing steady. In the latter case the workpiece should be dressed straight and mounted accurately centred in the lathe, or the workpiece can be preturned so that the collar fits snugly.

On very long workpieces multiple steadies can be used, and on automatic lathes carriage-mounted steadies which run just ahead of the cutters are common.

After turning and sanding of the steadied workpiece is complete, you have the problem of the area(s) on the workpiece which bore the steadying and which usually will be damaged and oversize. You can hand-finish these areas. If the workpiece is not too slender, you may be able to turn them off without again using a mechanical steady. If not you will have to use a steady, preferably of the collar type. However, a problem often arises which complicates turning off these areas—when you remove a steady the workpiece immediately bows. To overcome this, offset the ends with respect to the driving and tail centres, typically by half the magnitude of the bow so that the area to be turned off now rotates axially. (Similar offsetting is used when a bowed slender workpiece is initially mounted in the lathe).

Using steadies is slow, and often noisy, and usually results in damage to the workpiece. If very slender work is contemplated, preturning a cylindrical section on which to mount a steady may be difficult or almost impossible. Further, to turn off the damaged area left after using a steady may not easily be possible. If, therefore, it is impractical to turn a design in one piece because it is too slender, it may be best to redesign it or consider doing it in separate sections which are joined together later.

To lessen the slenderness of a profile. it is obviously necessary to increase the effective diameter and, if possible, reduce the workpiece length. The effective diameter will be

Figure 7.77   Using a small skew chisel to cut the long neck of a lace bobbin with the forefinger acting as a steady. The left-hand end of the bobbin blank is held in a Jacobs chuck.

Figure 7.78 Planing from right to left. The left hand is steadying the wood, the left wrist is pushing down onto and thus controlling the skew, and the left thumb is braced onto the toolrest. The hand and tool are moved along the toolrest as a unit.

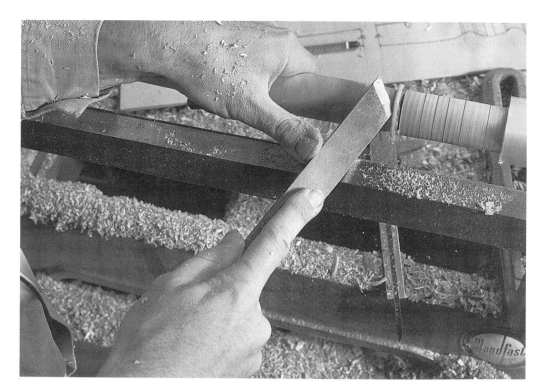

Figure 7.79 Completing a long slide cut. The left thumb is braced against both the toolrest and the skew chisel and the palm steadies the slender workpiece.

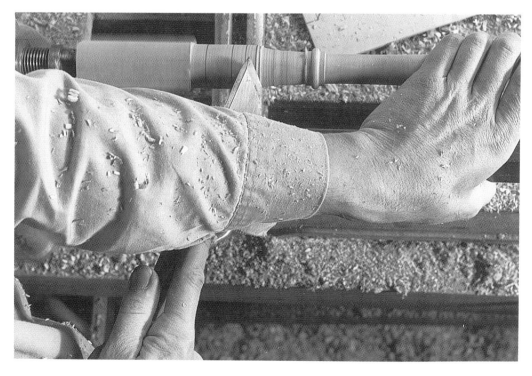

Figure 7.80 The left square section adjacent to the driving centre means that the workpiece has to be steadied to the right of the area being turned. The hand is steadying the workpiece and is braced onto the toolrest. The skew is pushed down onto the toolrest by the left forearm.

Figure 7.81   A simple wooden mechanical steady. Because the holes in the arms through which the bolt passes are slotted, a range of workpiece diameters can be accommodated. Abrasive paper is glued to the mating surfaces of the steady components so that slippage is reduced.

increased by making hollows shallower, by kicking-up fillets, and by making narrow sections greater in diameter; it can also be improved by relocating small diameter sections nearer to the ends of the work.

A long turning can be made up from axially bored separate sections threaded over a steel rod. For very slender work another alternative, albeit one which is weaker structurally, is to assemble the long turning from shorter turned sections joined end to end using sockets and spigots. Standard lamps are commonly manufactured this way. If the work is to be clear finished, then the joints need to be located at break points in the design such as at the junction of a bead and a fillet. To ensure maximum strength, have the pin's diameter somewhat greater than half of the minimum outside diameter of the work at the junction; also turn the pin on the section of lesser diameter. To ensure concentricity, predrill the sockets and use suitable centres or plugs to centre the drilled ends (Section 4.13).

Dowels

A particular case of slender turning is the production of special-diameter dowels. For mass production there are special machines, but there is a hand-held tool called a rounder or a stail engine. After you rough close to the required diameter, the rounder is pushed along the rotating wood from the tailstock end. Run your lathe at its lowest speed, ideally between 100 and 400 rpm. The rounder is a combination of steady and cutter, and various sizes are available commercially. Alternatively, you can make your own. A dowelling cutter can also be mounted on the end of the headstock spindle and the wood pushed through it providing that there is a sufficiently large hole through the spindle.

Figure 7.82   Inletting a ring into a groove. For turning the ring the wood was held in a cupchuck or similar.

7.18 SPLIT TURNINGS

Although a stone carving at Persepolis suggests that split turnings could have been made from about 500 BC, their heyday was the late seventeenth century. Split turnings can, of course, be made by sawing normal turnings in half and then, if necessary, planing the sawn surfaces flat. However, the halves are not truly semicircular in cross-section because of the thickness lost in the kerf and the shavings. Moreover, the planing and the sawing are sometimes easier said than done.

The alternative and better method is to glue two rectangular cross-sections of wood together, turn the assemblage, and then split it down the glue line. To enable a clean split to be made, a layer of heavy brown paper is sandwiched between the pieces of wood.

The two pieces of wood are prepared with any allowances for waste and their meeting faces planed true. These faces are then smeared with PVA glue. A piece of strong, heavy, uncreased brown paper is then placed between the mating faces and the assemblage firmly clamped until the glue has set. The object is to glue each piece of wood to the brown paper without forcing the glue through the full thickness of the paper and thereby preventing easy separation.

During turning, the centres will tend to rive the workpiece along the paper joint. Therefore, use a cup tail centre and position a four-prong driving centre so that two prongs grip each piece of wood. Additionally, you can mechanically fasten the ends of the two pieces of wood together in waste sections allowed for the purpose. After turning, the assemblage is separated by tapping a wide, acutely ground chisel down the centre of the brown paper, the remnants of which can then be sanded or soaked off if necessary.

A further technique taking advantage of wood's rivability is the inletting of oversize sections (Figure 7.82). A loose ring is cupchuck turned, neatly rived, and glued into a prepared recess.

7.19 MULTIPLE-AXIS TURNING

In the early 1990s, multiple-axis spindle and faceplate turning came in from the cold. The work of American Mark Sfirri received deserved attention. There was even a book, *Multi-*

Centre Woodturning by Ray Hopper. A special chuck was introduced by Craft Supplies for multi-axis turning, although you can use a four-jaw independent chuck or pack or improperly insert the jaws of a scroll-type chuck.

In multiple-axis spindle turning, because the wood is frequently mounted eccentrically, it will tend to whip and to come out of the lathe. Therefore ensure that the centres are in well. Further, a cup tail centre will hold better than a cone-shaped one. The lathe will also tend to vibrate, and hence the lathe speed should be reduced.

The simplest form of multiple-axis turning is the near ellipse. Figure 7.83 shows how the locations of the centres are determined. The principal can be developed further to enable sculptural effects to be realised.

Club Foot Turning

A still important application for multiple-axis turning is the production of club feet, often erroneously called cabriole leg turning. Two turning axes are used. Figure 7.84 shows some typical examples.

The chair front leg shown in Figure 7.85 will be used to illustrate the design and production of a club foot.

The usual first stage is to sketch a preliminary side elevation or diagonal section of the leg, bearing in mind the dimensions of the available wood. A preliminary selection of the two turning axes is then made. Axis B-B' is used to turn the bottom half of the club foot, and the pad if any. It is vertical through the leg and usually, although not necessarily, central through the blank. Axis A-A' is used to turn the upper part of the foot, the ankle, and sometimes the remainder of the leg. It is often vertical, but not always. Both axes lie in the diagonal plane through the leg.

The profile to be turned using axis B-B' is shown dotted. In this example, which is more extreme than most, the axis A-A' selected is not vertical and crosses B-B' about halfway up the leg. The profile to be turned using axis A-A' is shown dashed. The fixing of the axes' positions, the selection of the profiles to be turned, and the choice of leg shape result from a process of successive adjustment.

Although it is more common in the design stage to concentrate on the front or side elevation of a corner leg, it is the diagonal section which is critical with such a leg. At the

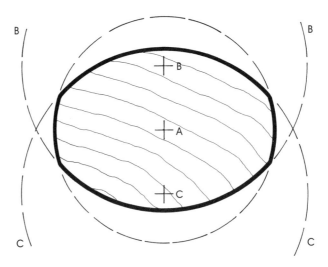

Figure 7.83 Multiple-axis turning of an elliptical cross-section. The workpiece is mounted in turn on axes A, B, and C. In-lathe sanding will blend the junctions between the surfaces.

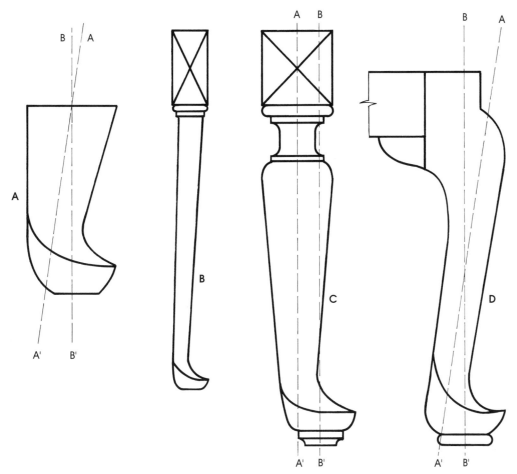

Figure 7.84 Examples of cabriole legs and pad feet. A, an ugly but common form of club foot; B, although economical, this form of leg makes furniture look weak and unstable; C, an elegant turned leg with a club foot and pad; D, a cabriole leg with club foot and pad. The top half of this leg has to be bandsawed and carved to shape.

back of the ankle at K on the diagonal section of Figure 7.85, the dashed and dotted curves must meet smoothly. However this apparently causes the same curves not to meet smoothly on the side elevation. But this is inherent in the geometry and the left half of Figure 7.85 is a true side elevation of the leg.

The adjustment process leading to the finalisation of the diagonal section and side elevation should only be done by adjusting the axes positions, projecting the adjusted axes on the side elevation onto the diagonal section as shown in Figure 7.85 or vice versa, and redrawing the turned profiles referencing them to the adjusted axes. Points on axes can be projected across horizontally. But if you project points on the outside of the leg from the diagonal section down and round and up, you will obtain a side elevation of the diagonal section, not of the leg (see Figure 7.86). Similarly if you project points down and round and up from the outside of the side elevation of the leg, you will obtain a diagonal projection of the side elevation. As you turn using the diagonal section as the reference, but bandsaw out the blank using the leg's side elevation, neither the side elevation of the diagonal section nor the diagonal projection of the side elevation are of use. Further, using the side elevation of the diagonal section as your bandsawing reference would result in an undersize blank.

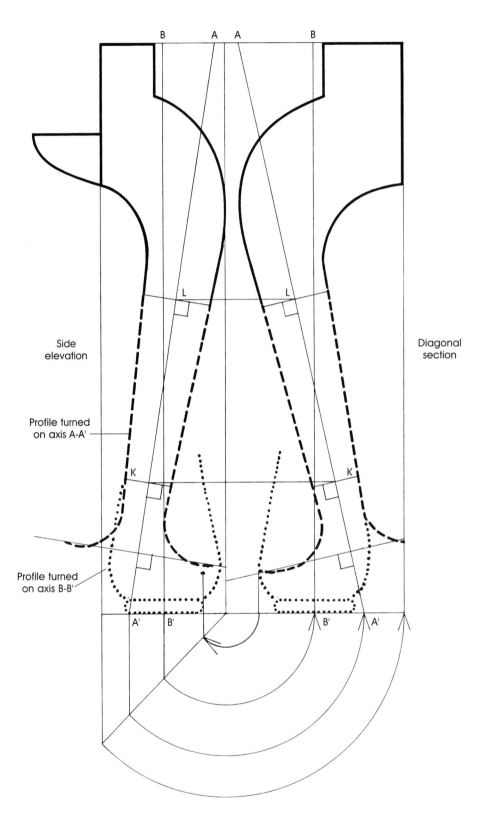

Figure 7.85 The finalised side elevation and the diagonal section of a cabriole leg with a club foot and pad. The diagonal section is here projected from the side elevation.

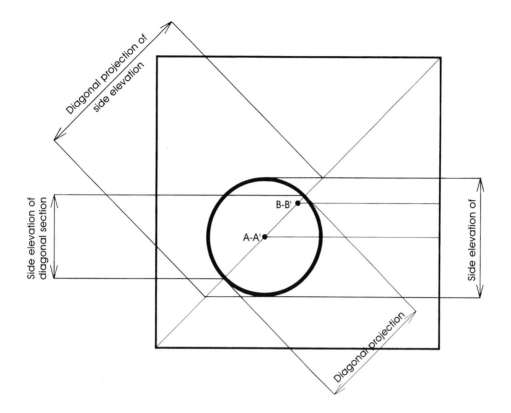

Figure 7.86   A horizontal cross-section through the ankle of Figure 7.85 showing the confusion which can arise with sections and elevations

Figure 7.87   The setting out for bandsawing the leg.

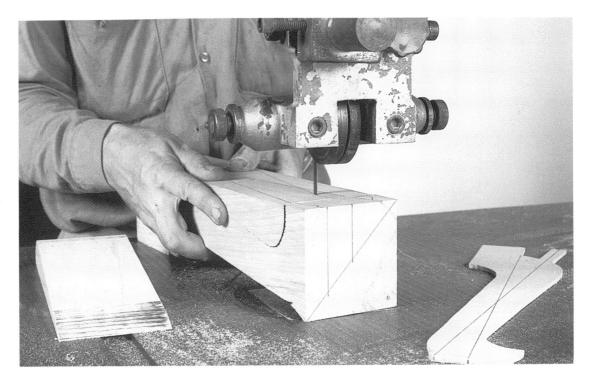

Figure 7.88   Bandsawing out the cabriole leg.

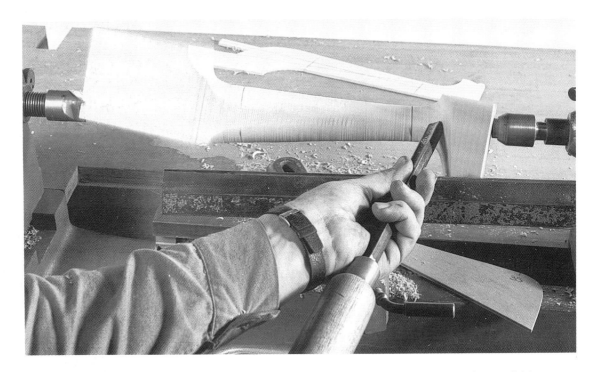

Figure 7.89 Turning on axis A-A' using a $1/2$-inch (13 mm) detail gouge. A template (bottom right) was prepared from the diagonal section and is helpful in getting the top part of the foot to the correct shape. If the bandsawing is accurate, the tapered part of the leg need only be turned until the flat areas have been cut away. Alternatively, you can mark (as shown) and calliper at specific positions. A template can be used to establish these callipering positions.

When it is required to match an existing leg, it is often possible to find the original centre imprint(s) in the bottom of the foot, and in the top of the leg if it was covered with upholstery or by the carcass.

To produce the blank ready for turning, the wood for the legs should be dressed to size on all four sides and cut cleanly and squarely to length, making any necessary allowance for waste at the top end. Cut a piece of thin plywood to the same size as a side of the turning blank and draw on it the side elevation of the leg. Using a narrow blade, bandsaw the plywood neatly along the outline of the leg. This will leave a template of the leg's side elevation, which can then be used for marking out on the sides of the blanks prior to bandsawing. Draw a diagonal on one end of the wood and the same diagonal on the other end. On two adjacent faces of each blank draw around the leg template. Note that the template will have to be turned over for drawing on the second face if that face is on the opposite side of the diagonal to the first. Mark A, A', B, and B' on one face, and project these points down onto the diagonals with a try square to establish the turning centres, which are then preferably punched.

As in the example, A and A' lie outside the finished leg, the wood in areas E and H (Figure 7.87) must not be sawed off. That in H will be turned off; that in E will be sawed off after all the turning is finished. Therefore, bandsaw areas G and F away with one marked face upwards. Turn the other marked face upwards and hold or tape the marked waste piece just sawed away back onto the blank; then complete the bandsawing (Figure 7.88). Alternatively you can saw in from each end of the appropriate lines so as to leave about $^1/_4$ inch (6 mm) in the middle not cut. This saves having to tape the waste back on. The short holding sections are cut through after the major bandsawing is complete. The blank is now ready for turning. Note that you might not bother bandsawing waste away for the fully turned legs such as those in Figures 7.84A and 7.84B.

In this Figure 7.85 example and in most cases, the turning is first performed on axis A-A' because A' will be virtually turned off when using axis B-B'. Therefore, mount the

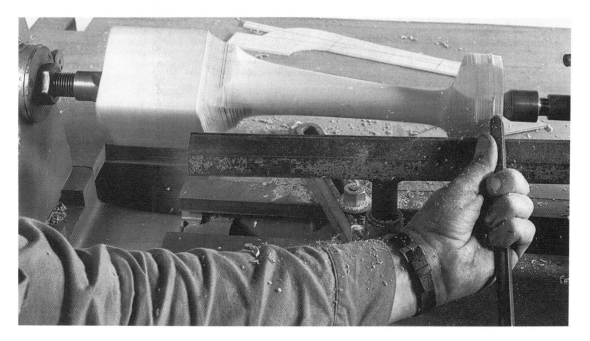

Figure 7.90 Turning on axis B-B'. It will be found easy to merge the curves at the back of the ankle. Because the grain is parallel to the lathe axis, a skew chisel can be used to cut the pad and the bottom of the club foot.

blank on axis A-A', preferably using a cup centre at A'. Ensure at the design stage that the centres will not be less than $^3/_8$ inch (10 mm) in from the edge of the wood. Check that the toolrest does not foul the eccentrically rotating wood and turn it at low speed (about 800 rpm) using a $^1/_2$-inch (13-mm) or larger detail gouge. Note that a skew cannot be used because the grain is not axial.

Although I do not usually favour the use of templates, with club foot turning proper curve shape is critical because the foot shape is determined by the intersection of two curves turned separately on two different axes. To turn the upper part of the foot and the ankle, the correct diameters need to be produced at L and K (see Figures 7.85 and 7.89), the upper and lower extents of the straight-sided section. Also, the cavetto from K downward needs to be turned accurately. Hence, a template is used which relates the positions of K and L to the end of the blank and defines the cavetto.

Having turned and sanded the blank on axis A-A', remount it on axis B-B'. Alter the position of the toolrest so that again it does not foul the work. The remaining turning is considerably easier (Figure 7.90), and all that may be necessary is to calliper the diameter of the pad. After this turning and sanding is completed, the sharp edge around the foot where the two curves intersect can be hand sanded. The upper waste (E) in Figure 7.87 is then sawed away, the ear pieces glued on, and the knee carved.

Chair Backs

Nonstraight chair backs with circular cross-sections may be made by bandsawing and carving, single-axis turning and steam-bending, dowelling two separate pieces together at an angle, or turning on one or more axes. In the simplest case of the last method, the wood is turned between centres and the waste bandsawed off afterwards (Figure 7.91). Figure 7.92 shows a more extreme example.

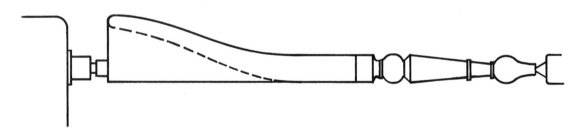

Figure 7.91   Turning a chair back leg. The back post above the seat rails is bandsawed later.

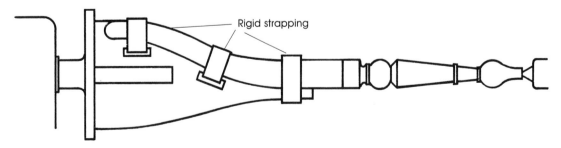

Figure 7.92   If the back post above the seat rails is bandsawed prior to turning, a rigid mounting system will enable the leg to be turned.

7.20 LAMINATING

Laminating to achieve colour and grain contrasts, patterns, and pictorial effects is becoming increasingly popular. Also, as large-size seasoned squares become rarer, laminating purely to achieve sufficient size will become more common.

Wood for laminating should be thoroughly seasoned, or failure will occur at some time. Laminating together pieces from the same length will assist with colour and grain match. Pieces should ideally be laminated front to back so that the pieces will cup in sympathy, and therefore minimise the tendency of the glue line to open. This will also show the joints least.

The faces to be glued should be jointed so that they meet truly. Use a glue which hardens, such as epoxy or urea formaldehyde, in preference to one like PVA which remains plastic.

Some table legs have a short bulbous section and sometimes a bulbous foot, both bulbous sections being greater in diameter than the sections left square. You can glue four pieces of wood around the square section. Alternatively, use wood large enough in cross-section to allow the bulbous sections to be turned normally and cut the square sections down to size locally. Another solution would be to dowel sections together longitudinally, but this could create a leg which is too weak.

7.21 TWISTS, SPIRALS, FLUTING, AND REEDING

The cutting of twists and spirals (Figure 2.5) is a carving process which follows turning, and I have therefore chosen not to describe it in detail. Two principles are used commercially. In the first, a router or other form of rotating cutter is passed slowly along the workpiece which is being slowly rotated. In the second, the workpiece is both rotated and moved longitudinally past the rotating cutter. The finish left after machining may require considerable sanding.

A proper twist lathe or overhead router with twist attachment is obviously not feasible for most of us. There is, however, an apparatus which utilises the first principle above and a portable electric router. Alternatively, the twist or spiral can be hand carved with help from a table saw, drilling machine, round Surform, carving tools, rasps, files, etc.

Fluting and reeding (Figure 2.5) may be hand carved, done on a spindle moulder, done with a drilling machine using a side cutting bit with ball-bearing guides, or scraped with a scratch gauge or routed. With the last two tools, the turned workpiece needs to be held in a cradle or proprietary guide system.

7.22 EXERCISES

This section gives a series of graded exercises in spindle turning for those who do not have access to professional tuition. You are advised to master each example fully before proceeding to the next. It is important to practice properly. Prepare pencil or pin gauges, if appropriate, and try to turn each piece accurately to the specified design. Do not rush the cuts and concentrate on performing each one correctly and rhythmically. Speed will come automatically. Exercises 1 and 2 are the most important. A full day spent on each is well worthwhile.

EXERCISE 1: FIGURE 7.93

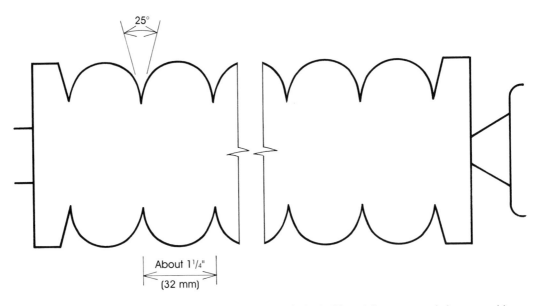

Figure 7.93 Exercise 1. A bead diameter of about 1¼ inch (30 mm) is recommended to start with because it will force you to make considerable lateral tool movements along the rest. Try the exercise with different bead diameters later. Almost any wood, whether seasoned or unseasoned, will do. Cut it a little shorter than your toolrest, ideally from 3 inch x 3 inch (75 mm x 75 mm) stock.

Tools Required: Roughing gouge
                           Large skew chisel, say 1 inch (25 mm)
                           Dividers set at 1¼ inch (32 mm)

Steps:

1. Rough, starting at the tailstock end.
2. Plane with the skew.
3. Mark the bead cusps with the dividers supported on the toolrest.
4. Perform the V-cuts and roll the beads.
5. Remove the toolrest. Sand using the first sanding method described in Section 6.8; that is, face the headstock with the abrasive paper held by both hands at the top of the workpiece.

Points to Note:

1. Try to get the profile produced by each rolling cut correct before taking the next rolling cut.
2. If a cut is spoiled, try to analyse why, and move to another half bead rather than attempt to correct the spoiled cut.

EXERCISE 2: FIGURE 7.94

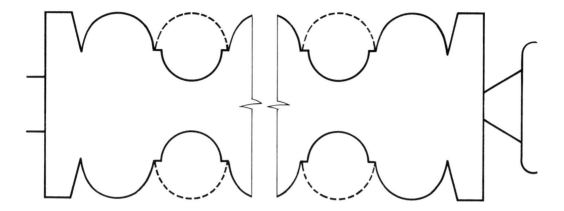

Figure 7.94   Exercise 2. A continuation of Exercise 1.

Tools Required: Roughing gouge
                           1-inch (25 mm) skew chisel
                           Dividers set at 1¹/₄ inch (19 mm)
                           ¹/₂-inch (13 mm) detail gouge

Steps:

1. Rough.
2. Plane with the skew chisel.
3. Set out with dividers.
4. Perform the V-cuts and steps 5 and 6 with the skew.
5. Roll the beads.
6. Cut the fillets with scooping cuts with the short point.
7. Cut the hollows with the detail gouge.
8. Sand.

Points to Note:

1. Once you have mastered cutting the fillets, try to cut them horizontal instead of
   canted.
2. Make the hollows semicircular; ensure therefore that the gouge is positioned correctly with its bevel perpendicular to the lathe axis and its axis pointing at the
   lathe axis for the start of the final cuts.
3. Start with bead diameters of 1¹/₄ inch (32 mm). Then try the exercise with bead
   diameters of ³/₄ inch and 1 inch (19 mm and 25 mm).

EXERCISE 3: FIGURE 7.95

Figure 7.95   Exercise 3. A side width of about 2 inches (50 mm) is recommended.

Tools Required: Roughing gouge
                                 1-inch (25- mm) skew chisel
                                 Parting tool
                                 Callipers

Steps:

1. Make a pencil gauge for the central turned section, a little shorter than that section (see Section 7.1).
2. Cut the dressed timber about ¹/₂ inch (13 mm) longer than the net length of the turning.
3. Mark the extents of square sections. Note that the waste is to be left at the headstock end.
4. Mark the centres accurately using a marking gauge and punch them.
5. Mount the wood accurately centred in the lathe.
6. With the long point of the skew, cut the extents of the square sections down to a diameter just below the width of a side.
7. Rough the centre and end sections to a cylinder.
8. Plane the inside section and mark out.
9. V-cut and roll the three beads.
10. Remove the bulk of the waste from the two conical sections down to the tops of the two fillets using slide cuts with the skew.
11. Define the ends of the fillets with the long point of the skew and then slide cut the two tapered sections and trim the cylindrical surfaces of the fillets.
12. Cut the two chamfers on either side of the central bead with the short point of the skew.
13. With the parting tool and callipers, cut the end pins.
14. Cut the fine bevel with the short point of the skew at the end of each pin.
15. Undercut the ends of the square sections adjacent to the pins very slightly with the long point. This will ensure that the spindle seats properly.
16. Sand.
17. Remove the spindle from the lathe and cut the waste off with a saw

EXERCISE 4: FIGURE 7.96

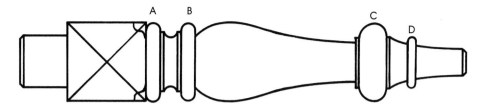

Figure 7.96   Exercise 4. A side width of about 3 inches (75 mm) is recommended.

Note that this exercise, sometimes to a larger scale, has been used extensively in this chapter to illustrate the various cuts.

Tools Required: Roughing gouge
                          1-inch (25 mm) skew chisel
                          ¹/₂-inch (13 mm) detail gouge
                          Parting tool
                          Callipers

Steps:

1. Make a pencil gauge for the turned section to the right of the left-square section.
2. Cut the dressed timber to the net length of the exercise.
3. Mark the extents of the square section.
4. Mark and punch the centres.
5. Mount the wood accurately centred in the lathe.
6. With the long point of the skew, cut the extents of the square section down to a diameter equal to that of the fillets between the two medium beads.
7. Rough the sections both to the left and to the right of the square section down to a cylinder just less in diameter than the side width.
8. Plane the right-hand cylindrical section with the 1-inch (25-mm) skew and mark out using the pencil gauge.
9. Roll the left-hand half bead adjacent to the square, V-cut down its right-hand edge, and V-cut and roll beads B and C. Cut the fillets between beads A and B using the skew's short point. Cant the fillets as little as possible.
10. Cut the tops of fillets adjacent to bead C with long slide cuts.
11. Cut the vertical face of the fillet to the left of C.
12. Plane and slide cut the baluster curve between B and C still using the 1-inch (25 mm) skew.
13. V-cut and roll bead D.
14. Roll the right-hand side of bead A using the detail gouge. You should not need to complete the cut with the long point of the 1-inch (25 mm) skew chisel.
15. Cut the hollow between beads A and B using the detail gouge.
16. Complete the tapered foot using the ³/₈-inch (10 mm) gouge. On the left-hand side of D, a short upward scraping cut will be needed to remove the waste which downhill cuts with the gouge cannot. For this scraping cut, the gouge flute must be facing horizontally to the left with the bevel at right angles to the lathe axis. A similar but downhill cut will be required on the right-hand side of bead D.

17. With the detail gouge, cut the ogee curve on the corners of the square. As the gouge is moved from left to right, it starts with the flute facing horizontally to the right, rolls onto its back, and rolls back fully onto its side with its bevel perpendicular again.
18. Using the parting tool and callipers, cut the pin.
19. With the 1-inch (25 mm) skew, slightly undercut the left-hand end of the left-hand square section and chamfer the left-hand end of the pin.
20. Sand.

8
Cupchuck Turning

In cupchuck turning, the wood has its grain parallel to the lathe axis as in spindle turning, is mounted over the bed, and is fixed by its left-hand end onto and in line with the headstock spindle. Cupchuck turning is so called because until recently the most common accessory used for holding the wood for such turning was the cupchuck.

Cupchuck turning is used where an end of the item is required to be fully finished and sanded in the lathe, as for a knob, or where an end is required to be hollowed, as in an egg cup. These two techniques may also be combined to enable production of items with lids.

Because the wood is held at its left-hand end, the turner should work from right to left, finishing each section in turn. This ensures that maximum stiffness is retained to enable the next section to the left to be turned without flexing beneath the tool. Normal spindle turning cuts are used with the addition of some special techniques, and these are illustrated by three examples which form the bulk of this chapter.

8.1 FIXING THE WORK TO THE HEADSTOCK

Cupchuck turning imposes severe forces on the headstock and will immediately show up any defects in the construction of the lathe. Possible problems are play or lack of preload in the bearings, racking of the headstock if lightly fabricated, and an overall lightness in construction. In lathes which have light unbraced beds, longitudinal vibrations may be transmitted through to the headstock giving the impression that there is play in the bearings.

There are a number of accessories which can be used to hold the wood for cupchucking and these have been described in Chapter 4. They comprise:
1. Screwchucks.

2. Cupchucks (Figure 8.1).
3. Jacobs chucks.
4. Screw cupchucks.
5. Engineer's scroll chucks or woodturner's scroll-type chucks with standard or special cupchucking jaws.
6. Collet-type chucks.
7. Homemade chucks (used for light work).

In addition, the lathe swallow (the Morse tapered hole in the right-hand end of the headstock spindle) may be used. As this is a very slow taper (approximately ⁵/₈ inch per foot or 1 in 20) it is self-gripping. Small work can be held by turning a waste section with a matching taper, and then gently hammering this into the swallow. On completion, the waste can be twisted out using a pipe wrench if sufficient wood is left projecting; otherwise, hammer out using a knock-out bar passing through the hollow spindle. Although effective, this method is rather slow.

Turners who do not have the appropriate chucks may still wish to try cupchuck work. This can be done by turning a parallel-sided spigot on the end of the wood and then gluing this into a hole in a disk of wood screwed to a faceplate. Alternatively, you can make a tapered wooden cupchuck using a faceplate-mounted disk.

Almost all cupchucking methods require preliminary turning of the end of the work which is to be chucked, see for example Figure 8.2. This is usually done with the work mounted between centres with the end to be chucked held by the tailstock (Figure 8.3). Parallel or tapered spigots are usually turned with the roughing gouge by experienced turners. Square shoulders can be cut with the roughing gouge rotated 90° so that its flute faces horizontally to the left. Any necessary callipering is done with the gouge held under

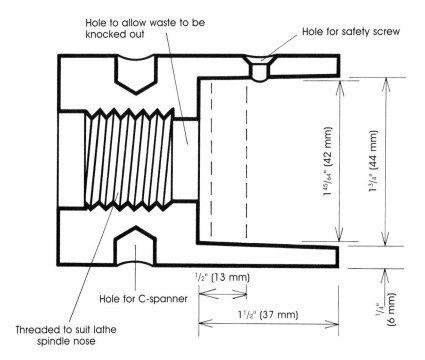

Figure 8.1   A longitudinal section through a 1³/₄-inch (44-mm) cupchuck. The right-hand vertical dashed line shows the end of the workpiece spigot when it is first entered into the bell. The left-hand dashed line shows where the end of the workpiece spigot should be after hammering in. There must be clearance between the end of the spigot and the bottom of the bell.

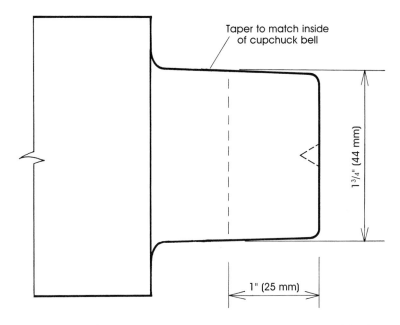

Figure 8.2   The dimensions of the spigot required to be turned on a workpiece which will then be held in the cupchuck illustrated in Figure 8.1.

the right forearm in the usual way (Figure 6.6). Less competent turners may prefer to use a parting tool or sizer for callipering and to turn parallel spigots, and a detail gouge for turning tapered spigots.

The maximum projection of the work from the chuck which can be turned without undue chattering is very variable. It will depend on the rigidity of the lathe, the efficiency of the chuck, the correctness of the turning of the spigot which goes into the chuck, and the diameter of the work. The projection must also allow waste for parting-off the work close to the face of the chuck.

8.2   CUPCHUCKING A KNOB

A knob is perhaps the most common example of an item which requires one end to be fully finished but not hollowed. A typical knob is used to illustrate the turning of this type of work.

Knobs can be turned between centres leaving a small-diameter pin projecting from the front of the knob. The knob may then be gripped by its rear pin in a Jacobs or other chuck so the front can be trimmed and fully sanded in the lathe. If the front of the knob is hand sanded, the fibres in the centre of the front of the knob will not be laid down in the same way as those earlier sanded in the lathe, and a dark patch will be visible after polishing. It is, however, more efficient to cupchuck turn such work and in this first example a cupchuck will be used to hold the wood. The cuts illustrated and numbered in Figure 8.4 are correspondingly numbered in the text, and are as follows:

1. Select square timber whose side width is about $^3/_8$ inch (10 mm) larger than the maximum diameter of the knob. Two knobs will be turned from each piece of wood. Therefore, cut the blanks about 3 inches (75 mm) longer then the net length of the two knobs.

Figure 8.3 Turning the right-hand end of the workpiece prior to hammering it into a cupchuck. The diameter at the mouth of the cupchuck is being callipered 1 inch (25 mm) from the right-hand end of the wood. Three sizes of cupchuck are shown in the foreground.

2. Mount the wood between centres, rough almost to a cylinder, and then, still with the roughing gouge, turn and calliper the spigot which is to be held in the bell of the cupchuck. Beginners will find it more certain to part down to the inside diameter of the open end of the cupchuck bell with a parting tool a set distance from the right-hand end of the spigot. The set distance (1 inch in Figure 8.2) should be such that after the workpiece is hammered into the bell, there is a little clearance between the end of the spigot and the bottom of the bell (see Figure 8.1).

   When turning the spigot for a cupchuck the tendency is to turn too steep a taper. Having a full-sized drawing of the required taper handy for reference will avoid this. Try the fit of the spigot in the bell. If the spigot is too thin, cut an appropriate length off its end, and if necessary remount the workpiece in the lathe and trim it as required.

   If you are turning a batch of knobs, turn all the spigots first, and then start on the detailed cupchuck turning.

3. Remove the blank from the lathe and hammer it into the cupchuck. A couple of sharp blows from a bricklayer's club hammer are sufficient. The back of the cupchuck should be supported and protected by a piece of wood on a solid bench or on the floor. Try to drive the wood in axially; if not, hammer it back into line.

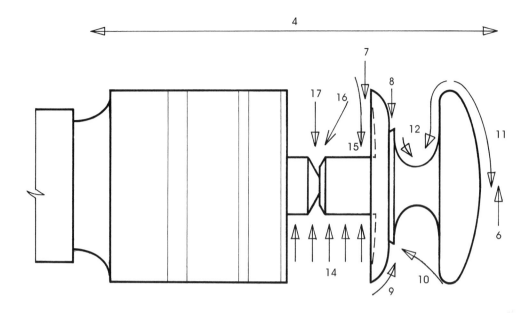

Figure 8.4   The steps in turning a knob. The numbering of the arrows corresponds with the step numbers in the text.

Note that if the wood bottoms in the cupchuck bell, it will not hold securely. A countersunk screw can be driven through the safety hole to prevent the wood being levered out through improper tool handling, but this should not be necessary for reasonably competent turners.

4. Screw the cupchuck firmly against the headstock spindle's right-hand flange to prevent the cupchuck locking-on when the lathe is started. Check that the lathe speed is correct, position the toolrest as if spindle turning, and rough the wood down to a cylinder of the correct diameter. Do not be too heavy with the roughing.
5. Mark out the two knobs from a pin or pencil gauge leaving about $^{1}/_{2}$ inch (13 mm) of waste between them. The front of the right-hand knob should be about $^{3}/_{8}$ inch (10 mm) back from the end of the wood so that the imprint of the driving centre will not be left in the front of the knob.
6. Face off the end of the wood with the long point of a skew back almost to the mark defining the front of the knob. Several cuts of the squaring shoulder type (see Section 7.12) may be required. Leaving a little waste on the front of the knob allows you to roll the whole front of the knob in cut 11 and thereby achieve a consistent surface finish.
7. With the long point, cut an offset V-shaped recess at the left-hand edge of the knob's flange. The recess should be about $^{1}/_{4}$ inch (6 mm) deep and its right-hand side should be perpendicular to the lathe axis. 8. Cut a similar but oppositely-handed recess at the right-hand side of the flange down to the fillet.
9. Roll the half bead forming the flange with the short point of the skew.
10. Cut the fillet with the short point of the skew.
11. With a small detail gouge, roll the front of the knob. At the end of the cut, the bevel should be perpendicular to the lathe axis with the flute facing horizontally to the right. This cut can be performed with a skew, but it is a little more risky.
12. Cut the hollow with the detail gouge.
13. Sand, starting with 150 or 180 grit.

14. With a parting tool, cut the pin to the required diameter, working from right to left to a little to the left of the end of the pin.
15. Trim and undercut the back of the knob with the long point of the skew.
16. Cut a small bevel at the left-hand end of the pin with the skew's short point.
17. Part-off with the long point of the skew, or a parting-off tool. You catch the knob in your left hand, thus having to work cross-armed. As you part through, the knob will drop gently into your expectant left hand (Figure 8.5).
18. Turn the second knob, remove the cupchuck from the lathe, and hammer the waste out of the chuck. Use a soft-faced hammer and a hard wood knock-out bar so that the internal thread and back of the chuck are not damaged. Ideally the knock-out bar should be of two diameters. The smaller fits neatly through the threaded section of the cupchuck and is about 3 inch (75 mm) long. The length of the other section is similar, but its diameter is larger so that the back of the cupchuck and your fingers are protected. If you cannot hammer the waste out, replace the chuck in the lathe and turn the waste out.

An alternative to the above slow process of chucking the wood and driving out the waste is to have the cupchuck mounted on the spindle, hammer the wood in with one or two crisp blows, and turn the waste out with a gouge or hammer it out using a knock-out bar passing through the headstock spindle. Although quicker, this alternative method is very harmful to the lathe bearings.

Note that during the turning, cut 7 is taken down only a short way, the hollow is cut after the front of the knob, and the pin is cut last. This procedure ensures that the section being turned can be turned without flexing beneath the tool because the wood to the left has not been prematurely weakened.

Figure 8.5 Parting-off the knob. The special series of deepening and clearing V-cuts described in Section 7.15 has been used to part down.

Figure 8.6 Hollowing with a hook tool. (This one made in Sweden by Kurt Johansson). To ensure a good surface the edge is applied without clearance but with about 45° side rake.

8.3 TURNING AN EGG CUP

In cupchuck hollowing, the end grain is usually *scraped* prior to sanding. During this scraping, some woods bruise, crush, or tear to various extents. By taking light cuts with freshly sharpened tools, this damage to the end grain can be skimmed off, but with looser woods only by switching to *cutting* with a hook or ring tool applied with side rake can you obtain a good surface (Figure 8.6). Hook and ring tools also leave a superior surface on woods which scrape well.

The hollows in egg cups need to be accurately sized at the rim of the cup. Also, when egg cups are made in sets, the hollows must be of a consistent depth and shape. This example details the appropriate techniques (Figure 8.7), and employs a collet chuck to hold the work:

1. Prepare a blank about 2 inches (50 mm) longer and about $^3/_8$ inch (10 mm) greater in side width than the maximum diameter of the egg cup.
2. Mount the blank between centres, rough almost to a cylinder, and then turn a parallel-sided spigot of the diameter required for the collet chuck. This spigot diameter should not be too much smaller than the outside diameter of the egg cup or the spigot will tend to flex during the turning. Alignment and gripping is assisted if a shoulder is turned on the spigot, and that shoulder is butted hard against the face of the collet. The projection of the spigot into the collet should generally be about 1 inch (25 mm), but should be varied according to the collet design and the workpiece size and hardness.
3. Lock the spigot into the collet chuck and rough the workpiece to a cylinder.
4. Flush the end of the wood with the long point of the skew.
5. To ensure consistency of hole size, the wood can be roughed down to exactly the outside diameter of the egg cup in step 3 and the rim thickness eyed when the hollow is turned. Alternatively, the diameter of the hole can be marked with dividers after step 4 and the outside diameter of the egg cup estimated by eyeing the rim

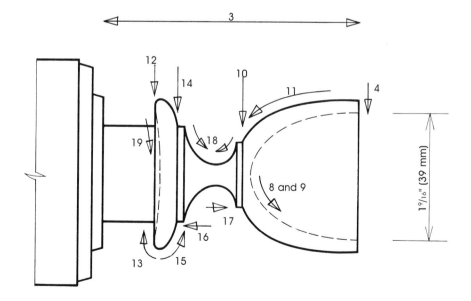

Figure 8.7   The steps in turning an egg cup. The numbering of the arrows indicates the order of cutting and also corresponds with the step numbering in the text.

thickness.

6. Set the rest at right angles to the lathe axis, about 1 inch (25 mm) from the end of the work. Use a long-and-strong $^3/_8$- or $^1/_2$-inch (10- or 13-mm) detail gouge for preliminary hollowing. The toolrest height is set so that the bottom of the gouge flute is at lathe axis height when the gouge is horizontally on its back.

7. If the diameter of the hole is to be marked, set the dividers to the hole radius. Support both arms of the dividers on the toolrest, locate the left-hand point in the centre of the work, and bring the right-hand point into contact with the wood. As the toolrest is below the lathe axis, the right-hand divider point will be trailing and will not be grabbed by the wood.

8. Turning the hole is usually a two-stage operation. Firstly, the hole is pulled out with the detail gouge, and then the surface is frequently cleaned up using a scraper. The hollowing cuts with the gouge are illustrated in Figures 8.8, 8.9, and 8.10. When making them it is best to remove the tailstock from the lathe, or at least the tail centre, so that you do not injure your elbow.

The hollowing method described cuts the wood as it descends onto the gouge tip. There is another method in which cutting is performed as the wood ascends, but this method is more difficult to master and less generally applicable. In hollowing the gouge is positioned along the lathe axis and firmly pushed straight in on its back until a suitable depth of cut is achieved. The objective is then to maintain this approximate thickness of cut while horizontally moving the gouge tip to your left and simultaneously withdrawing it so as to cut a smooth surface of the desired shape. Concurrently with these two com-

Figure 8.8   The detail gouge is on its back with the bottom of its flute coincident with the lathe axis. The cut is started by pushing the gouge into the wood. The gouge nose is then forced to the left and the gouge rotated anticlockwise. A Vicmarc VM 140 scroll chuck is holding the wood.

Figure 8.9   To keep the cutting just on the left side of the gouge nose, the handle has been swung to the right a little. The rotation of the gouge is about 20° anticlockwise.

bining movements, the gouge is progressively rotated anticlockwise. While the tip movement is mainly at right angles to the lathe axis, the gouge rotation is approximately 20°, increasing to about 45° when the cutting is parallel to the lathe axis. The feeling should be of shear scraping the bottom of the hole and of 'hooking' the wood from the sides. When the sides are being cut, it is the cutting edge on the left-hand side of the nose which is cutting, albeit with a significant clearance angle. Also, during these hollowing cuts, the gouge handle will often need to be moved away to your right to keep the unsharpened top of the left-hand flange clear of the wood.

If the gouge is not pushed in truly axially, a little spike of wood will be formed. To eliminate this, position the gouge nose, flute up, below the spike and push the handle down.

For hollowing cuts, you should face the end of the wood with your head low. You will find it helpful if a light shines down the hollow so that the cuts can be clearly seen. This is further assisted by using the tied-underhand grip in which the left hand is beneath the tool blade. Ideally you would hollow, skim and sand in layers, starting at the rim of the hollow, but inevitably you will need to trim a thin wall which will chatter as it flexes. This chattering can be damped by locating the tool with your left thumb while using your fingers on the outside as dampers (Figure 8.11).

When it is required to hollow to a specific depth, pencil a reference mark in the flute of the gouge. The correct depth is reached when the mark lines up with the rim of the workpiece.

Initially, heavy cuts can be taken, but try to form the correct hollow shape early on. Towards the end, use lighter cuts which will leave a better surface finish. In some cir-

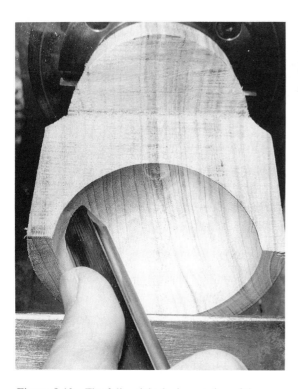

Figure 8.10 The full anticlockwise rotation of the gouge (about 45°) has been reached and the wood is being hooked off as the gouge is being pulled out. The cutting should feel quite sweet and is at lathe axis height.

Figure 8.11 Hooking out the inside of a hollow (the lid in Figure 8.13) with a $^1/_2$ inch (13 mm) detail gouge, the fingers being used as they would be to damp chattering.

cumstances the gouge will leave a finish suitable for sanding, but normally a scraper properly used will improve the finish in a hollow
(Figure 8.12). Again, as with the gouge, cutting should be *downhill* so that the scraper
should be made to cut when being pulled out
of a hollow which widens toward the right-
hand end of the work. Conversely, where a
hollow narrows towards its right-hand end,
skim the walls on the push.

The length of cutting edge used in scraping which a turner can control will depend on
the wood's hardness, the tool overhang, the
direction of cut relative to the grain direction,
and especially the thickness of the cut. As the
final shaping of a hollow can be most accurately achieved using a scraper whose left-
hand plan profile conforms closely to the
desired shape of the hollow, the scraping cuts
should be fine even when the overhang is fairly small. As the tool overhang becomes
greater, the active length of burr must be
reduced. But although flat scraping is the
technique most commonly used to finish-turn
a hollow, wide and shallow hollows can be
shear scraped. As the hollow becomes relatively deeper, specially-angled shear scrapers
would be needed. Hook and ring tools (Figure
8.6) also suffer similar access problems
which require specially shaped tools, but they should leave an excellent finish.

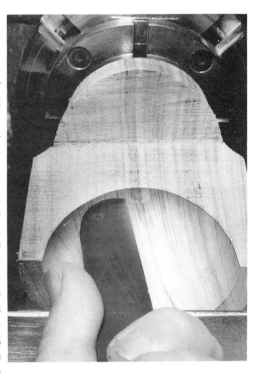

Figure 8.12 A finishing cut with a scraper. The
toolrest has been raised a little (this is often
dispensed with for short hollows) so that the
scraper is safely pointing slightly downwards. The
cut is very light and the scraper is sharp with the
burr left on.

During the turning of a hollow, you will wish to monitor progress. It is quite safe to
feel inside the hollow if the toolrest is moved out of the way. Contact the left-hand side
of the hollow with the forefinger or second finger of the right hand. It is also sensible to
stop the lathe and examine the hollow visually.

9. Sand the hollow. Depending on the off-the-tool finish achieved, the starting grit
    may be between 80 and 150. Use quarter sheets which are then torn into strips
    about 2 inches (50 mm) wide and each folded lengthways into three. The abrasive
    paper is held in the right hand, supported behind by the forefinger and/or second
    finger. Be careful not to round over the edge of the hollow at the rim unless this
    is desired.
10. After sanding the hollow, V-cut down to the right-hand fillet.
11. Roll the outside of the cup. You will find it easier to cut the area near the rim with
    a detail gouge, changing to a skew for the remainder. A skew can certainly be used
    to slide cut the whole of the outside of the cup, but there is tendency to split wood
    off at the rim and for the tool to be grabbed as it enters the wood.
12. The remainder of the turning is similar to that of the knob described in Section
    8.2. When parting-off, take care to leave a good finish with the long point on the
    undercut base of the egg cup. The finish to the bottom of the foot can be further
    improved by skimming cuts and/or sanding with the egg cup being held by its top
    rim (see step 16, Section 8.4).

8.4   TURNING LIDDED BOXES

One method of turning lidded boxes requires the wood to be chucked only once. However, there is a grain mismatch between the lid and the base (Figure 8.13A). The preferred method (Figure 8.13B) ensures excellent grain matching, but takes longer and requires two chucking operations. These chucking operations should therefore utilise chucks which give good axial mounting alignment or else the grain match will be reduced.

Lids may fit inside or outside the top rim of the base (Figure 8.14). Whichever is outside should normally be thicker because it will be subject to circumferential tensile stresses. These are greatest when the lid is held by a tight friction fit onto the base so that the lid's top can be finish-turned and sanded. For this the mating sections of both lid and base should ideally be exactly parallel-sided. How much this fit is subsequently eased will depend on whether the lid of the finished box is intended to be removed with the base hand-held or not. But not all fits are parallel. For example, in Japanese tea boxes the base spigot is incurved so that a partial vacuum is not created as the lid is removed and the green tea powder does not therefore billow into the air.

For a box in which the fit of the lid and base remain true in the long term, both lid

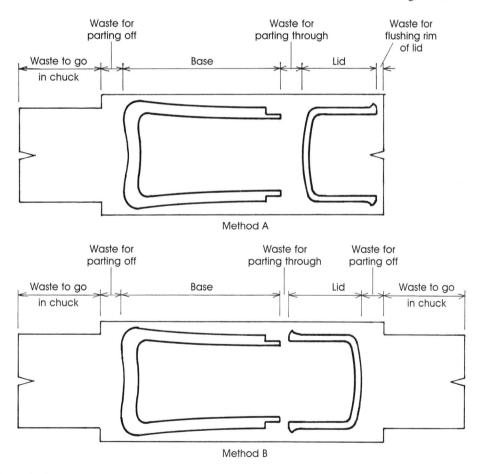

Figure 8.13   Two methods for cupchuck turning lidded boxes. In method A the lid is first hollowed. After turning its outside, the lid is then parted-off. The mating spigot is then turned on the right-hand end of the box base either before, during, or preferably after hollowing the base. The lid is fitted and the lid and base then finished. Although quicker than method B, method A results in a grain mismatch between the lid and base.

and base should be rough-turned somewhat oversize and allowed to season completely and relax. With well seasoned wood of below 2 inches diameter this is often not done, but the long term fit will not remain quite as good. After seasoning and relaxation, the lid and base will need to be axially and securely rechucked by their waste spigots—your chucking procedure will need to accommodate this two-stage turning process. Where the wood is expensive, chucks which require only a short waste spigot will be preferred. In general such chucks demand less vigorous turning techniques.

An important aesthetic consideration is that there should be some uniformity of wood thickness throughout the box so that the external shape and internal hollowings are related. This will also maximise tactility and minimise weight.

For the example of box turning which follows, a Nova scroll chuck will be used with special cupchuck jaws:

1. Prepare a blank with a side width about $^3/_8$ inch (10 mm) greater than the greatest diameter of the box. Depending on the size of the box and the chucking methods to be used, the blank will need to be between 1 inch (25 mm) and $4^1/_2$ inch (120 mm) longer than the sum length of base and lid (Figure 8.13B). The extra length needs to allow for chucking, separating the lid from the base, and parting-off the lid and base at the face of the chuck. As described in Section 8.3, the strength and axial accuracy of chucking is improved if the spigots project from shoulders which are butted against the chuck face.

2. Mount the blank between centres, rough almost to a cylinder. Turn the parallel-sided or dovetailed spigots at each end. Make a fine V-cut where the blank is to be cut into two and accurately saw through. Alternatively, part down using a thin parting-off tool to a diameter of about $^3/_8$ inch (10 mm) and then twist or saw the two sections apart.

3. Ideally with a chuck guard in place, mount the lid blank by its spigot, ensuring that the jaws exert high pressure. Rotate the blank by hand to check that it is held axially.

4. Rough the workpiece to a true cylinder.

5. Flush the end with the long point of a skew.

6. Hollow the lid to the required shape with a $^3/_8$ inch (10 mm) or larger detail gouge using the techniques described in Section 8.3. Clean up with fine scraper cuts, taking care to leave the mating surface parallel sided (see Figure 8.14) and with the best possible off-the-tool finish. Two differently shaped scrapers may be required for the insides of some lids. Always take care to cut *downhill*. When the lid is fairly wide and shallow, you may be able to use a ring or hook tool for the

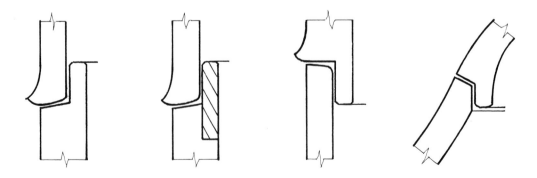

Figure 8.14 Four alternative junctions between base and lid. *Left to right:* the most common; inletting a separate spigot to minimise external grain mismatch; with a lid spigot projecting down, the base cannot be completely filled with contents; the preferred design when the box sides slope.

finishing cuts. You can hollow to the required depth using a pencil mark in the gouge flute as described in Section 8.3 to monitor progress. You can also readily transfer the depth of hollowing to the outside of the lid using the steps shown in Figures 8.15 and 8.16. when you come to turning the workpiece's outside.

7. Turn the outer surface of the lid, sand its inside and rim, and part-off (Figure 8.17). An offset skew or a parting-off tool may be required if room is restricted. When sanding the inside take great care at the right-hand end of the hollow. Sanding tends to make turnings elliptical in cross-section, so minimise sanding of the area which will mate with the base spigot, and take care not to round it over.

8. Chuck the box base blank axially.

9. Rough to a true cylinder.

10. Flush the right-hand end.

11. Hollow the base and sand its inside. This can also be done after the mating spigot is finish-turned, but because of stress relaxation, a better long-term fit will be achieved if the mating spigot is finished after base hollowing. Another reason for hollowing first is that it is during hollowing that you are most likely to disturb the workpiece's axial alignment. If you do so and cannot restore perfect axial alignment of the base spigot, the lid will not be perfectly aligned with the base.

    You will need to closely monitor the hollowing so that the intended base exterior is not compromised. You will also need to take care that the designed mating spigot can be achieved after hollowing. To ensure this you can mark the designed outside diameter of the base hollow at its top on the right-hand end of the base before starting hollowing.

12. Cut the mating spigot. There are several methods by which you can achieve the objective of a mating spigot with a uniform and correct diameter. All these methods require skill and care, and it is wise to practice beforehand on some scrap

Figure 8.15 Before sanding the inside, the inside depth of the lid is measured by aligning the end of your thumb nail with the right-hand end of the lid when the blunt end of a pencil is in contact with the bottom of the hollow. This is done while the lathe is running, and by keeping the thumbnail on the pencil, the point at which to part-off the lid can be measured (Figure 8.16).

wood. The method described in Figure 18*A* requires you to first cut cavettos with a small detail gouge. The action is that used for the final cuts when turning a semi-circular hollow (Section 7.14). With these cuts you are trying to cut a very slow taper adjacent to the right-hand end of the spigot. By cautiously offering up the lid with the lathe running you can monitor progress. As you get close to the required diameter it is safer to stop the lathe and try the fit. When a tight fit is achieved just back from the right-hand end of the spigot, a series of deepening, shoulder-squaring cuts with the long point should be alternated with exactly horizontal slide cuts with the shaving taken on the short point presented with 45° side rake (Figure 8.19). These slide cuts should not cut below the bottom of the preceding deepening cuts or a ruff is formed and damage could show on the finished vertical shoulder. To ensure that the finished shoulder has a clean surface, it should be formed by a single, final deepening cut.

The lid to spigot fit required is one tight enough to hold the lid while you complete its turning, but it should not be so tight that you split the lid in forcing it over the spigot. If you have turned the spigot only just too big, you can lightly sand. However heavy sanding will make the spigot elliptical and so is not recommended.

The most likely mistake is to reduce the spigot diameter too far. If the lid is shallow you may be able to pack the spigot with tissue paper or masking tape prior to finish-turning the lid, but the final fit of the lid will unavoidably be a loose one. If packing the spigot is not a suitable option, you will have to cut a new spigot—this usually means that the base will be shorter than originally intended and that there is more grain mismatch between lid and base.

The horizontal slide used to form the spigot cuts require the wood to be straight and axially grained. If the wood is not cooperative you will need to direct all horizontal and near-horizontal cuts from right to left, and the finishing cuts

Figure 8.16 Marking where the lid is to be parted-off. To the reference measurement taken in Figure 8.15 an allowance for the thickness of the top of the lid is added. Again there is no need to stop the lathe. This measuring method can also be used for the base of the box.

Figure 8.17 Parting-off the lid. The parting-off tool's left-hand point is longer and therefore avoids pulling out fibres from what will be the finished top of the lid.

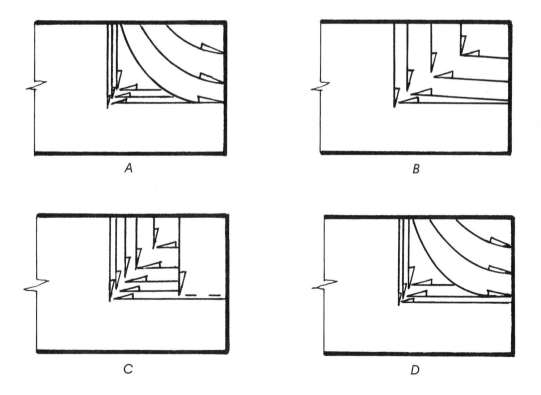

Figure 8.18 Four procedures for cutting the outside of a box base spigot. In *A* and *D* the cuts are made first with a detail gouge and then with a skew. In *B* all cutting is done with the skew. In *C* use the skew after a parting tool or a skew used as a parting tool. *B* and *C* are my preferred methods.

may need to be shear scraping cuts. They can be made with the very tip of a spindle gouge on its side, or with a small shear scraper (a scraper with a burr presented at about 45° side rake).

A variation on the previous method is shown in Figure 8.18*B*: it enables you to use a skew throughout, but requires cooperative grain. Early cuts are deepening and slide cuts, the slide cuts being right to left and slightly uphill so that the spigot diameter increases from right to left. Once the required fit is achieved at the right-hand end of the spigot, deepening and exactly horizontal right to left slide cuts are used.

If you have vernier callipers, these can be used to establish the spigot diameter more quickly. If you calliper with a parting tool or a skew used as a parting tool (Figures 8.18*C* and 8.20) you will need to set the callipers about $^1/_{16}$ inch (1.5 mm) oversize because of the torn surface left by the parting tool. If you calliper with a detail gouge (Figure 8.18*D*) less margin is needed. Final trimming is then as previously described. There are also available devices for cutting excellent threads on lids and bases, and brass lid and spigot liners which you glue in. These devices are not detailed here, but add to the range of box possibilities.

13. Push the lid onto the base with the grain aligned. Finish-turn the top of the lid (Figure 8.21). If you have doubt whether the lid will hold on, augment the hold with adhesive tape around the junction of the lid and base.

14. If adhesive tape was used, remove it. Finish-turn the outside of the base, but without reducing the diameter of the spigot connecting the base into the chuck. Sand the outside of the lid and base. Stop the lathe and remove the lid.

Figure 8.19 Fine trimming of the spigot using small slide cuts. The cuts perpendicular to the lathe axis which define the shoulder should always be kept ahead of the slide cuts. The pencil line which defined the diameter of the hollow is still visible.

Figure 8.20 Callipering the base spigot using a skew as a parting tool.

Figure 8.21   Finish-turning the top of the lid using a detail gouge on its side to remove the waste left after Figure 8.17.

Figure 8.22   Finish-turning of the bottom of a reverse-chucked box base. This press fit chuck is turned from the waste left in the chuck after parting-off the base. As the bottom is concave, the preferred tool is a convex-bevelled detail gouge on its side.

15. You may need to slightly reduce the spigot diameter to achieve the required lid fit. A fine finishing cut followed by a light sand is preferred. A nice touch is to form very small bevels on the inside and outside of the right-hand end of the spigot.

16. Part-off the box base. As you reduce the diameter of the holding spigot, finish-turn and sand as much of the box bottom as you can. If the box bottom is required to be concave, you can skim it during parting-off with a convex-bevelled detail gouge or offset skew. You can also reverse chuck the base as described in step 17.

    As you finally part through there is a tendency to pull out fibres from the centre of the base bottom. To avoid this, leave a tiny spigot of waste projecting from the bottom. If you use a parting-off tool, grinding its right-hand point a little shorter will cause the pull-out to be avoided.

17. No matter how good your finish-turning and parting-off, the surface of the bottom of the base can be improved by reverse-chucking in which the base is held by its spigot thus allowing unimpeded access to the base bottom. If the waste left in the chuck after parting-off the base is large enough it can be used for reverse chucking (Figure 8.22). Otherwise chuck some waste in the chuck you have first used or screw a waste disk of wood, plywood, or fibreboard onto a screwchuck or faceplate. If you are producing a batch of boxes, do the finish-turning of the base bottoms together at the end, working from the smallest spigot diameter to the largest.

    Skim the right-hand face of the waste vertical and cut an annular recess a little deeper than the length of the spigot (Figure 4.16). The recess must be parallel sided and its diameter such that the spigot is a tight fit within.

    Force the spigot into the recess so that the shoulder bears hard against the outer face of the chuck. If you have vacuum chucking it can be used to increase the security of the hold, but this is not usually necessary. Finish-turn the bottom. If the bottom is to be concave, a gouge with a convex bevel is ideal (Figure 8.22).

    If you sand the bottom with the base being mounted on the right-hand side of a lathe spindle rotating forward, the fibres will be laid down in the reverse direction to that in which the earlier sanded fibres lie. This often shows in the finished box. To avoid this, reverse chuck on the left-hand end of the headstock or, if mounted inboard, sand the bottom of the base in reverse.

18. Some turners polish their boxes in the lathe after steps 7, 16 and 17, and during steps 13, 14 or 15. They use quick-drying French polish or nitrocellulose lacquer. If you wish to polish this way, properly exhaust the fumes and wear vinyl gloves to prevent skin damage.

8.5   HOLLOW TURNING

Hollow turning is an ancient technique, but one which has been advanced enormously since 1980. David Ellsworth and Dennis Stewart were in the van, but have since been joined by many others. Aesthetic developments in hollow turning have lead to a focus on the vessel, and they have promoted and been promoted by developments in techniques and equipment. As a worthwhile treatment of hollow turning would require a major chapter I have, as in earlier editions, given it merely a mention.

In hollow turning, the form is basically an enclosed one with a relatively small hole in the top to allow tool access (Figure 8.23). Superior examples have walls of $1/8$-inch (3-mm) thickness or even less.

The form being incurved is more rigid than that of a bowl, and the outside is turned first. The general grain direction in the wood will determine whether the outside is treated as an example of cupchuck turning or of bowl turning. The inside is generally scraped;

straight, bent, and curved tools may be used. Bent and curved scrapers will be difficult to control because of the moments induced. However, this can be alleviated by judicious toolrest positioning, and by using specially shaped toolrests, narrow scraping tips, and bent-back scrapers. When scraping, as far as possible try to preserve workpiece stiffness, cut *downhill*, and have the tool trailing.

Wall thicknesses can be measured as for bowls, and their constancy of thickness can also be judged by tapping. The sounds emitted during turning will also be a good guide. Especially fragile wood may be bound with tape. Shavings and sanding dust are best removed using a vacuum cleaner.

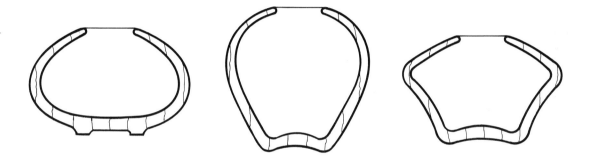

Figure 8.23   Sections through typical hollow turnings.

9
Faceplate Turning

The general term for turning in which the grain runs in a plane perpendicular to the lathe axis is faceplate turning, and it is then split into the turning of basically flat or convex disks or annular mouldings (faceplate turning) and the turning of concave shapes, the most common examples of which are bowls.

Faceplate turning is often, though not necessarily, traditionally detailed and therefore the most-used tool is a spindle detail gouge—the slim nose allowing good access to areas with fine detail, and the cutting edges along the sides of the ladyfinger nose enabling side rake cutting even in difficult access situations. The tools and techniques particularly associated with bowl turning can also be used for faceplate turning and are described in Chapter 10.

9.1 HOLDING THE WORKPIECE

The workpieces for faceplate turning are generally in the form of disks cut from planks. Such workpieces are most frequently held by screwchucks. Faceplates, vacuum chucks, glue chucks, and chucks which grip by expanding their jaws into holes or shallow recesses are also used. When the workpiece is thin and large in diameter relative to the metal faceplate, a wood, plywood, or MDF backing disc of a similar large diameter is used between the workpiece and the chuck to prevent the workpiece flexing.

Faceplate turning was traditionally done inboard, probably because few commercial lathes had an outboard facility. If the design of the turning is basically convex, inboard turning is fine. If hollowing is entailed, the turning is better done outboard because tool handle movements will not there be restricted by the lathe bed. A swivelling headstock can also overcome this problem associated with inboard hollowing. Note that if you want to use a screwchuck outboard, the screw will need a left-hand thread if you intend to turn with the lathe running forward.

9.2   PREPARING THE WORKPIECE

Most chucking methods require that the back of the workpiece which bears against the chuck be flat. Ideally this is done on a planer, and the plank brought to the finished thickness with a thicknesser before the disks are bandsawn out.

If you do not have a planer you can hand plane the workpiece's back, but it can be more efficient to do it in the lathe. The workpiece is held by what will be its top when the detailed turning is in progress—take care that any fixing holes will not be visible in the finished turning. The bottom is then finished with a detail gouge or scraper using the appropriate techniques described in the next section, and any required chucking recess is turned. The bottom is then sanded if required, and the mounting then reversed ready for finish-turning the top.

9.3   THE BASIC FACEPLATE TURNING CUTS

In spindle turning the wood grain runs parallel to the lathe axis. In faceplate and bowl turning the wood grain is essentially radial, perpendicular to the lathe axis. Also, even though you turn *downhill* (with the grain) as defined in Figure 5.23, it is impossible to avoid turning against the grain in two zones, each bounded by end and long grain, for about half of each workpiece rotation (Figure 9.1). It is this unfortunate truth which dictates the special cuts and procedures, the special tools, and the need to use higher side rake presentations than in spindle turning.

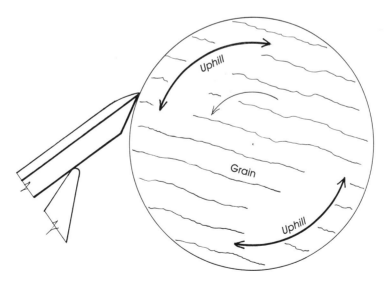

Figure 9.1   Cutting *uphill*. In the two opposite zones marked, turning *uphill* (against the grain) is unavoidable, and therefore the need to use high side rake presentations.

Most faceplate turning uses up to four distinct presentations with a detail gouge, and consists of using them alone for straight cuts, and of gradually transferring from one to another to cut curves. The basic faceplate detail gouge and scraping cuts are:

1. *Peripheral skimming* (Figure 9.2) has the tool in a near-vertical presentation. The flute should be rotated into the cut, that is turned to face partially in the direction in which the tool is being moved. The toolrest should be relatively close to limit tool overhang and to encourage a near-zero clearance angle presentation. The toolrest also needs to be approximately parallel to the surface being cut. Although the tied-underhand grip is preferred, the overhand grip may be used where the surface to be cut is wide.

2. *Radial scraping* (Figure 9.3) is used when the toolrest is positioned approximately parallel to the lathe axis and at about a right angle to the surface to be scraped. If the gouge were used with its flute facing vertically upwards taking the shaving well back from the tip, control would be difficult to retain. The gouge would tend to be yanked over onto its side. You therefore 'go with it' and use the cutting edge behind and below the tip as a scraper with the flute facing about 20 above horizontal.

   The cut is useful because it avoids having to move the toolrest from being parallel to the lathe axis. The drawbacks are that the finished surface will have noticeable subsurface damage, and that if too long an overhang is used, blade flexing and chattering results.

3. *Radial peeling* (Figure 9.4) avoids the problems associated with radial scraping. The toolrest needs to be close to the surface and $^{1}/_{2}$ inch (13 mm) or possibly more below lathe axis height. As in spindle roughing an overhand grip with the thumb atop the blade is used. Using a side rake of about 45°, the shavings are peeled away by the leading cutting edge back from the gouge tip.

Figure 9.2 Peripheral skimming.

Figure 9.3 Radial scraping.

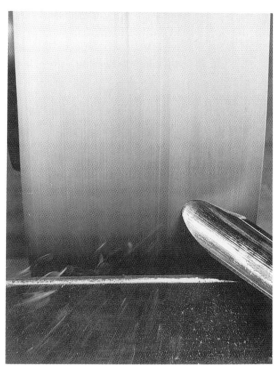

Figure 9.4   Radial peeling. The top of the toolrest is
5/8 inch (16 mm) below centre height. The pencilled
circle shows good side rake. Because the toolrest is
close, the overhand grip is used.

Figure 9.5   The pointing cut.

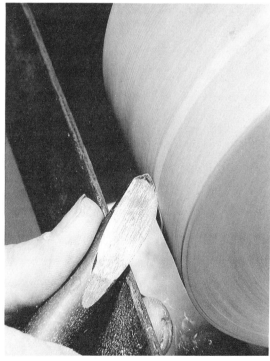

Figure 9.6   Flat scraping the front of a disk.

Figure 9.7   Shear scraping.

4. *Pointing* is the final basic cut (Figure 9.5). The flute faces a little above horizontal and cutting is performed just above the nose tip. This type of near-horizontal presentation is especially common in bowl turning, and with zero clearance angle leaves an excellent finish. If the surface to be cut is convex or straight, use a hollow-ground and honed bevel at zero clearance. If the surface to be cut is concave in plan, it is better to use a convex-bevelled gouge, or steepen the gouge presentation and cut on the side of the nose.

5. *Flat scraping* (Figure 9.6) can be used in faceplate turning, but is best used only on faces perpendicular to the lathe axis where it will leave a reasonable surface finish. Shear scraping, scraping with side rake, causes far less subsurface damage and can therefore be used on surfaces other than those perpendicular to the lathe axis (Figure 9.7). Shear scrapers have to be dragged along.

9.4 TURNING A BASE

Figure 9.8 shows a base. This section describes its turning and thereby demonstrates the use of the basic faceplate turning cuts. The blank has a planed back, is held on a screwchuck, and is oversize in thickness and diameter.

1. Use peripheral skimming cuts (Figure 9.2) working towards the centre from both faces to smooth the outside so that the finished thickness (line E) can be pencilled onto the rotating periphery. Use a conservative lathe speed at first. After cut 1 or 2 the disk will be trued and the lathe speed can be increased if required.

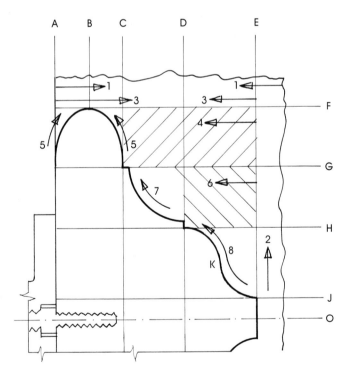

Figure 9.8 A vertical section through a base mounted on a screwchuck. The numbers and letters in the Figure are referred to in the text, each cut numbered being described in a correspondingly numbered paragraph in Section 9.4.

Figure 9.9 Pencilling on lines F,G,H, and J.

2. Bring the disk to finished thickness. The overhang is too large for radial scraping, so the toolrest is repositioned along the front of the disc and well below centre so that radial peeling can be used (Figure 9.4) The front of the disk can then be marked out by pencilling on the rotating wood (Figure 9.9). The toolrest is then returned to a position parallel to the lathe axis.

3. Having marked the radius OF, the remaining peripheral waste can be skimmed off as in cut 1. Take fine finishing cuts with plenty of side rake between A and C. Then pencil on lines C and B.

4. The objective of this cut is to remove the outer hatched ring of wood in Figure 9.8 and thereby establish CG, the base of the bead or torus. The cut starts into face E as a peripheral skim. Part way along, the movement of the blade along the toolrest slows and stops (Figure 9.10), but the nose continues on. As it does so, there is very little anticlockwise axial rotation of the gouge (Figure 9.11). The clearance angle in plan is near zero. If the cut is completed properly you will be able to produce a nice sharp corner at CG using the leading cutting edge on the low side of the tip. As the tool overhang increases, you have to slow and stop the gouge on the toolrest earlier.

   If necessary, face C can be radially scraped back exactly to the line using the gouge in the presentation shown in Figure 9.3.

5. To cut the bead joining AG, BF and CG you do not use a skew. Although it is possible, I do not advise *cutting* with a skew in either faceplate or bowl turning as the consequences are likely to be disastrous. Instead you continue with the detail gouge. To work with the grain the gouge nose has to work up from CG to BF, and from AG to BF. As in bead rolling in spindle turning, you do a series of increasingly larger cuts, developing the shape early, rather than attempting to remove all

Figure 9.10   About to start transferring the peripheral skim into the position in Figure 9.11.

Figure 9.11   The cut started in Figure 9.10 almost completed.

Figure 9.12   The completion of the bead cut CG to BF. The cut was started in a radial scraping presentation similar to that in Figure 9.3.

Figure 9.13   Cutting the cavetto.

the wood in one go.

For the final cut for the right-hand half of the bead, the gouge starts in the radial scraping presentation (Figure 9.3). The tip is then levered up the bead. As it comes up, the gouge is rotated clockwise, and the handle drops down and moves to the left so that at completion it is as shown in Figure 9.12 with the flute rotated about 30° into the cut.

The left-hand half of the bead is cut similarly.

6. Line D is eyed and marked onto surface G, and the smaller hatched ring in Figure 9.8 is cut away as in cut 4 to thus define DH. For this the toolrest can be repositioned as shown in Figure 9.13, about parallel to DF, EG.

7. You could be purist and cut the cavetto with the toolrest parallel to the lathe axis, starting with peripheral skimming and transferring to a radial scrape. If the gouge overhang is large, the radial scrape will be accompanied by chattering as the tool blade flexes. It is generally better therefore to shift the toolrest into the closer, more diagonal position suggested at the end of the previous paragraph (Figure 9.13). Then the cavetto can be cut starting with a peripheral skim which is converted into a radial peel by axially rotating the gouge about 20° clockwise as it follows the required curve. The widths of the fillets along G and D are eyed in.

8. With the toolrest aligned practically parallel to face E, the cyma reversa can be cut by peripheral skimming transferring to radial peeling, in turn transferring back to peripheral skimming, finally transferring to the presentation shown in Figure 9.11. With this toolrest position the axial gouge rotations required are small.

If the toolrest is positioned parallel to the lathe bed, much greater axial rotations are required because instead of the radial peeling you will need to use radial scraping along the part of the curve labelled K.

9.5   HOLLOWING IN FACEPLATE TURNING

Producing a half-hollow or cavetto has been covered in the previous section. This section considers turning a hollow in the rim of a disk, and then in the face of a disk.

In order to cut the hollow ABC in Figure 9.14 properly *downhill*, the gouge nose should work from B to A and from B to C. To get the nose in deep, you thrust in towards the lathe axis with a pointing cut. For pointing cut 2 the tool blade should point a little above the lathe axis and the flute should face to your left a little above horizontal (Figure 9.15). After pushing firmly in, the gouge is rotated a little anticlockwise and a curved outward radial skimming/scraping cut is made with a slightly lowered handle (figure 9.16).

A series of such cuts, alternating from one side to the other, is made to deepen and widen the hollow. As the hollow becomes wider, the bottom of the hollow can be cut with a peripheral skim which is then rolled into a radial scrape as the nose is moved towards A or C. With a narrow gouge flute it can be possible to improve the surface finish by varying the axial rotation of the tool as the nose is brought towards A or C so that the latter part of the cut is more of a radial peel.

When hollowing the front of a disk, if you are turning inboard the presence of the bed dictates that you use your tools in a near-horizontal presentation. Pointing cuts (Figure 9.5) from D to E and from F to E are often used, but ideally the bevel of the detail (or bowl) gouge should be convex to avoid bevel heel crushing damage. You could also flat scrape or better shear scrape to form or finish-skim the hollow.

If hollowing outboard, you have the additional option of using a detail gouge in the near-vertical presentation of a peripheral skimming cut. This presentation can be maintained as the nose goes round the curve. Again a convex bevel avoids bevel heel contact.

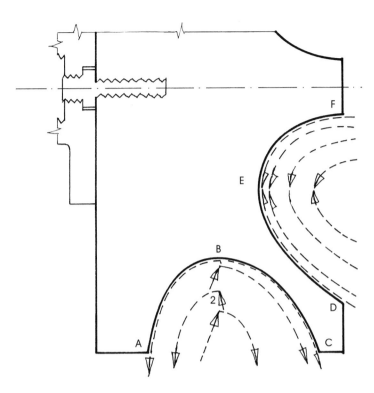

Figure 9.14   A horizontal cross-section through a disk hollowed in its rim and front. The paths of the tool tip during cuts are indicated by the arrows.

Figure 9.15   Deepening with a pointing cut. Notice the fine ribbon-like shavings produced with high side rake *cutting*.

Figure 9.16   Cutting *downhill*. The action is converting here from a peripheral skim into one which will be about 70 percent radial peel and 30 percent radial scrape.

9.6 TURNING A RING

Curtain and other rings are a common faceplate turning job, and an example is described in Figures 9.17 to 9.25.

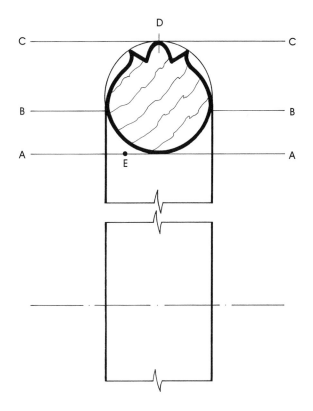

Figure 9.17 A section through a profiled ring, the turning of which will be described in Figures 9.18 to 9.25.

Figure 9.18 A disk has been mounted on a screwchuck with a small-diameter packing piece between. This will allow tool access to the left-hand side of the workpiece. The disk was bandsawed a little oversize in diameter from a plank which had been planed and correctly thicknessed. Using the axis of rotation of the disk as a reference, the radiuses to the inside (A), outside (C), and maximum thickness of the ring (B) are marked with a pencil.

Figure 9.19   The bead D and the adjoining fillets are quite fine. It is therefore difficult to cut them all *downhill*. Cutting the fillets *uphill* and then cutting the sides of the central bead *downhill* using the usual hooking type of cut will be found to be the best.

Skim the outside of the disk down to the finished outside diameter (C): mark the top of the bead at D. To cut the fillet and half bead on the left-hand side of the disk, put the gouge into the near-horizontal presentation. Use your smallest fluted detail gouge—it will be found better to have a smaller than usual sharpening angle and a more pointed ladyfinger nose. Have that part of the bevel in contact with the wood in line with the desired finished surface of the fillet, and push the nose of the gouge down to the base of the bead with a pointing cut. Then hook the side of the bead away, axially rotating the gouge a little anticlockwise to transfer cutting from the tip to the right-hand side of the nose. Ideally when the gouge reaches the top of the bead it is in the peripheral skimming presentation.

Figure 9.20   Cutting *downhill* from B towards C. Similar cuts will then be performed on the left-hand side of the workpiece. Here the presentation is being converted from a radial scrape to a radial peel.

Figure 9.21 Cutting parallel to the lathe axis along A as far as E. The gouge is fully on its side with the back of the bevel parallel to the lathe axis for the final pointing cut. Prior to that it is necessary to make space by making a couple of similar cuts with the gouge fully on its side and facing alternatively to your left and your right as you look along the lathe bed.

Figure 9.22 One of the making space, pointing cuts referred to in Figure 9.21.

Figure 9.23 The gouge is still in the near-horizontal presentation and is almost fully on its side to cut *downhill* from B to A. Notice that the pencil line at B is not cut away. The cutting takes place on the top of the tip of the nose. All cut surfaces are then carefully sanded. Reversing the lathe occasionally can speed the sanding.

Figure 9.24 Using dividers to set the outside diameter of the ring on a disk of waste wood which will be used for a press fit chuck. A recess is then cut out with a gouge so that the ring is a tight fit within.

Figure 9.25 A press fit chuck has been made from a disc of scrap wood. The recess need not be much deeper than half the thickness of the ring. Instead of a press fit chuck you could use a scroll- or collet-type chuck with suitable supplementary jaws (see Sections 4.7 and 4.8).

With the lathe running, the lines at A and B have been marked from the pencil gauge. The series of pointing cuts described in Figures 9.21, 9.22 and 9.23 are being repeated.

When a waste disk is cut free it can jam against the toolrest and cause damage. You could tack or screw it to the chuck, or hold it in with the striking part of your hand until the lathe stops. After removing the waste disk, complete the sanding, ideally with the toolrest removed, and lever the completed ring out of the chuck.

10

Bowl Turning

The dominant feature of late twentieth century woodturning has been the concentration on bowl and vessel turning. While there is nothing wrong in specialising in one branch of woodturning to the exclusion of the others, a somewhat broader view would do nothing but good, and would further the progress of the specialist. Yet there is an impression that bowl turning is special; the wood is treated differently, the tools and equipment used are different, the techniques are different. Therefore there has been a tendency to ignore the innate and strong interconnections between bowl turning and the rest of turning. Bowl turning is not a distinct entity, it is part of a greater whole.

The modern hand-turned wooden bowl is more often conceived as a decorative item or work of art than as a functional piece. The particular properties of wood and the relatively high cost of hand-turned wooden bowls mean that the purely functional role is now largely the prerogative of materials which can be cast or pressed, such as metal, plastic, clay, and glass.

The decorative role of the wooden bowl is based upon the form of the bowl and, of course, on the appearance of the wood itself. Hence, bowls have now become perhaps the main vehicle for showing the unique example of natural creation that each piece of wood is. Certainly each piece of wood is not equally attractive, so that the search for desirable species and especially attractive grain and colour examples within those and other species is now of major importance in bowl turning.

A major feature of contemporary bowl turning is the growing use of non-turning techniques so that in some cases the turning occupies less than five percent of the production time. Laminating, special finishes, carving, coloured staining, charring, cutting apart and reassembling, mixed media additions, etc.; anything is valid even if it is not always convincing or successful to individual observers.

Note that throughout this chapter, unless otherwise stated, the work is assumed to be turned outboard with the lathe rotating forwards, that is clockwise when viewed from the left of the headstock. The compromises that you have to make to bowl turn over the bed are described in Section 10.9.

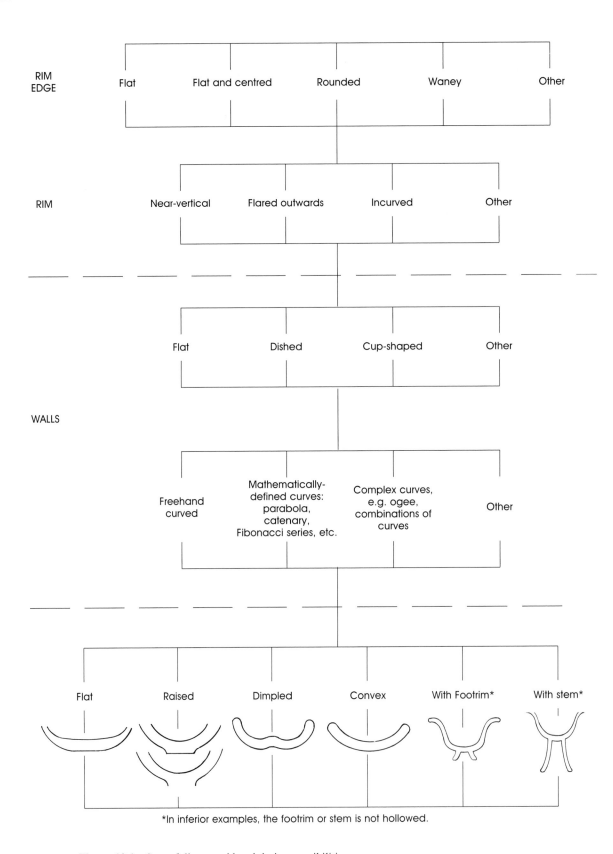

RIM
EDGE

Flat   Flat and centred   Rounded   Waney   Other

RIM

Near-vertical   Flared outwards   Incurved   Other

WALLS

Flat   Dished   Cup-shaped   Other

Freehand curved

Mathematically-defined curves: parabola, catenary, Fibonacci series, etc.

Complex curves, e.g. ogee, combinations of curves

Other

Flat   Raised   Dimpled   Convex   With Footrim*   With stem*

*In inferior examples, the footrim or stem is not hollowed.

Figure 10.1 Some fully-turned bowl design possibilities.

10.1 BOWL DESIGN

Much of Chapter 2 is relevant to bowl design, however neither it nor this section pretend to do the subject full justice. But while no longer the poor relation of technique, design, including bowl and vessel design, is still treated superficially. There are two main approaches: the first promotes the falsehood that success is merely a matter of applying geometric rules; the second approach seeks to inspire (or at least offer material to plagiarise) by just displaying a range of alternatives and gimmicks.

A particular bowl is the product of the specific intents of its creator. It communicates, however imperfectly, those intents to those who experience it. The appreciation of a bowl is not solely a matter of judging its success as a geometric object or a vehicle for wood display, especially when neither of these factors were considered important or relevant by the creator. The inquiring 'experiencer' has to attempt to discover the creator's intents. He then has to judge the merits of those intents and how successfully they are manifested in the bowl. This is at best an imperfect process as the experiencer will have a different mental make-up to, and have had different experiences from, the creator. Further the creation and experiencing are separated by time and geography. The thorough experiencer should therefore attempt to make three separate but related judgements on the bowl. He will judge its merits:

1. In the context of the time and place in which it was made.
2. In the context of the time and place in which the bowl is being experienced.
3. As a timeless object. The experiencer will attempt to exclude or separate the influences of such as changes in fashion or developments in technology.

The success of a bowl both to the creator and to later experiencers is largely dependent on the worth and clarity of the creator's intents. Those intents are not necessarily to create an object of aesthetic beauty or one which successfully fulfils a utilitarian purpose. They may even be intended to be private to the creator and thus hidden from future experiencers. When the creator's intents are intended to be public, they may be communicative, intended to even shock or horrify experiencers. The first step therefore towards producing a successful bowl is to clarify your creative intents. The second step is to decide how to manifest those intents. And the third is to produce the bowl. In many cases the three steps are neither separate nor serial, but without clarity the chance of success is small.

One of the attractions of bowl turning for many is that formal prior design is considered unnecessary, even undesirable. The rarity of good bowls, alas, confirms that most turners should be taking a more structured approach. While I am not advocating that for every bowl you turn you should draw a carefully considered full-size cross-section and make inside and outside templates, I believe that such an approach could do nothing but good. It would enforce clarity.

The possibilities for bowl and vessel shapes are infinite (Figure 10.1). I have chosen not to give pages of profiles or cross-sections, but describe below factors which influence appearance and tactility.

1. Bowls may vary in thickness in themselves or be of constant thickness which may itself be thin, medium, or thick.
2. Bowls may be turned from single pieces of wood or from laminated blanks, or they may be assembled from two or more turned components. In addition to simple butt laminating of seasoned sections to enable larger bowls to be turned, decorative laminating is also practiced. This is largely an exercise in precision sawing, drilling, sanding, and planing. It can be taken to extremes, and result in gar-

Figure 10.2 The Flag Bowl was made to celebrate Australia's victory in the 1984 America's Cup yacht race. It is made from paperbark *(Melaleuca quinquenervia)*, a wood much used in boat building.

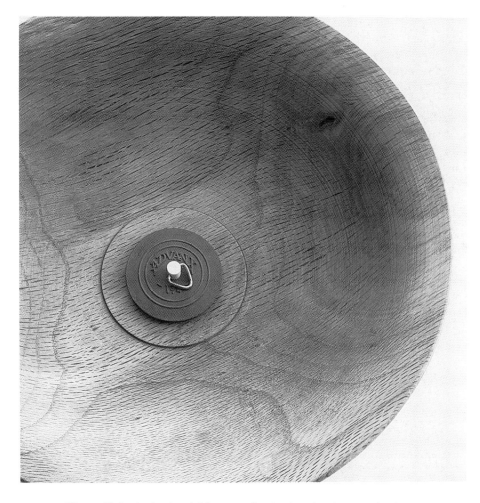

Figure 10.3   A plug bowl. Many people take these bowls too seriously.

Figure 10.4   The rippled finish left on English oak (Quercus robur) by using a gouge with a $^1/_{16}$-inch (1.5-mm) flute diameter in a near-vertical presentation.

ish multicoloured horrors. Besides laminating before turning, laminating may be used between stages in multiple-stage turning. The approach popularised by Stephen Hogbin has resulted in many fine and original works. Turnings are segmented, the segments sometimes being reshaped, and the segments reassembled, but not in their original relationships, to produce quite new shapes.

3. Carving or other processes may be applied during or after turning.
4. Bowls may be open or lidded.
5. There may be special design features which make the bowl unusual. For example, Figures 10.2 and 10.3 display communicative intents.
6. It is not necessary that the whole surface of a bowl be tooled. Waney or natural-edged bowls were fashionable in the late 1980s, but the bark or cambium surface left need not be restricted just to the rim.
7. Although most bowls are simply clear finished, unusual stains, charring, opaque finishes, and mixed media additions are being applied, particularly to manifest communicative intents.

The above merely gives a framework within which to discuss bowl design, but it is, I believe, possible to provide some specific advice:

1. When a bowl is to be utilitarian, such as a salad bowl, there are certain design constraints. The bowl should have a relatively wide base for stability, should not be too thick so that it can be lifted easily, and should be free of knots and cracks so that it does not leak.
2. For a given diameter and height, a bowl's capacity is substantially greater if the sides are steep.
3. A bowl should be designed wherever possible to show off the best figure (see Section 10.3), although this is not always compatible with other objectives.
4. Some woods—oaks (*Quercus* species) are perhaps the most common—are hard and turn crisply. With such woods, a rippled off-the-tool finish (Figure 10.4) is an alternative to the usual finely sanded surface. This rippled finish is more 'woody' to many people and blends well with country-style furniture. It is especially effective with bowls which are finish-turned when wet (Section 10.4), therefore warp during seasoning, and hence have an antique character. Much more expressive tooling has also been developed, notably by Mark Lindquist.
5. The curves in a bowl should be strong and definite, not weak and vague. Sudden changes in direction such as the projection of a footrim look best when at 90°.
6. The underside of a bowl is as important as the upper surfaces. There is no excuse for bowl bottoms with screw holes or crude coverings of felt or cork. Do not let your equipment dictate design.
7. Turned bowls with waney edges are not often aesthetically successful. If the bark is to be left on, ensure that no bits are missing.
8. Integrity of wall thickness is important. All too often you see bowls with walls thick at the base and razor sharp at the rim. The walls and base should be of equal and constant thickness unless there is a specific reason otherwise. Similarly, footrims and stems should be hollowed.
9. Lidded bowls are rarely completely satisfactory because of differential shrinkage coefficients and stress relaxation (see Sections 1.6 and 1.7). To minimise lack of fit, ensure that the wood is fully seasoned and that the bowl lid are cut from the same piece of wood and have the growth rings facing the same way. If the wood is quartersawn and, even if seasoned, can be rough-turned and allowed to further season and relax prior to finish-turning, then stability will be maximised.

Turned bowl design should be a two-way process. You should be in sympathy with the wood so that you can utilise its full potential. Therefore, the first major step described, that of selecting and preparing the wood for turning, implies that you can visualise the finished bowls within the tree, log, or plank from which you start, and further, that you have a good idea of the turning processes which will be used.

10.2 WOOD FOR BOWLS

Although for most woodworking timber is bought seasoned and dimensioned, bowl turners commonly use raw wood straight from the tree. It is not that trees may be obtained cheaply or at no cost, because of course harvesting your own wood is expensive—there is time, transport, and wear and tear on equipment. It is rather that the sizes, species, and grain configurations which a turner prefers or can use are just not available from most commercial timber outlets.

There is a strong correlation between species which spindle turn well and those which faceplate turn well. Certainly, however, the turnabilities of individual species are highlighted in the bowl turning situation. These show particularly when cutting *uphill*, that is, in the zone immediately after cutting at right angles to the grain (Figure 9.1). The difficulties associated with particular species and grain configurations are:

1. *Hardness.* Obviously, the bowl will take longer and your tools will blunt sooner. However, hardness and the attendant weight are not undesirable features in a finished bowl.
2. *Silica inclusions.* Some woods contain up to 1.5 percent of free silica grains. These rapidly blunt tools.
3. *Long fibres.* When you are turning woods with long fibres, there may be a tendency for wood to be torn out when cutting both against and parallel to the grain. Considerable extra sanding may therefore be the penalty for using such species.
4. *Large, brittle, medullary rays.* In some species, these rays have a tendency to chip out rather than be cut.
5. *Crushing or bruising.* Some species, and perhaps especially the softer fine-grained hardwoods, tend to crush under the tool rather than stand up and be crisply cut. To minimise this, your tools must be sharp and be *cutting* with plenty of side rake. Tool presentation should be such as to avoid heel of bevel contact which causes circles of paler crushed cells. In some species this crushing damage can penetrate surprisingly deeply.
6. *Hard and soft grain.* Some species are composed of alternating layers of hard and soft tissue. Douglas fir is a well-known example. When being turned, the soft tissue often tends to crush and the harder tissue tends to prevent the sandpaper abrading the damaged soft tissue between unless the sanding is heavy and prolonged.
7. *Knots.* Knots will often chip out or be pulled out altogether during the turning process.
8. *Interlocked grain and grain not in a plane radial to the lathe axis.* Obviously the areas in which the tool is cutting *uphill* may not then be concentrated in the two zones showed in Figure 9.1.
9. *Spalted woods* (Figure 1.11) *and woods of very low strength.* With these woods, the finish left by the tool is very poor and special abrasion processes such as power sanding have to be used to produce an acceptable surface finish. In addition the wood may need to be hardened by being saturated with hard-setting glues or finishes.

10. *Shrinkage coefficients.* A major concern in bowl turning is the shrinkage and degrade which accompanies seasoning. It is particularly relevant to bowl turning because the process frequently involves you starting from freshly felled timber or from blanks which because of their size are relatively wet in the middle. Therefore unless you particularly desire the cracking and excessive warping associated with high shrinkage coefficients, you are better to concentrate on lower coefficient species.

11. *Internal stresses.* Section 1.7 discussed the warping and possible cracking associated with internal stresses. Bowl turners who are tempted to use wood which grew in a highly stressed state should be aware of the increased tendency to warping and cracking.

10.3 WOOD PREPARATION FOR ROUGH-TURNING OF BOWLS

About half the wood felled in the world is used for fuel. Woodworking processes tend to be just as wasteful, and when you are turning a thin-walled bowl, at least 90 percent of the precious wood ends up as shavings. However, one saving grace of bowl turners is that they can use, and may actively prefer, the contorted sections of a tree which are unsuitable for use by cabinetmakers and carpenters.

When you go to your local commercial timber yard, you may tend to forget that wood comes from trees. You can become annoyed when the wood is cracked, distorted, and not free from knots because you have not been associated with the stages prior to its being offered for sale. Bowl turners, however, tend to be prime examples of industrial vertical integration in that they often fell the tree, season the wood, turn and finish the bowls, and sell them direct to the general public! This section therefore considers the various stages and decisions implicit in converting the living tree into disks ready for the lathe.

Tree Felling

Tree felling, particularly of large specimens, is potentially hazardous to both persons and property, and a woodturner is well advised to leave it to those with the necessary equipment, skills, and insurances. However, for the more adventurous, felling need not be dangerous if care is exercised. Figure 10.5 shows the procedure. Two cuts are made to form either a conventional or a Humboldt undercut. The wedge which comes free should be about one-third of the tree diameter deep and one-fifth high with the intersection of the two cuts horizontal and at right angles to the intended lay (direction of fall). Make the backcut about 2 inches (50 mm) above the horizontal part of the undercut, and when it is sufficiently deep, drive in wood wedges to prevent the tree falling backwards. Continue to back-cut until a narrow strip of holding wood remains. If the tree has not started to fall, drive the wedges in further. The holding wood and undercut direct and control the fall so that the tree slips rather than jumps off the stump and is thereby prevented from kicking back over it.

Some trees grow with a lean or have lost major branches on one side. In these cases, the unskilled should attempt to fell the tree only in the direction of the lean or out of balance. If this is not possible, the tree should be taken down by a professional. Similarly, it is not recommended to attempt to fell a tree in windy conditions unless the wind is in the felling direction required.

Ropes can be useful to guide a small tree down, although their effect is negligible on larger trees. Ensure that the rope is long enough so that the luckless person pulling is not engulfed.

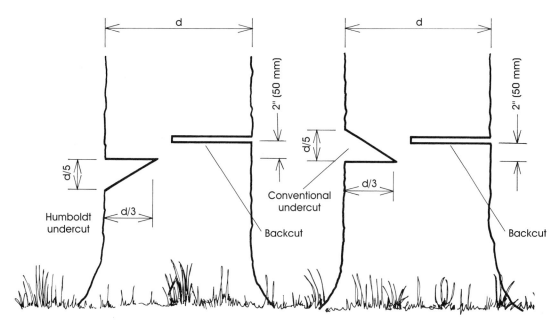

Figure 10.5 The steps in felling a tree.

Finally, take care in selecting the height of the felling cuts so that a desirable feature is not ruined—some tree fellers seem to specialise in cutting through the centre of large burls.

Dimensioning

The woodturner may wish to convert part of the tree into planks and square sections. Preferably, these should be cut from straight and vertical trunk sections. After cross-cutting with a chain saw, planks may be ripped with a chain saw alone (virtually impossible to produce planks straight and of even thickness), ripped with a chain saw mill, or band-sawed. If required, the planks may then be sawed into squares. Logs may be rived with wedges if of a species which will rive well. Alternatively it may be worthwhile to get the log converted at a nearby sawmill. Ensure that the sections have ample cross-sectional allowance for shrinkage and dressing, and that waste is also allowed at the ends for the inevitable end splitting which occurs during seasoning.

There are several ways to mill logs and the choice depends largely on the size of the log, the end uses anticipated, the figure, and the properties of the wood. With small logs, the wood may merely be halved or quartered, either by sawing or by riving.

With larger diameters, several criteria will be relevant to choosing the milling method:

1. With prominently rayed timbers, quartersawing is preferred as it shows the best figure and also minimises the tendency of such woods to split parallel to the rays.
2. With timbers with high shrinkage coefficients, quartersawing will again minimise distortion and splitting.
3. For woods without prominent rays, plainsawing (sawing through and through) often gives the best figure, but the planks will tend to cup.
4. If maximum width of plank is the main criterion, sawing through and through will be preferred.

5. The pith area is unstable, will always be a source of cracking, and so is usually boxed out.
6. In milling, allow ample for the inevitable end splitting and thicknesses which will have to be dressed off to eliminate cupping and other distortions which will occur during the seasoning.
7. Milling should be done as soon as possible after felling to minimise splitting in the log, damage due to insect attack and other causes, and fungal staining.

After milling, the wood should be end sealed and stacked under cover with stickers and weights if air seasoning is to be used. Alternatively it can be seasoned by kilning or by some other process.

Sectioning for Bowls

The easiest way to obtain disks for turning into bowls would be to cross-cut the tree to produce disks each with the pith running perpendicularly through the centre and bark around the cylindrical periphery. The major reason why this is not done is that cracks develop radially outwards from the pith during seasoning. Such cracks commonly and suddenly appear whenever you cross-cut a log due to instant internal stress relaxation. A less important reason is that the appearance of the bowl would be somewhat boring when compared with a bowl with the normal grain orientation. And the normal orientation has the grain running about parallel to the rim of the bowl; that is the bowl is turned from a disk cut from a plank. It is not uncommon for a bowl to have the grain running axially, but the turning process is then one of cupchuck turning.

In cutting up a tree for bowls, you may cut for figure, for stability, for colour effects, for shape, or for size. Sometimes these objectives will conflict. As outlined in the section on bowl design, as you cut up a tree you must visualise the finished bowls within. You must therefore be able to visualise the grain configuration, although sometimes faults or features hidden within the log may thwart your intentions. Each cut with the chain saw is irreversible, a step into the unknown. Sometimes you will be rewarded, sometimes your hopes will be dashed.

In a tree there are certain areas which typically have significantly greater figure: burls, crotches, and the butt or stump. In some species, sapwood and heartwood colour contrasts are a major feature.

Burls (Figure 10.6) are protuberances on the surface of the tree, often with a mass of fine twigs growing from them. The 'radial' grain directions within a burl are irregular and contorted so that burls are generally stable, although they may season with a great number of very fine, irregular cracks. It is the contortions of the grain and the eye figure which occur throughout that make burls so ornate. However, the burl figure goes well into the thickness of the basic log diameter, so merely cutting off the protuberances wastes much of the highly prized wood. Also if the tree is alive, pests and disease may enter through the wound and in time kill the tree.

A *crotch* (Figure 10.7) is the point where a single stem divides into two (or more) smaller stems. The figure can be very ornate, but is commonly more so in some species than others, and may vary in ornateness in crotches from a single tree. The ornate figure is concentrated in a narrow band between the piths. In addition, zones of fiddleback figure often occur in the outer wood where the single stem widens into the multiple stems.

The *butt* is the base of a tree, and contortion of figure occurs where the roots combine to form the trunk(s). A particularly ornate type of butt is the lignotuber, a large burl-like mass occurring just below the ground's surface from which both roots and trunks spring. These occur notably in the mallee trees in outback Australia. From time to time, fires destroy all the above-ground parts of these trees which then regenerate from the lig-

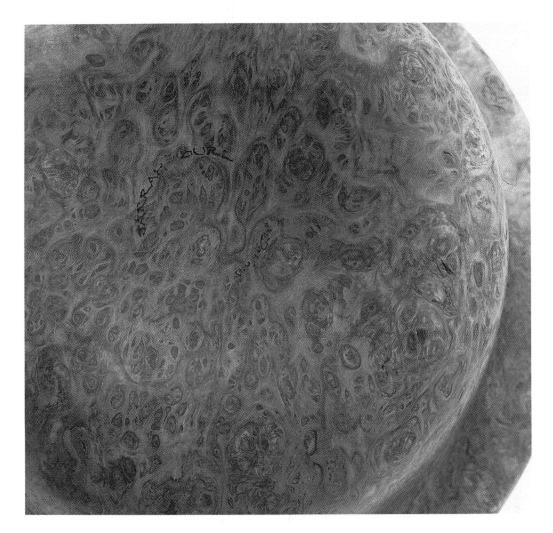

Figure 10.6   The dimpled bottom of a jarrah (*Eucalyptus marginata*) burl bowl showing the characteristic eye figure.

notuber. Another special case of the butt is the grass tree root. The grass tree is a true species of grass which occurs in Australia, and its underground root is sufficiently dense to be turned (Figure 10.8).

Obviously, the underground portion of the butt will contain stones, etc., and so chain saws are used with discretion—wedges, bow saws, and axes being preferred. However, the above-ground sections of trees are useful as notice boards, fence posts, etc., and so nails, wire, and even bottles may lurk unseen to damage your saws. Inspection of the trunk's surface may suggest hidden debris, but the damage caused to cutting equipment by foreign bodies in trees is part and parcel of bowl turning.

Besides the parts of a tree described above which reliably yield ornate figure, some trees yield special figure such as bird's eye (Figure 10.9), fiddleback (Figure 10.10), or colour banding (Figure 10.11). Some species can also show spectacular but often transient red colour banding due to insect attack (Figure 10.12).

In addition to being able to use the non-straight grained parts of the trunk, the bowl turner is well able to use branch wood. Branch wood is unsuitable for cabinetmaking as it grows in a highly stressed condition, is therefore unstable, and machines poorly.

Figure 10.7 The top of a raised platter showing crotch figure.

Figure 10.8 A bowl made from the root of the grass tree (*Xanthorrhoea arborea*). The base of the cone-shaped root is left unturned to form the rough rim.

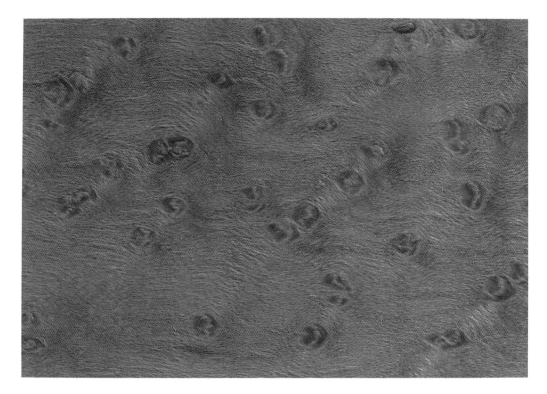

Figure 10.9 Bird's eye figure in maple (*Acer* species).

Figure 10.10 Fiddleback figure in Queensland maple (*Flindersia brayleyana*).

Figure 10.11   Characteristic colour banding in New Guinea walnut (*Dracontomelum mangiferum*).

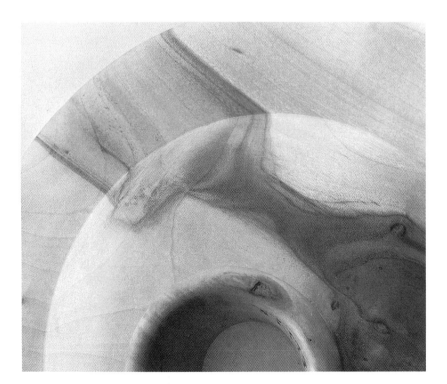

Figure 10.12   The result of insect damage to cream-coloured box elder (*Acer negundo*), a bright crimson stripe. On the underside of the stemmed bowl the colour remains vibrant, but it has faded inside the bowl due to sunlight.

However, it does turn satisfactorily, although the bowls produced may distort more than usual. The characteristic of branch wood, the growth of reaction wood, is described in Section 1.7.

When you are cutting up log cross-sections for bowls, the following points should be borne in mind:

1. If maximum size is the main consideration, split the log through a diameter to produce two semicircular blanks (Figure 10.13A).
2. If a quartersawn figure is desired, cutting as in Figure 10.13 C1, C2, C3, D2, or D3 will be suitable. However, cutting as in Figure 10.13B will give two quarter-sawn areas on the bowl sides if care is taken to keep the side grain parts of the

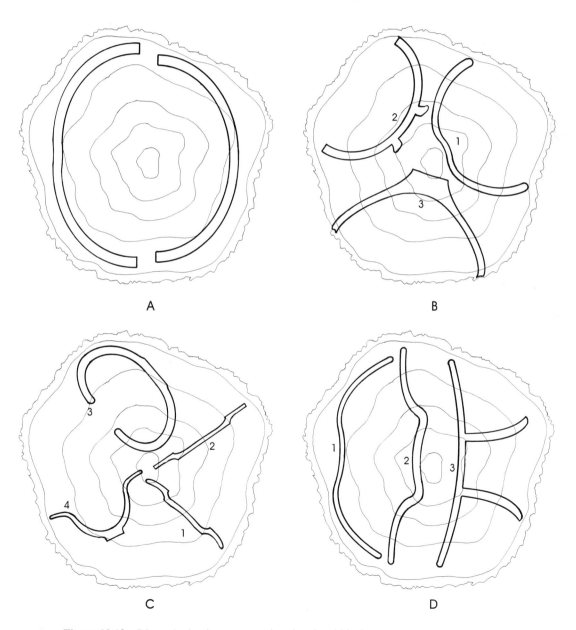

Figure 10.13 Dimensioning log cross-sections into bowl blanks.

walls within a radial plane as much as possible.
3. If the characteristic figure of the tree is annular bands of differing colours or of coarse and fine cells, the backcut surfaces in Figure 10.13A will show very ornate watery figure.
4. If a waney-edged rim is desired, then the log should be split as in Figure 10.13B3.
5. If there is a sharp colour contrast between sapwood and heartwood, then cutting as in Figure 10.13B3 is especially recommended.

Obviously, cutting up a tree for bowls requires both knowledge and thought. Unless you are able to identify and are familiar with the wood of the species, cut through a large branch and examine the grain and colour characteristics. The steps in cutting the tree into sections ready for final bandsawing are roughly as follows:

1. Fell the tree as previously described or bring it down in sections, taking care where the sections are cut; or start from a tree felled by others.
2. Saw out the sections with special figure allowing 20 percent waste per diameter of length. Separate logs which will be milled into planks.
3. Chain saw into lengths which are an integral number of diameters plus 20 percent. The 20 percent allowance per diameter allows for some end checking and the waste required during bandsawing.
4. Logs quickly develop star checking from the pith due to the changed internal stress conditions. To minimise this and also checking due to drying, saw or split the logs down the pith as soon as possible. Note that areas of contorted wood will not split cleanly and should therefore be sawed.
5. If bluestaining is to be avoided in prone species, the wood can be brushed with or immersed in a suitable chemical solution (see Section 1.8). It should be milled and seasoned quickly.
6. End checking of the log sections can be minimised by sealing the ends. It is also sensible to seal side-grain areas of contorted figure such as crotches. Mobilcer M, a proprietary wax emulsion, is easily brushed on. Wrapping in plastic bags or sheeting may also be used to prevent cracking prior to rough-turning.

The log sections should then be transported back to the workshop as soon as possible so that turning can commence with the minimum of delay and therefore the minimum of degrade.

Bandsawing into Disks

An essential part of the serious bowl turner's equipment is a bandsaw with a narrow blade width (that is up to $1\frac{1}{2}$ inches (37 mm)). Depth of cut is important and 20 inches (500 mm) is not unusual for a bandsaw with two 36-inch (915-mm) wheels. If a large bandsaw is not available, use a smaller one and one of the very handy small chain saws (electric chain saws are very useful inside the workshop).

Any woodworking machine is potentially dangerous, and a bandsaw is no exception. In cutting bowl blanks, you may be tempted to cut at the limit of the saw's capacity, the support of the wood being cut is not always optimum, and the length of blade exposed during a cut is variable even if the top guides are adjusted to be as low as possible. In short, take great care, ensure that your footing is secure, wear a face shield in case the blade breaks and spears back up off the table, and use a sharp blade with skip teeth and, if possible, more set than usual.

The procedure for cutting a bowl disk is illustrated in Figures 10.14 to 10.20. Do not cut up too many disks at a time, or they may start to crack before they can be turned.

Figure 10.14   Using an electric chainsaw to cut off a length of *Cedrus deodara* log about one-fifth longer than the log diameter.

Figure 10.15   Cutting along a diameter containing the pith. Ensure that the log will be stable when being sawed—a plywood cradle can be used for this.

Figure 10.16 The half log is placed cut face down on the bandsaw table, and a flat face is sawed on one end which will hence be at right angles to the face on the table.

Figure 10.17 The half log is rested on the squared end just cut, and a cut is taken parallel to the diametrical cut.

Figure 10.18 The wood is placed on the face cut in Figure 10.17 and a circle drawn. The circle's centre should be clearly marked if it is going to be used later to centre the blank on a faceplate. If it is appropriate or safer to cut the wood diametral face down, tack a thin, suitably sized disk on top and saw around it.

Figure 10.19 Cutting out the circular disk. Be careful to keep your hands well clear of the blade.

Figure 10.20   Trimming the base of the disk. A somewhat risky cut which can be omitted, or made safe by sloping the bandsaw table or by using an adjustable sloping cradle.

10.4 OUTLINE TURNING PROCEDURES

There can be a variety of starting points for turning a particular bowl. Figure 10.21 outlines the basic, possible, subsequent procedures, of which there are three:

1. Starting from a wet or unseasoned disk, to rough-turn a thick-walled version of the final bowl, season or stabilise it, and then finish-turn the final bowl which will largely retain its turned shape long-term.
2. Finish-turn directly from the wet or unseasoned disk. The resulting bowl will warp, perhaps grossly (Figure 10.22), during subsequent seasoning and stress relaxation.
3. If starting from a fully seasoned disk, to finish-turn directly. After the turning there will be some minor warping and a small risk of cracking due to stress relaxation and further seasoning, but this is generally accepted. If long-term true circularity is required, a preliminary rough-turning operation as in procedure 1 would be necessary.

Bowl Rough-Turning

The purposes of rough-turning prior to seasoning or stabilisation are:

1. To speed the turning. Wet wood cuts more easily and can therefore be turned off more quickly.
2. To reduce the likelihood of degrade during seasoning and stress relaxation. Because the bowl is seasoned in a bowl form rather than a disc form, the walls of

the rough-turned bowl have some, albeit limited, flexibility and cracking is therefore less likely.
3. To improve the dimensional stability of the finished bowl.
4. To speed seasoning and stabilisation (see Sections 10.5 and 10.6).

To speed seasoning and reduce the chance of cracking, the rough-turning should take the blank down to near the minimum wall thickness which will still allow you to finish-turn your desired bowl. After seasoning the blank will be oval. Therefore the roughed wall thickness must be sufficient to accommodate a circular bowl of the prescribed thickness being finished-turned from the seasoned oval. What this rough-turned wall thickness should be depends primarily on the bowl size and the wood's shrinkage coefficients, but the required research to enable definitive recommendations has yet to be done. However for a bowl diameter of about 12 inches (300 mm), a wall thickness of between 1 to 2 inches (25 to 50 mm) depending on the shrinkage coefficients would be usual.

Finish-Turning

If you finish-turn directly from a wet disk, the finished wall thicknesses must have sufficient flexibility to allow the inevitable warping to occur without unacceptable cracking. The maximum wall thickness which will give an acceptable result varies according to the:

Moisture contents through the wood
Shrinkage coefficients of the timber
Dimensions of the bowl
Presence of sap wood
Seasoning process after turning
Directions and contorted nature of the grain

Typically the wall thicknesses chosen would be between $^3/_4$ and $^1/_4$ inch (19 and 6 mm) for a bowl of about a foot (300 mm) diameter. The chosen thicknesses should be fairly constant over the whole bowl surface, if not cracking will be more likely. Cracking

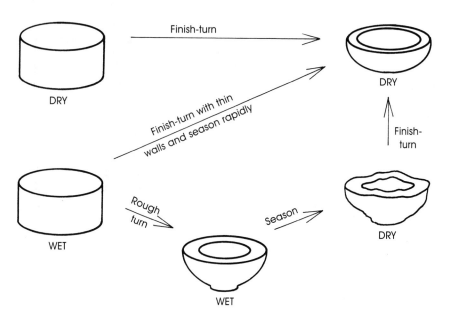

Figure 10.21 The basic procedures for turning wooden bowls.

Figure 10.22   A pappadum bowl. Turned very thinly from a crotch, a wood with high shrinkage coefficients will warp like this if turned green.

Figure 10.23   A large bowl turned green. The outcurving rim leads to more interesting shrinkage effects.

Figure 10.24   A seasoned bowl blank of peppermint gum (*Eucalyptus piperita*).When turned from the green wood, the bowl was round and flat-topped. Even though the walls are 1¹/₂ inches (37 mm) thick, the bowl has gone oval in plan and has cupped in cross-section. (Seasoning bowls will cup in a fashion opposite to the end-grain arcs of the annual or growth rings).The top of the bowl shows the corrugated surface caused by collapse and also cracking from the pith.

will also be less likely: if highly unstable zones are absent—therefore the pith zone is usually excluded, if the wood is sealed immediately after the turning, and if the seasoning (which may only take a day or two) is taken carefully.

Warping will occur during the turning. You will therefore need to modify your turning method. Freshly turned areas should be sanded before significant warping occurs. The sanding of wet wood will be considerably slower owing to clogging of the abrasive paper or cloth—an off-the-tool finish eliminates this problem (Figure 10.4).

As warping is perhaps the most prominent feature of green-turned bowls, you may wish to emphasise it. It can be increased by using species with high shrinkage coefficients and by cutting the blanks from areas of contorted grain (Figure 10.22). Warping can be made less regular and therefore usually more attractive by shaping the bowls sympathetically. For example, if turning a green bowl from a semicircular trunk cross-section (see Figure 10.13A), a bowl with an outcurving rim (Figure 10.23) or an incurving rim will warp more interestingly than a shallow U-shaped one. However if the axis of the bowl is not radial in the log, or if the grain structure is grossly asymmetrical, the bowl will probably warp into a unbalanced shape which may or may not be attractive.

10.5 SEASONING

Several seasoning factors affect the magnitude of shrinkage, cracking, and other degrade defects:

1. Degrade is reduced if the drying rate is not reversed.
2. Degrade will be reduced if moisture-content gradients (that is change in moisture content per unit thickness) through the wood's thickness can be kept gentle. These gradients are however necessary for there to be moisture flow through the wood.
3. Degrade should be less if the wood can be held in a more plastic state during the drying.

Drying in the natural atmosphere can be slowed by partially sealing the bowl or by keeping it enclosed. The bowl will then dry out gradually, but once below 25 percent moisture content it may absorb moisture on humid days. Obviously any reversals to the drying will tend to increase degrade. Section 1.6 noted the very rapid evaporation through end grain. Degrade can be reduced, while maintaining a fast seasoning rate, by sealing the exposed end grain only.

Atmospheric drying can be made more gentle and even by:

1. Keeping the bowls out of drafts, out of direct sunlight, in cupboards, or in paper bags.
2. Keeping the bowls in dry sawdust that is changed from time to time.
3. Sealing the surface with paste wax or a wax emulsion such as Mobilcer M. This treatment is also effective in preventing Lyctid attack.

Rough-turned bowls unsealed or lightly sealed will take a minimum of three months to reach equilibrium moisture content (in average coastal areas 12 to 15 percent). This can be checked with a moisture meter or by weighing regularly. Fully sealed bowls may take at least twelve months to dry to this state. The actual duration taken for roughed bowls to reach equilibrium moisture content will vary considerably.

Fungal attack and the inherent staining start as soon as the tree is felled. They will be increased if the drying rate is slowed by the means described above and if there is no air movement. Whether attack is desirable or not will influence the choice of seasoning method (see Section 1.9).

Seasoning can be accelerated and degrade can be reduced by using small evaporative heating kilns. These keep the wood at a raised temperature so that the lignin is softened and the wood is therefore much freer to distort. Seasoning done in microwave ovens uses microwave energy to heat the wood, soften the lignin, and increase the evaporation of the water. However steam forms and causes cracking if too high a temperature is generated inside the wood. Microwave seasoning is therefore generally done at defrost, and in stages with cooling between. It is not effective with very dense woods or thick walls as the microwaves do not penetrate sufficiently.

A process in which temperature control is more certain uses 'external' heating and vacuum. Heat is applied to soften the lignin and a partial vacuum is used to hasten evaporation. Temperature and pressure need to be controlled so that the lignin is softened without the water in the wood boiling. This form of seasoning is commercially available and has a high capital cost, but it is very effective.

10.6 STABILISATION

An alternative to seasoning is stabilisation, but this process does have its drawbacks.

The recommended stabiliser is polyethylene glycol in the form whose molecular weight is 1000. It is known as PEG 1000 or simply PEG. PEG is a white, waxy chemical at room temperature, which is slowly but completely water soluble. PEG melts at 104°F (40°C) and can then be mixed immediately. Aqueous solutions containing 30 to 50 percent by weight of PEG are used. The fully green rough-turned bowls are immersed in PEG solution for a few days to several weeks depending on the wood species, the PEG solution temperature, and the wood thickness. When the moisture in the wood has been replaced by PEG, the wood is stable, that is, unable to degrade by evaporation. It may then be turned, sanded, surface dried, and polished.

PEG treatment prevents distortions and cracking due to drying. It will not affect distortions which rough-turning initiates because of the need of the wood to relax into a new equilibrium internal stress pattern.

PEG acts by displacing the water in the cell walls, the combined water, by the process of diffusion. PEG penetration is rarely greater than 2 inches (50 mm), and in hard, dense woods it may not penetrate at all. When the wood is saturated with PEG, it is still wet because the free water is still in the wood. Therefore, after the bowl has been finish-turned and sanded, it must be dried so that a finish will take. There are no additional problems that the presence of PEG introduces into the turning process except that abrasive papers will clog very quickly.

Because the PEG held in the wood is still water soluble, it will come to the wood's surface in humid weather. The wood should therefore be sealed, polyurethane is recommended.

PEG is also useful for large turnings such as lamp bases which are turned direct from green logs. Multiple holes are drilled from the bottom to enable full PEG penetration.

I am conscious that this and the previous section avoid giving much quantitative information, but can only admit that I have not undertaken any worthwhile research.

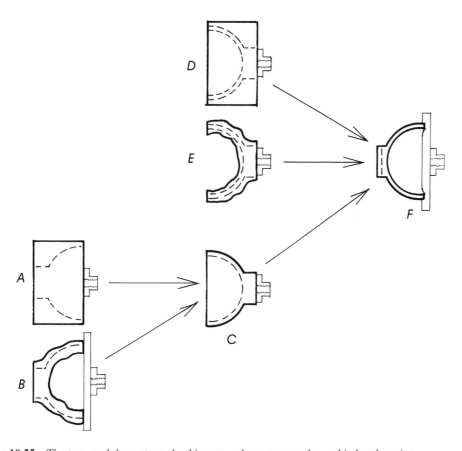

Figure 10.25 The two- and three-stage chucking procedures commonly used in bowl turning.

Further details may be found in Patrick Spielman, *Working Green Wood with PEG*, Sterling Publishing, New York, 1980, and in R. Bruce Hoadley, *Understanding Wood, A Craftsman's Guide to Wood Technology*, Taunton Press, Newtown, Connecticut, 1980.

10.7 BOWL CHUCKING

During the rough-turning and finish-turning procedures outlined in Section 10.4 the wood has to be held in the lathe. The area being held cannot be turned during that turning operation. Therefore for that and for other reasons special chucking methods and equipment have been developed. This section seeks to describe them.

Figure 10.25 outlines two- and three-stage chucking procedures. The three-stage is not redundant because it enables unrestricted access to the outside of the bowl when mounted as in *A* and *B*. The disadvantage of three-stage chucking is that the re-chucking by the bowl bottom at *C* must be truly axial or the bowl outside will need to be skimmed in order to obtain an even wall thickness.

Many turners choose to omit the final chucking at *F* in Figure 10.25. The reasons why a finished bowl which retains features only there for chucking cannot be first-rate are discussed in Section 10.1.

When bowl bottoms have suitably shaped shoulders, stems, or footrims, the final stage *F* need not be used. In this situation, *A* and *B* in Figure 10.25 become stage 1 of 2, and *C* becomes stage 2 of 2.

A feature of bowl turning is the continuing development of chucking equipment. None of the new chucks make anything new possible, for all chucking can be accomplished with the humble faceplate. What the chucks do to varying degrees is allow the wood to be chucked more quickly.

The remainder of this section outlines the chucking methods which can be used in *A* to *F* in Figure 10.25: it is comprehensive but not exhaustive, and concentrates on chuck types rather than brands.

Turning the Outside of a Disk, Stage 1 of 3, Figure 10.25A

There are five major chucking options for rough- or finish-turning the outside of a bowl starting from a wet or a seasoned disk:

1. Turn between centres. The tail centre (ideally a ring centre) holds the bottom of the bowl. Your normal driving centre will probably be too small to hold securely and consistently, especially if the wood is wet—the special faceplate in Figure 10.26 shows an easily made and superior substitute.
2. Screws through a faceplate. This is probably the most common method. Screw penetration can be deep as you are screwing into what will be waste. If the top of the disk is slightly uneven, plane it flat or use packing washers on the screws between the faceplate and the bowl's top. If you are turning inboard, the tailstock can be brought up until the workpiece has been turned sufficiently for it to be in reasonable dynamic balance.
3. Drill a suitably-sized hole into the top of the disk and use with:

   a. A pin chuck (Figures 10.27 and 10.28). Note that the disk can tend to slide off the early pin chucks with smooth spigots.
   b. The outer surfaces of expanding jaws. Such jaws are often dovetailed (Figure 10.29) and are supplied with:
   i. Engineer's scroll chucks.

Figure 10.26 A bowl driving centre held by a scroll chuck. If the face of the blank is uneven, packing washers can be slipped over the prongs. Alternatively the projections of the prongs can be varied as they screw through tapped holes in the plate.

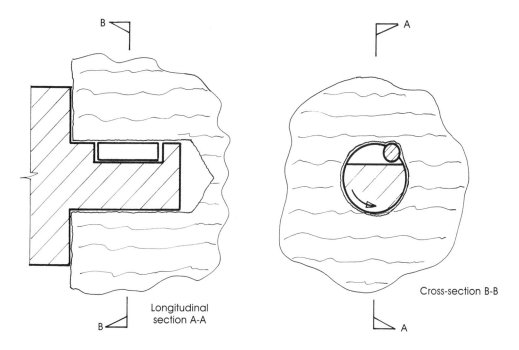

Figure 10.27 The early form of pin chuck. Tool applied forces further wedge the loose pin.

Figure 10.28   The 1 inch (25 mm) pin chuck jaws of a Maxi-Grip 2000 chuck. The ridges prevent the blank sliding off, a problem with the earlier form in Figure 10.27.

  ii.   Woodturner's scroll-type chucks
 iii.   Collet-type chucks.
 iv.   The Woodfast Super Chuck.

   c. A screwchuck. This is only suitable for small workpieces. You may be able to supplement its hold with screws if your screwchuck allows this.
   d. A Woodfast Screw Spigot Chuck (a larger version of a screwchuck).
4. Some chucks have supplementary steel rings which are screwed directly to the workpiece. The supplementary ring usually has some form of dovetailed recess into which particular chuck jaws are designed to expand, and therefore acts similarly to the recess in the workpiece in method 3b.
5. If the top is flat, by high-vacuum chucking.

   If you are chucking inboard, the tailstock should be used to give greater security, at least until the workpiece is in reasonable dynamic balance. You should also note the precautions described at the end of method 15 later.

Turning the Outside of a Seasoned Blank, Stage 1 of 3, Figure 10.25*B*

Chucking a seasoned blank by its rim is a little more demanding because you do not want to lose bowl height by screwing in at the radius of the finished bowl rim, and because the top of the blank is unlikely to be flat. There are five main holding methods.

6. If the top can be flattened, by high-vacuum chucking as in method 5 above.
7. Plane the top flat, either by hand or with care on a planer. Because the top of the

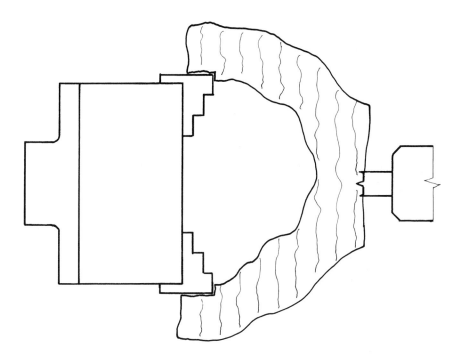

Figure 10.29 Gripping a seasoned blank inside the rim with a scroll chuck. The jaws should not be expanded too strongly. With the tailstock against the bottom, the outside and bottom can be trued and the bowl thus be prepared for being held by its bottom.

blank is roughly elliptical there will be waste areas inside and outside the intended bowl rim which you can screw into, either through a faceplate or through a supplementary disk mounted on a faceplate.

8. If you have engineering chuck jaws which will spread wide enough, by gripping the outside of the rim of the blank. Depending on whether the chuck is three or four-jaw and on how the rim has warped, there may be difficulty in centring the blank.

9. Adrian Hunt in Tasmania has a novel method. At the previous roughing stage he turns a short section of the inside bowl wall to a uniform diameter. After seasoning he then expands his scroll chuck jaws to grip against it (Figure 10.29).

10. Glue the blank onto a supplementary disk. Various forms of gluing have been developed. The difficulty has been to de-chuck without having to saw the workpiece free. Methods 10a. and b. allow you to quickly chuck a series of workpieces without having to change or remove the supplementary disk.

    a. Use hot melt glue. This glue never sets hard and the workpiece can be prised or jolted off.

    b. Double-sided tape is an increasingly popular holding medium. It does however not hold too strongly and has a flexibility.

    c. Use a paper joint. The process is similar to that described in Section 7.18.

Turning the Inside, Stage 2 of 3, Figure 10.25C

After roughing the outside as at *A* or finish-turning the outside at *A* or *B*, there are several chucking choices at *C*, the rough- or finish-turning of the bowl inside. Depending on the method chosen there may have to be some particular feature turned on or in the base at *A* or *B*. For woods such as seasoned burl which are crumbly and do not hold screws, etc. well, you may need to glue on a supplementary plywood disk and chuck onto that. The major chucking alternatives at *C* are:

11. Holding using high-vacuum as in method 5. Take care that the area of bowl bottom within the sealing ring of the vacuum chuck is large enough to give sufficient hold.
12. Screws through a faceplate. Try to select the largest radius at which to install the screws which does not cause you to lose bowl height. In general screw penetration need not be more that $^1/_2$ inch (13 mm). It is usually better to use more screws than deepen their penetration.

    The problem with this method is to ensure the truly axial mounting required if the bowl rim is to be even. Assuming that the bottom of the blank has been turned true you can:

    a. Eye the faceplate centrally onto the blank. To assist, pencil a circle on the bowl bottom either a little smaller than the hole through the faceplate or a little larger than the outside diameter of the faceplate. This can be done with the lathe running at *A* or *B*.
    b. At *A* or *B*, turn a shallow spigot projecting from the bowl bottom which can mate with the hole through the faceplate. Alternatively you can turn a shallow recess with a diameter equal to your faceplate's outside diameter in the bowl bottom.
    c. Use a supplementary wooden plate on the faceplate, and turn a shallow recess in it. The diameter of the recess in this press-fit type chuck should match that of the diameter of the bowl bottom turned at *A* or *B*, or that of a shallow waste

Figure 10.30   Trimming a dovetailed recess in a bowl bottom with a side- and end-cutting scraper. The expanding dovetail jaws of a Nova scroll chuck are shown on the right.

spigot. You can rely just on a friction fit, supplement with vacuum, or screw through the supplementary plate (and if possible the faceplate) to hold the bowl. If a bowl is to have a hollowed stem or footrim (see Figure 10.1), you can use deeper-than-normal fixings or even a screwchuck into the waste inside this feature as the waste will be turned away at stage *F*. Alternatively, although few aesthetically successful bowl designs allow it, if the whole bowl outside and bottom are finished at stages *A* or *B*, it may be possible to avoid the need for stage *F*. To take advantage of this option, the finished bowl bottom needs a definite feature such as a stem, footrim, or shoulder. Ideally the feature should have a constant diameter where it will be gripped within the press fit or other chuck.

13. Use method 12c above, but hot melt glue the bowl bottom into the recess.
14. Turn or drill at *A* or *B* a shallow recess in the bowl bottom and use with expanding jaws as in methods 3bii, iii, and iv (Figure 10.30). As discussed in Section 10.1, I do not believe that such a recess is compatible with a first-rate bowl, however many turners turn decorative mouldings in these recesses and display them with pride in their finished bowls, thereby avoiding stage *F*.
15. An alternative to jaws expanding into a recess is jaws contracting onto a suitably-shaped footrim, stem, shoulder, or a shallow spigot surrounded by an annular recess. This method can be more secure as there is no tendency to split the wood asunder. As in chucking method 12c, if the whole bowl outside is finish-turned at *A* or *B*, this method 15 can be a final stage and stage *F* is not required.

   To ensure in methods 14 and 15 that the hold is secure and the bottom of the blank is truly perpendicular to the lathe axis:

   a. Use the largest diameter of chuck jaws feasible and safe.
   b. The chuck jaws should ideally exert the same pressure over almost the whole wall of the spigot, shoulder, or recess. Therefore turn the holding feature to the correct, specified diameter for this, and if the jaws are dovetailed similarly dovetail the feature.
   c. The back of the blank should bear against the face of the chuck rather than the faces of the jaws. Jaws which can be used include those of: scroll, scroll-type and collet-type chucks; and the Woodfast Super Chuck.However the area of jaw/wood contact is too small for a really secure hold with engineer's scroll chuck standard jaws and the jaws of some other chucks. When using these you should be less vigorous in your turning.

Turning the Outside and Inside, Stage 1 of 2, Figure 10.25*D* and *E*

When mounting a wet or a seasoned disc at *D*, or a roughed and seasoned blank at *E*, you will need a plane base. You can then use for *D* and *E*:

16. High-vacuum chucking as in method 11.
17. Screwing through a faceplate as in method 12a. Ideally the faceplate should be small so that there is good tool access to the lower wall outside.
18. Expanding chuck jaws into a shallow detailed recess (method 14) or a supplementary ring (method 4). For *E*, with both methods 17 and 18 you may be able to reuse the fixing features used to hold the blank in the earlier roughing.
19. Gluing onto a supplementary wooden disk as in method 10. (For a rough-turned blank you may have to plane the bottom flat). Note that most glues hold poorly onto wet wood.

Figure 10.31 Taping a bowl into a press fit chuck prior to finish-turning the bottom. The fly does not seem to be too impressed.

At the top right a crude but effective bracket is shown. The outer edge of the chuck is chamfered and a small piece of plywood screwed on. A piece of carpet protects the bowl surface. Two or more such brackets are sufficient. Instead of the continuous chamfer you could chisel a recess.

Figure 10.32   Reverse chucking a waney-edged burl bowl in the cage of a funnel and annular ring chuck. The tailstock is used to axially align the bowl. The rings can be used with a press fit chuck and without a funnel for bowls with plane rims.

Finish-Turning the Bottom, Final stage, Figure 10.25*F*

This stage can be done inboard or outboard, although inboard allows you to use the tail-stock for additional safety (and for axially aligning the bowl).

If the rim is reasonably complete and plane, the basis of the reverse-chucking methods is the press fit chuck which automatically locates the bowl's axis truly along the lathe axis. The various ways in which the press fit chuck (Section 4.9) can be used are:

20. Alone (Figure 4.16). In this case the rim of the bowl must be a really tight fit or else the bowl will come out. The advantage of this method is that you have full access to the bowl outside. Its disadvantages are the ever-present risk of the bowl flying out and the impossibility of holding bowls with incurved rims or similar.

    If the fit of the bowl rim within the recess is as tight as it needs to be, the bowl will be hard to de-chuck. You can squirt compressed air through a hole in the supplementary plate, tap the chuck while it is on the lathe, or tap the rim of the chuck, bowl down, on the edge of the lathe bed or a bench.

21. With additions. To increase the security of the previous method 20, and fortuitously to lessen the need for a such a tight fit, you can use:
    a. Packaging tape wrapped around the bowl and chuck (Figure 10.31).
    b. Informal supplementary brackets (Figure 10.31). I use two or more rectangular bits of thinnish plywood or similar screwed onto the face of the chuck. Use padding to protect the bowl surface.
    c. Formal brackets which slide and are fixed in radial slots.
    d. Annular loose rings. These are bolted back to the press fit chuck (Figures 10.32 and 10.33). To give maximum tool and visual access to the bowl bottom have the hole through the ring as large as possible. The major applications for this method are for incurved bowls or those with thick, round rims.
    e. High vacuum.
    f. Low vacuum. Domestic vacuum cleaners which do not use the sucked air to cool their motors can be used to apply a low vacuum. A crude form of union can be readily made using a sealed bearing (Figure 10.34). Vacuum chucking is a very quick chucking method, but any loss of seal is catastrophic unless you take extra precautions such taping (method 21a).
    g. A press fit chuck which grips by contraction. Dale Ross in the August 1995 *Fine Woodworking* magazine details such a device.

Other methods for stage - include:

22. The chuck plate principle detailed in Section 4.7 (Figures 10.35 and 10.36). Several brands of scroll and collet-type chuck offer this.
23. Supplementary sector shaped plates with radially adjustable studs (Figure 10.37). This extension of the chuck plate principle is again offered by several chuck brands,
24. The Longworth chuck. Invented in New Zealand, this chuck works somewhat like a scroll chuck.

Waney or natural edged bowls, often with the bark attached, are still popular to turn. The non-plane top complicates their chucking at *A*, *B*, and *F*. At *A* and *B* chucking on a faceplate may be difficult. The pin chuck or between centres options are preferred for *A*, but the former is not an option for *B*. Turning the back off at *F* cannot be done using a press-fit chuck; however there are several options:

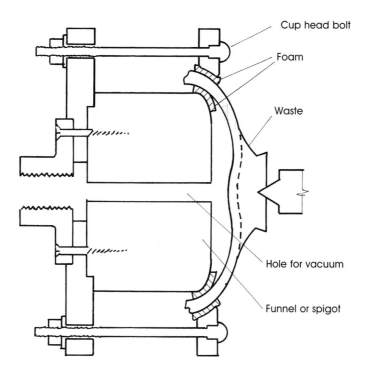

Cup head bolt

Foam

Waste

Hole for vacuum

Funnel or spigot

Figure 10.33   A longitudinal section through a funnel and annular ring chuck. By having replaceable funnels of various shapes, and by having several annular rings each with a different internal diameter, a wide variety of bowl shapes and sizes can be held. Ideally the ring should press onto the outside of the bowl opposite where it is supported internally by the funnel.

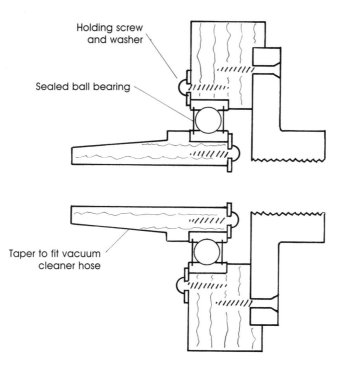

Holding screw and washer

Sealed ball bearing

Taper to fit vacuum cleaner hose

Figure 10.34   A homemade vacuum union based on a faceplate and sealed bearing. Leakage is relatively high so that only about 20 percent of full vacuum is attainable.

Figure 10.35   Cutting a slightly dovetailed annular recess in the supplementary plates which are attached to the chuck plates pictured on page 65.

Figure 10.36   A bowl is about to be gripped by its rim in the recess turned in Figure 10.35.

25. Instead of a press fit chuck use a funnel or spigot as the basis for several chucking options. These options are:

   a. High vacuum.
   b. Annular loose rings as in method 21d. Ideally the rim of the funnel should be directly resisting the force applied by the ring (Figure 10.33). Both this option and 25a are best done inboard so that the tailstock can be used to ensure axial alignment of the workpiece and give added support and security during the reverse-turning.
   c. Use the unorthodox turning procedure in Figure 10.38. Note, this procedure can also be used for bowls with plane rims.

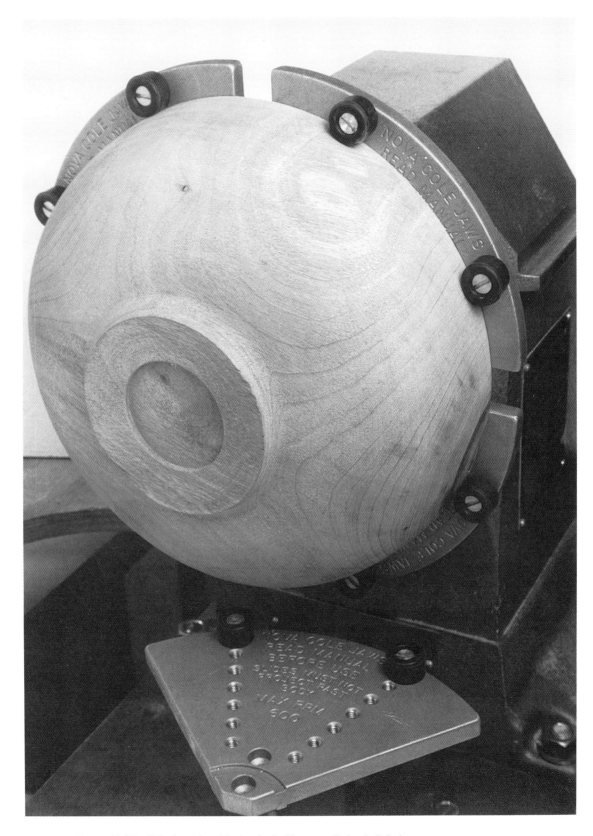

Figure 10.37   Gripping a bowl by its rim in Nova scroll chuck Cole jaws.

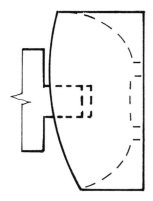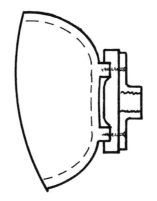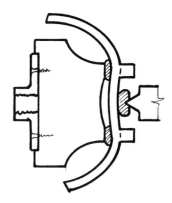

Figure 10.38   An alternative and unorthodox chucking procedure. *Left*: chucking the blank on a pin chuck to turn the outside. The bottom within the annular ridge of waste is finish-turned and sanded at this stage. *Middle*: the bowl is held by the ridge of waste while finish-turning the inside. *Right*: the bowl surfaces are protected by padding on the tail centre and spigot while the waste ridge is turned off.

10.8 TOOL CHOICE AND PRESENTATIONS

The major tools used in bowl turning are: bowl gouges, spindle detail gouges, hook tools, ring tools, flat scrapers, and shear scrapers. All except bowl gouges were discussed in Chapter 5.

Until the mid-1970s the bowl gouge was little known and bowl turning was generally done with spindle gouges and scrapers in the English-speaking world. Whether the few turners who specialised in bowls used special gouges or specially sharpened detail gouges, I know not. Elsewhere hook tools were widely used. Now the English- and non-English-speaking worlds are learning the advantages of each other's techniques. But what are not generally clarified are the advantages of bowl gouges for bowl turning, and their differences from spindle gouges. These advantages and differences are listed below, and are discussed at length in this section:

1. For a given nominal size (outside diameter), a bowl gouge is stiffer due to its high flanges.
2. A bowl gouge is intended to be mainly used in a near-horizontal presentation. Spindle gouges are less presentation specific.
3. A detail gouge is a *cutting* tool. When taking heavy cuts in a near-horizontal presentation, the bowl gouge tends to sever the shaving by *cutting*, and *scrape* or *shear scrape* it out of the way with the base of the flute so as not to impede tool progress. A bowl gouge is therefore superior for taking heavy cuts approximately parallel to the lathe axis.
4. The flute of a detail gouge approximates to semicircular in cross-section. Most bowl gouges have a U- or V-shaped flute giving a central section of high curvature, the insides of the two projecting flanges having low curvature.
5. Detail gouges are often used for cutting details, their pointy noses help in this. Bowl gouges are less suited to detail cutting because their nose shapes are generally much blunter.
6. The desirable side rake for bowl finishing cuts is greater than that for spindle finishing cuts. This and the advantage of being able to work at long tool overhangs largely explain why bowl gouges are used in horizontal presentations.

7. By varying the axial rotation of most bowl gouges, the curvature of the active length of cutting edge can be varied. With other than a bowl gouge sharpened square-across, varying the axial rotation also alters the side rake. Similar active cutting edge curvatures and side rakes can usually be achieved by presenting a bowl gouge in different ways.

There is little consensus on either the optimum blade cross-section or nose sharpening of bowl gouges. Why? Because the use of bowl gouges does not readily lend itself to the clear, theoretical treatment which can be applied to spindle turning tools. Give a competent bowl turner almost any bowl gouge sharpened in almost any recognised fashion and he or she will be able to perform competently with it. But this is not a reason for ducking the challenge of providing at least some specific advice.

It is convenient to split bowl turning into two: rough-turning in which the major intent is to rapidly turn-off unwanted waste wood; and finish-turning in which you are normally trying to achieve the best possible surface finish, usually a finish with minimal rippling and subsurface damage. In addition both rough- and finish-turning are applied to surfaces which are convex or concave, or a mixture in plan and in vertical section. There can be access problems, for example when hollowing deep bowls. And finally, how many bowl gouges are you prepared to buy? One only, or, at the other extreme, one for each particular bowl turning situation.

In Chapter 9 the versatility of the spindle detail gouge was demonstrated. The bowl gouge is at least as versatile; a strength to the user but a complicating factor to the theoretician. There are two extremes of presentation, both of which were described in Chapter 9: the near-horizontal presentation (Figure 9.5), and the near-vertical presentation (Figure 9.2). In the main, bowl gouges are used in the former. This is because:

1. A much greater tool overhang can be safely used.
2. If control is lost, the consequences are far less serious.
3. A more advantageous cutting edge support is possible if a high side rake presentation is used.
4. Nose sharpening is easier and there is more scope to use more of the cutting edge.

In Section 5.1 the problems of bevel support were discussed. Too much support and you get glazing, crushing, bevel bounce, and rippling; too little and the cutting edge stutters. Just $1/8$ inch (3 mm) movement of the handle is enough to materially effect the quality of the bevel support. And you judge the quality of the cut largely through the feeling transmitted from the nose and along the blade and handle to your right hand. The sound produced is also relevant. The competent turner is much more likely to present the tool well at the start of a cut, and is then sufficiently attuned so that he can make any presentational adjustments required during the cut's duration.

In my attempt to be at least somewhat definitive, I shall split bowl gouge design into three (Figure 10.39): the blade cross-section, the nose profile and the bevel curvature.

Bowl Gouge Cross-Section

For the few reasons described earlier, bowl gouges are mostly used in near-horizontal presentations. Hence the irrelevance of the circular cross-section flutes preferred for spindle detail gouges, tools which are primarily used to cut hollows with curvatures little smaller than those of their flutes.

Bowl gouges are subjected to strong and varying forces. The tall flanges contribute substantially to blade stiffness while creating three lengths of cutting edge: two of small curvature between which is one of high curvature at the base of the flute.

In Figure 5.17 it was shown that as the side rake increases, the length of *cutting* but unsupported cutting edge increases. Therefore the minute cutting edge pivoting and oscillations (page 87) increase and in turn increase the non-circularity of the surface being cut. This undesirable effect is stronger in bowl turning because of the higher variations in shaving and severance forces.

It is tempting to suggest that suddenly shortening the cutting edge by abruptly increasing the curvature at the base of the flute decreases the unsupported length of the low curvature length of cutting edge without decreasing the length of its support. However in practice the change is imperceptible, at least to me.

A bowl gouge has two slightly curved chisels at the ends of its flanges. Commonly one is mainly used on bowl outsides, the other mainly on bowl insides. If it were possible to determine the optimum relationship between the vertical curvature of a surface and the curvature of the cutting edge applied to it at a high side rake, there might be a case for having the two flange cross-sections with different curvatures. However this is an unlikely prospect, and I merely state my subjective preference for a U- rather than a V-shaped flute. I also prefer that the flute sides be curved rather than straight in cross-section.

The desirable radius of curvature of the base of the flute is largely governed by how you want to use the gouge. If your cuts will be made by a flange and about half the flute base, the radius of curvature of the latter can be small. If you want to use all of the flute base for a particular cut, as say in heavy roughing, then a larger flute radius is desirable.

To keep costs down, bowl gouges are normally machined from round bar of diameters up to 1 inch (25 mm). For general bowl turning the ⅝ inch (16 mm) size seems about right.

Nose shape

Figure 10.39 shows the three most commonly recommended bowl gouge nose shapes:

1. *Square-across.* When a gouge is used in a near-horizontal presentation, this nose profile helps achieve a high side rake. It is therefore the preferred nose for finishing cuts.
2. *Ground-back.* In roughing there is no need for a high side rake, a larger cross-section of shaving being more important. The ground-back nose is therefore preferred for roughing and for general purpose use. The angle in profile between the bevel at the base of the flute and the ends of the flanges is just less than 90°.
3. *Swept-back.* The sharpening angle varies along the cutting edge, being about 55° near the base of the flute and 30° or less along the flanges. While varying sharp-

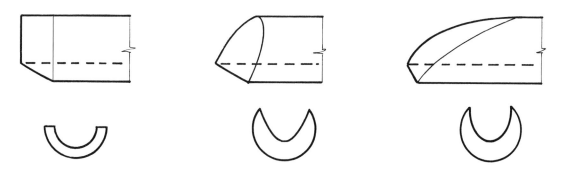

Figure 10.39 Bowl gouge nose profiles and cross-sections. *Top, left to right:* square-across, ground-back, swept-back. *Bottom, left to right:* annular, V-shaped, and U-shaped blade cross-sections.

ening angles along an edge can be beneficial, here it seems to be futile. A short shear scraper is created at the base of the flute. The use of the flange cutting edges is limited to peripheral and radial skimming cuts, cuts of limited usefulness. In short, turners who sharpen this way for general use succeed despite rather than because of it.

These basic nose shapes can be modified or even made asymmetrical. Most commonly varied are the profile angle between the bevel at the base of the flute and the ends of the flanges, the bevel profile and sharpening, and the sharpening angle which does not have to be uniform along the whole cutting edge. So, for example, if you use the right-hand flange of a particular bowl gouge just for cutting bowl insides, by angling the flute back (Figure 10.40), scraping a shaving away occurs after rather than before severance by the trailing cutting edge. You could also coarsen the

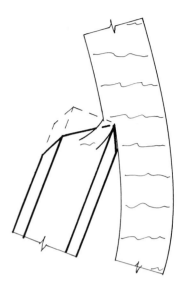

Figure 10.40 An asymmetrically sharpened bowl gouge.

sharpening angle on the left-hand side of the base of the flute, and use this in zone 2 of Figure 10.69.

Effect of Access and Sharpening Angle

A bowl gouge's preferred sharpening angle is governed by the importance of minimising subsurface damage, and by the problem of access.

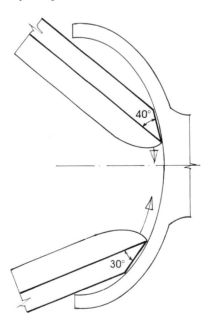

Figure 10.41 The effect of the sharpening angle on the length of cut inside a bowl. The nose of the lower gouge with the 30° sharpening angle can go no further without undesirable bevel heel contact due to the fouling of the blade on the bowl rim. When the bowl wall is very steep the fouling of the blade on the rim causes a clearance angle to arise. The upper gouge with the 40° sharpening angle avoids the fouling, but the surface finish will be slightly poorer and you have to exert greater force on the gouge.

As described in Section 5.1, a reasonable minimum sharpening angle is 30°. But if you are turning a deepish or squarish bowl inside, as your gouge goes round the bend into the bowl bottom, the blade or handle will contact the bowl rim (Figure 10.41). To continue the cut you can:

1. Continue, but thin the cut so that you can retain reasonable control despite the clearance angle.
2. Drop the handle into a more near-vertical presentation. The efficacy of this for finishing cuts depends on whether by axially rotating the gouge a high side rake can be retained.
3. Change to a hook or ring tool, shear scraper, or flat scraper.
4. Change to a gouge with a coarser sharpening angle. The coarseness of the required sharpening angle will of course depend on the internal shape of the bowl, but typically the sharpening angle could be increased to 50° or more. As the sharpening angle is increased, the subsurface damage increases, and so the action of the tool tends towards shear scraping and it becomes preferable to leave the burr on.
5. Use a bowl gouge with a convex bevel. It will allow the gouge to proceed a little further towards to the bottom.

Producing a Convex Bevel

In Section 5.1 the advantages of a convex bevel were described. For surfaces concave in plan, bowl insides and saddle shapes on bowl outsides, a convex bevel avoids the problem of bevel heel support. On the convex-in-plan outsides of bowls, a hollow ground and honed bevel still avoids undesirable instep and bevel heel support, while giving a clearer line of sight.

A true convex bevel can be produced on a bench grinder. Substitutes for a convex bevel can also be readily produced.

In the good old days professional turners used large diameter, wide, natural stone grinding wheels. Part of the wheel periphery was kept flat for grinding chisels and plane irons, while semi-circular-sectioned grooves of various sizes were allowed to wear in the remaining width. In these grooves gouges were ground, the gouges being axially rotated within a plane perpendicular to the axis of rotation of the grinding wheel. The grinding method used was therefore the rotate-and-push method (page 119), which when done

Figure 10.42 Grinding a square-across bowl gouge with a convex bevel for internal bowl finishing cuts. The angled presentation is retained while the gouge is axially rotated. The hollowed grinding wheel rim gives the convexity.

within a groove also gives a smoother bevel more easily. Fortuitously grinding a gouge in a groove also enables you to produce a convex bevel if you angle the tool (Figure 10.42).

The more you angle the handle to the side the greater the convexity of the bevel. Grinding convex bevels on bowl gouges is therefore relatively simple.

Square-across and ground-back gouges with hollow ground bevels can be ground by the method used for roughing gouges (page 117). When grinding the bevels along the flanges there is no necessity that the grinding scratches be square to the cutting edges—if this is thought desirable (and I cannot see any sound reason why it should be) some fanning of the tool will be necessary. To achieve a convex bevel you first need to grind a hollowed rim in a wheel—this is of course why grinders have two wheels. Use a dressing stick to produce a groove with a flute radius of about 1 inch (25 mm). The convexity of the gouge bevel is varied by altering the angle of presentation. An approximation to a convex bevel can be created by grinding or honing a microbevel adjacent to the cutting edge.

Bowl Turning Tool Kit

Below I suggest a number of alternatives. Which one you adopt will depend on how seriously you wish to treat bowl turning, the range of sizes and shapes you hope to turn, and how much you wish to spend on tools.

Minimum kit
General purpose bowl gouge, ⁵/₈ inch (16 mm), nose ground-back, 40° sharpening angle, preferably a convex bevel.
1¹/₄ inch (30 mm) domed scraper.

Two bowl-gouge kit
Bowl roughing gouge, ⁵/₈ inch (16 mm), nose ground-back, 50° sharpening angle, convex bevel.
Bowl finishing gouge, ⁵/₈ inch (16 mm), ground square-across, 30° sharpening angle, convex bevel.
1¹/₄ inch (30 mm) domed scraper.
Shear scraper.

Extra tools
Heavy hook tool or ring tool.
Outside finishing gouge, ⁵/₈ inch (16 mm), ground square-across, 30° sharpening angle, hollow-ground and honed bevel.
Special-purpose scrapers.

10.9 THE TURNING OF BOWLS

Bowl turners use widely varying methods, in part because they have different intents. Some like to exert maximum force; some seek the quickest method even if the quality of the finished bowl suffers somewhat; for others the challenge may be to almost eliminate sanding by trying to achieve the very best off-the-tool surface. All these intents have validity, and hopefully this book is relevant to all, even though my preference is for the more purist, more aesthetically satisfying, final intent.

A comment made about pre-1994 editions of this book was that its sales might have been restricted because bowl turning was pictured outboard. Bowl turning continues to be pictured outboard in post-1994 editions because it is the superior way. Many turners have lathes which force them to turn inboard with the bed restricting their gouges' access. Lathes with pivoting headstocks are significantly better, but although in total cheaper than comparative lathes with double-nosed spindles, my preference is definitely for the latter.

The problems associated with bowl turning over a conventional bed are obviously avoided with the special bowl lathes which have very short beds or equivalents.

To save the expense of having separate accessories or adaptors for each nose of a double-nosed headstock you may be able to have the left-hand nose with a right-hand thread. This arrangement makes hollowing more awkward for a right-hander, requires a reverse on the motor, and means that the lathe cannot be positioned against a wall.

If you have to turn inboard how do your techniques have to be adapted? The major effect is that hollowing, etc. have to be done with the tools in near-horizontal presentations with you leaning over the bed.

The chucking procedures described in Section 10.7 are based upon the outside of the bowl wall being turned first and the inside being turned second, the inside's shape being referenced to the outside by monitoring the wall thickness. You can reverse this order. Doing so has three benefits:

1. There is more chance of a dig-in when turning the inside. If so the walls are still relatively thick and you can turn-out the dig-in because you are not yet committed a finished bowl outside.
2. Because of better tool access, it is easier to turn the outside with reference to the inside.
3. The inside can be readily turned to a smooth flowing shape. As the bowl outside is usually turned in two separate stages (the wall, then the bottom), turning the outside first may not yield the intended unified whole due to carelessness or miscalculation.

Despite these three factors, however, it is generally best to turn the outside first, both during roughing and finish-turning, because:

1. If you turn the inside first, the wall has to be left thick enough so that the outside can be turned without the wall flexing. You can therefore get a bigger bowl if you turn the outside first.
2. If you turn the inside first there is a tendency to be too safe, to not realise the full potential of the blank.
3. Most turners will be more confident in visually monitoring the bowl's design from the outside profile than from the inside's shape which has to be monitored by a combination of sight and feeling.

Bowl turning is wasteful of wood if only one bowl is produced from each disk-shaped blank. The solution is to turn nests of bowls. The component nesting bowls were roughed and separated from a wet block using long, curved-bladed hook tools or mechanically pivoted blades shaped like an eighth of the surface of a sphere mounted with a scraping cutter. Curved-bladed, hand-held scraper systems have been developed by Bruce Leadbeatter in Australia and Kel McNaughton in New Zealand. A mechanically pivoting scraper system is now manufactured by Craft Supplies in Britain.

When turning bowls, the tools and manipulations used are usually similar irrespective of whether you are roughing or finish-turning. Often finish-turning is just a thinner, slower, more careful, higher side rake version of roughing. The following detailed treatments of the stages in turning a bowl therefore describe the roughing of a particular area before detailing how it might be finish-turned.

Turning the outside and bottom

Figure 10.43 illustrates the cuts used in turning the whole outside of a bowl mounted by

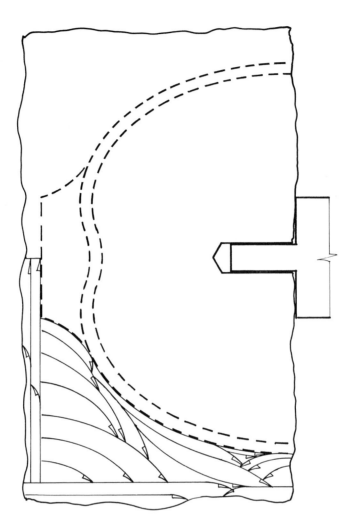

Figure 10.43   The cuts for turning a bowl outside. Here the bowl is held outboard by a pin chuck. At a slow speed, first the cylindrical periphery, then the bottom, are flushed. The lathe speed can then be increased.

its top.

The usual first step of truing the blank should be done with the lathe at a conservative speed. Once the bowl is in good dynamic balance you can increase the lathe speed. An uneven blank will tend to bounce away a bowl gouge presented in a near-horizontal presentation, and a nearer-vertical presentation would be more efficient at waste removal (Figure 10.44). You can use a heavy peripheral skimming cut with a heavy detail or bowl gouge, but this requires the tool overhang to be kept low and the toolrest therefore fairly parallel to the surface being cut. As the blank is trued, you can increase the side rake of these roughing cuts, ideally now made with a ground-back bowl gouge. As there is unrestricted tool access you should prefer a small, say 30°, sharpening angle.

After truing the blank periphery, true the bottom. Start with the toolrest about ¹/₂ inch (13 mm) below axis height and close and parallel to the bowl bottom. To true the bottom start with a bowl gouge in a near-vertical presentation, making the tool presentation more horizontal as the cuts proceed. For finishing, take slow cuts with at least 60° side rake (Figures 10.45 and 10.46). The alternative of using a flat scraper leaves a better macro cut

Figure 10.44 Truing the cylindrical periphery of a disk. At the start, peripheral skimming cuts, here with a ground-back gouge, remove projections faster.

Figure 10.45 A large side rake finishing cut with a ground-back gouge

Figure 10.46 A large side rake finishing cut with a square-across gouge. Any axial rotation will give the large side rake, but using the less curved cutting edge at the end of the trailing flange will lessen the rippling of the macro cut surface.

Figure 10.47 Starting an outside shaping cut. The toolrest is approximately parallel to the wall. The bowl roughing gouge has its flute facing about 30° above horizontal, thus producing a 60° side rake cut. The convex bevel avoids bevel heel ontact during the early part of the cut.

Figure 10.48   The outside shaping cut continues.

Figure 10.49   Almost at the completion of the cut started in Figure 10.47.

Figure 10.50   A finishing cut with a square-across bowl finishing gouge. A superb finish results from a slow traverse along the toolrest, high side rake and rake angles, a cutting edge with a small curvature, and a small depth of cut.

Figure 10.51   An inverted presentation with a bowl roughing gouge results in a similar cutting edge shape and presentation to that in Figure 10.50.

surface, but there will be noticeable subsurface damage. Shear scraping may be the preferred option for some woods.

If the bottom is to be nominally flat, you should turn it slightly concave. If the bowl is to be later chucked by its bottom, pencil on any required circles to aid concentric remounting, or cut any required recess, spigot, or shoulder. The sides of the recess or shoulder are best trimmed with a pointing cut with a detail gouge on its side or a side cutting scraper (Figure 10.30). The bottom of a recess is often skimmed with a scraper with a skewed, slightly convex end.

The development of the outside wall profile can be started with the toolrest still parallel to the bowl bottom. Start a bowl roughing gouge in a vertical presentation with the flute facing about 30° above horizontal and slowly thrust it forwards along the wall towards the rim. During these shaping cuts the presentation becomes more horizontal as the tool overhang lengthens. As you approach the final shape reposition the toolrest parallel to the wall (Figures 10.47, 10.48 and 10.49). Do not continue these cuts as far as the top rim of the blank or you will splinter it out. Cut the very top of the bowl working from the top towards the bottom. If access is a problem at the rim, you may need to use a peripheral skim with a detail gouge.

For finishing the bowl outside wall I generally prefer a square-across bowl gouge in a near-horizontal presentation with both a high rake and side rake. If the surface is convex in plan, a hollow-ground and honed bevel will give a better line of sight. For a surface concave in plan, a convex bevel with the flute honed and the bevel buffed is ideal. Have the toolrest close and parallel to the surface. The cuts should be slow, fine, and taken on the trailing edge (Figure 10.50). Any risk of a dig-in can be avoided by using the gouge flute-down (Figure 10.51), but visibility is reduced and I therefore prefer flute up. If the grain is uncooperative, try a dragging cut with a shear scraper.

With bowl turning you always have the risk of warping due to seasoning and internal stress relaxation. It is therefore best to sand the outside immediately after finish-turning it.

Turning the Outside, the Bowl Chucked by its Bottom

When turning the outside of a bowl chucked by its bottom, access is usually restricted by the headstock. You can use the leading edge of a swept-back bowl gouge (Figure 10.52) or of a detail gouge, both in a near-vertical presentation. The swept-back gouge has greater reference support and therefore leaves a less rippled macro cut surface. You may also be able to use a shear scraper. As soon as access permits, revert to the cuts described in the previous section.

Turning a Bowl Between Centres

The chucking of bowls between centres was described in Section 10.7. Until the adoption of the two-bearing headstock,

Figure 10.52 Using the swept-back cutting edge of an asymmetrically sharpened gouge to overcome the access restriction caused by the headstock.

Figure 10.53 Roughing between centres. The detail gouge is working *downhill.*

Figure 10.54   Scraping out the inside leaving a spigot. The spigot was cut with pointing cuts.

Figure 10.55   The spigot has been tapped to break it off. A homemade driving centre is shown behind.

all bowls were turned between centres.

On the outside the cuts and procedures are as described previously (Figures 10.43 and 10.53). If using a pin chuck or similar with the bowl inboard and with its top facing the headstock, keep the tail centre in contact except when it prevents tool access.

After rough-turning the outside, the bowl is usually remounted by its bottom for turning the inside. But if you choose to turn the inside between centres, tool access is impeded by the tailstock. On the outside of the waste cone held by the tail centre you can use pointing cuts with a gouge. Unless you have special-purpose tools for *cutting*, you will have to scrape the inside (Figure 10.54). Take care that the bottom of the cone is not narrowed so much that it snaps—it is easily broken off after the turning (Figure 10.55).

Turning a Bowl's Inside

When you are finish-turning the inside, the bowl should be mounted as truly as possible. If you cannot get the outside to run true, you will need to skim the top part of the outside wall and the top of the rim.

If the bowl inside has not been roughed-out, you can 'mark' the required depth of hollowing by drilling along the lathe axis (Figure 10.56). Use the point of a skew or of a

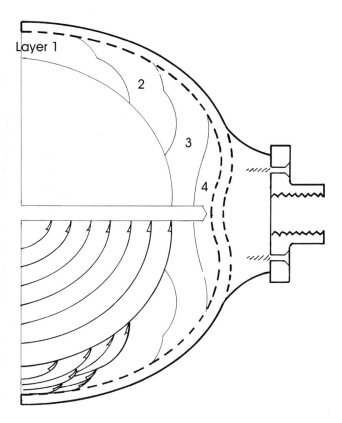

Figure 10.56 Turning the inside of a bowl. Drilling to the hollowing depth is optional. The inside is roughed out leaving still rigid walls. If the next stage is finish-turning it should be done in layers, each layer being finish-turned and sanded before you proceed to the next. The insides of thick-walled bowls need not be finish-turned in layers, but even medium-thickness walls tend to flex beneath the tool and so are best finished in layers.

detail gouge on its side to form a little central conical starting recess for the drill. A hand-held twist drill of about $^3/_8$ inch (10 mm) diameter can then be pushed into the rotating wood to the required depth. This is a sensible first step, but one I rarely use.

Although bowl gouges can be used at long overhangs, control lessens as the overhang grows. By angling a straight toolrest into the bowl, overhangs can be greatly reduced. For greater reductions, particularly worthwhile during finishing cuts, curved toolrests are required (Figure 10.57). For roughing cuts use a convex-bevelled, ground-back bowl gouge. The objective of preliminary roughing is to remove waste rapidly and develop the required shape of hollow. If seasoning or stabilisation are to follow, a thick wall of even thickness will be required. If you are finish-turning, the objective of preliminary roughing is to quickly remove as much waste as possible without leaving the walls perceptibly flexible, so that the duration of the finishing cuts is minimised (Figure 10.56).

Pointing cuts with a detail gouge can be used for inside roughing, but because the waste is not scraped free as it is with a bowl gouge, cuts have to be lighter when near-parallel to the lathe axis or they are blocked.

Beginners frequently, and experienced turners occasionally, find that on entry the gouge nose skids radially outwards across the top of the blank creating a spiral dig-in all too reminiscent of those experienced in spindle turning. The causes are similar. If the bit of cutting edge which first contacts the wood is not in line with the wood's velocity the edge will tend to skate away just as with a spindle gouge in Section 7.14. If in addition

Figure 10.57   Two bowl turning toolrests. If you will be turning large bowls, several toolrests of different curvatures will be found beneficial. The S-shaped toolrest can be used for turning both the outside and the inside; however, a straight toolrest will probably be preferred to turn the outside of most bowls.

the turner-applied movement of the cutting edge is such that there is no or insufficient cutting edge support generated immediately on entry, the tendency to skate away becomes a certainty. Therefore for absolute certainty of entry you need to have the relevant bit of cutting edge in line (for example vertical if you contact the wood at axis height), and the presentation such that proper cutting edge support is generated immediately on entry. Experienced turners are able to achieve a stable entry with a confident thrust because they depend on the second criteria coming into play before their non-conformation to the first has time to manifest. There are however three ways to achieve a foolproof entry:

1. Have the gouge fully on its side and in a horizontal plane so that the cutting edge at the tip of the nose runs vertically. The gouge should then be pushed in at axis height. Once in, the presentation can then be changed to the normal roughing presentation described below.
2. If the gouge is on its side, is in a horizontal presentation, and is angled far to your right if you are turning outboard, the skating tendency is nullified. After entry the handle is swung to your left until the bevel is pointing along the line of the wall. The tool tip thus cuts a tight quarter-circle on the inside of the rim (Figures 10.58 and 10.59).
3. Once a reasonable hollow has been developed, you can safely enter by using a

Figure 10.58   Starting to cut a tight quarter circle.

Figure 10.59   The quarter circle completed and the gouge about to be thrust forwards and upwards.

Figure 10.60   The toolrest being curved is parallel to the inside bowl wall near the rim. The risk of the gouge nose being yanked to the right is greatly reduced, and even eliminated if the tool is in a near-vertical presentation. Here a finishing cut is being taken on the trailing flange of a square-across gouge.

Figure 10.61   Starting to cut a tight quarter circle as in Figure 10.58 with a bowl roughing gouge.

Figure 10.62   The flute is facing about 30° above horizontal, and the gouge is being thrust forwards and upwards.

Figure 10.63   This bowl wall is slightly incurved and therefore the upwards component of the thrust is larger than usual for a roughing cut.

Figure 10.64   The gouge is starting to come 'round the bend' towards the botttom of the bowl. The gouge will be axially rotated slightly anticlockwise as it goes round.

Figure 10.65   The blade is about to contact the rim. This is as far as the 30° sharpening angle will allow this gouge to go.

Figure 10.66   To complete the cut a 40° sharpening angled convex bevelled, bowl roughing gouge is being used with zero clearance.

Figure 10.67 Descending towards the centre.

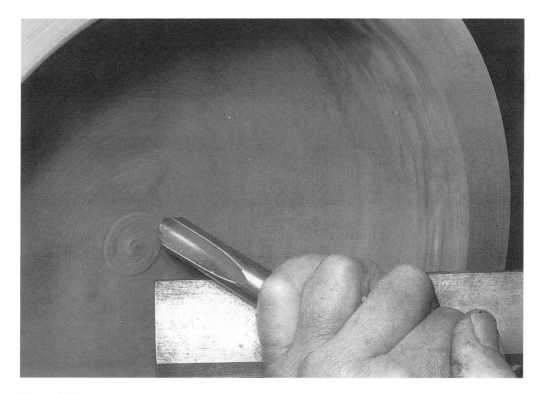

Figure 10.68 The cut almost completed.

peripheral skimming or other presentation (Figure 10.60) if the toolrest is positioned parallel to the bowl wall.

Once entry is achieved at axis height, the gouge flute should be axially tilted to about 30° from the horizontal. The ground-back nose is traditionally thrust along a slightly rising path until it comes around the bend into the bottom; it then gradually descends until it reaches the lathe axis (Figures 10.61 to 10.68). The advantage of the rising path is that it slightly increases the clearance between the bowl rim and the gouge blade or handle. It allows you to compensate for the longer tool overhangs in zone 2 (Figure 10.69) which occur when you use a straight toolrest. It also varies the side rake because the wood velocity becomes more horizontal as the cut is taken higher above the lathe axis. It may also obviate the need to change to a gouge with a coarser sharpening angle.

Inside a bowl there are up to four turning zones (see Figure 10.69), the extents of the zones being governed in the main by tool access.

Zone 1. Access is unimpeded and a gouge with a 30° sharpening angle can be used.

Zone 2. A gouge with a 30° sharpening angle used in a horizontal presentation fouls the rim. By steepening the gouge's presentation you may be able to avoid changing to a gouge with a coarser sharpening angle. Access for hook, ring, or shear scrapers is often impeded. Flat scrapers leave significant subsurface damage.

Zone 3. The bottom of the inside. The grain is approximately parallel to the surface and more conducive to flat scraping, although hook tools, ring tools, shear scrapers, and bowl gouges with coarse sharpening angles leave less subsurface damage. If the centre of the bottom has a dimple as has that in Figure 10.69, work *downhill* from the top of the dimple to the bottom of the annular valley even with a scraper.

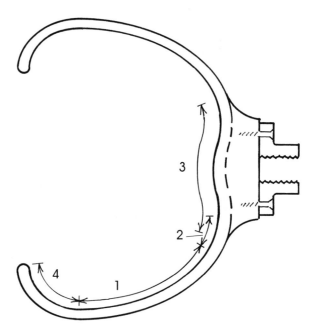

Figure 10.69   The four turning zones inside a bowl.
Zone 1: access is good. *Zone 2*: access is restricted and a coarser sharpening angle than 30° is required.
Zone 3: the bottom of the inside. *Zone 4*: an incurved rim.

Zone 4. An incurved section of wall, usually adjacent to the rim. Although it leaves significant subsurface damage, a flat scraper with a suitably shaped nose is frequently used. An often better option is to turn against the grain with a convex-bevelled gouge.

Finish-Turning the Inside

In this finish-turning there are four basic objectives.

1. *To minimise warping during the turning*
   The major minimisation measure is to turn efficiently and without stopping for tea or lunch breaks. If the bowl is huge and will take a long time to turn, maintain the bowl's moisture content by wrapping it, if appropriate, with wet fabric or in plastic sheeting when not being turned.

2. *To produce the desired off-the-tool surface*
   For roughing in zones 2, 3 and 4 where tool access is restricted you can use just a bowl gouge with a coarse sharpening angle or a flat scraper because the standard of the surface finish is unimportant. For finishing cuts, however, you should consider a greater range of options and test them. Your choice will be influenced by the reaction of the wood to the different edges, the tools available, how you might sand, the intended finished surface, your personal intents (discussed at the start of Section 10.9), and the bowl shape and tool access. If you intend an off-the-tool surface, you should choose your method for the zone with the poorest access, and you will have to use that method for the bowl outside and the rest of

Figure 10.70 Working *downhill* with a square-across bowl finishing gouge in a dimple bottomed bowl.

Figure 10.71   A hook tool works well in zones 2 and 3.

Figure 10.72   Cutting down a dimple with a convex-bevelled detail gouge in a near-vertical presentation tends to leave a rippled macro cut surface.

the inside.

For finishing cuts for conventional finished surfaces (Figure 10.70):

a) Slow the rate of tool transverse.
b) Thin the depth of cut.
c) Minimise tool overhang.
d) Maximise the rake angle unless you are scraping or shear scraping.
e) Unless flat scraping, use a higher side rake than for roughing.
f) Use a small cutting edge curvature to reduce rippling.

Where access is restricted in zones 2, 3 and 4 you have several options:

a) A gouge with a coarse sharpening angle used in a near-horizontal presentation.
b) Flat scraping. However this usually causes significant subsurface damage.
c) Shear scraping.
d) Hook or ring tools (Figure 10.71).
e) A detail gouge or similar in a near-vertical presentation rotated into the cut (Figure 10.72). Loss of control is usually catastrophic, so the tool overhang needs to be restricted to under 1 inch (25 mm), and requires the use of curved toolrests. This presentation is particularly relevant to off-the-tool finished surfaces. A small bowl gouge sharpened like a detail gouge and with a convex bevel will give the desirable small flute radius with greater blade stiffness.

3. *To minimise the tendency of the bowl wall to flex due to the forces applied during turning*
Figure 10.56 explains the turning procedure used to retain bowl wall stiffness. The waste is turned off in radial layers, typically $1\frac{1}{2}$ inch (40 mm) thick, and the inside wall bounding each layer is finish-turned and preferably sanded before you commence to turn away the next layer. Thus the ring of wall you are finish-turning is stiffened by the still thick wall immediately adjacent. Note that the bowl rim is part of the first layer and should be completed with it, not left until later when the warping and flexibility will cause problems.

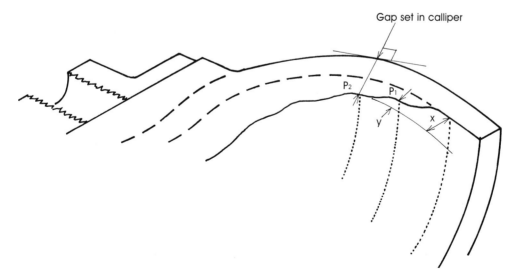

Figure 10.73 Measurement of bowl wall waste thickness. P_1 and P_2 are pencil lines (see Figure 10.74 also). The thickness to be cut away at P_2 is x. The thickness to be cut away at P_1 is x-y.

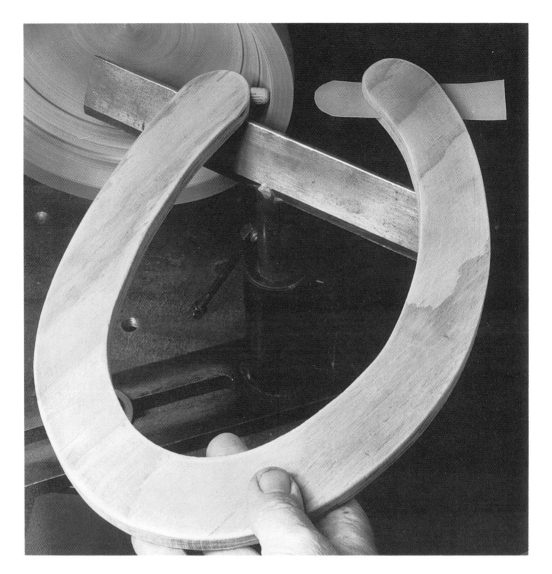

Figure 10.74 A simple homemade calliper. The body is ³/₄ inch (19 mm) plywood. A dowel is housed in a drilled hole on the left. A strip of flexible plastic is housed and can be slid in a saw cut on the right: it is based upon a hollow-turning device of Dennis Stewart's, and can be safely used with the lathe running.

When turning very thin walls to overcome the rapid distortion and wall flexibility, you can use a hand to damp the flexing. If using wet wood you can dampen it occasionally during the turning to prevent it seasoning on the lathe. But perhaps the most effective means is to reduce the thickness of the layers.

4. *To produce the designed wall thickness*
The layered turning procedure described above is readily mated with a measuring and comparing procedure for wall thickness. The procedure is explained in Figures 10.73 and 10.74. Conventional callipers should be used with the lathe stopped. The callipers in Figure 10.74 can be used with care with the lathe running.

With the turning in layers and wall thickness measuring procedures exceedingly thin bowls can be turned. As the wall thickness is reduced, the sound produced by the turning is a useful guide to thickness. Very thin walls, particularly in pale woods, are translucent and shining a light through can be a useful aid to judging thickness. You can also monitor using the perceived distance between the tips of your thumb and forefinger.

10.10 TURNING THE WASTE FROM THE BOTTOM

Section 10.7 detailed the bowl chucking methods appropriate when you come to finish-turning the bowl bottom. In this final bowl-turning operation you can eye-in the shape of the bottom, and this is helped of you finish-turn the outside walls as far down and across the bottom as you can during the earlier turning. But rather than take the risk of just eying

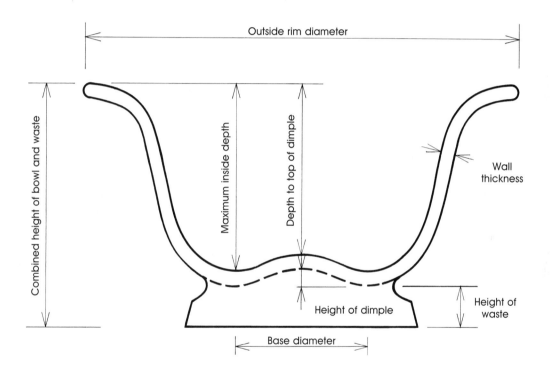

Figure 10.75   The following measurements need to be taken in order to finish-turn a bowl's bottom to a specific thickness:

1. The outside rim diameter is measured with a rule or tape and is usually required to size the annular recess in your press fit chuck.

2. The base diameter is taken by spreading your thumb and forefinger inside the bowl. Without altering their spread, they are then held against a rule.

3. The wall thickness is measured using firm-joint callipers with shielded ends.

4. The combined height and the two depths are measured down from a straight edge lying across the top of the bowl.

Height of waste =   Combined height of bowl and waste - Maximum inside depth - Wall thickness

Height of dimple = Maximum inside depth - Depth to top of dimple

Figure 10.76 The height of the waste which has to be cut away was determined as described in Figure 10.75 and this height is now being marked.

Figure 10.77 The waste is being cut away using a bowl roughing gouge in the near-vertical presentation. When a flat surface within the pencilled circle has been produced, the base diameter is marked.

Figure 10.78 The inner pencilled circle is the base diameter. The dimple bottom is being cut. The height of the dimple has been calculated as in Figure 10.75 and therefore the proper depth of cutting can be achieved. Outside the base diameter, cut wood away as necessary to achieve the correct smoothly curved surface; the outer pencil circle will usually be cut away during this.

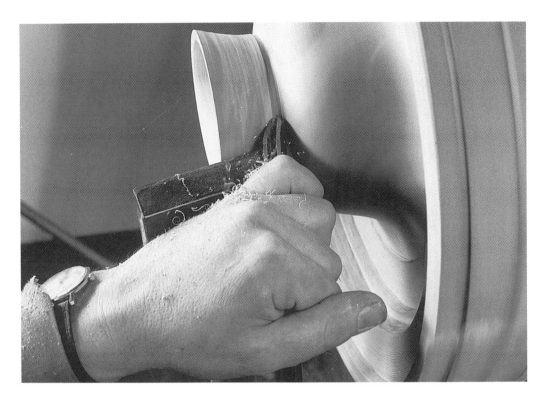

Figure 10.79 A small bowl gouge sharpened like a detail gouge being used to cut *downhill* from right to left on the outside of a footrim.

Figure 10.80 Flat scraping the bottom of the bowl within a footrim.

the bottom, there is a simple procedure which you can follow, and which is demonstrated below, This procedure also avoids the need to check wall thicknesses during the final turning stage. Such checking would require the bowl to be dechucked and rechucked, an interruption both time-consuming and carrying the risk of inaccurate re-chucking.

Before preparing the reverse chucking, the simple measurements described in Figure 10.75 are taken and noted. The steps are then:

1. Chuck the bowl by its rim after turning a recess equal in diameter to the maximum diameter at the bowl rim (Figure 10.76). If the rim is not plane, you will have to use other methods detailed in Section 10.7. If you are turning a series of bowls, do the smallest first because this will maximise the life of the supplementary plates or disk.
2. With the lathe running, pencil in a line at the height of the waste from the bottom of the wood (Figure 10.76).
3. Turn the waste off (Figure 10.77) leaving a flat bottom on the bowl.
4. Mark the base diameter with a pencil.
5. Turn off the remainder of the waste, both inside and outside the pencilled circle, to form the dimple, footrim, recess, etc., without turning off the pencil line (Figure 10.78).
6. Sand and make any guidelines or fine V-cuts prior to signing and labelling the bowl.

Figure 10.1 showed that there is a variety of different turned bowl bottoms. A variety of techniques may therefore need to be used (Figures 10.79 and 10.80).

10.11 BOWL SANDING

Unless there is some particular reason for not doing so, bowls are sanded after the best possible off-the-tool finish has been achieved. Because the off-the-tool finish is usually poorer than for spindle turning, the starting grit grade will normally be coarser, in the range of 60 to 120 grit. You then proceed through the grits to the chosen finest, usually between 220 and 400 grit.

For hand sanding the paper is folded into three, as for spindle turning. Abrasive cloth rather than paper may be preferred for the coarser sanding. Be careful to keep the fingers holding the abrasive paper or cloth trailing or else they will experience a painful whip. Rotary sanding may also be used and is especially effective on difficult or spalted woods. The direction of motion of the abrasive disk at the interface should oppose that of the wood. Pneumatic or electric drills and angle drills can be employed, but they should ideally have two handles so that sufficient control can be exercised (Figure 10.81). The most used disk backings are circular pads faced with thick foam which is itself faced with Velcro: they are available in a range of diameters. Cloth-backed abrasive disks in a full range of grit sizes are available for them.

In sanding, the fibres being sanded *downhill* will tend to be pressed down rather than cut off. Regular reversal of the lathe rotation will make sanding more efficient; stop the lathe first before putting it into reverse. Stop the bowl occasionally and examine it under a good light. Awkward spots may require some hand sanding.

Wet woods are a problem to sand—drying the surface with a heat gun is well worthwhile otherwise the abrasive will rapidly clog. Clogging will also occur with oily woods. Therefore, use light pressure and remove the caked wood before it becomes baked onto the abrasive—a brass-wire brush can be used with hand-held abrasives. Abrasive restoring compound in stick form is ideal for sanding disks.

As explained in Section 6.8, soft wood is abraded at a faster rate than hard wood. Therefore, where a bowl has areas of rot, holes, or bark inclusions, heavy and prolonged sanding will not only preferentially abrade the soft tissue, but will also locally abrade the surrounding areas of hard tissue, leading to depressed areas which disturb the true circularity of the bowl and which are therefore undesirable. To prevent this effect, a rigid sanding head, preferably a rotating one, would be required which would be positioned not by pressing it against the rotating bowl, but by using an independent moveable mounting system. As such a system is not usually feasible, use light sanding pressure and, if possible, a shaped support for the abrasive.

A bowl is often chucked more than once during finish-turning. The final sanding operation before a bowl is rechucked or removed should be with the same grit and in the same direction as the other final sandings on the same bowl. For example if a bowl is held by its base, and its inside and outside sanded with 400 grit with the bowl spinning clockwise, then when that bowl is held by its rim on the same end of the headstock spindle, the 400 grit sanding should be done with the bowl spinning counterclockwise.

Figure 10.81   Sanding with an abrasive disk held in an electric drill.

References

The multinational publisher which produced (but did not publish) the orginal edition of this book advised against the inclusion of references. I have always regretted accepting that advice. The practice of not acknowledging sources continues to be widespread, perhaps because it is thought to intimidate readers or to detract from the achievement of an author.

I list below the references that I can recall after five years, and apologise to the authors of any sources that I have omitted.

Chapter 1
Keith R. Bootle, *Wood in Australia*, McGraw-Hill, Sydney, 1983.

Chapter 2
Victor Chinnery, *Oak Furniture*, Antique Collectors' Club, Suffolk, 1979.
John Gloag, *A Short Dictionary of Funiture*, George Allen & Unwin, London, 1969.
Joseph Gwilt, *The Encyclopedia of Architecture*, Bonanza Books, New York, 1982.
Wallace Nutting, *Furniture Treasury*, MacMillian Publishing Co Inc, New York, 1928.
Edward H. Pinto, *Treen and Other Wooden Bygones*, G. Bell Sons Ltd, London, 1969.
Maureen Stafford and Dora Ware, *An Illustrated Dictionary of Ornament*, George Allen & Unwin, London, 1974.
William H Varnum, *Industrial Art Design*, Manual Arts Press, Illinois, 1933.

Chapter 3
Douglas Alan Fisher, *The Epic of Steel*, Harper & Row, New York, 1963.
Eric Oberg and F.D. Jones, *Machinery's Handbook*, The Industrial Press, New York, 1964.
L.T.C. Rolt, *Tools for the Job*, B.T. Batsford Ltd, London, 1965.
Robert S. Woodbury, *History of the Lathe to 1850*, M.I.T. Press, Massachusetts, 1964.

Chapter 4
Woodturning Course Notes, Sydney Technical College, Sydney.
Leaflet PB 1580, Pratt Burnerd International, Halifax, England.

Chapter 5
P. Afanasyer, *Woodworking Machinery and Cutting Tools*, Higher School Publishing House, Moscow.

Chapter 6
Handbook on Grinding, Australian Abrasives, 1975.
F. Pain, *The Practical Woodturner*, Drake Publishers Inc., New York, 1972.

Chapter 7
Mike Darlow, *Turning Thin Spindles*, Fine Woodworking, July/August 1980, pp.70-71.
Mike Darlow, *The Taming of the Skew*, Fine Woodworking, September/October 1982, pp. 70-75.

Chapter 8
John David Ellsworth, *Hollow Turnings*, Fine Woodworking, May/June 1979, pp. 62-66.

Chapter 10
Patrick Spielman, *Working Green Wood with PEG*, Sterling Publishing, New York, 1980.
R. Bruce Hoadley, *Understanding Wood, A Craftsman's Guide to Wood Technology*, Taunton Press, Connecticut, 1980.

Gallery

Photographs of woodturnings tend to be especially boring. I hope that the pieces shown here will be of interest and will illustrate that there is more scope in turning than you perhaps thought.

A chess set made of silver ash and Queensland walnut. I wanted to make a fully turned chess set in which all the pieces would be recognizable. The knight was a problem. My solution: a medieval war helmet.

The *Bush Potty*, my first major sculptural piece. The ends of the horizontal rails and stretchers were turned to fit into drilled holes in the legs. The paper (the bark of a paperbark tree) is held within the lever-operated dispenser. A banksia tree flower becomes the brush head.

A boot jack. If you do not have a serving wench to remove your boots, this is the next best thing. The flap that holds down the toe of the boot is pivoted.

A whip and crop stand, made of Brazilian mahogany. There does not seem to be much demand for these, but it gives an excuse to do some club foot turning.

The *Green Submarine*. Emu eggs are very large and a deep viridian green in colour.
All wood except the stand is painted to match.

The *Elephant Table*. Zoologists will be able to confirm its lineage because it has five toes on each foot. Anyway, if you have a really large, beautifully figured plank of Australian red cedar, what do you do with it?

The *Russian Caravan Teapot*. It is richly painted and runs along on its wheels.
It works too, the inside being sealed.

A traditional gavel (right), made of Tasmanian blackwood, and my attempt to do something a little different—a contemporary gavel made of live oak.

Index

Abrasive cloth, 132,134
  bowl turning, 319-20
Abrasive grits, 132, 134,138
Abrasive paper, 132-37
  clogging, 273, 275, 319
  sanding,132-38
  screwchucks, 59
  steadies, 200
  see also Sanding
Abrasive restoring compound, 319
Abrasive stick, 115, 117, 294
Abrasive wood:
  lathe speed reduction, 49, 91
  see also Silica
Absolute humidity, 7
Acanthus carving, 22
Acceleration of electric motors, 50
Acer negundo, 264
Acheson, E.G., 35
Acorns, 2
Adhesion of glue, 6
Adhesive tape:
  chucking, 230, 282, 284
  depth guide, 46, 74
  roughing,143
Aesthetics, 28
Agathis alba, 8
Allergic reaction to wood, 6, 123
Aluminium oxide:
  grinding, 35, 114
  sanding,132, 134-35
American Iron and Steel Institute, 94
American long taper spindle nose, 42, 44
Amino acids, 4
Ammonia, 6
Angiosperms, 3
Angle of skewness, 97, 99
Angles:
  clearance, 77-90
  effective sharpening, 84-85
  effective rake, 84-85
  rake, 77-90
  sharpening, 77-90, 292, 293, 308, 310
  side rake, 83-90, 101-3, 109, 220
Annealing, 94

Annual rings, 4-5, 257, 261, 266
  centring, 147
  sanding, 133
Antique restoration turning, 131-32
Appendage, 26
Arbors, 42, 61-62
Arrising edges, 98, 107
Ash (from burning), 6
Ash (species), 2, 131
Astragal, 17
Attacks on wood, *see* Fungal attack;
          Insect attack
Auger, 44-46, 73, 75
Automatic lathes, 31, 35-37, 196
Axial thrust, 80
Axial hole drilling, 45-46, 73-75, 110, 145

Backcutting, 160
Ball, 17
Ball and ring, 20
Ball foot, 19
Ball bearings, 34, 35, 42, 43, 196, 209,
          285
Ball foot, 19
Ball turned spindle, 20
Balusters, 18, 21, 139, 142, 161, 194
Bamboo turning, 20
Bamboos, 3
Band,17
Band of cutting edge support, 78-90
Bandsaw, 30, 35
Bandsawing, 30
  bowl turning, 266-70
  chair back legs, 208
  club feet, 203, 205-7
  safety, 123
Banjo, 33, 37, 38, 45, 46, 47, 52, 53, 54
  positioning, 147, 154
Bark, 4
Bead cutting, 98, 128, 168-79
  exercises, 209-14
  long point, 178-79
  short point, 168-78
Bead forming tools, 113
Beading and parting tool, 98

331

Beads, 16, 28, 29

Bearings (lathe), 34, 35, 42, 43, 215, 220

Bed, bedways, 33, 34, 36, 37, 38, 41, 215

Bench lathe, 39, 40, 53

Bevel (chamfer), 17

Bevel (tool), *see* Sharpening angle

Bevel:

    blocking, 96-97, 155, 303

    bounce, 84, 181, 194

    convex, 90, 293-94, 299, 303, 312

    heel contact, 89, 100, 257

    profile, 90-91

    support, 78-90

Bine, 18, 21

Binomial nomenclature, 2

Birch, 131

Bird's beak, 17

Bird's eye figure, 261, 263

Birmingham Museum and Art Gallery, 16

Biting cuts, 154-56

Bits, *see* Drill bits

Blackbean, 5

Blacksmiths, 82, 121

Blanchard, Thomas, 35

Bluestain, 11, 13, 266

Blunting of tools, 6, 91

Bobbin,17

Bobbin turning, 20

Bolection moldings, 58

Bone,130

Borers (insect), 12, 28, 75

Boring, 29, 45-46, 73-75, 145

Boring bits, 73

Bostrychids, 12

Bottle, 21

Bouncing beneath tool, 84, 181, 194

Bowl design, 29, 251-57

Bowl pricing, 13

Bowl sanding, 319-320

Bowl turning, 251-320

    between centres, 276, 299-302

    chucking, 275-89

    finish-turning, 271-73, 295

    gouge, 95, 104, 108, 289-94

    inboard, 294-95

    inside hollowing, 299-315

    nests, 295

    outside and bottom, 295-99

    procedures, 270-73, 287, 289, 295

    reverse-chucking, 315-319

    rough turning, 270-71, 273, 295,
        297-99, 302-03

    sanding, 257, 319-20

    stance, 125

    tool choice and presentation, 289

    tool entry, 303-6

    tool kit, 294

    toolrests, 48, 303-4

    wall thickness, 313-319

    wood, 257-58, 260-65

    wood preparation, 258-70

    wood seasoning, 273-74

    wood stabilisation, 274-75

    zones, 310-13

Bowls, lidded, 256

Bowstring lathe, 34, 36

Box elder, 264

Box turning, 70, 225-32

Brad point drill bits, 73, 75

Brainstorming, 14

Braking of headstock spindle, 50

Branch wood for bowls, 261, 265

Brazil, 2

Breadboards, 69

Brezil, 2

Brown paper for split turnings, 201

Brown tulip oak, 2

Bruising, 83, 84, 86, 257

Bruzze, 111

Buffing, 82-83, 121

Bun foot, 19

Burl, 259-61, 280

Burnishing by tool bevel, 154

Burr on steel, 82, 106, 119, 224, 230

Butt, 260-61

C-spanner, 60, 61

Cabinetmaker's plane, 165

Cabriole leg turning, 202-8

Caesalpinia echinata, 2

Caesalpinia sappan, 2

Caesalpinus, Professor, 1, 2

Callipering, 29, 129, 130, 139, 140, 143,
      144, 156-57, 181-82, 208, 216-17

    bowl walls, 313-15

    grip, 129

    minimization, 29

    parting tool, 129

    roughing, 156-58

    skew, 230

Callipers, 56-58, 158, 314

Cambium, 3, 4

Candlesticks, 27, 29

Canted fillets, 28, 200

Cantilever bed, 37

Cantilever plate outboard stand, 53, 54

Capacitor motor starter, 50

Carba-Tec grinding jig, 115

Carbohydrates, 5

Carbon, 92, 93

Carbon dioxide, 4

Carbon steel scrapers, 107

Carbon steel tools, 108
  grinding, 94, 119
Carbon tool steel, 34, 35, 91, 92-94, 116
Carborundum, 35
Cardwellia sublimis, 2
Carpenter's auger, 75
Carriage, 33, 44, 55, 196
Carving, 131, 149, 208, 209, 251, 256
Cast iron, 38, 40, 41
Castanospermum australe, 5
Casuarina, 2
Cavetto, 17, 162, 190, 208, 228, 241
Cedars, 2, 131
Cedrus deodara, 267
Cellulose, 5
Centre finder, 57-58
Centre punch, 145, 146
Centring old turnings, 148, 149, 207
Centres:
  marking, 144-46
  mounting between, 147-49
Chain saw mill, 259
Chain sawing, 259-69, 266
Chair backs, 208
Chair legs, 9, 144
Chamfer, 17, 150, 211, 213
Chatter tool, 113
Chemical treatment of wood, 11-12, 266
Child, Peter, 11
Chip, 78, *see* Shaving
Chitham, Robert, 18
Chlorophyll, 4, 11
Chuck plates, 65-67, 284-87
Chucks:
  annular ring (cage), 283-87
  choice, 70-71, 194-95, 215-16, 225,
    234-35, 276-89
  collet, 67-68, 70-71, 195, 216, 221-234,
    278, 281
  cup, 61, 70, 101, 216-20
  faceplate, 42-43, 58-60, 70, 234, 276
  glue, 234
  homemade, 60-70, 216
  Jacobs, 61-62, 74, 110, 195, 197, 216,
    217
  loose dovetailed ring, 278
  Longworth, 284
  mandrel, 71, 72, 74
  Maxi-Grip 2000, 67, 278
  multi-axis, 202
  Nova, 67, 226-32, 280, 284
  paper joint, 234, 279
  pin, 276-78, 284, 302
  press fit, 69-70, 231-32, 249-50, 280-84
  screw, 59-60, 70-71,81, 215, 234-35,
    278, 281

Screw Cupchuck, 216
Screw Spigot, 278
scroll, 62-67, 70-71, 101, 195, 216,
    226-32, 234, 276, 278-81
  6 in 1, 68, 72
  Super, 278-81
  supplementary plate, 279-81
  swallow, 195, 216
  vacuum, 69-70, 234, 278, 280, 284, 287
  Vicmarc, 222
Citrus limonia, 12
Class, 2-3
Clear finishes, 6
Clearance angle, 77-90, 99, 101
Club foot, 18-19
  turning, 202-8
Cluster leg, 22
Clutch, 50
Coil, 17
Collapse, 273
Collet chucks, 67-68, 70-71, 195, 216,
    221-34, 278, 281
Colour banding, 261, 264
Colour of wood, 5-6, 11, 30
Columns, 18, 19, 21-23
Combined water, 8, 275
Commercial lathe, 36, 37
Compasses, 57-58, 269
Compression of wood in chucking, 69
Compression wood, 9-10
Concave surface, *see* Hollow
Conifers, 3
Contour enrichment, 25
Convex surface, *see* Bead
Copy-lathe, 35, 36
Copy turning, 58, 194
Corundum, 35
Cove, *see* Hollow
Cracking of wood, 6, 8, 266, 270
Cradle for turned work, 209, 267, 270
Craft Supplies
  Maxi-Grip chuck, 67, 278
  multi-axis chuck, 202
  nesting appartus, 295
  sizer, 111
  6 in 1, 68-72
Creative Woodturning, 118
Cross-slide, 44, 55
Crotches, 260, 262
Crucible Particle Metallurgy, 94
Crushing under tool, 30; *see also*
    Subsurface damage
Cup and cover, 22
Cupchuck, 61, 70, 101, 216-20
Cupchuck turning, 131, 192, 201, 215-33,
    260

box, 225-32
chucking, 215-17, 225-26, 231-32
egg cup, 221-24
hollow turning, 232-33
hollowing, 125, 220-28
knob, 217-20
Cupping, 29, 273
Curve matching, 58
Curve nomenclature, 17
Curved toolrests, 48, 303-5, 311-12
Curving corners of square sections, 162, 165, 191
Cuts:
clearing, 161, 172, 192-93, 220
deepening, 161, 172, 192-93, 220
Cutting, *see also* Turning
downhill, 91-93, 108, 149, 158, 160
forces, 78, 149
speed, 78, 91
theory, 77-92
uphill, 91, 149, 160, 235
Cutting edge, 82, 83, 92
support, 78-90
Cutting theory, 77-93
Cycloid, 98
Cyma curve, 17
Cyma reversa, 17

Darning mushroom, 143
De Plantis, 1
Decay, 11; *see also* Fungal attack
Degrade, 8-11, 270, 273-74
Dent repair, 138
Depth measurement:
bowl turning, 302-3, 315
cupchuck, 223, 227-28
drilling, 46, 74-75
Dermatitis, 123
Design, 14-32
aesthetic considerations, 28-29
bowl, 252-57
guidelines, 25-28
influences, 29-30
limitations, 29-30
nomenclature, 16-22, 24
practical considerations, 28-29
process, 14, 24
production, 15
rationalization, 149
sources, 15-16
structural, 25-28
Design for the Craftsman, 25
Detail gouges, 95, 101-4, 108
bowlturning, 289-90, 296, 300, 303, 312
cupchuck hollowing, 221-23
spindle turning, 182-92

Diagonals:
drawing to find centre, 144-45
Diameter gauges, 56-58, 139, 144
Diamond-patterned surface, 194
Dicotyledons, 3
Differential shrinkage coefficients, 8, 11
Diffuse porous woods, 4
Dig-in, 176-78, 295, 303
Dimensioning of a log, 259-60
Diminution, 18
Dimpled bowl base, 252, 315-19
Dining table, 27
Dioscorides, 1
Disk preparation for bowl turning, 260-70
Distance between centres, 36-37
Dividers, 57-58, 69, 221-22, 249
Divisions in plant taxonomy, 2-3
Douglas fir, 257
Dowels, 29, 55, 200
Downhill cutting, 91-93, 108, 149, 158, 160
Dracontomelum mangiferum, 264
Drafting, 25
Double-sided tape, 279
Dovetailed recess, 280, 281
Dressing stick, 115, 117, 294
Drift, 44, 62
Drill bits, 43-44, 46, 61, 73-75
Drilling, 44-46, 61, 73-75, 110, 302-3
Drilling machine, 29, 75
Drilling tailstock, 44
Driving centre, 43, 45, 51-53, 144-45, 201
Driving pulleys, 41-43, 63
Drops, 23
Drying:
glue or finishes, 6, 138
wood, *see* Seasoning
Dundas, James, 35
Durability of wood, 6
Dust, wood, 6, 12, 122, 123

Ear pieces, 208
Ebony, 131
Eccentric spindle turning, 49, 201-8
Effective diameter, 194
Egg cup, 221-24
Egypt, 34
Electric motors, 35
Electrical resistance of wood, 7
Elliptical cross-section, 202
Ellsworth, David, 232
Elm, 131
Emery grinding wheel, 35
End fixity of a spindle, 61, 195
End grain, 5, 8, 13, 96, 235
checking, 260, 266

Engineer's chucks, 62-66; *see also*
    Chucks, scroll
Engineer's face driver, 52
Entasis, 18,19, 23
English oak, 4
Epoxy resin glue, 209
Equilibrium moisture content, 7
Equipment, influences of, 30
   measuring, 56-58, 313-15; *see also*
    Callipering; Callipers
Eucalyptus marginata, 261
Eucalyptus piperita, 8, 273
Exercises in spindle turning, 209-14
Extension socket, 62
Extractives, 5-6, 137
Eye figure, 260-61
Eye protection, 113, 122, 123, 266
Eyes, use of, 58, 144
Faceplates, 42-43, 58-60, 70, 234, 276
  modified as a driving centre, 276-77, 302
Faceplate turning, 58, 69, 92, 140, 234-50
  base, 238-41
  basic cuts, 235-38
  chucking, 234-35
  hollowing, 241-42
  ring, 243-50
Fairburn, William, 35
Family, 2-3
Fashion, 30-31
Feed shaft, 33, 55
Feeling if round, 156-157
Feet:
  club, 18-19, 202-8
  turned, 18-19
Felling of trees, 258-59
Ferrules, 110-11
Fibre saturation point, 8
Fibreboard (MDF), 59, 232, 234
Fiddleback grain, 130, 260-61, 263
Files for turning tools, 94
Fillets, 17, 28, 132, 140; *see also*
    Spindle turning
Filling during finishing, 138
Fine Woodworking, 284
Finials, 23-24, 131
Finishing (polishing), 6, 132, 136-38
Firm-joint callipers, *see* Callipers
Flag bowl, 254
Flange thickness (*t*) of a gouge, 97, 102-4
Flanges, 17, 219
Flat belt, 35, 43
Flexible steel rod for callipering, 57-58
Flindersia brayleyana, 263
Flush bead, 17, 28
Flute angle, 102, 103

Flute radius, 88-89, 94, 96, 101-4, 155,
    290-91
Fluting, 22, 131, 209
Flywheel, 34
Folding abrasive paper, 134, 135
Footrim, 252, 256, 281, 318
Forces on tool, 78-81
Forstner bit, 73, 75
Four-prong driving centre, 51, 52
Free water, 8, 275
Friction disk speed variation, 50
Friction polish, 138, 232
Fungal attack, 5, 6, 11-12, 260, 274;
    see also Degrade
Furniture beetles, 12
Gadrooning, 21
Gap in bed, 37-38
Gauge line, 42
Genus, 2
Ginko, 3
Glaser
  screwchuck, 59
  sharpening jig, 113, 118
  skew, 95
Glass, 32, 251
Glazing, *see* Subsurface damage
Gluing, 6, 131, 209
Going round-the-bend, 307
Golden Proportion, 25
Good practice, 28-29
Gottshall, F.H., 25
Gouges,
  bowl turning, *see* Bowl turning gouge
  detail, *see* Detail gouge
  hybrid, 64, 97-98
  roughing, *see* Roughing gouge
  sizing nomenclature, 104
Grain mismatch in boxes, 225-26
Gramme, Theophile, 35
Grass tree, 261-62
Great Wheel drive, 34, 36
Green-turned bowls, 6, 256, 270-73
Grevillea robusta, 2
Grinding, 82, 113-19
  gouges, 117-19
  scrapers, 119
  skews and parting tools, 116, 117
Grinding wheels, 35, 113-15
Grinding wheel dressing, 113-16, 294
Grips, *see* Turning grips
Guard for scroll chucks, 64
Gun drills, 45
Gymnosperms, 3
Hand as a steady, 74, 195-99
Hand brace, 75

Handles, 108-11, 125
  making, 110-11
Hard and soft tissue, 133, 147, 257, 320
Hardening of tool steel, 94
Hardwoods, 3-6, 9
Headstock, 34, 35, 41-43
  swivelling, 35, 42, 125, 234, 294
Heartwood, 4-6; *see also* Sapwood/
      heartwood contrast
Heat treatment, 94
Hemicelluloses, 5
Heritiera trifoliata, 2
High-speed steel, 35, 92, 93, 94, 103, 106,
      107, 111, 116
Hoadley, R.B., 275
Hobby lathes, 35, 36, 39, 49
  bearings, 64
Hogbin, Stephen, 256
Holding bowl by rim, *see* Reverse
      chucking
Holes in spindles, 145
Hollow cup centre, 46, 53
Hollow grinding, 90, 100, 113, 116
Hollow turning, 232-33
Hollowing (cupchuck), 55, 220, 222-24
  faceplate, 241-42
Hollows, 16-17, 28-29
Homemade chucks, 60-70, 216
Honing, 82, 83, 90, 101, 119-121
Hook tools, 82, 105, 112-13, 220, 221,
      224, 226, 289, 293-95, 310, 312
  sharpening, 121
Hopper, Ray, 202
Horizontal borer, 29
Hose clips, 68, 69
Hot melt glue, 279, 281
Hourly rate, 32
Humboldt undercut, 258-59
Hunt, Adrian, 279
Huntsman, Benjamin, 34
Hybrid gouges, 64, 97, 98

Inboard turning, 39
  bowl, 278, 284, 294-95
  faceplate, 39, 234
Increasing effective flute diameter, 190
Incurving rims, 252, 273, 310-11
Indexing, 41, 43
Indonesian kauri, 8
Industrial Art Design, 25
Industrial Revolution, 35
Influence of equipment, 30
Inletting a ring, 201
Inorganic compounds, 6
Insect attack, 5, 6, 11, 12, 30, 134, 260,
      264; *see also* Degrade

Intentional staining, 13
Intents, 253
Interference angle, 100, 175, 177
Interlocked grain, 30, 134, 165, 257
Internal stresses, 9-11, 258
Inverted finials, 23
Investment in equipment, 30
Iron, 6
Iron-carbon diagram, 93
Ivory, 130

Jacobs, C.B., 35
Jacobs chuck, 61-62, 74, 110, 195, 197,
      216, 217
Japanese tea boxes, 225
Jarrah, 261
Jeans cloth, 132
Johansson, Kurt, 105
Judging by eye, 58, 144
Judgment of wall thickness, 313-15
Junction of turned and square sections,
      132, 161

Kilns, 274
Knee of leg, 208
Knobs, 23-24, 131
  turning, 217-20
Knots, 144, 240
Kerosene, 120
Knock-out bar, 44, 216, 220

Lace bobbins, 196
Ladyfinger-nosed gouge, 102, 118-19, 234
Laminating, 209, 251, 253, 256
Laminations, 31
Lamp bases, 69, 275
Lamp standard auger, 45-46, 73, 75
L 'art du tourneau, 34
Lathe, 33-55
  accessories, 56-75
  axis, 37, 38, 43-44, 125
  bearings, 34-35, 42-43, 215
  bed, bedways, 32, 38, 39
  capacity, 36-37
  carriage, 33, 37, 44, 55
  defects in construction, 215
  equipment, 56-75
  headstock, *see* Headstock
  height, 40
  history, 34-35
  metal turning, 34, 37-38, 42
  motor, 39, 49-51
  patternmaker's, 33, 34, 36, 37, 44, 55
  reversing for sanding, 232, 320
  rigidity 91

speed, 41, 78, 84, 86, 90-92, 123, 134, 148, 194, 195
stand, 39-41
swallow, 42, 216
tailstock, *see* Tailstock
types, 35-37
vibration, 161
Leadbeatter, Bruce, 295
Leather belting, 35
Leather glove, 196
Leaving squares, 161-65
Lee, Leonard, 114
Left forefinger as a steady, 196, 197
Left hand as a steady, 196, 198, 199
Left-handed turners, 125
Left-square section, 140, 142-45, 161-65, 190-94, 199
Legs (furniture), 18, 21-22, 131
    lowboy, 27
Lemon wood, 12
Lidded box, turning of, 225-32
Lids, 29, 216, 225-32, 256
Lighting, 123
Lignin, 5, 274
Lignotuber, 260-61
Line of sight, 90, 100, 102, 299
Lindquist, Mark, 256
Line-shafting, 35
Linnaeus, Carolus, 2
Long-and-strong tools, 108, 128, 130, 222
Long edge of skew, 97-101, 161
Long fibres, 257
Long hole boring, 44-46
Long point of skew, 97-101, 149, 178-79
Longhorn beetles, 12
Longworth chuck, 284
Loose rings, 112
Lyctids, 12, 274

McNaughton, Kel, 295
Macro cut surface, 83, 86, 87, 157, 190, 296-97, 299
Mahogany, 2, 131
Mallee trees, 260-61
Mandrel, 34, 71-72
Maples, 2, 131
Marketing, 31-32
Marking gauge, 144-45, 212
Marking out, 139-146, 239
Marlboro' foot, 18-19
Masking tape, 143
Measurements for finish-turning bowl bases, 315-19
Medullary rays, 2, 4, 30, 133, 257, 259
Melaleuca quinquenervia, 254
Melon bulb, 21

Metal turning, 34, 38, 62, 68, 77, 106, 130
Methodus Plantarum, 2
Microwave seasoning, 274
Mildew, 6
Milling logs, 259-60
Mimic, 57-58, 139
Mineral turpentine, 138
Minimisation of turning time, 29, 149, 311
Mobilcer M, 266
Mohs' scale, 132
Moisture content, 6-9, 30, 274
Moisture meter, 7
Moisture movement, 8, 274
Mould attack, 11
Mouldings, 16-17, 58, 234
Molybdenum, 93
Monocotyledons, 3
Morse taper, 36, 41-43, 51, 61, 195, 216
Morse taper arbor, 61-62
Morse taper shank, 74
Motors, 35, 39, 49-50
Mounting work between centers, 147-53
Multi-centre woodturning, 201-2
Multiple-axis turning, 201-8
Mushet, R.F., 35

Near-horizontal presentation, 254-55, 257, 263-68, 270-71, 286, 295, 299-301, 304-7, 318, 322
Near-vertical presentation, 39, 125, 236, 241, 290, 293, 296, 299, 305, 312, 317
New Guinea walnut, 264
Newbury, William, 35
Nish, Dale, 118
Nitrocellulose lacquer, 232
Nitrogen compounds, 6
Nonaxial grain, 144, 154, 158, 165
Norton Company, 35
Norton, F.B., 35
Nose shape in bowl gouges, 291-93
Nova scroll chuck, 67, 226-32, 280, 284

Oaks, 2, 131, 256
Objet virtu, 134
Off-the-tool finish, 9, 133, 255, 256, 311, 313
Offset skew, 100-1, 227
Ogee, 17, 29, 162, 190, 191
Oil exudation, 30, 137
Oilstone, 120
Oleoresins, 6
One-handed grip, 125-30, 158, 181, 182. 196, 198-99, 218, 230
Onion foot, 19
Order, 2
Order of turning, 149, 194, 195

Original finish, 132
Orites excelsa, 2
Ornamental turning lathes, 34-36
Outboard turning, 31, 37, 58, 123, 137,
        234, 294-5
Outboard turning rest, 40, 54
Outboard turning stands, 52-55
Oven drying, 7
Overhand turning grip, 149, 154-56
Overhang of tool, 48, 129, 149, 181, 224,
        289, 313
Overloading of motors, 50
Ovolo, 17, 190

Pad of club foot, 18-19, 202-8
Paint, 134, 137
Palm trees, 3
Paper joint, 201, 279
Paperbark, 254
Pappadum bowl, 272
Parting-off, 100, 101, 105, 106, 130,
        192-94, 220, 224, 225, 227, 229, 232
Parting tool, 98, 105-6, 108, 172, 192,
        217
Pasteur, L., 14
Patina, 136
Pattern books, 28
Patternmaker's lathe, 33, 34, 36, 37, 44, 55
Pecking, 83, 132, 133
Pedestal lathe, 36, 37, 40
Peeling, 77-81
Peg, 17
PEG, 274-76
Pencil gauge, 58, 139-44, 194, 239
Peppermint gum, 8, 273
Permeability to moisture, 8
Pernambuco, 2
Persepolis, 201
Phenols, 5, 6
Photosynthesis, 4
Pin, 17, 131, 200
Pin chuck, 67, 71, 276-8
Pin gauge, 58, 139-41, 144, 194
Pinhole borers, 12
Pinto, E.H., 16
Pinus radiata, 5, 8
Pith, 4, 260, 266, 273
Pivoting, 178
Plainsawing, 4, 30, 133, 259
Planing, 87, 88, 125, 165-67, 198
    detail gouge, 190
Plant Kingdom, 2-3
Plastic, 29, 130, 251
Plastic wrapping, 13, 266
Pleasure and Profit from Woodturning, 119
Plug bowl, 255

Plugs, 74-75, 145, 200
Plumier, Charles, 34
Point of inflection, 28
Pole lathe, 34, 36
Polishing, 132, 134, 136-38, 232; *see also*
        Finishing
Polyethylene glycol, 274-76
Polyurethane, 111, 138, 275
Pommel, *see* Section left square
Pores, 4, 5, 12
Port, Ken, 113
Powder-post beetles, 12
Preload, 43, 215
Press fit chuck, 69, 70, 231-32, 250,
        280-84, 287
    with brackets, 282, 284
Primary mass, 25-28
Profile curves, 139, 144
Projection from cupchuck, 217
Protective clothing, 122
Public reaction to woodturning, 31
Punching centres, 145-46
PVA glue, 201, 209
Pyrograph, 32

Quartersawing, 4, 29-30, 133, 259, 265
Queensland maple, 263
Queensland walnut, 6
Quercus robur, 4
Quercus species, 2, 256
Quirk, 17

Racal ventilated face shield, 123
Racking of headstock, 215
Radiata pine, 5, 8
Raffan, Richard, 101
Raised platter, 262, 265
Rake angle, 77-85
Rattle, 112
Ray, John, 2
Reaction wood, 9-11
Recommended tools, 108, 294
Record ventilated face shield, 123
Redesign to overcome slenderness, 195,
        197, 200
Reeding, 22, 55, 131, 209
Reference support, 87-89, 299
Reference points for gauges, 140
Regester, David, 112
Relative humidity, 7-8
Relaxation of internal stresses, 11
Removing spindles with the lathe running,
        192-4
Removing tool handles, 111
Removing waste with the skew, 181
Repetitive turning, 148, 194

Resin, 6, 134
Restoration turning, 131-32, 148
Reverse chucking, 224, 231, 283-85
Reverse ogee, 17
Rhythm in turning, 154, 162, 209
Ring, 17, 29, 107, 129, 157
Ring porous, 4
Ring scrapers, 112
Ring tools, 82, 105, 112, 113, 121, 221, 224, 226, 293, 294, 310
Ring turning, 112
Rippled finish, 194, 255, 256
Riving, 96, 105, 144, 165, 201, 259
Rocking parting tool, 182
Rolling cuts, 168, 169, 172-79
Rose countersink, 75
Ross, Dale, 284
Rosewoods, 131
Rot, 11
Rotary sanding, 319-20
Rotational stability:
    detail gouge, 101-4
    roughing gouge, 94-96
Roughing:
    bowls, 270-71, 273, 295-99, 302-3
    cupchuck, 215-18
    spindle turning, 154-65
Roughing (spindle) gouge, 94-98, 101, 104, 108
Rounder, 200
Router, 55, 139, 209
Roy Child parting tool, 105-6
Rubber, 130

Sabre Sharpening Centre, 114
Saddles, 90
Safety, 121-23
Salad bowl, 2
Sales, 31-32
Sanding, 128, 132-37
    bowl, 273, 313, 319-20
    faceplate, 248, 319-20
    in reverse, 232, 248, 319-20
    rattles, 112
    square section, 134
    spindles, 132-37, 202
    twists, 209
Sandpaper, 132; see also Abrasive paper
Sandpaper rack, 38
Sap, 4, 6
Sapwood, 4 – 6, 11
Sapwood/heartwood contrast, 266
Satinwood, 131
Sausage turning, 20
Sawtooth bits, 73, 75
Schuler, L., 35

Scooping action with skew, 179-80
Scotia, 17
Scrapers, 105-8, 224, 233, 280, 294
    grinding, 94, 106-8, 113, 119
    side-sharpened, 280
Scraping, 9, 78, 81, 82
    bowl turning, 289, 292, 293, 295, 296, 299, 301, 302, 310, 311, 313, 318
    cupchuck, 9, 221-32
    faceplate, 235-38, 241, 245
    spindle turning, 190-92
Scratch gauge, 209
Screw holes in bowls, 256
Screwchuck, 59-60, 215, 234-5, 238, 243, 278
Scroll chuck, see Chucks, scroll
Sculptural multiple-axis turning, 202
Sealing to reduce degrade, 8, 273, 274
Seasoning, 6-13, 226, 273-74
Section left square, 29, 132, 154, 160, 161, 165, 199
Sectioning for bowls, 260-66
Self-centring center punch, 145-46
Self-centring chuck, see Chucks, scroll
Self-gripping taper, 216; see also Morse taper
Selling, 31-32
Set-over adjustment, 44-45
Setting diameters, 56-58, 105, 129-30, 181-82, 222, 227-30, 216-18
Sexual organs of plants, 2
Sewing needle, 29
Sfirri, Mark, 201
Sharpening, see Grinding; honing
Sharpening angle, 77-78, 80-89, 94, 99, 292, 293, 308, 310
Sharpening jigs, 113-18
Sharpness, 82-83
Shear scraper, 105, 108
Shear scraping, 105, 224, 292-94, 299, 313
Sheoaks, 2
Sherwin, Reg, 119
Short edge, 97-98
Short point, 97-98
Shoulders, see Cutting shoulders
Shrinkage, 8-9, 258-59; see also Cracking of wood; Degrade
Shrinkage coefficients, 8, 258-59, 271-72
Side-grain abrasion, 133
Side table, 27
Side rake, 83-90, 101-3, 108, 220
Silica, 6, 30, 83, 91, 257
Silicon carbide, 35, 132, 134
Silky oaks, 2
6-in-1 chuck, 68, 72

Sizers, 111, 112, 130, 139, 217
Skew chisel, 87-89, 97-101, 108
  bead cutting, 99, 168-79
  bowl turning, 239
  convex cutting edge, 101
  fillets, 179-81
  geometry, 97-101
  ground straight-across, 98
  long point, *see* Long point of skew
  oval, 98
  offset, 100
  parting, 181, 230
  parting-off, 192-93
  planing, 98, 165-67, 198
  removing waste, 181, 230
  sharpening, 116-17, 119-21
  short point, *see* Short point
  slide cutting, 167, 199, 228-30
  square across, 98
  squaring shoulders, 99, 101, 181
  V-cutting, 160-64, 168-72, 192-94
Skewed cutting, 83-90
Skills, 30
Sleeves, 43, 62
Slender turning, 29, 154, 194-200
Slide cut, 167, 179-80, 199
Slide rest, 34
Slipstone, 120-21
Smith, Vin, 105,113
Sloping cradle, 270
Small-scale turning, 130
Sockets, 17, 131, 200
Soft-faced hammer, 220
Soft-metal bearings, 34
Softwoods, 4, 6, 9, 12, 131
Spacing disk, 60
Spade bit, 73, 75
Spade foot, 18
Spalting, 11, 12, 257
Special-purpose chucks, 69
Species, 2-3
Species Plantarum, 2
Speed (cutting), *see* Lathe speed
Speed changing, 35, 49-50
Spermatophyta, 3
Spielman, P., 275
Spigots, 17, 200, 216-32
Spike removal, 223
Spindle (headstock), *see* Headstock spindle
Spindle gouges, *see* Gouges
Spindle moulder, 209
Spindle turning, 139-214
  bead cutting, 168-79
  copy turning, 194
  cutting fillets, 179-81
  detail gouge, 182-92

  exercises, 209-14
  gauges, 139-44
  hollowing, 167, 182-89
  laminating, 209
  leaving squares, 161-65
  mounting wood between centres, 147-53
  multiple-axis turning, 201-8
  parting, 181-82
  parting-off, 192-94
  planing, 165-67,190, 198
  preparation for, 139-46
  principles, 149-54
  removing waste, 181, 230
  roughing, 154-60, 164, 165
  slender, 194-200
  split, 201
  squaring shoulders, 99, 101, 181
  twists, spirals, fluting, reeding, 209
  V-cutting, 160-64, 168-72, 192-94
Spindles, 18, 20, 29
Spiraled surface, 80
Spirals, 18, 21, 209
Splintering away front of bowl, 296, 299
Split chucks, 68, 69, 72
Split turnings, 201
Spool, 17
Spool turning, 20
Spores, 3, 11
Sprung center pin, 70
Square section, *see* Section left square
Squaring a shoulder, 90, 99, 101, 181, 219
Stability of tools:
  detail gouge, 101-4
  parting tool, 105
  roughing gouge, 95-97, 154-56
Stability of wood, 7, 289-90; *see also*
        Seasoning; Shrinkage
Stabilisation, 8, 137, 274-76
Stail engine, 200
Staining, 6, 11, 13, 134, 138, 260
  intentional, 13
Stair balusters, 18, 21, 139, 142, 161, 194
Stance for turning, 124-25, 134
Stand (lathe), 33, 37-40
Standard lamps, 200
Star checking, 260
Starches, 4, 12
Steadies, 195-200
Steam bending, 5, 208
Steaming, 138
Stearate, 132, 135
Steel wool, 138
Steels, *see* Tool, steels
Stepped pulleys, 34, 49, 50
Stewart, Dennis, 232
Stopping, 134

Straightened fingers with roughing gouge, 154-55
Strength of wood, 6, 9, 11, 30
Stress relaxation, 11, 197, 227, 270
Stropping, 120
Structural design, 25
Stubbs, Del, 50
Stump feet, 18-19
Styles, 30-31, 119, 234
Subclass, 2
Subkingdom, 2, 3
Subsurface damage, 83, 86, 101, 160
Suitability for use, 29
Supplementary plates, 65-67, 286-87
Supporting disk, 59-60
Surface enrichment, 25
Surface finish, 84-90, 255, 256, 294
Surform, 209
Swallow, 41-43, 51, 195, 216
Swing, 35-37
Swing arm diameter setter, 139, 144
Swing arm seat, 40
Switchgear, 39, 49-50
Switching lathe on, 148
Syncarpia glomulifera, 8

Table legs, 161, 209
Table saw, 209
Tail centres, 45, 46, 53-54, 92, 144, 145
Tailstock, 33, 36-37, 43-45
    bowl turning, 276, 278, 279, 283, 285, 289, 299, 302
    drilling, 44, 74-75
    handwheel, 44-45
    long-hole boring, 45-46
    quick-acting, 44
    spindle, 41, 43-45
    spindle swallow, 61
Tailstock end of work, 139, 140
Tang, 108-10, 111
Tannin, 5, 6
Taper:
    cupchuck, 61
    Morse, 42
    turning, 44, 165
Taste, 30-31
Taxonomy of plants, 2-3
Taylor, F.W., 35
Teak, 6
Tear-out, 83, 89, 90, 160, 165
Techniques, influence of, 30, 31
Temperature:
    during cutting, 78
    effect on wood strength, 9, 78
Tempering, 94
Templates, 139, 144, 206-8

Tension wood, 9-10
Termites, 12
Terpenes, 5
The Classical Orders of Architecture, 18
The Complete Guide to Sharpening, 114
The Craftsman Woodturner, 11
Theophrastus, 1
Therming, 18
Thread cutting, 37
Threaded lathe spindle nose, 41, 42
Threads, 131
Three-cornered file, 140
Ticketing, 107
Tied-underhand grip, 48, 125-29, 162, 188
Tool:
    grinding, 113-19, 293-94
    handle, 30, 108-11, 154
    post, 55
    rack, 39-41
    sharpness, 82-85
    stability, *see* Displacement or Stability
    steels, 35, 91, 92-94, 104, 106-8
Toolrests, 33, 47-49, 303-4
    bowl turning, 48, 303-4
    cantilever, 49
    cross-sections, 48
    curved, 48, 303-4
    holders, *see* Banjos
    nicks in, 98
    positioning, 125-28, 165, 222, 299, 303
    right-angled, 49
Tools:
    high-speed steel, 92-94, 108
    recommended set, 108, 294
Torus, 17
Toupie, 18-19, 140
Toxicity:
    chemicals, 11, 137
    wood, 122, 123
Trammel heads, 57-58
Transmission, 49-51
Treacle mould, 17
Treadle, 34, 36
Tree:
    felling, 9, 258-59, 274
    growth, 3-4
    nomenclature, 1-3
Treen, 16, 131
Treen and Other Wooden Bygones, 16
Trumpet foot, 18-19
Trumpet leg, 21
Try square, 140, 145
Tungsten, 93
Tungsten carbide, 94
Tungsten tool steel, 35
Turning:

bowl, 251-320
cupchuck, 215-32
egg cups, 221-24
faceplate, 234-250
furniture restoration, 131-32
grips, 125-30, 172-76
knobs, 217-20
lidded boxes, 225-32
materials other than wood, 130
spindle, 139-214
Turnip foot, 19
Turnability, 13, 30
Turning grips, 125-30
one-handed, 129-30
overhand, 125-27, 236
right hand, 128-30
tied-underhand, 48, 125-29, 223, 236
underhand, 128, 129
Turpentine, 8
Twist drill, 46, 73-75
Twists, 18, 21, 209
Two-bearing headstock, 34, 299

Ultraviolet inhibitors, 6, 137
Ultraviolet light, 6
Undercutting, 101, 110, 220, 224
Underhand grip, 128, 129
Understanding Wood, A Craftsman's Guide to Wood Technology, 275
Uphill cutting, *see* Cutting uphill
Uphill scraping, 190, 192
Urea formaldehyde, 209

V-belts, 35, 49-50
V-cuts, 28, 161, 168, 169
V-cutting, 98, 160-64, 168-72
Vacuum chucks, 69-70, 232, 234, 278, 280, 284, 287
Vacuum seasoning, 274
Vacuum union, 70, 284-85
Varnum, W.H., 25, 28
Vase, 21
Veranda post, 134, 149
Vernier calipers, 57, 58, 230
Vibration of lathe, 38, 40, 41, 161, 215, 296
Vicmarc scroll chuck, 222

Vinyl gloves, 232
Waisting of columns, 18
Wall thickness, 239
Walnut, 2, 131
Waney-edged bowls, 254, 256, 283, 284
Warping, 8-11, 29, 131-32, 258, 270-74
Wastage of wood, 28
Waste allowance, 145, 192-93, 216-17, 221, 225-26
Water marks, 6
Watt, James, 35
Waxing, 13, 136
Wet and dry paper, 132
Windsor chair legs, 9
Wood, 1-13
bowl, 2
chemical composition, 5
classification, 1-3
colour, 5, 6, 30
extractives, 5-6
hardness, 6, 91
internal stresses, 9-11
movement, 9-11, 29
nomenclature, 1-3
planing research, 77
preparation for turning, 144-46
properties, 6-9, 13, 30
sources, 13
spindle turning, 144
strength, 6, 9, 30, 78
supply, 30, 131
value, 32
Wooden tray, 154
Woodfast
headstock, 41
Screw Cupchuck, 216
Screw Spigot Chuck, 278
Super chuck, 278, 281
Working Green Wood with PEG, 275
Workshop procedures, 122-38

Xanthorrhoea arborea, 262

Yellowing of finishes, 6
Yews, 3